THE OECUMENICAL
MOVEMENT
AND THE UNITY OF
THE CHURCH

By THOMAS SARTORY, O.S.B.

Translated by
HILDA C. GRAEF

THE NEWMAN PRESS
WESTMINSTER, MARYLAND
1963

Translated from the German edition 1955, published by the Kyrios Verlag, Meitingen bei Augsburg, with additions by the Author.

Oecumenical Movement and
the Unity of the Church

translated from the German of Thomas Sartory, O.S.B.

Nihil Obstat: Ricardus Roche, S.T.D.
                                                          censor deputus

Imprimatur: + FRANCISCUS
                                          Archiepiscopus Birmingamiensis

Datum Birmingamiae, 23rd Octobris, 1962.

Printed in Great Britain

CONTENTS

II. Systematic Part

AUTHOR'S PREFACE TO THE
ENGLISH EDITION

The present book appeared in Germany in 1955 under the title *Die ökumenische Bewegung und die Einheit der Kirche. Ein Beitrag im Dienst einer ökumenischen Ekklesiologie.* It was well received in the German speaking countries, by both Catholics and Protestants. Many reviewers confirmed that I had used the right method for working out the actual distinctions between Catholic and Protestant doctrine in a truly oecumenical spirit. Considering the difficulty of the subject it is only natural that this can be no more than a preliminary attempt; I am well aware that there is a long way to go before we can achieve something like Johann Adam Möhler's *Symbolik.* One of the difficulties is that we Catholics have to try to make contact with the whole of reformed Christianity as represented in the oecumenical movement. Such conversations would be simpler with Lutherans, Reformed or Anglicans separately. But even Lutherans do not all hold the same views, much less Anglicans. Nevertheless, there are many cross currents among the Protestant communions and denominations, which today, in view of their oecumenical engagement, take on a new significance. On the other hand, it is not easy, either, to present Catholic doctrine in a way readily intelligible to non-Catholic Christians on account of the great variety of theological schools of thought. One thing we know for certain, that today our old-style apologetics is no longer convincing.

The present English version of the book has been adapted and enlarged. The English-speaking public has already become acquainted with the oecumenical problems in the books of Congar, Dumont, Bouyer and van de Pol, to mention only some names of Catholic representatives of the movement on the Continent. My book is meant to be a modest contribution to the subject and may perhaps be regarded as a complement to the work of E. Duff, S. J., *The Social Thought of the World Council of Churches* (1956); it is chiefly concerned with the systematical aspect. For a detailed introduction to the history of the oecumenical movement and the World Council of Churches the reader is referred to the *History of the Ecumenical Movement* edited by R. Rouse and S. C. Neill (1954). In 1955 I was introduced to the Anglican Church through the Church of England Council on Foreign Relations and had conversations with several of its authorities. Everywhere I met the desire for closer contacts with the Catholic Church. One Anglican clergyman wrote to me: "Can you come over into Macedonia and help us? (Acts xvi. 9)". Perhaps this book may provide such a help. I have always been impressed by the exegetical and patristic scholarship of Anglican theologians, but even more by that 'pietas Anglicana' about which Henry St. John, O.P., has written so beautifully in *Essays on Christian Unity* (1955). And nowhere have I been so painfully conscious of the tragedy of a divided Christendom as in England. Here both Anglicans and Catholics possess an exponent of the oecumenical spirit *par excellence* in John Henry Newman, whose life and work no Catholic oecumenist can disregard. Newman is of such special importance for us because he represents a Catholicism which is truely catholic, that is to say all-embracing, and thus integrates legitimate concerns of the reformers into Catholicism. Moreover, he always retained a sincere respect for our separated brethren, teaching us the fundamental principle of all oecumenical work: "doing the truth in charity" (Eph. iv. 15).

I dedicate this English edition of my book to my Anglican confrères, the Benedictines of Nashdom Abbey. Ever since I visited them we have been united by the bond of Christian friendship which has been visibly expressed in the candle lit in both our respective houses each Thursday in commemoration of the Highpriestly prayer of Christ (John xvii) as a living gesture of prayer: ut omnes unum sint.

Abtei Niederaltaich,　　　　　　　　Dom Thomas Sartory, O.S.B.
Easter 1960.

The subject index is the work of Dom Martin Symons, O.S.B., to whom I am grateful, both for this, and for the reading of the proofs.

T. S.

FOREWORD

The words of Jesus Christ at the Last Supper, with His prayer for the unity of all who believe in His name, are so clear that there have always been a few bold spirits who have dared to hope that, even in our day, a beginning of a restoration of unity among all who bear the name of Christ might be made. A few years ago their number was small. It is true that, as this book shows, the roots of the oecumenical movement go far back into the past. But it is chiefly in our own century that the movement has steadily advanced from strength to strength. It is well known that it has made more rapid progress among non-Catholics. One might have been surprised, or even scandalized, that the Church that claims the greatest unity has hesitated to join in a movement for increasing unity. Yet our Catholic unity is perhaps the very reason for our hesitation. Possessing, as we do, international unity and solidarity to so remarkable a degree, we did not quickly become sufficiently aware of the great number of Christians outside the Catholic fold. Nor was it easy for us to realize that we Catholics might share the responsibility for what actual division exists. Today every Catholic knows that the faults were not all on one side. But the history taught in the post-reformation period was not so objective and calm. It was the age of polemic, and each side saw only the faults of the other. Protestants took up oecumenism sooner than we did, perhaps largely because they already knew the phenomenon of division and schism as existing between their own Protestant communions. No doubt this experience helped them to turn their minds more quickly than we did to the need to strive for reunion between Catholic and Protestant.

To these psychological reasons we must add others which spring from Catholic doctrine. The Catholic's unshakable faith in the presence of the Holy Spirit guiding his Church, and the visible nature of that Church with the very audible nature of its creed, is not an easy basis for dialogue with Christians who do not admit the Holy Spirit's guidance in the same way. In the nature of things dialogue is difficult where one side is more wholly committed in doctrine than the other. The field of what is regarded as Christ's teaching, guaranteed by the Holy Spirit, is larger for the Catholic than for the Protestant. So that, even while both parties to the dialogue may agree that they will in no way compromise on essentials, this means that the Protestant has a greater field of non-essentials in which compromise is possible than the Catholic. It is this fact that is at the root of the occasional Protestant complaint that dialogue with Catholics is difficult or useless since Catholics have decided before the dialogue begins what view they must hold. Where the Protestant would hope for a certain amount of give-and-take, the Catholic appears only to offer 'take it or leave it'.

In this latter respect, the Protestant and Orthodox observers at the first Session of the Vatican Council have been much surprised and relieved to discover, as they listened to the discussions in St Peter's, what an astounding freedom of thought and discussion still remains to the Catholic. They have found that, although we do agree on a very full common creed, our Church is by no means monolithic in its theology or its practical applications of doctrine.

In addition, thank God, well before the Second Vatican Council, so many prayers had been offered up, and so great has been the growth of good will and mutual understanding, that, in spite of immense difficulties felt sincerely by both Catholics and Protestants, dialogue has begun in many countries, and more and more theologians on both sides are convinced that it is both possible and useful. The early dialogue, and much that still takes place, has been confined to a statement of one another's beliefs in such a way as to give the opposite party a sympathetic understanding of one's position. More and more Protestant theologians are at least beginning to understand why a Catholic believes what he does, and even to enter into his mind. In the same way, many Catholic theologians have learnt to understand why Protestants cling so firmly to their views, and even why Protestants find it difficult to accept the Catholic position.

In the course of these early dialogues, which had as their purpose no more than mutual understanding, each side became more and more aware that these new contacts were helping each side to understand more clearly his own faith. Inevitably, as in the case of Justification, it was often discovered that the Catholic and Protestant were not saying things that were mutually exclusive. Sometimes they were saying the same thing in different language. At other times they came to discover that their differences were a question of different emphasis. Each side was insisting on the aspect of doctrine most opposed to what he conceived as the position of the other. Thus the Protestant, in defending the doctrine of *sola gratia* was underestimating the active human co-operation or response. On the other hand, the Catholic, in opposing the Protestant, tended to overstate the part of man's co-operation and good works. Dialogue in this province has often helped both Catholic and Protestant in the understanding of the original true Catholic scriptural doctrine.

It was, of course, fortunate that all this happened at a period of theological revival. One of the characteristic features of this revival was that Catholics have been less tempted than in a less theological age to think that defined statements of Christian belief exhausted the whole content and meaning of Christian doctrine. The Catholic theologian was ever more ready to admit that any dogmatic definition is no more than the beginning of full theological understanding. It was a source, a principle, from which, and on the basis of which, theology advances. Theology is *fides quaerens intellectum*. For the Catholic the *fides* is outwardly expressed in the doctrinal definition. But the full understanding of this *fides* is a

matter for the theologian; and theology will continue to progress and
deepen in its understanding as long as the world lasts. It will not be true
theology if it is false to its principles. But it will not be theology at all
unless it grows in its understanding of those principles.

It is precisely here that we are beginning to realize that there is a possibility of ever more fruitful dialogue with Protestants, Anglicans and
Orthodox. As long as there is no hope of their accepting, or learning to
accept, our basic principles, dialogue must be fruitless. But many of our
principles, such as the Creed, a great number, if not the greater number,
of Christians with whom we have dialogue will accept already. Since we
believe that ultimately the whole of our faith must stand or fall together,
there must be some hope where there is even partial agreement on the
basic Christian creed. It is on the basis of this measure of agreement that
theological dialogue becomes possible. Just as the Catholic theologian
can advance in his understanding of the Creed by dialogue with other
Catholic theologians, is it not possible for such understanding to grow in
dialogue with Protestant theologians who also accept the Creed, or even
an important part of it?

It is on principles such as these that Father Thomas Sartory approaches
the question of Oecumenism in this volume. He agrees that the great gulf
between Catholic and Protestant comes from our not-yet-reconcilable
views on the nature of the Church. He believes, and surely he is right, that,
when a Catholic discusses with a non-Catholic any other doctrine, the
dialogue is liable to be frustrated by different basic doctrines on the
Church. Where the Protestant feels thwarted by the fact that he knows
the Catholic is not free to reject a doctrine that his Church has defined, the
tension between the two comes from their undiscussed beliefs regarding
the Church. Nothing then is, from an oecumenical view, more important
than a dialogue on the nature of the Church. The main contribution of
this book, it seems to me, is the author's attempt to initiate such a dialogue.
So that it be true dialogue, Fr. Sartory does not simply tell non-Catholics
what Catholics hold. This has value, but cannot be said to have immediate
oecumenical value. He goes further, in that he considers many of the views
of Protestants on the nature of the Church and allied doctrines. He considers these views, not with the object of refuting them, but in order to
discover what is in these Protestant views which will fill out or even
deepen our own Catholic doctrine of the Church. At the same time, it is
his hope, as I understand it, to point out to the Protestant how much there
is in Catholic ecclesiology which is theologically demanded by the best
Protestant insights into this subject. He finds ground for oecumenical
hope in the contribution that the theologians of each side can make to a
more profound ecclesiology. This more profound ecclesiology will not
be a new one for the Catholic, since it will still be built on the Catholic
Creed. But it will be a deeper one, for it will help us to understand that
Creed more deeply, and in a more balanced way. I say 'more balanced';

for we now recognize that the demands of polemic have frequently led us to stress one side of the truth so as to risk the underestimation of the other.

This approach is, I believe, new in the English language, at least in relation to the question of oecumenism. Our continual prayers for unity, and our interest in the cause, must urge us to examine our conscience to see what we can do, with God's grace, to help forward the cause for which we pray. The kind of dialogue here exemplified is perhaps the most that we can do in the theological order. Since finally there will never be reunion except on a basis of doctrine, this method must surely in the long run be more important than the method of mere social friendliness and charitable co-operation.

I have known Fr Sartory well for many years, and my wishes for the success of his book are increased by my appreciation of his life-long dedication to the cause of unity. It must give him great joy to know how wonderfully our beloved Pope John XXIII is leading his Catholic children to work and pray for the same cause.

H. FRANCIS DAVIS

ROME, *Advent 1962*

Introduction

PRINCIPLES OF METHOD

Today the Christian communions, separated from one other for so long, have again been brought into touch with one another. This is proved by the existence of the Protestant *Oecumenical Movement* whose aim is to make contact between the various denominations so that they may clearly recognize both their affinities and their differences and thus seek ways to re-establish unity. Even though the Catholic Church does not take part in these 'oecumenical' Conferences, the words of the *Instructio* of the Congregation of the Holy Office[1] (20th December 1949) on the Oecumenical Movement remain valid: 'It emerges from several Papal pronouncements that the Catholic Church has never ceased, nor will cease in the future, to follow with a lively interest and further with its incessant prayer all efforts that seek to attain the end which is so near to the heart of Christ our Lord, namely that all who believe in Him "may be made perfect in one" (John xvii, 23).' This interest is shown also by the many conversations which have been held between theologians and laymen of the separated denominations under the auspices of the *Una Sancta* Movement. The participants in these conversations aimed in the first place at getting to know one another, recognizing one another as brethren and removing the prejudices and misunderstandings that spoiled the relations between the various communions after their centuries-old separation. The tenor of these conversations shows that much progress has already been made, and the very fact that they have become possible may surely be regarded as a special grace of God, a gift of the Holy Spirit who conducts the 'dialogue' between the Father and the Son in the internal life of the Trinity.

Nevertheless, inter-denominational talks must not be confined to the statement of uniting and separating elements. The debate between the denominations cannot escape the question of truth, because this is also the question of the way of salvation. Thus the dialogue is inspired by a *telos*, an end, which is to find the truth, to bear witness to it and to acknowledge it. Now in inter-denominational conversations the partners on both sides are each convinced of possessing the truth; hence it is the acknowledged or unacknowledged aim of each to try to lead the other partner to his own point of view.

[1] *AAS* XL (1948), 142-7.

This characteristic of inter-denominational conversations throws light also on their method. It may cause surprise that we speak of the method of a conversation in this context, since a conversation is something living that ought not to be pressed into the forms of a predetermined method.

Now the method of any activity is largely determined by its object, in the present case by the object of the conversation. In an inter-denominational talk there is certainly no lack of 'objects' to be discussed. There are enough controversial points between the separated communions, and ever since the Reformation innumerable discussions have been held on these points. But surely the effect of such talks has been that the distinctive doctrines have become even clearer. It was felt that there had been movement only on the surface of the different opinions and views. Something must have been 'behind' them which could not be grasped and which was the real ground of division. Hence, if we speak of applying method (*Methodik*) to inter-denominational discussion, we are primarily concerned with the subject to be discussed and the manner in which we approach it. Realization of this fact cannot but help the debate, if it is indeed to be fruitful and to lead to open confession of the truth.

The inter-denominational debate already has a history (indeed, it would be a rewarding task to study this in all its detail), and in considering this history several possible methods can be distinguished.

There is first the possibility of denominational controversy. As a typical example of this we may consider the method of the first post-Reformation[1] generation of theological controversialists, that of attack. 'At this stage, each side assumes that it fully understands what the other side means and is only concerned to refute it.'[2] One disputes—the term is significant—in the context of hostile polemics. To the Catholic side it appeared that its own faith was attacked by false doctrines and had consequently to be defended. From the Protestant point of view, the Christian faith had been falsified by the Catholics and had therefore to be corrected, which was possible only by attacking false teaching. This method has survived the Reformation for centuries and it cannot be said even today that it no longer plays an important role in our apologetic and controversial theology. This exaggeratedly pedantic apologetic lacked particularly personal

---

[1] Cf. J. Lortz, *Die Reformation in Deutschland*, vol. ii 154–75.
[2] Skydsgaard, 'The Roman Catholic Church and the Ecumenical Movement', in *The Universal Church in God's Design*, 159.

contact with the dissidents. Its theology was largely book learning, by which, as a theologian once expressed it in a conversation, 'one defeated an absent opponent all alone in one's study'. These theologians were, above all, incapable of understanding the terminology of their adversaries. They argued deductively without taking account of historical data and circumstances. It was characteristic of this method that particular controversial points were taken in isolation; on the Catholic side for example, the 'sola fide' or 'sola scriptura' of the Reformers, on the Protestant side, for example, the dogma of the primacy or transubstantiation in the doctrine of the Eucharist. This isolation resulted in an obstinate defence of one's own position which destroyed the capacity for listening intelligently to the other side.

Now these denominational controversies were not only futile with regard to inter-denominational discussion; they also had unfortunate effects on personal theological insight. Here we can only point to some examples in the Catholic sphere. There is a wise saying that it is a great misfortune to have learned one's catechism in opposition to somebody. In the last four centuries Catholics have learned their catechism far too much in opposition to Luther or Baius. Consequently, the truths of the faith were no longer seen in all their fullness. Controversy necessitated definition, which in its turn was conditioned by a defence reaction. Thus walls were erected which had to be defended, and men were compelled to remain on the walls, while losing sight of what they enclosed. They also no longer looked over the wall in the right way, and especially did not dare to admit that many of the fine flowers in their own garden blossomed also in their neighbour's. In fact, they only stared at the other's fast-growing flowers and got so excited that they failed to perceive their scent. And because they kept peering into their neighbour's garden so aggressively they forgot to attend to their own flowers, which therefore only too often languished and withered. The extreme on the one side called forth the extreme on the other. The Reformers, for example, attacked the hierarchical structure of the Church. Consequently Catholic ecclesiology came to be little else but hierarchology,[1] even to our own day. Theologians confined

---

[1] Congar, *Vraie et fausse Réforme*, 59ff. How much the Church has been equated with the hierarchy in the catechisms and thus in the instruction of the people has been shown by the study of Martin Ramsauer, 'Die Kirche in den Katechismen', in *ZKTh*, 73 (1951), 129; 169; 313–46. Cf. also F. X. Arnold, *Grundsätzliches und Geschichtliches zur Theologie der Seelsorge*, Freiburg 1949, 8ff. and 106ff. ; id., 'Die Stellung des Laien in der Kirche', in *USR*, 9 (1954), No. 4, 8–26.

themselves to proving the divine realities that constitute the Church, but neglected the truth of their temporal and human actualization, and the tension between the absolute and the relative resulting from this. The Reformers preferred the language of religious experience. To obviate the dangers of this tendency Catholic theologians found themselves increasingly compelled to speak in metaphysical abstractions and, for the sake of greater certainty and precision, to present the data of faith in terms of Aristotelian scholasticism rather than in the words of the Bible. Hence they frequently succumbed to the danger of using the same terminology for God and for the mysteries of salvation, thus divorcing the facts of the Redemption from the theological concepts. Luther's theology was influenced by Augustinianism—consequently a Catholic theologian was suspect of 'Protestantizing tendencies' as soon as he based himself on St Augustine and the Fathers rather than on the late medieval Schoolmen. We realize today what a loss this has been to theology, since Augustinian thought has only recently been readmitted to its rightful place in Catholic theology. To give another example: J. A. Jungmann draws attention to the fact that, owing to the controversy with the Reformers, the Eucharist has almost exclusively been regarded from the point of view of the presence of Christ, while its other aspects have been neglected. Since the Reformers denied the particular priesthood, Catholic theologians felt obliged to stress not the common traits, but the differences between priest and people.[1] Examples of such disastrous consequences of Christian polemics might be multiplied.

We have said that it was a methodological mistake of these denominational polemics to select and treat particular controversial points in isolation. This does not mean that these particular points should not be approached directly; but they must not be considered apart from the whole. Now this is precisely what has happened only too frequently in inter-denominational discussions. The successes of this method were deceptive. If a Protestant theologian professed a 'Catholic' opinion on a controversial point this was triumphantly celebrated as a 'victory'. Catholics imagined that the 'others' needed only to admit the Catholic doctrine of justification, the primacy, or the veneration of saints and relics, in order to be Catholics. They overlooked the fact that particular Protestant doctrines rest on a different foundation, that the material differences are based on formal ones. Catholic theologians like K. Rahner and H. Urs von Balthasar, who take part in inter-denominational conversations have recognized

[1] *The Mass of the Roman Rite*, vol. I, 180f.

this. The latter writes for example: 'Nothing whatever is gained if such a [inter-denominational] discussion produces material agreement on particular doctrines. The essential point in all this is the formal principles that determine all the theological details. If the discussion did not concern these, everything would be useless.'[1]

There is another factor which makes inter-denominational conversations difficult from the start. This is that the positions of the partners differ. Because of the difference in their conception of the Church the Catholic is in a different situation from the Protestant. 'If, for example,' writes K. Rahner, 'a Lutheran and a Catholic discuss the right conception of the doctrine of justification, the situation is different on the two sides. It is true, each of them has his own conviction and presupposes that of the other; comparing and defending their respective points of view both aim at mutual understanding and at convincing their partner. . . . Yet the position of the Catholic differs from that of the Lutheran. The conviction of the Catholic regarding this or that controversial point is always in the first place determined by his faith in his Church and in the infallibility which he ascribes to its doctrine in certain well defined conditions. The Catholic can take part in such conversations only with constant regard to the teaching office of his Church.'[2]

Hence many Protestants consider conversations with Rome futile, or even impossible from the start. On the other hand, such conversations are made difficult by an often only too obvious inconsistency of the Protestant theologians. To begin with, the Catholic can never be sure whether his interlocutor actually represents the doctrine of his denomination, or whether he is perhaps in the position of an outsider. This introduces a permanent element of uncertainty into the inter-denominational discussion, which is enhanced by the fact that Protestant theologians frequently fail to draw the consequences from their theological insights. This was recently pointed out by E. Peterson who wrote: 'Recent theologians have hit on the expedient of developing ideas as "historians" while taking no notice of them as "theologians". This seems impossible to me. One cannot

---

[1] *Karl Barth, Darstellung und Deutung seiner Theologie*, 176. Cf. also K. Rahner, who asks 'whether it is reasonable to talk about particular doctrines of a material kind while we are so profoundly divided on the formal principle of faith. This question ought not to be treated lightly. The problem undoubtedly overshadows all conversations, so that little seems to be gained even if we more or less "agree" on a question of theological detail . . . . Hence we ought to be sufficiently sober and honest not to exaggerate the importance of such material rapprochements.' 'Gespräche über den "Zaun". Offener Brief an Hans Asmussen', in *W.u.W.*, 5 (1950), 176.

[2] ibid., 175f.

assert, as does Holl . . . that the primitive community in Jerusalem had been "Catholic", equipped with ecclesiastical law, etc., and yet refuse to draw any theological consequences from this. One cannot write, like Mundle . . . that the Acts of the Apostles presupposes the idea of the Apostolic Succession and then perhaps attack this very idea. One cannot say, as Lietzmann does . . . that St Paul regarded the Last Supper as a sacrificial meal, i.e. as the Mass, and yet disregard this completely in the sphere of dogma. Finally, one cannot, as is generally done, regard the New Testament as the reflection of Church tradition and nevertheless oppose the former to the latter. We must demand that the facts that admittedly appear in the New Testament should not be separated from the doctrinal statement by too large a gap; else the Protestant Church in Germany will be in danger of becoming a sect, because it moves farther and farther away from the New Testament.'[1] All these are subtle difficulties besetting inter-denominational conversations.

A further possibility in the conduct of such discussions would be the eirenical method, which is only concerned to establish peace among the denominations. Here, too, it is presupposed 'that positions on both sides were known and fixed, but that they merely represented a beneficial variety of outlook within the infinite range of truth'.[2] This method has been a temptation to the Oecumenical Movement wherever theologians have held that the different elements of truth within the Churches could be combined by way of addition. Nevertheless, the representatives of this eirenical method soon realized that such an attempt could be made only at the expense of truth. The same must be said of the idea of including only certain fundamental truths of the faith in the conversations and thus reaching unity on the basis of a minimum creed. This, too, has proved to be a Utopian delusion. In conversations with the Catholic Church this has sometimes been regarded as profitable, since certain of its doctrines were seen merely as 'Catholic exaggerations' which need only be discarded for agreement to be reached. Such opinions have occasionally been supported by certain Catholics who developed a one-sided conception of what is to be considered as 'Catholic'. Here we would only point to the controversy between Adam Fechter and Josef Lortz on writing the history of the Reformation.[3]

[1] *Die Kirche.*

[2] Skydsgaard, loc. cit., 159.

[3] A. Fechter, 'Die Reformation im ökumenischen Gewissen. Vor neuen Aufgaben einer katholischen Geschichtsschreibung'. In *W.u.W.* 7 (1952), 11–19.

This eirenical spirit had gained admission especially in certain circles of the *Una Sancta* movement which tried to base these conversations on a 'unity in charity' which was to be achieved by synthesis and based on common experience. All these attempts contain a right motive and a nucleus of truth. But this method lacks final validity, for a conversation, however fraternal and understanding, which aims at a compromise cannot be considered fruitful. There can be no compromise with truth.

The method of a discussion of isolated controversial points has already been mentioned, and we would not maintain that this approach is necessarily superficial. While distinguishing it from the methods of denominational controversy and eirenics we have found that the distinctive doctrines rest on underlying basic assumptions and should never be considered in isolation from one another.

As we have seen, K. Rahner and H. U. von Balthasar distinguish between material and formal oppositions. We would adopt this distinction, because it may lead to the right method of inter-denominational conversations. K. Rahner sees in the 'formal principle of faith' the basic factor that determines all else. Hence the formal distinction is to be found in a principle that is the cause of the various particular affirmations. We would not confine the term 'formal' to a theological principle, but would take material and formal difference in the sense of the scholastic distinction between matter and form. According to this terminology matter is something indistinct that waits to be stamped with a form, the form being the determining factor. Now, in the question under discussion the material and formal distinction of faith is not quite adequate, for the material points of detail are already determined by a formal background. But the form can be extracted from these material data, and the material details can be examined with a view to discovering their basic *'forma'*.

The present work attempts to clarify this formal, actual, ground of division between the denominations. In our discussion of the struggle for the unity of the Church we have chosen the 'Oecumene' as our point of departure. The question of what constitutes the Church is the most pressing problem in inter-denominational conversations today. And the Oecumenical Movement is a fact with which the Catholic theologians, as the vanguard of their Church, must concern themselves. For this movement struggles for the unity of the Church in both theological discussion and practical experiment. The results achieved are important also for our own ecclesiology. We hope to prove in this work that the latter can only gain from them. Our method is neither polemical controversy nor eirenics; we would rather listen to our separated brethren than incur the reproach of Karl Barth who asserts that the Catholic 'partner speaks rather than listens, that he takes up the attitude of one who is in the right even before the discussion begins'.[1] It is true, that as Catholics, we take as our starting-point the doctrine of the Church such as it is today, based on Scripture, tradition and *magisterium*, yet by so doing we would not take up the attitude of those happily in possession. We would listen to our separated brethren, conscious of a possible incompleteness in our faith such as we live it,[2] or even of the fact that the Church's vision and interpretation of the faith have not yet reached their ultimate degree of perfection.[3] The Catholic theologians are confronted with the warning of Y. M.-J. Congar cited by H. U. von Balthasar in his book on Karl Barth:[4] 'Against the one-sided deformation of the truth the Church does indeed stress not merely the corresponding particular truth, but the truth in its totality, which overrides both particular truths and errors. Yet it is inevitable that in its relevant statements it should point out just those aspects that are denied by the heresy; it is above all impossible that her apologists should not attempt to restore the rights of the truths that have been denied, that her theologians should not be concerned to elaborate the relevant doctrine in all its aspects. Thus the theology of the Church loses as well as gains by heresy; for on the one hand the latter stimulates its progress, on the other it causes it to become one-sided. Whenever a certain error begins to spread, the organism of the Church stiffens and its forces are concentrated in order to counteract the evil. A false statement which exaggerates a truth is opposed by its carefully-defined correction; but generally this is not referred to the Church's doctrine as a whole, and the theologians are satisfied if the truth that has been denied or mis-understood has been defined more precisely. Moreover, since the error will always be partial, the opposed doctrinal truth is also in danger of being a partial truth, inasmuch as it is content merely to assert the opposite. Now, as the Schoolmen say, contrary truths are

---

[1] H. U. von Balthasar, *Karl Barth* . . . , 26.

[2] ibid, 26.

[3] Cf. Pius XII in *Humani generis*: Accedit quod uterque doctrinae divinitus revelatae fons tot tantosque continet thesauros veritatis, *ut numquam* reapse *exhauriatur*. Quapropter sacrorum fontium studio sacrae disciplinae semper *juvenescunt ;* dum contra speculatio, quae ulteriorem sacri depositi inquisitionem neglegit, *ut experiundo novimus*, sterilis evadit'.

[4] op. cit. 23–25.

of the same species. Then it is easy, whether from habit, principle or indolence, to be more concerned with the official texts than with life; such is the way of the lazy and not infrequently opportunist theologians who are content to consult their Denzinger instead of studying Scripture, the Fathers, the Liturgy and the living faith of the Church. Such, also, are the apologists who have to oppose the errors that arise day by day and who regard the Church from its most external side, and this means the majority, at least the majority of those who speak, write and make themselves heard: all these oppose error by a hardened and imperfect truth (if they remain attached to a chance definition or formulation of the moment), i.e. a one-sided and partial truth. There is much progress in precision, much specialization, but also much rigidity and contraction of the content of Revelation in such dogmatic reactions as the condemnation of Baius, the definition of the Seven Sacraments, the anti-Protestant insistence on tradition alongside Scripture and the condemnation of Modernism. The gain in doctrinal precision, in certainty in matters of faith, is indeed valuable and even necessary. But, on the other hand, perspectives have surely been greatly narrowed and problems have been over-specialized by the condemnation of Baius, when the supernatural was considered merely under its aspect of being "not due" and thus other relations between nature and grace were in danger of being neglected and disregarded. Further, the massive crystallization of the sacramental reality in the Seven Sacraments involving extreme theological and canonistic affirmations surely tends to make us forget the sacramental character of the whole Church and its life, to the detriment of the understanding of symbolism and liturgy. Moreover, the necessary anti-Protestant reaction in favour of tradition will increase the difficulties even further and suggest the idea that, if it is wrong that the Church is founded on Scripture, it is consequently true that Scripture is founded on the Church—which would be a very bad way of approaching the question. Has not the very necessary reaction against Modernism actually led us to generalize certain true but incomplete aspects of doctrine, for example, the doctrine of the teaching Church? For this has led to a certain elimination and misunderstanding of the complementary positive aspects, of all that means life and historical development within the Church; an elimination and a misunderstanding which actually affect the true concept of tradition and thus of Christian doctrine.'[1]

[1] *Chrétiens Désunis*, 34–36.

We hope we shall not be thought arrogant if we desire to help our separated brethren in their search; for we are convinced and believe that the Roman Catholic Church is the true Church and that true unity willed by God can be found only in her. But we should like to treat of these things with our separated brethren in a discussion that is truly oecumenical. In choosing the 'Oecumene' as the subject of the conversation we can consider particular communions only in so far as they give it its character, and the views of individual theologians only if they bear witness to their Church or point to such witness. It is very doubtful whether the 'Oecumene' itself can yet be considered a genuine interlocutor of the Roman Catholic Church; in fact we think that this must be denied. But we hope that this may one day be achieved, and if this study offers a humble contribution to this end it will have fulfilled its purpose despite its shortcomings. For it would not claim to give a final presentation of the doctrine of the Church whether from one point of view or from the other; indeed it is doubtful whether this could ever be done. We would consider the problem from every side, in an attempt to form a concept, for 'because the Church is the mystery of Christ traversing the ages . . . she cannot actually be defined; she can only be described and depicted.'[1] But the theology of the 'Oecumene' has suggested new questions. From their angle we would consider the question of the unity of the Church in the service of 'a new theology of the Church that has arisen among us and is as yet far from its goal'.[2] Today we can no longer say with M. D. Koster, 'The ecclesiology of our time is still in a pre-theological state.'[3] What concerns us today is 'to work out more clearly the reality "Church", to see it more distinctly than hitherto as a *corpus sui generis*. Pius XII's encyclicals *Mystici corporis* and *Mediator Dei* have greatly encouraged theological thinking in this respect.'[4]

If we want another term for 'method of oecumenical discussions' we may well choose G. Söhngen's 'method of the open system'.[5] This method, we hope, will afford the most fruitful start for a positive approach to the Christians separated from the Mother-Church, so that our Lord's words 'that all may be one' may become reality.

---

[1] Schmaus, *Katholische Dogmatik*[2] III, 1, 6.
[2] *HK* III (1948–9), 216.
[3] *Ekklesiologie im Werden*, Paderborn 1940.
[4] K. Rahner, loc. cit. in *W.u.W.* 5 (1950), 184.
[5] *Die Einheit in der Theologie*, 63 f.

I. Historical Part

1. THE OECUMENICAL MOVEMENT AND 'OECUMENE'

We must first of all define the term 'oecumenical', which has almost become a slogan.[1] People speak of an 'Oecumenical Movement', of 'Oecumene' pure and simple, of a 'non-catholic' and a 'catholic Oecumenism', of 'oecumenical Christians and theologians', of an 'oecumenical theology' and an 'oecumenical problem'; hence we have first to ask what non-Catholics mean by it. O. Tomkins speaks of a modern use of the old term oecumenical. In the New Testament, Oecumene means the inhabited part of the earth where the Gospel must be preached.[2] Later the Church gave to this word in such expressions as 'Oecumenical Councils' and 'Oecumenical Symbols' the meaning of geographical completeness, i.e. of representing all regions where the Church had proclaimed its message, but also that of doctrinal unity, implying a common witness to the faith. G. F. Vicedom has rightly drawn attention to the fact that, if we go back to the original meaning of the term, it at once becomes frighteningly clear 'that we have no reason to use it so naturally and with such a claim to totality as we actually do'. The Oecumenical Movement comprises only part of the Christian churches, and precisely that part 'which least emphasizes tradition and doctrine' and which is interested in internal and inter-Church questions rather than in the apostolate. Vicedom therefore concludes: 'Hence the term "oecumenical" is not applicable to it (i.e. the Oecumenical Movement)'.[3] If, therefore, Protestants use this term today it must have a new meaning, which O. Tomkins describes thus: 'Its modern use in this setting was obviously dictated by the need to express the idea of Catholic without its partisan associations.' The word 'ecumenical' is used to denote *'interest in Christian unity and church union.*[4]' Thus 'oecumenical' would mean the opposite of 'denominational' used in a derogatory sense. Hence a definition of the term will not lead to the essence of the Oecumene and of the Oecumenical Movement. But a definition of the essence also involves great difficulties.

[1] W. Menn speaks of a 'glut of the term oecumenical since the end of the war', so that it is time 'to strive to use the word more sparingly' (*Die Ökumenische Bewegung 1932–1948*, 8).

[2] Michel, *ThWzNT*, V, 159–61.

[3] 'Credo unam, sanctam, catholicam et apostolicam,' *ELKZ*, 7 (1953), 33.

[4] *The Church in the Purpose of God*, 8.

Pastor G. Lagny said at the World Conference of Churches (1937) at Edinburgh: 'Even the principles which lie at the starting-point of every search for oecumenicity are obscure to many. One of the most striking indications of this fact is the widely differing and even contradictory way in which the term "oecumenism" itself is used. For some, it seems to imply above all universal, or perhaps merely interconfessional or international relations between the churches. For others, true oecumenicity is only possible when the whole world has been converted to Christ. It seems to us a matter of urgency that the principles which mark our starting-point and the fundamental terms we use should be defined.'[1] Since Amsterdam, the word 'Oecumene' has been used only with trepidation. The term 'Oecumenical Movement' is used much more frequently, since it expresses a certain dynamism and development, that is to say a beginning of unity, the intention and aims of which will emerge only gradually.

In order to understand what Protestants mean by the unity of the Church it is best to pursue the history of this movement; then we shall also be able to make clearer what contemporary Protestantism means when using the terms Church and unity.

The roots of the Oecumenical Movement go far back into the past. W. Menn speaks of a 'pre-history', by which he means 'the period . . . in which the desire for unity was expressed in the form of international Christian associations without influencing the Churches as such'.[2] He mentions as examples of such international associations of the first period the 'Evangelical Alliance', founded in 1846 as 'Bruderbund des Gebetes und des Kampfes für den Glauben', the Young Men's Christian Association (1844) and the Young Women's Christian Association (1855), the 'Jugendbund für entschiedenes Christentum' (1894) and the international missionary conferences, the first of which took place in London in 1879, and among which that of Edinburgh in 1910 became particularly important for the further history of the Oecumenical Movement.[3] During this first period national frontiers were transcended; churches of the same faith drew together. Thus, in 1867, the Anglican bishops of the whole world gathered together in the Lambeth Conference; the Allgemeine Evangelisch-Lutherische Konferenz soon assumed an international character and became the Lutheran World Convention at Eisenach in 1923; the Oecumenical Methodist Conference came

[1] L. Hodgson, *The Second World Conference on Faith and Order*, 212.
[2] Menn, loc. cit., 9.
[3] ibid., 10.

into being in 1881, the International Union of Congregational Churches in 1891 and the Baptist World Convention in 1905.

The Anglican Church in the United States, the Protestant Episcopal Church, was the first Protestant body to suggest a supradenominational association (if we leave out of account the German Evangelical Kirchenausschuss of 1903 and the North American Church Association which had a national basis). In October 1910 the Rev. W. T. Manning sponsored a motion at the General Convention at Cincinnati in which he made the following request: 'To take under advisement the promotion by this Church of a Conference following the general method of the World Missionary Conference (i.e. Edinburgh), to be participated in by representatives of all Christian bodies throughout the world which accept our Lord Jesus Christ as God and Saviour, for the consideration of questions pertaining to the Faith and Order of the Church of Christ.'[1] This Committee reported its conviction 'that such a Conference for the purposes of study and discussion, without power to legislate or to adopt resolutions, is the next step toward unity.'[2] The moving spirits of this committee were above all Charles Brent of the Protestant Episcopal Church of the United States and Robert H. Gardiner, with whose names the Oecumenical Movement has since remained indissolubly linked. There was now a definite goal to which all efforts were directed, the World Council of Churches.

FAITH AND ORDER

Thus, the Oecumenical Movement owes its origin partly to the group of men who worked on questions of faith and Church order and was therefore called the Commission on Faith and Order. The slogan Faith and Order was first pronounced at the General Convention of 1886. We must now examine its meaning.

Faith is used in the sense of *fides quae creditur*. It means the content of faith, not its function (belief) or the formulation of its contents, i.e. the Creed, though both, of course, belong to the content of faith which, in fact, cannot be conceived without its formulation. Faith is the essence of the revealed truths that are formulated in the oecumenical symbols and belong to the substance of Christianity.

The concept of Order is more difficult. It is intimately related to the questions of the nature of the Church as a visible community, of the Church's ministry and of the Sacraments. Order is the sum total

[1] *Faith and Order*. Lausanne, 1927, ed. H. N. Bate, 1927, p. vii.
[2] ibid.

of the divinely instituted outer forms which belong to the essence of the Church. Hence it cannot be equated with the 'constitution of the Church'; for this includes also matters not instituted by God, while on the other hand not including the Sacraments.[1]

It is evident that the 'programme' of Faith and Order originated in Anglican circles.[2] The one faith, the God-given means of grace and the ordained ministers, i.e. the triad of faith, sacraments and ministry appears wherever Anglicans define their classical conception of the Church. But this began to change in proportion as the Anglican Church took part in the Oecumenical Movement. Whereas in the middle of the nineteenth century its term of reference had still been the old undivided Church, it now began to visualize the 'united Church of the future' characterized by its universality expressed in a variety of forms. H. Sasse in his official German report on the World Conference of Lausanne states that 'this expresses a special characteristic of English and American thought, viz. the desire for comprehensiveness'.[3] Thus this idea of Anglican theology left its mark on the Oecumenical Movement.

LIFE AND WORK

The Oecumenical Movement has still another root, the so-called Life and Work Movement. This was the name of a group of men more interested in the practical side of the Christian life and mission in the world and deeply affected by the unhappy social consequences of the First World War, which brought the Churches more closely together. The soul of this movement was the Archbishop of Uppsala, Nathan Søderblom.[4] The First World Conference on Life and Work held at Stockholm in 1925 was above all the fruit of his labours; its Continuation Committee called itself (after 1929) 'Oecumenical Council for Life and Work'. 'It left questions of faith and order to the movement of Lausanne (as the Faith and Order Movement is sometimes called, because it first met at Lausanne in Switzerland), but devoted itself to practical questions currently occupying the

[1] On the concept of Order cf. Pribilla: 'Order concerns not so much the constitution (hierarchy) of the Church as the performance of the sacred actions (divine service and sacraments), i.e. the question whether a special ordination is necessary and of what kind it should be' (*Um kirchliche Einheit*, 137).

[2] Cf. 'An Appeal to All Christian People', of the Lambeth Conference of 1920, in G. K. A. Bell, *Documents on Christian Unity*, 1 ff.

[3] *Die Weltkonferenz für Glaube und Kirchenverfassung*, Berlin, 1929, 16.

[4] Congar characterizes Søderblom as 'a man of extremely able mind, though somewhat complex and eclectic, strongly influenced by the modernism coupled with relativism of Schleiermacher, A. Sabatier and Troeltsch' (*Divided Christendom*, 117).

attention of the world as well as the churches, and established the "Institute of Social Science" at Geneva to deal with social problems. This Institute convoked Church conferences which considered, among other things, questions of unemployment and economic crises, but increasingly also the fundamental theological and moral social problems connected with them.'[1]

This Oecumenical Movement for Life and Work held a second World Conference at Oxford in 1937 on the subject 'Church, Community and State'.[2] Here an amalgamation of the two movements of Lausanne and Stockholm to form a World Council of Churches was proposed. This desire was to be fulfilled at Amsterdam in 1948.

(a) LAUSANNE

The Oecumenical Movement has sometimes been held to 'owe its inner and outer growth to the hard pressure to which the Church was subjected during the past epoch', 'expressing the ideological internationalism of the years after the First World War'.[3] Though this view contains elements of truth, the Oecumenical Movement cannot be explained in this way. Menn rightly observes that the Church 'does not live in a vacuum, but, as a community of beings bound up in history, is subject to a multitude of influences. . . . Nevertheless it has the *Deus vult* behind it'.[4] We, too, would agree that 'The Oecumenical Movement is a movement of a spiritual nature, in which God Himself takes all the Churches and brings them to one another for mutual encounter and discussion'.[5] There

---

[1] W. Menn, 13 ff. On the Stockholm Conference, its preliminaries, course and results cf. Pribilla, loc. cit. 40 ff. The theological roots of the Life and Work Movement have been well set out by Congar (*Divided Christendom*, 116 f.). According to him it was founded on a combination of nominalism, Lutheran dualism, philosophical rationalism and a pragmatic position, which ideologies produced their doctrinal effects: 'It practically reduces the Christian position to a philosophy of religion; it fails to understand the true nature of faith, and the fact that this faith is the very substance of the Church and of its unity' (127). Thus, at Stockholm it was possible for Salvationists, Unitarians, Orthodox and Anglicans to sit peacefully round the same table. 'At Stockholm the most diverse and irreconcilable ideas underlay the common use of the Christian terms' (130). 'Stockholm emanated from a pragmatist and chiefly English-speaking milieu assembled under the aegis of a Protestant modernist' (131).'However grateful we may be to the pioneers of Stockholm, we cannot and dare not go back to the "as if" theology which demands that we should act "as if" we were one in faith.' (Visser't Hooft in *The Universal Church in God's Design*, 184.

[2] Cf. J. H. Oldham, *Church, Community and State*, SCM Press, 1934.

[3] Menn, 7.

[4] ibid.

[5] Cf. Sasse, loc. cit. 11.

can be no doubt that the will to union springs from a profound *religious* motive.

Evidence of this is the confession of guilt of the Churches, which deplores the divisions of Christendom as a sin and which trustingly turns to the prayer of Christ before His death *'Ut omnes unum sint'* (John xvii) as it is expressed in the preamble to the Resolutions of the First Lambeth Conference of 1867: 'We desire to express the deep sorrow with which we view the divided condition of the flock of Christ throughout the world, ardently longing for the fulfilment of the prayer of our Lord: "That all may be one, as Thou, Father, art in me, and I in Thee, that they also may be one in us: that the world may believe that Thou hast sent me." '[1]

But this religious motive also finds a widespread response just where the need for unity in Faith and Order is most felt, that is in the mission field. The young Churches constitute the vanguard of the Oecumenical Movement, because they realize most keenly how the native peoples' esteem for the Christian message is lowered by the divisions of Christendom.[2]

But to return to Faith and Order, which is the best guide to the development of the Oecumenical question. The First World Conference on Faith and Order was held at Lausanne from 3rd to 21st August 1927. Its preparation had been seriously hampered by the First World War;[3] nevertheless 450 members of approximately ninety churches finally assembled. Its presidents were Charles H. Brent (Anglican, USA), A. E. Garvie (Congregational Union of England and Wales), and vice-presidents were the Archbishop of Uppsala, Nathan Søderblom, the Archbishop and Metropolitan of Thyatira, Germanos (Orthodox), Professor A. Deissmann (Evangelical Church of the Old Prussian Union) and M. le Pasteur Charles Merle d'Aubigné (Union Nationale des Églises Réformées Évangéliques de France). The following Churches were represented either by official delegations or by delegates appointed as 'visitors':[4]

Orthodox Churches: The Oecumenical Patriarchate of Constanti-

---

[1] *The Six Lambeth Conferences,*[2] SPCK, 1929, p. 9.

[2] Cf. the address of the Anglican Bishop of Dornakal (India), Dr. Vedenayakam Samuel Azariah, in the third plenary session in the cathedral of Lausanne. His main points were: 1. Unity is necessary in view of the world opportunities open before the Church today. 2. Unity is necessary for a common witness before the non-Christian world. 3. Unity is necessary for the life of the Church in the mission field (Bate, p. 491 ff.).

[3] Cf. ibid., viii ff.; M. Pribilla, 135–61.

[4] In Bate. These Churches are mentioned here so that the reader may know which Churches take part in the Oecumenical Movement.

nople, the Patriarchates of Alexandria, Jerusalem, Roumania, Serbia, and the Churches of Greece, Cyprus, Bulgaria, Poland, Russia and Georgia.

Other *Eastern Churches:* The Apostolic Church of Armenia.

The Old Catholic Church in the Netherlands, The Christ Catholic Church in Switzerland, the Polish-National Catholic Church, The Czecho-Slovak Church.

Anglican Churches: Church of England, Church of Ireland, Episcopal Church in Scotland, the Church in Wales, Protestant Episcopal Church in USA, Church of England in Canada, Province of the West Indies, Anglican Diocese in Argentina and Eastern South America, Church of England in India, the Holy Catholic Church of China, the Holy Catholic Church of Japan, Church of the Province of South Africa, Church of England in Australia and Tasmania.

Lutheran Churches: United Lutheran Church in America, Lutheran Free Church of America, Norwegian Lutheran Church of America, Église Évangélique Luthérienne de France, Church of the Confession of Augsburg (Alsace and Lorraine), Church of Sweden, Church of Finland, Church of Latvia, German Evangelical Church in Bohemia, Moravia and Silesia, Evangelical Church in Slovakia, Evangelical-Lutheran Church in Hungary, Evangelical-Lutheran Church in Holland, Tamil Evangelical Lutheran Church.

Reformed and Presbyterian Churches: Church of Scotland, United Free Church of Scotland, Presbyterian Church of England, Presbyterian Church in Ireland, Presbyterian Church in Wales, Presbyterian Church in the USA, United Presbyterian Church of North America, Reformed Church in the United States, Reformed Church in America, Presbyterian Church in Canada, Reformed Churches of Switzerland, Union Nationale des Églises Réformées de France, Reformed Church of Alsace, Église Chrétienne Missionnaire Belge, Dutch Reformed Church, Czech Evangelical Church, Reformed Church in Hungary, Italian Evangelical Church, Waldensian Evangelical Church, Presbyterian Church of South Africa, Presbyterian Church of New Zealand.

Congregational Churches: Congregational Union of England and Wales, National Council of Congregational Churches in the United States, North China Kung li Hui, Congregational Union of South Africa, Congregational Union of Australia and New Zealand.

Methodist Churches: Wesleyan Methodist Conference, United Methodist Church, Primitive Methodist Church, Methodist Church in Ireland, Methodist Episcopal Church in USA, Methodist

Episcopal Church, South (USA), Primitive Methodist Church, USA, Église Évangélique Méthodiste de France, Wesleyan Methodist Church of South Africa, Methodist Church of Australia, Methodist Episcopal Church in Portugal.

Baptist Churches: Northern Baptist Convention, USA, Seventh Day Baptist General Conference, Baptist Union of Ontario and Quebec, Seventh Day Baptist Churches of Holland, Union of German Baptists.

Disciples: Disciples of Christ in North America, Churches of Christ in Australia.

Christian: General Convention of the Christian Church, USA, Churches of Christ in America.

Church of the Brethren, USA, Conference of South-German Mennonites.

Quakers: Society of Friends in Great Britain and Ireland, Society of Friends in America.

A great multitude indeed. Yet not really a multitude, if we take into account that 'more than one third of the Evangelical Lutheran Communion in the world had not sent representatives to this gathering'.[1]

The following subjects had been proposed for discussion:

I.   The Call to Unity.
II.   The Church's Message to the world: the Gospel.
III. The Nature of the Church.
IV.   The Church's common confession of Faith.
V.   The Church's Ministry.
VI.   The Sacraments.
VII. The Unity of Christendom and the relation thereto of existing Churches.

Subjects II–VII were discussed by specially formed sections which were to give their reports to the full session.

Here we are concerned especially with the seventh subject, which expresses the aim of the Oecumenical Movement most clearly. Archbishop Søderblom presided over this section. In the fourteenth full session he stated, *inter alia*, that the unity of the Church ought to be expressed in love, in faith and in the constitution of the Church. Søderblom considered that there were 'three general answers to the questions about unity in Creed and Order':

1. Institutionalism ("The primary thing is, according to this

1 Bate, 325.

conception, the sacramental institution'[1]), which Søderblom calls 'a hindrance to unity'.[2]

2. Spiritualism. Søderblom says: 'If I am bound to choose between Institutionalism and Spiritualism I prefer the latter.'[3]

3. Incarnationalism. 'This third group emphasizes, as against the first, that religion is not essentially a body, a fixed form, a doctrine, a hierarchy, but primarily a soul, a spirit. It emphasizes as against the second group that for us, in this earthly existence, every spirit must receive bodily form, be incarnated in words, in deeds, men, institutions, doctrines and forms of service in order to become active and lasting.'[4] Søderblom hopes for the 'miracle' of a 'future united Church' by 'a new expression of faith in the living God . . . in the language and fabric of the thought of these times',[5] and thus he actually expected the Conference to provide an *experience* of spiritual unity as well as an expression of it. But the members of the Conference regarded Søderblom as too much a representative of the Stockholm thesis of 'unity in love'. The Anglican and Orthodox opposition was stronger.

As noted above, the Faith and Order Movement is of Anglican origin. The Anglican idea of the unity of the Church was represented at Lausanne especially by Dr A. C. Headlam, Bishop of Gloucester. He said in his address: 'The ideal that we have put before us is a unity which should have in it great possibilities of diversity.[6] The following must be the principles of this unity:

1. The unity of faith, including a confession of faith in the doctrines of the Incarnation and the Trinity handed down in the Apostles' and the Nicene Creeds.

2. A sacramental union. Headlam holds that 'this unity in sacrament means the acceptance of the sacraments and not any particular teaching about them'.[7] 'Each worshipper will receive the sacrament with the meaning that he himself attaches to it.'[8]

3. Union in ministry. Dr Headlam has no doubt 'that this union in the ministry must mean the acceptance of the traditional form of the Christian ministry, the acceptance of episcopacy and of episcopal ordination'.[9]

Apart from this, however, great variety was demanded: (1) in the manner of worship, (2) in the particular confessions of particular Churches which are seen as 'different interpretations of the one

---

[1] Bate, 322.
[2] ibid., 324.
[3] ibid., 324 f.
[4] ibid., 323.
[5] ibid., 331.
[6] ibid.
[7] ibid., 332.
[8] ibid., 333.
[9] ibid., 333.

truth', (3) in the exercise of the ministry: 'Episcopacy may be autocratic, constitutional or democratic', so that 'the adoption of episcopacy does not mean the adoption necessarily of one particular type',[1] (4) in the types of national Churches which spring from their relation to the national life. As regards 'those societies which have organized themselves apart from national Churches ... the only thing that we should demand is that these societies, whether Anglican, Roman, Methodist or whatever they may be, should not call themselves Churches'.[2]

Thus the ideal is to leave much room for difference and variety; the fundamental demands made on a united Church are freedom and tolerance. Hence the Church of the future is based on the presupposition that the Church does not yet exist but can be founded on a 'rational minimum basis',[3] or a *via media* between Catholicism and Protestantism governed by the Anglican conception of the Church.

This must have sounded strange, indeed, to the Orthodox members. In his reply to Archbishop Gardiner's invitation to the World Conference Archbishop Anthony of Kharkov had stated that 'there can be only *one* true Church and the only way to unity is submission to this Church'.[4] The archbishop's secretary drew attention to several articles in periodicals which were published at the time as semi-official pronouncements of the Holy Synod and which criticized the plans for the World Conference from the point of view of the Orthodox Church: 'According to orthodox teaching, unity is not only a goal to be aimed at but also a fact. ... We believe in the *one* existing Church but do not strive to construct this one Church. ... The only way to reunion is the conversion of the heterodox to this Church. The union of Churches is something of an Utopia, but the communion of the Churches, the mutual rapprochement can ... be a living reality.'[5] In the name of the delegates of the Orthodox Church, Archbishop Germanos therefore read a declaration which, according to Pribilla, represents 'probably the most important event of the Conference of Lausanne'. The Orthodox speak of a 'compromise between, in our view, contradictory thoughts and opinions. ... But there is no possibility of a compromise in matters of faith and conscience.' The Orthodox Church holds firmly to the principle that the limits of private opinion are circumscribed by the

[1] ibid., 336.
[2] ibid., 337 f.
[3] Cf. Heiler, *Im Ringen um die Kirche*, vol. ii, Munich, 1951, 294.
[4] Cf. Sasse, op. cit., 31.
[5] Sasse, p. 32, note 69.

definition given by the universal Church. . . . . Hence the Orthodox Church is of the opinion that reunion can take place only on the basis of the common faith and confession of the old, undivided Church of the seven Oecumenical Councils and the first eight centuries. (Hence) . . . we cannot support the idea of a reunion limited to a few common tenets and external declarations; for, according to the Orthodox Church, there can be no *communio in sacris* where the totality of faith is lacking.'[1] This was a clear pronouncement, by which the Orthodox opposed a maximum basis to the Anglican minimum programme.

Surveying the Lausanne Conference as a whole three points can be made. (1) 'The greatest and most important aspect of the Conference is that it took place at all.'[2] (2) A positive gain was above all the confession that the divisions were a matter of sin and guilt. (3) But the Conference failed to bring out the differences. It 'suffered from the mechanical imitation of the parliamentary method which was applied rather high-handedly according to the Anglo-Saxon custom.'[3]

Two types of faith, one institutional and traditional, the other spiritualistic and prophetical, opposed each other.[4] 'The method of the Lausanne Conference could not embrace such polarities, because it was a method of the surface and not of the depth (*Flächenmethode, nicht Tiefenmethode*).'[5]

The opposition between 'Catholic' and 'Evangelical' within the Oecumene was to be formulated only later, at Amsterdam; but it made itself felt already at Lausanne. The slogan 'Church of the Future' was proposed by the Anglicans, but the Conference opposed any sort of Anglican 'institutionalism'. The Oecumenical Movement is characterized by this concept of the 'Church of the Future'. None of the existing 'Churches' is *the* Church of Christ as a present reality, 'but all Christian bodies which preserve a minimum of ecclesiastical order and doctrinal tradition are in some measure, though imperfectly, the Church of Christ'.[6] 'The future "ecumenical" Church will be a synthesis of all the confessional Churches at present separated in practice but united in origin and substance, broadly diversified as to doctrine and discipline in non-essentials.'[7]

The Anglican ideal of synthesis and 'comprehensiveness' was

---

[1] *Um kirchliche Einheit*, 177.
[2] Heiler, *Im Ringen um die Kirche*, ii, 289
[3] Pribilla, loc. cit., 188.
[4] Heiler, loc. cit., 292.
[5] ibid., 310.
[6] Congar, *Divided Christendom*, 132.
[7] ibid., 178.

influenced, as is noted by Congar and Pribilla, by the 'Constitution of the British Empire—the administrative and cultural autonomy of different states with equal rights, united by common loyalty to the Crown'.[1] It was expressed theologically by the 'Branch Theory'[2] and designed to shape the 'Church of the future'.

The concept of the Incarnation, which appeared several times during the Conference, was, indeed, important; it did not, however, signify Incarnation in its full Biblical sense of *incarnatio continuata* but was used in a vague sense of embodiment, a 'taking-on shape', so that the spirit might 'become active and lasting' (Søderblom). This concept had to accommodate the spiritualistic and eschatological tendencies which, as we shall see later, are attached to Protestantism. Even at Lausanne the problem of variety and division became a burning question in the matter of inter-communion. 'With our eyes upon this goal, we cannot but see how distant it is, and what obstacles beset the road to it. . . . Christendom will be near its goal on the day when members of all Churches can approach the same altar, to kneel there with one heart as brothers in the Lord, brought thither not merely by individual sentiment, but by the inward moving of the Spirit of their own Church, to celebrate there the sacrificial feast of communion with Christ and the brotherhood, to the glory of God.'[3] The word 'compromise' occurs in almost all speeches made at the Lausanne Conference; its members were afraid of compromise and felt it as an invisible pressure. Yet they could not escape from it. This was due not only to a wrong method used at the Conference, but also to the failure to clarify the formal foundations of this faith and theology. 'Most members of Lausanne were incapable of recognizing that the way on which they had started led nowhere; that there "unity in Christ" was asserted and sought by Christians who believed in totally different Christs, without ever realizing that, in the history of Christianity, Satan and false Christs also play a part (as was remarked even then by Pfarrer Hans

---

[1] ibid., 181.

[2] The theory was developed by the theologians of the Oxford Movement, 'who refused allegiance to Rome' (ibid., 173). 'In its narrower form, this theory asserts that the true Church of God on earth is one, but with several branches, the Roman Catholic Church, the Holy Greek Orthodox Church, the Old Catholics, and the Church of England, and certain other communions which retain the Apostolic Succession. In a wider form, the Branch Theory seems to be expressed in the Doctrinal Basis of the Free Church Federal Council of England and Wales (1917). ('The sentence: of this visible Church, and every branch thereof, the only Head is the Lord Jesus Christ, expresses this view.') Cf. R. N. Flew, *The Nature of the Church*, 36.

[3] Bishop Küry, Bate, 355.

Asmussen).'[1] One thing, however, became clear at Lausanne: the problem of reunion is the question of the nature of the Church.

(b) EDINBURGH

The Conference of Lausanne set up a continuation committee whose task it was to receive reports from the Churches on their attitude to the findings of the Conference and to devote itself to studying the doctrine of Grace, of the Ministry and the Sacraments, of the Church of Christ and the Word of God as well as the unity of the Church in life and worship.[2] This continuation committee decided to convoke the next World Conference of Churches at Edinburgh (1937), proposing as a provisional programme the subject 'The Church in the Purpose of God'. This theme, however, was severely criticized. 'It became clear that whereas in England and some other parts of the world, questions of ministry and church order stood out as providing the most serious obstacles to unity, on the continent of Europe disagreements concerning the theological doctrines of Grace and the Word of God were felt to be of much more vital importance, while in America a most acute problem was presented by divisions based on psychological, social and cultural factors and owing their origin to the course of the historical development of the New World.'[3]

One hundred and twenty-three Churches had sent 443 representatives.[4] The first chairman, Bishop Brent, had died in 1929; Dr William Temple, Archbishop of York, was appointed to succeed him. The following were elected Vice-Presidents: Gustaf Aulén, D.D., Bishop of Strangenas, Pastor Marc Boegner, President of the National Union of the Reformed Churches of France, A. E. Garvie, D.D., Archbishop Germanos, Metropolitan of Thyatira and J. Ross Stevenson, D.D. Canon L. Hodgson, D.D., was the secretary of the Conference. As at Lausanne, the Conference was again divided into sections, devoted to the following subjects:

I. The Grace of Our Lord.

II. The Church of Christ and the Word of God.

III. The Ministry and Sacraments.

IV. The Church's Unity in Life and Worship.[5]

[1] J. P. Michael, 'Der dritte Versuch', in *Orientierung*, 16 (1952), 152.
[2] Cf. O. Tomkins, *The Church in the Purpose of God*, 22 f.
[3] L. Hodgson, *The Second World Conference on Faith and Order*, 9.
[4] List of Churches, ibid., 281 ff. 'The German Evangelical Church . . . was prevented from participating by police' (Menn, *Ökumenischer Katechismus*, 14).
[5] Hodgson, 35 f.

A new method was adopted: the reports of the commissions were at once laid before the individual sections; after these had worked on them the Conference was to discuss the results.

How did the Edinburgh Conference view the Oecumenical problem, and what was the aim of the Oecumenical Movement at this Conference? The final version of the report says: 'Our goal is to realize the ideal of the Church.'[1] At the opening service Archbishop Temple preached the sermon on Eph. iv, 13, in which he said: 'The unity of the Church of God is a perpetual fact; our task is not to create it but to exhibit it . . .,' but 'our surrender is not absolute; our allegiance is not complete. Consequently the historical form and outward manifestation of the Church is never worthy of its true nature . . . and for the impotence which our sin has brought upon the Church through divisions in its outward aspect we should be covered with shame and driven to repentance'.[2] The Archbishop said further that 'the second great evil of our divisions . . . is that through the division each party to it loses some spiritual treasure, and none perfectly represents the balance of truth'.[3] Looking back on the ten years since the first Conference met at Lausanne, he declared 'that period can fitly be called . . . a decade of objective progress in church unity'.[4]

Several conceptions and possibilities of Church unity were now proposed:

1. Unity as Alliance: 'The unity which we seek may be conceived as a confederation or alliance of Churches for co-operative action.'[5] Such a confederation, however, was considered unsatisfactory: 'We are agreed that co-operative action between Churches unable to achieve intercommunion or to look towards corporate union . . . is not our final goal, since co-operative action in itself fails to manifest to the world the true character of the Church as one community of faith and worship, as well as of service.'[6]

2. Unity as Intercommunion: 'We regard sacramental intercommunion as a necessary part of any satisfactory Church unity.'[7] 'We believe that "regularity" and "mutuality" belong to the full meaning of intercommunion, ' hence all Churches sharing in intercommunion are 'true Churches, or true branches of the one Church'.[8]

3. Unity as Corporate Union. This is described as 'the final goal of our movement'.[9] Corporate union may also be called 'organic

[1] ibid., 250.
[2] ibid., 15-17.
[3] ibid., 17.
[4] ibid., 19.
[5] ibid., 250.
[6] ibid., 251.
[7] ibid.
[8] ibid., 251 f.
[9] ibid., 252.

unity'. So here appears again the 'Church of the Future' mentioned at Lausanne. 'What we desire is the unity of a living organism, with the diversity characteristic of the members of a healthy body.'[1] Bishop E. J. Palmer made an important contribution to this subject in the discussion; he preferred the term 'organic reunion'. This, he said, 'has a definite meaning. It means reunion of the churches in such a way as will enable them to live together the life of an organism. That organism is the Body of Christ. It has a history of over 1,900 years'.[2] He understood organic unity, the ideal of the Church of the future, as the Body of Christ; this provided an access to history, to a vertical unity. Unfortunately Bishop Palmer did not succeed; the Oecumenical Movement was already committed to other ideas.

The Conference now laid down conditions for arriving at inter-communion or organic unity:

1. Essential unity in faith and confession, by which 'many of the Churches' understand 'the Apostles' Creed and the Creed commonly called the Nicene as witnessing to and safeguarding that faith', though 'remembering that these documents are sacred symbols and witnesses of the Christian faith rather than legalistic standards'. Further 'that there has been in the Church through the centuries, and still is, a divinely sustained consciousness of the living Christ' (this was due to the influence of the Orthodox). Here, however' appears a difficulty in that some Churches considered Holy Scripture as the *only* norm and source of the Christian faith, rejecting tradition as an equal source beside it.

2. Likeness in non-sacramental worship is not demanded.

3. Likeness in sacramental faith and practice. The liturgical movement that is growing everywhere is a cause of encouragement to attaining unity.

4. Likeness of Orders as a basis for unity. Here, as in the doctrine of the Sacraments, 'it will be necessary to reconcile the differences between Churches'.[3]

5. Likeness in polity. Here only the existing unlikeness can be stated, 'whether as a matter of existing practice or as a matter of rival doctrines'.[4]

We see that the conditions are clearly recognized. But how are they to be realized? This sober question reveals that the ideal of an organic union cannot be achieved except by undesirable comprom-

---

[1] ibid.
[2] ibid.
[3] ibid., 253–6.
[4] ibid., 257.

ises. This is recognized quite distinctly as formal differences emerge: 'We find that the obstacles most difficult to overcome consist of elements of "faith" and "order" combined, as when some form of Church government or worship is considered a part of the faith'.[1] If an organic unity is to be achieved in these circumstances, then the order of the sacraments, the ministry and constitution must cease to be regarded as divinely given. This can be done only if the desired unity is split in two, viz. the inner spiritual unity, known in its fullness only to God, and the outer unity expressed in mutual recognition, common action and corporate or institutional unity. If concrete unity makes shipwreck on the Creed, the Ministry and the Sacraments then it may surely be doubted if the Conference could really affirm, *nemine contradicente*: "We are one in faith in Our Lord Jesus Christ, the incarnate Word of God".[2]

The question of grace was one of the central subjects at Edinburgh, and the Conference achieved astonishing agreement on this matter.

'The sovereignty of God is supreme. By the sovereignty of God we mean His all-controlling, all-embracing will and purpose revealed in Jesus Christ for each man and for all mankind. . . . But, on the other hand, it is the will of God that His grace should be actively appropriated by man's own will and that for such decision men should remain responsible.'[3] On the point of *sola gratia* the Report says: 'We do not . . . hold that the action of the divine grace over-rides human freedom and responsibility; rather, it is only as response is made by faith to divine grace that true freedom is achieved'.[4] Another unanimous statement said that 'justification and sanctification are two inseparable aspects of God's gracious action in dealing with sinful men'.[5]

J. P. Michael observes that this agreement 'is not to be treated lightly, because it removed a *virus protestanticus*'.[6] 'However', he adds, 'the German Lutherans were absent because the political authorities had refused them permission to leave their country!' We may wonder whether the above declaration could have been made *nemine contradicente* if they had been present.

It may, however, be asked how the Conference understood the nature of grace. After what has been said above it is evident that grace was held to be uncreated. 'When we speak of God's grace, we

[1] ibid.
[2] ibid., 275.
[3] ibid., 225.
[4] ibid., 227.
[5] ibid., 224.
[6] *Orientierung*, 16 (1952), 152.

think of God Himself as revealed in His Son Jesus Christ.'[1] 'The whole sphere of "created grace" which reformed spiritualism finds so difficult to understand, the gifts of grace to which belong also the Church, its law, its ministry and sacraments, remain obscure, because the doctrine of grace could not start with a universal Christology. The description of the Real Presence in the Eucharistic Sacrifice also remained essentially spiritual, and the idea of sacrifice was excluded because the one sacrifice of Christ on Golgotha was held to be unrepeatable.'[2] The agreement on the doctrine of grace regarding human activity is the more important as Archbishop Temple in his presidential address had posed this question in connexion with the decree of the Council of Trent: 'If any one says that sinful man is justified by faith alone, and understands it thus that nothing else is required for co-operating to obtain the grace of justification, and that it is in no wise necessary to prepare and dispose oneself by the activity of one's own will, let him be anathema.'[3] The Archbishop remarked on this: 'We may be very much concerned with the thought expressed in that decree. And I wish to ask my friends of the Protestant and of the Reformed traditions whether by "faith" they mean a determination of the whole person or a response of the intellect alone. For if they mean the former, faith includes the co-operation of the will, and this doctrine is not touched by this decree; but if they mean the latter, then I am one who needs to learn from their experience before I can assent to their doctrine.'[4]

Orthodox pressure had forced the Fourth Section at Edinburgh to occupy itself with the *Communion of Saints*, and so the Conference had also to define its attitude to the veneration of Our Lady in the Eastern Church. The following resolution was put before the Conference: 'The place of the Mother of Christ was considered by this Section, and all agreed that she should have a high place in Christian esteem. We commend further study of this question to the Churches.'[5] Were the Orthodox satisfied with this? Professor Bulgakoff, who had put the question of the Communion of Saints

---

[1] Hodgson, p. 224.

[2] *Orientierung*, 16 (1952), 152.

[3] Sess. VI, can. IX: 'Si quis dixerit, sola fide impium justificari, ita ut intelligat, nihil aliud requiri, quo ad justificationis gratiam consequendam cooperetur, et nulla ex parte necesse esse, eum suae voluntatis motu praeparari atque disponi, anathema sit.'

[4] Hodgson, 64.

[5] ibid., 153.

and of Our Lady already at Lausanne[1] remarked on this resolution: 'The general question of the Communion of Saints belongs with us to our doctrine of the Church; it is an ecclesiological question. In the Section it was not discussed dogmatically, but only practically.'[2] Was that not meant to be an important reminder to Faith and Order, especially as the delegate of the Evangelical Lutheran Augustan Synod of North America, C. A. Nelson, said that with this subject they had felt they were 'at the centre and heart of the oecumenical movement'?[3]

Generally it may be said that the practical points of view predominated at Edinburgh; 'practical' not in the sense of the Life and Work Movement, but 'in the realms of experience and purpose. Deeper than intellectual interpretations have been fellowship in an experience of God and dedication to His will'.[4]

'Nevertheless, the final result of the year 1937 is this, that the non-Roman Catholic communions have set out on a road from which there is no return. It means that certain effects of the Reformation and of its understanding of revelation have been revoked. The right of separate and national churches and denominations to exist in isolation has been rejected; in fact this is acknowledged to be a sin. The Christian communities officially represented in the Oecumenical Movement have admitted in principle that their doctrines and experiences, despite their historical justification, are only part of the whole truth and need to be examined both in the light of the fullness of the Old Church and of the experiences of the other communities. The only exception was the Orthodox who believe themselves to be the one true Church according to the will of the Saviour and who bear an impressive witness to the Catholic faith at these Oecumenical Conferences. If the Protestant communions consciously soften up their own doctrinal position this is by no means due only to a nineteenth-century tendency to compose dogmatic differences and simplify the faith in a rationalist manner—this is largely true of American Protestantism—but it shows an extraordinary guidance of conscience, betraying the desire for the whole revelation and the fullness of Christ. The Oecumenical Movement is governed by both these tendencies. In any case, the historical confessions and new churches of the sixteenth and seventeenth centuries have begun to

[1] Bate, 208 f.
[2] Hodgson, 153.
[3] ibid.
[4] C. T. Craig in *The Report of the American Theological Committee*. 'The Nature of the Church', 249.

move, partly towards a synthesis or union, but partly also towards the dogma and liturgy of the Old Church before the great schism'.[1]

The World Council of Churches

In another way, too, Edinburgh was to be an important event in the Oecumenical Movement. Even before the World Conferences of Oxford and Edinburgh 'the conviction had been growing that "Life and Work" and "Faith and Order" had too much in common to justify their remaining apart. Both were manifestations of the same deep desire for greater unity within the family of Christ. In "Life and Work" it was proving increasingly necessary to deal with theological issues that had first been regarded as the province of "Faith and Order". In "Faith and Order" there was a heightened feeling that the ultimate problems of unity could not be solved unless the churches began to work together effectively in those areas in which a substantial measure of agreement is already found'.[2] In 1936, therefore, a 'Committee of Thirty-five' was formed to which were elected leading personalities of the associations interested in the Oecumenical Movement, e.g. of the YMCA, YWCA, the International Missionary Council and the World Alliance for International Friendship through the Churches. This Committee met before Oxford and Edinburgh at Westfield College, Hampstead. As a result of their consultations the Committee proposed to both World Conferences at Edinburgh and Oxford that both movements 'should be more closely related in a body representative of the Churches and caring for the interests of each movement'.[3] The Archbishop of York, explaining this proposal to the Edinburgh Conference, said: 'Advantage is taken of this to provide the Oecumenical Movement as a whole with a more effective means of self-expression. This takes the form of a World Council of Churches functioning through (a) a General Assembly—meeting every five years, (b) a Central Council meeting every year, (c) Commissions dealing with special interests or departments'.[4]

It was stressed, however, that the Churches were to preserve complete freedom of action, for 'the new organization which is proposed shall have no power to legislate for the Churches or to

[1] 'Das Glaubensbewusstsein der "Ökumenischen Christenheit" ' in *Der Grosse Herder*, vol. X, col. 1438.

[2] W. A. Visser't Hooft, *The First Assembly of the World Council of Churches*, Man's Disorder and God's Design, vol. v, 13.

[3] Hodgson, 273.

[4] ibid., 194.

commit them to action, without their consent'.[1] Faith and Order and
Life and Work were to continue their work through independent
commissions; these were to be nominated by these movements
themselves and were to be members of the World Council. This
organization of the World Council 'would do something to provide
a voice for non-Roman Christendom'.[2] The Conferences of Oxford
and Edinburgh agreed to this proposal of the Committee of
Thirty-five and appointed a 'Committee of Fourteen'—seven members representing Life and Work and seven Faith and Order—who
were authorized to convene the first meeting of the Council.[3] In
1938 this Committee held a conference at Utrecht 'at which a
provisional constitution was drafted for submission to the churches.
The Utrecht Conference also created a "Provisional Committee" . . .
to whom was entrusted the responsibility of carrying on the work
of "The World Council of Churches—in Process of Formation" '.[4]
Some members of Faith and Order viewed this development with
misgivings. Thus the delegate of the Church in Wales, Archdeacon
A. E. Monahan, stated that Faith and Order had been built on a
trinitarian foundation. The report of the Committee of Thirty-five
seemed to imperil this basis, for 'The Life and Work Movement has
on its notepaper a list of participating churches which includes
Unitarian churches. That is the great question at stake. Are we going
to transform our work from a trinitarian to a unitarian basis?'[5]
Hence the essence of the World Council of Churches had to be
formulated dogmatically, and thus the aims of the Oecumenical
Movement had to be restated. This was to exercise the minds of the
theologians for many years.

W. A. Visser't Hooft attempted to define the nature and task of
the Oecumenical Council in his essay on 'The Significance of the
World Council of Churches'.[6] He does not intend to give a final
definition of this 'new phenomenon in Church history', because
room must be left for the guidance of the Holy Spirit. Nevertheless,
the Council answers the question of its nature implicitly through the
criteria of its membership, the defining of its functions, etc. Sum-
marizing the problems of the World Council we might ask: Does this
Council represent the *Una Sancta*, is it its embodied institution, can

[1] ibid., 273.
[2] ibid., 196.
[3] Visser't Hooft, 14.
[4] ibid.
[5] Hodgson, p. 202 f.
[6] *The Universal Church in God's Design*, 177–99.

it speak in the name of the Universal Church and legislate for the individual churches? We have seen that Archbishop Temple had thus understood the task of the Edinburgh Conference: as representing the already existing unity. We have also seen that the Conference of Lausanne, though content to study only the prospects of reunion, yet tried, on the other hand, 'to confess the faith of the churches in the measure of unity already attained'.[1] Visser't Hooft then speaks of a 'dualism' characteristic of the Oecumenical Movement, being both 'an agency of the churches to prepare the way for unity' and 'an organ which declares the unity already achieved'.[2] The Council is a body representing the Churches directly and officially. Is this body in process of realizing what has been described above as corporate unity? Visser't Hooft observes that 'the proposed constitution makes it abundantly clear that the Council is in no sense a super-church. The Constitution says: "The World Council shall not legislate for the Churches," and the official explanatory memorandum comments: that the Assembly and Central Committee "will have no constitutional authority whatever over its constituent churches" and that the Council exists "to serve the churches, not to control them" '.[3]

Here again the question of the nature of the Church becomes relevant. Visser't Hooft proves his thesis that the Council is not the *Una Sancta* by denying it the necessary *notae ecclesiae*. Both the complete testimony of a common faith and the community of the sacramental life are absent. 'The churches are at the moment not able to manifest the *Una Sancta* in a way which corresponds to the reality of its nature. The unity which would be seen ... would be far too much a unity of compromise. There is still in much of our present ecumenism a strong element of relativism and of lack of concern for the truth of God. And so our unity would not be the biblical unity *in truth*.'[4]

Visser't Hooft goes on to ask: 'Is the World Council then just an organization?' He refuses to understand it in the sense of the Stockholm Movement. 'The World Council cannot be a mere organization simply because it is a Council of *Churches*. For the Church in the churches insists on asserting itself. Wherever two or three churches are gathered together, the *Una Sancta* is in the midst of them and demands to be manifested.'[5] But does this not mean that the author abandons his own principle? He himself must admit that 'the whole

1 ibid., 180.
2 ibid.
3 ibid., 181.
4 ibid., 183.
5 ibid., 185.

existence of the Council is dominated by a "dilemma" ',[1] and he thinks one can escape from it only by the way of faith. Since unity can only be given, the living Christ—God and Saviour—is the only basis of the World Council of Churches, and the Council itself is 'but a means and a method which have no other *raison d'être* than to be used for the building of the *Una Sancta*'.[2] Thus the World Council is without authority, and 'it is open to any member church, and indeed to every church member to decide whether, in each given case, it recognizes in the World Council a manifestation of the one Body which fulfils the will of the Head'.[3]

Thus, from the ecclesiological standpoint, the World Council of Churches remains a very questionable affair, seeing that it lacks both spiritual and juridical power. 'We have no canonical authority.'[4] Its pronouncements cannot bind the churches. In the following sections Visser't Hooft discusses the conditions of membership. 'It must be and indeed is, possible to enter the World Council without compromising on any fundamental confessional points of faith and order.'[5] But 'each church should recognize at least in its sister churches in the Council the *vestigia ecclesiae*, that is, the fact that in some sense the Church of Christ exists also in them and that the Lord of the Church is at work in their life'.[6] This says very little about the terms of reference of membership. The basis is the common faith in Christ as God and Saviour, that is to say, it is definitely Christocentric, but there are few more definite references to Jesus Christ. E. Schlink rightly says that this theological basis '. . . is not necessarily an expression of a common faith in Christ, for the interpretation of the basis is left to each individual church. Moreover, the basis is insufficient; it can, for instance, be understood in an antitrinitarian, i.e. in a modalist and patripassian sense. This is an empirical and not strictly theological conception of the Church . . .'.[7]

The *Herder-Korrespondenz* has observed that Visser't Hooft shows up the 'eschatological dialectic' in which the Oecumenical Movement

[1] ibid., 186.

[2] ibid., 187.

[3] ibid., 188.

[4] In the criticisms of this essay of Visser't Hooft this statement was welcomed particularly; on the other hand, however, questions put from the ecclesiological point of view require a definite answer, and these questions are asked again and again by German Protestant theologians.

[5] loc. cit., 191.

[6] ibid., 192.

[7] 'The Church and the Churches', *ER* I (1949), 151.

sees itself.[1] We shall return to this later, in connexion with the Toronto-Statement, in which Visser't Hooft's views are strongly reflected. But first we would continue to trace the oecumenical developments.

In 1945 the Provisional Committee of the Council decided that the principal subject of the next World Conference, to be held at Amsterdam in 1948, was to be 'Man's Disorder and God's Design'. It was to be divided into four sections: I. The Universal Church in God's Design; II. The Church's Witness to God's Design; III. The Church and the Disorder of Society; IV. The Church and the International Disorder.

(c) Amsterdam

Amsterdam was not a Conference of Faith and Order or of Life and Work, but was meant to be the first assembly of the World Council of Churches, its principal task being to constitute this Council officially. On 23rd August 1948 Archbishop Fisher declared the formation of the World Council to be completed: 'There was a wave of applause. But a deeper realization of the significance of this moment came when the chairman asked all to stand in silent prayer, and then asked God's blessing upon this solemn decision of the constituent churches.'[2] In his report the General Secretary, Dr W. A. Visser't Hooft, called the present situation of the Council an event without precedent in the history of the Church. On the tasks of the Council he said this: 'What then is the true function of our Council? Our name gives us the clue to an answer. We are a Council of Churches, not *the* Council of the one undivided Church. Our name indicates our weakness and our shame before God, for there can be and there *is* finally only one Church of Christ on earth. Our plurality is a deep anomaly. But our name indicates also that we are aware of that situation, that we do not accept it passively, that we would move forward towards the manifestation of the One Holy Church. Our Council represents therefore an emergency solution—a stage on the road—a body living between the time of complete isolation of the churches from each other and the time—on earth or in heaven—when it will be visibly true that there is one Shepherd and one flock.

'The functions of the Council follow from this situation. We are a fellowship in which the churches after a long period of ignoring each other come to know each other. We are a fellowship in which the

[1] *HK* III (1948/9), 93.
[2] Visser't Hooft, p. 28.

churches enter into serious and dynamic conversation with each other about their differences in faith, in message, in order. . . . We are a fellowship in which common witness is rendered to the Lord-ship of Christ in all matters in which a common word for the churches and for the world is given to us. We are above all a fellowship which seeks to express that unity in Christ already given to us and to pre-pare the way for a much fuller and much deeper expression of that unity.'[1]

Roughly 160 Christian communions were to represent this 'oikumene'. This is how Karl Barth characterizes the Churches assembled at Amsterdam: '. . . I see a right and a left wing; on the extreme right there are our friends of the Orthodox Church, who are very difficult to understand, as if they threatened to disappear in a mist. On their left, nearer towards the centre, there are the Anglicans with a wealth of different possibilities, then the Old Catholics, and after them our next-door neighbours on the right, the Lutherans. We see on our left a great variety of Congregationalists, Methodists, Baptists and Disciples of Christ. Beyond them begins a misty region, inhabited by Mennonites, Quakers, the Salvation Army, who have neither baptism nor the Lord's Supper. It is doubtful whether they are still Churches or not, even whether they still want to be. This whole array is the "World Council of Churches", this long front from right to left, with all its differences and secret as well as open contradictions.'[2]

The first section of Amsterdam was to discuss the question of 'the Church in God's design' under the chairmanship of Bishop Hanns Lilje. Its report ('received by the Assembly and commended to the churches for their serious consideration and appropriate action') first mentions 'the unity given to us'. 'God has given to His people in Jesus Christ a unity . . . we . . . discover that, notwith-standing our divisions, we are one in Jesus Christ.'[3] 'It is in the light of this unity that we can face our deepest difference. . . . We would draw special attention to a difference to which, by many paths, we are constantly brought back. Historically it has been loosely des-cribed as the difference between "Catholic" and "Protestant" . . . the emphasis usually called "Catholic" contains a primary insistence upon the visible continuity of the Church in the apostolic succession of the episcopate. The one usually called "Protestant" primarily

---

[1] ibid.
[2] 'Amsterdamer Fragen und Antworten'. *Theologische Existenz heute*, No. 15, 12.
[3] Visser't Hooft, 51.

emphasizes the initiative of the Word of God and the response of faith, focused in the doctrine of justification *sola fide*.[1] Thus G. Florovsky observed that there 'were two completely different *blocs* of belief, which could be reconciled only by a compromise'.[2]

But the American theologians disagreed with this dichotomy.[3] Thus Douglas Horton 'suggested to the Drafting Committee that they include a reference to a further type of church, the "gathered" church, the church of the Covenant, the church of the community of the Holy Spirit'. Bishop Angus Dun further characterized this type as 'the fellowship of experience, or the community of the perfect way'.[4] This proposal was rejected by vote, Bishop Lilje giving two reasons for this: 'One was that it would have broken up the logical structure of the whole document. The second was that this was a first attempt to speak *as churches*," therefore it was necessary to abstain 'from emotional terminology'.[5] Nevertheless, this proposal is noteworthy because a third type of Church must be considered if the Protestant-evangelical conception is to be shown in its fullness. G. Florovsky had proposed 'to describe these differences as the conception of apostolic succession and the conception of the gathered Church'.[6] This proposal was rejected by the Committee 'because the doctrine of the gathered Church did not cover the whole Protestant field'.[7] Now this is, indeed, true, yet it seems to us a necessary auxiliary concept complementing the 'evangelical-Protestant' type.

The second section had been entrusted with working out the subject 'The Church's witness to God's design'. This meant something new within the framework of the Oecumenical Movement, outside the scope of Edinburgh and Oxford, Stockholm and Lausanne, though it had been considered by the World Missionary Conference.[8] The report of this section mentioned the purpose of God, the present situation and the Church's task in the present day, which is understood as 'missionary and evangelistic strategy'. According to this report, the Church 'has largely lost touch with the dominant realities of modern life, and still tries to meet the

[1] ibid., 51 f.
[2] ibid., 61.
[3] 'The majority of American theologians thought on phenomenological lines and demanded a descriptive definition', *HK* III (1948/9), 130.
[4] Visser't Hooft, 58.
[5] ibid., 63.
[6] ibid., 61.
[7] ibid.
[8] Cf. W. Menn, *Die Ökumenische Bewegung 1932–1948*, p. 76.

modern world with a language and technique that may have been appropriate two hundred years ago'.[1] Therefore 'the Church must find its way to the places where men really live. . . . It can be done fully only if, by the inspiration of the Holy Spirit, the Church recovers the spirit of prophecy to discern the signs of the times . . .'.[2] It was emphasized especially that the laity has an important role in this task.[3]

The themes of sections III and IV were 'The Church and the Disorder of Society' and 'The Church and the International Disorder'. Here the members of the Conference considered the historical situation, discussing capitalism and communism, as well as problems of peace, international law and religious freedom.

It has been asserted that the reports of the sections were inferior to the results obtained at the earlier World Conferences. This is certainly true, as Schlink says 'with regard to the doctrine of the Church'.[4] For Amsterdam was not a Faith and Order Conference, nor a 'vanguard of ecumenically-minded individual Christians from the various churches',[5] but here the churches themselves were present. 'The Churches are members of the Oecumene, or . . . the Oecumene itself is composed of the Churches. Thus the whole heavy "apparatus" which unfortunately belongs to most churches is drawn into the Oecumene.'[6] We are once again faced with the weighty question: If the World Council is the Council of the Churches, what is the *authority* of its pronouncements? It has 'no legislative authority over the Churches'. O. Tomkins has illustrated this problematic situation by a 'case'. 'Suppose the World Council of Churches had existed in 1937 and the so-called German Christian Church under Reich-Bishop Müller had applied for membership. That would have raised another problem in the comprehensiveness of the World Council. Can the constituent churches of the World Council, met in assembly, designate another Christian body as an apostate church and refuse it their fellowship? Certainly the World Council exists in order to be comprehensive, but it is not easy to see what price it should pay for its comprehensiveness.'[7]

[1] Visser't Hooft, 65.
[2] ibid., 67.
[3] ibid., 68 f.
[4] 'The Church and the Churches', ER I (1949), 161.
[5] ibid.
[6] Amsterdam, 1948. 'Die Bedeutung der ersten Vollversammlung des Ökumenischen Rates der Kirchen', by G. Brennecke in Die Zeichen der Zeit, 2nd year, p. 353.
[7] CNL., No. 297 (29th October 1947), 15.

'Something, however, conquered theological consciences at Amsterdam in critical moments, and this, so it was said, was the experience of Pentecost,'[1] or, as we would say more soberly, yet sympathetically: the new experience of a happy, truly oecumenical (hence so to speak Catholic) fellowship. 'In this particular historic hour, threatened by a third World War, it was intensified to a prophetical consciousness wanting to avert the calamity by a word of God addressed to the Powers.'[2]

Viewing the conference of Amsterdam as a whole we are struck by the fact that here theological currents met which were destined to influence the further development of the 'Oecumene'. We can discern the dualism of a 'Catholic' and an 'evangelical' type of belief, a right and a left wing, old and young churches. But there is even more than that. For at Amsterdam different possibilities of Christian existence made their appearance, which the *Herder-Korrespondenz* calls 'the dramatic encounter of "prophets" and Christian activists'.[3] Here is truly a tension which is reflected even in the 'Message of the Assembly'. We would cite two characteristic sentences. There is, on the one hand, an emphasis on the action of God and His eschatological rule: 'The end of history will be the triumph of His Kingdom. . . . Often we have . . . confused the Gospel with our own economic or national or racial interests. . . . Till the day of that victory our lives are hid with Christ in God.' And, on the other hand: 'But, by our acts of obedience and faith, we can on earth set up signs which point to the coming victory.'[4]

* * *

DIGRESSION:

Continental and Anglo-Saxon Thought in the 'Oecumene'

The prophetic side was represented at Amsterdam above all by Karl Barth. He put the whole emphasis on God's action and uttered a warning: 'On this first day of our deliberations we should at once give up the idea that the care for the Church and the world is *our* care . . . for this ultimately is precisely the root and ground of all human disorder: a frightful, godless, ridiculous idea as if man were an

---

[1] 'God has called us to another Pentecost here' says the declaration of the youth delegation. Cf. Visser't Hooft, 183.
[2] J. P. Michael, 'Der dritte Versuch', *Orientierung*, 16 (1952), 153.
[3] *HK* III (1948/9), 94.
[4] Visser't Hooft, 9–11.

Atlas ordered to carry the world on his shoulders.' Barth is concerned to show that ' "God's design" is not to be understood as a kind of christian Marshall Plan'.[1] When referring in his speech to the work of the third and fourth sections his language is very clear: 'The disorder of the world is today . . . not less, but also not greater than it always has been. In the midst of this disorder it is the prophetic task of the Church to show forth the kingdom of God as the realm of justice and peace, the task of its political guardianship and its social service of charity. . . . Now, first of all, the kingdom we show to the world must be the kingdom of God and not of some ideas and principles we happen to approve. . . . We must be certain that, in carrying out our prophetic task, we really show forth the kingdom of God and not, even though in good faith, some other kingdom. . . . And secondly, we shall have to realize that we can only *show* His kingdom. . . . We do not await . . . a future liberal or authoritarian state to be erected with the help of Christians. The world passes away.'[2] The other view was represented most clearly by the late American Secretary of State J. F. Dulles. He spoke in the fourth section, which sought for an answer to the question of peace among the nations and which therefore had to consider the political tension between Soviet Russia and the West. Now this was a political subject that suited Mr Dulles. In his speech, the subject of which was 'The Christian citizen in a changing world',[3] 'he developed . . . the American and—in his view—Christian counter-problem to Soviet Imperialism.[4] This was the opposite of prophetism, this was Christian activism in the guise of an "Americanizing" of the social gospel'.[5] Here we speak of Americanizing, and it is indeed a fact that the American Free Churches gained increasing influence in the Oecumenical Movement. Thus the latter developed a tendency which because of its practical outlook was too much inclined to disregard the theological and doctrinal difficulties of the continental Churches and to insist on a unity which, in the eyes of an objective observer, could only be a compromise. These Free Churches hold an individualistic conception of the Church that is opposed to the institutional one; it is based on a purist notion of the Church which rejects the existence of good and bad men in the Church and upholds the notion of a 'spiritual succession' which is diametrically opposed to the historical

[1] 'Amsterdamer Fragen und Antworten', loc. cit. 4 f.
[2] ibid., 8 f.
[3] Cf. *HK* II (1947/8), 521.
[4] *HK* VII (1952/3), 238.
[5] *HK* III (1948/9), 96.

apostolic succession.[1] 'Compared with the national churches these sects have one advantage: they prove their beliefs by a life of works and thus are able to convince.'[2]

Apart from this extreme Americanizing in the Oecumene the members of the Amsterdam Conference also thought they could see a difference in the theology of the Continental and the Anglo-Saxon Churches, expressed by the notions: here a continental, there an Anglo-Saxon approach to theology.[3] In a controversy between Barth and the American theologian Reinhold Niebuhr after Amsterdam this difference of theology was discussed. In his essay 'We are men, not God', Niebuhr has attempted to describe this 'most noticeable difference in the first Assembly of the World Council of Churches at Amsterdam'.[4] 'The first theological position will best be described as distinctly "eschatological". This, however, does not mean that the emphasis here is especially on *hope*, on the end of all history that comes with the Second Advent of Christ, the final Judgement and the General Resurrection. The position would better be described as "realized eschatology".'[5] This should be compared with the words of Karl Barth cited above. Niebuhr thinks that no Christian would doubt this, but that the conclusions drawn from this position beg the question. 'If drawn in the way in which they were drawn here (at Amsterdam), they would surely deprive the Christian life of its sense of responsibility.' Niebuhr holds that this theology fails to interpret the whole Gospel, however much it might destroy the illusions of Churchmen, theologians and moralists. This 'continental theology needs to be corrected; for it has left to themselves those spheres where human life should be lived'.[6]

Barth replied to Niebuhr in his essay 'Präliminare Gedanken zu Reinhold Niebuhrs Darlegungen über die "kontinentale" Theologie'.[7] To begin with he stresses that he felt impelled to take up his position when examining the subject-matter of sections II to IV. He thought he could perceive 'that there was a desire to ascend from

---

[1] Cf. H. Townsend, *The Claims of the Free Churches*, London, 1949, esp. pp. 26, 63, 67.
[2] Adam Fechter, 'Die getrennten Brüder', *W.u.W.* 3 (1948), 753.
[3] These concepts are considered as 'not quite exact' by the partners of the discussion, 'because many " Continentals" did not subscribe to the first theology, and again the second can be called "Anglo-Saxon" only because, apart from all differences of the denominations, the Anglo-Saxon world was united in rejecting the first position' (Niebuhr 25; cf. K. Barth, 30).
[4] *Theologische Existenz heute*, No. 15, p. 25 f.
[5] ibid., 25.
[6] ibid., 29.
[7] ibid.

the "disorder of the world", i.e. from certain opinions about this disorder, to the "purpose of God", though it did not even seem altogether certain whether "God's purpose" did not simply mean one's own opinions and proposals for conquering that disorder'.[1]

Barth admits that there were misunderstandings on both sides; but at Amsterdam he had not found the contrast between Continental and Anglo-Saxon theology where Niebuhr saw it. 'I think it is simply the different relation to the Bible from which we start on either side.'[2] 'I was struck by a strangely nonchalant attitude in our Anglo-Saxon friends towards "an attention to the Bible determining theological thought". They preferred to theologize according to their own lights, i.e. without asking themselves on which Biblical foundation they wanted to base this or that supposedly "Christian" view. Scripture was cited, but selectively. . . . This loose relation to the Bible was the reason why it seemed to me as if the thought of the "Anglo-Saxons" lacked a whole dimension. Two dimensions were evidently familiar to it: such as the opposition between good and evil, freedom and necessity, love and selfishness, spirit and matter, person and mechanism, progress and stagnation—and in this sense also God and world or God and man. . . . But this schema leaves me cold, I am not at home in it. And I quite understand that people who insist on these formulae fail to understand me. But I find comfort in the fact that the Bible knows not only these two, but a third dimension, and this the decisive one: the Word of God, the Holy Spirit, the free election of God, His grace and judgement, creation, atonement, kingdom, sanctification, community—all these not as principles, hence not to be interpreted in the sense of the first two dimensions, but all this as a description of *events*, of a concrete, unique divine action, signifying the majestic mystery of God that cannot be dissolved by any pragmatism. . . . The "Anglo-Saxon" theology, as far as I can see and understand it, is in principle strangely devoid of mystery . . . .'[3]

So here appear formal 'background' oppositions within the Oecumene. Though, as Barth observes, these were never explicitly discussed at Amsterdam, yet it has to be asked 'whether (this difference) will not greatly trouble and exercise the oecumenical community in the future'.[4] Nevertheless, it is always profitable if such background differences are seen at all.

Thus Amsterdam is shot through with a profound dialectic. The

[1] ibid., 31.
[2] ibid., 34.
[3] ibid., 34 f.
[4] ibid., 30.

question is whether the Oecumenical Movement will become accustomed to this dialectic, a temptation to which Protestantism may easily succumb. 'The dialectic tension is inevitable, and we cannot reject it in spite of the ambiguity it produces in the fields of dogma and church order. We cannot unduly stress the one side: "The Oikumene is *Una Sancta, koinonía*, its basis is the confession that makes us one," nor can we limit ourselves to the other: "The Oikumene is an office, a relief organization, etc., and its basis is a signboard, an attempt to make the circle as wide as possible." Yet neither can we leave this dialectic in a state of suspense; we must continue with this dialectic tension on the road that leads to the day of the *parousia* of the Lord. For this dialectic is, ultimately, a dialectic with an eschatological reference.'[1] If only this eschatological dialectic were not a flight from the fullness of the incarnate Christ and from the effective operation of the Holy Spirit![2] And if only it did not tempt its exponents to an abstraction of unity that escapes from space and time into the invisible sphere of the risen and returning Christ!

This abstract 'unionism' was also mentioned in the resolution of the Moscow Conference of Churches addressed to the World Council in July 1948.[3] It is true, the refusal of the Patriarchate of Moscow and the autocephalous churches attached to it had political implications and was due to a misunderstanding of the World Conference of Churches; nevertheless they realized the insufficient doctrinal basis and thus added weight to the protest of the Orthodox at Lausanne and Edinburgh. They saw the danger of relativism which was also mentioned by the Evangelicals.[4] Thus the Oecumene 'has not yet made the basic decision whether the unity of

---

[1] E. Schlink, 'The Church and the Churches', loc. cit., 153.

[2] There has been criticism of this 'eschatological dialectic' which 'fails to do sufficient justice to the historical and doctrinal obligations of the churches of the World Council'. Already at Amsterdam this dialectic, which would liquidate the doctrinal differences of the churches, had been opposed by Professor Florovsky (Paris) on behalf of the Orthodox, by Canon Ramsay for the Anglicans and by Professor Skydsgaard for the Lutherans. 'At this year's (1949) assembly of the British Council of Churches at Edinburgh the Dean of Chichester, Dr. Duncan Jones, dramatically reiterated this warning. Dean Jones observed that the dialectical method of the Geneva Council was neither "supernatural" nor truly "eschatological" but was rather the way of Barth's "Christian Community", i.e. a mere analogue of the civic community' (*HK* IV (1949/50), 85). On the 'dialectical method' of Amsterdam which wants to solve ecclesiological questions by means of a 'phenomenological consensus' cf. D. C. Lialine, 'Le Dialogue Théologique à Amsterdam', *Irénikon*, XX (1950), 2ᵉ et 3ᵉ Trimestre.

[3] Text in *ER* I (1949), 190 f.

[4] E. Schlink, 'The Church and the Churches', loc. cit., 166.

the Church is to be viewed as an historical tradition or an eschatological datum. In the meantime the oecumenical managers are very busy dissolving the Incarnation into eschatology, and creating facts of organization which are to become habits outweighing theological arguments.'[1]

*   *   *

(d) FROM AMSTERDAM TO LUND

The World Council delegated part of its functions to commissions; these were to work 'under the authority of the Assembly . . .' and 'between meetings of the Assembly, report annually to the Central Committee'.[2] Thus was nominated a 'Commission on Faith and Order' which was to continue the work of the Movement of the same name. This commission was to concern itself especially with questions of the nature of the Church, of divine worship and of the Eucharist. Oliver Tomkins[3] now Bishop of Bristol, was appointed its secretary. The 'Study Department' of the World Council was to examine the questions hitherto dealt with by Life and Work. The programme of this department was drawn up at a conference held at Oxford in 1949; it took as its first subject the question of the authority of Holy Scripture as applied to the social and political message of the contemporary Church. This conference worked out the hermeneutical principles of Scriptural exegesis. Ten years after Amsterdam Visser't Hooft said in his report to the Central Committee in 1958 (*Ecumenical Review* XI, 1, Oct. 1958). . . . 'Both movements stood for unity. The one for visible unity in faith and order. The other (as expressed in its Latin title "*communio in serviendo ecumenica*") for ecumenical communion or fellowship in service to humanity. Now it has become increasingly clear that these two types of unity cannot be promoted independently from each other. A unity in faith and order sought for its own sake can easily become a self-centred unity. At the same time unity pursued outside the context of the Church's task in the world lacks the proper dynamic and remains unconvincing. On the other hand a unity that is so exclusively concerned with service to the world that it neglects the basic question of truth or the true understanding of the Christian revelation, is in danger of becoming a sentimental and superficial unity.'

---

[1] J. P. Michael, *Orientierung*, 16 (1952), 153.

[2] Visser't Hooft, 200.

[3] Today (1960) the chairman is Dean Douglas Horton (United Church of Christ, U.S.A.). Bishop Tomkins is chairman of the Working Committee.

'So 1948 meant in fact that we chose an oecumenical movement which would not minimize the serious doctrinal issues of unity, but which would seek to work at these issues in the setting of the common calling of the churches to humanity. Thus the unity we stand for was characterized as a *pastoral* unity—a unity, nor merely for the sake of the Church, but for the sake of mankind.'

Catholics ought not only to take note of this aim but also to learn from it. The Oecumenical Movement is a spiritual fact. If the *Instructio* of the Holy Office says of it that it originated 'under the grace-filled breathing of the Holy Spirit', then we must take account of the impulse and the direction of the Holy Spirit gathering what had been scattered. Otherwise the Catholic effort at re-uniting the separated Christians might risk losing itself in abstractions somewhat remote from real life. It would be too little if the practical collaboration of the separated Christians in questions of a social or political ethics would, for example, be carried out only on the basis of the natural law, in the same way as the Church must cooperate e.g. with Islam against communism. For Protestants differ essentially from Muslims because, as Pope John XXIII said in his Christmas Allocution of 1959 'they bear on their foreheads the name of Christ, read his holy and blessed Gospel and are open to the suggestions of piety and of charitable neighbourly love'.

Nevertheless, it should not be overlooked that the position of the new Commission on Faith and Order within the structure of the World Council of Churches after Amsterdam and especially after Evanston is not an easy one. The danger in which the World Council of Churches finds itself was pointed out by Visser't Hooft at a meeting of the Commission on Faith and Order at Spittal (Austria) in 1959. 'There is a danger', he said, 'that the whole oecumenical movement should become accepted in the minds of the large majority of churchmen as merely an existing movement of cooperation—a useful piece of ecclesiastical machinery' (Paper 27, p. 5). And the Working Committee on Faith and Order on the future of faith and Order made it quite clear: 'It is our strong conviction that to proclaim the essential oneness of the Church of Christ involves facing the question, what kind of unity does God demand of His Church? We agree that no one definition of the nature of unity can be a condition of membership in the WCC, but Faith and Order exists in order to stand for the unity of the Church as the will of God and for a ceaseless effort to know what obedience to that will means concretely. Only so can it be "manifest". The WCC can have no "neutrality" on whether that question is answered or not.' The chief interest of Catholic theologians in the Oecumenical Movement is obviously directed to the work of the Commission on Faith and Order. The question whether Faith and Order is of central importance in the structure of the WCC is decisive for the relation between the Catholic Church and the WCC. But interest should not only be directed towards Faith and Order. Both sides have a pastoral responsibility for the salvation of the world that transcends the work of the theologians. J. P. Michael's article 'Pius XII politische Prophetie und die Ökumene' (*Wort und Wahrheit* 14 (1959), pp. 5–15) is a very instructive contribution to these questions, on which the author remarks that 'a dogmatically relevant event need by no means be inaugurated primarily by dogmatic formulae'. The Oecumenical Institute at Bossey in Switzerland was closely connected with the work of this study commission.

The Commission on Faith and Order prepared the third World Conference at Lund in 1952. Faith and Order was faced with a new situation, for now the 160 churches of the World Council were to send their official delegates to this conference. Faith and Order had appointed a theological commission which, as we have already seen, was to devote itself to the question of the Church, of worship and of intercommunion.[1]

What were the opinions reflected in these accounts regarding the unity of the Church? From what we have already said it can be seen that no unanimity could be expected. 'Some big differences remain. To the Roman Catholic Church, the Orthodox Church, the Old Catholic Church and to many Anglicans, the unity of the visible Church includes unity of visible order as an integral part of itself; the breach of visible order, as for instance by the abandonment of ministerial succession, is of itself a part of the meaning of schism, and the healing of such a breach is the necessary prelude to the restoration of full communion. To those who follow the main Reformation tradition the unity of the visible Church is essentially constituted by the faithful congregation and the presence of the Word and the Sacraments within it, and breaches of order do not necessarily have the character of schism. To other Protestant communions the unity of the Church is the fellowship in faith and life of those who acknowledge Jesus Christ as Lord and Saviour.'[2] It is a very important aspect of this report on the Church that its authors examined the various formal backgrounds for these contra-

---

[1] Cf. the relevant volumes published by the SCM Press.
[2] *Die Kirche*, 16.

dictory views on the Church. Since the expression 'non-theological factors in the division of faith' had been uttered at Amsterdam, the importance of this background came to be increasingly realized. We would further mention that this new impulse in the Oecumene originated among laymen. The report speaks particularly of the 'systematic differences . . . which are of a philosophical character'. The influence of Neoplatonism and Aristotelianism in the patristic and scholastic periods was well known. 'Leibniz', it is stated, 'detected rival philosophical assumptions beneath the theological disputes' of his time, and the influence of idealist philosophy and existentialism on modern theological systems was evident. The report on forms of worship, too, castigated the (fundamentally neo-platonist) 'persistent error, according to which spiritual and material things are seen as absolutely opposed . . . : It is increasingly understood that faith embraces the life of the whole man, body, soul and spirit. . . . For God created not only spirits but men. He re-creates not only our souls but ourselves.'[1] This hit the mark.

Did these activities of the theological commissions mark a progress towards the unity of the Church? Are they more than merely a comparative presentation of the various conceptions of the nature of the Church? The criticisms of the *Ecumenical Review* are significant: 'These papers will shatter any illusion about an imminent realization of Christian unity. We are up against a stone wall and no amount of comparative ecclesiology will break it down, for precisely those who understand the grounds of disagreement best, who most desire Christian unity, who appreciate the best in other Churches and understand the weaknesses of their own, see no easy way out or any smooth road forward. This may indicate that the ecumenical consideration of the Church has gone as far as it can, as a study and discussion.'[2]

The differences remain; they concern the frontiers of the Church, the way of defining it, the unity of the Church, the Sacraments and their relation to the Church, and the relation of the Church to the Kingdom of God. There remains, above all, the disagreement on the apostolic ministry and the resulting impossibility of celebrating the Eucharist together. 'The time for that (a synthetic doctrine of the Church) is not yet, and the roads towards it are more in number than a Commission of theologians can tread,' as R. Flew remarked with regard to the intention of the report on behalf of the theological

[1] *Die Kirche*, 12.
[2] *ER* IV (1952), 313.

commission on the Church.[1] Yet there is some progress, despite the 'stone walls'. The position becomes clearer, the true dogmatic problems are raised and at times the actual background of these questions is touched. Moreover, the report of the theological commission speaks of 'trends in theology today which may prove to be of great significance for our thought on the Church or for the hastening of its unity'.[2] These are:

1. The Laymen's movements: 'they are a reaffirmation of the unity of "laity" and ministry, together constituting the *laós* or People of God.'

2. A return to Biblical theology, 'to a new Biblical realism'.[3] Here the study of the history of salvation, the greater importance of eschatology and the re-discovery of the doctrine of the Church are emphasized particularly.

3. A 'confessionalist' revival, an awareness of the specific tradition combined with a new 'acknowledgment of the centrality of dogma in the life of the Church. One dogmatist may respect another dogmatist, whilst both look askance at the man whom they suspect of basing his view of the Church upon expediency, sentiment or secular fashion. Because a man takes his own dogma seriously, he recognizes the right of his opponent to have his dogma taken seriously, too'.[4]

4. New ways of philosophy. The report notes that theology has always been influenced by certain categories of philosophy. 'There comes a point when a period may become aware of its unconscious assumptions, as a man may suddenly realize that he is wearing spectacles with a certain tint.'[5]

New philosophical categories are recognized in a new cosmological way of thought: the world 'is characterized by the constant emergence of new things, a world in which the *esse* of anything is its *fieri*'. This means for the Church that 'it is to be thought of as a process. . . . It is in process of becoming itself as it grows up into that which God is giving it to be'.

'Seen from below it is the Church growing into its true self as it becomes more truly the body of Christ; seen from above it is Christ communicating its true self to the Church.'[6]

---

[1] *Die Kirche*, 12.
[2] ibid., 39.
[3] ibid., 42.
[4] ibid., 47.
[5] ibid., 48.
[6] Hodgson, 'Modern Thought-forms and the doctrine of the Church', *Die Kirche*, 60.

In this way an attempt is made to grasp the divine and the human side of the Church, e.g. the fact that she is holy and sinless, yet at the same time consists of sinful members. Existentialism, too, is used to clarify the nature of the Church. Being must be seen and interpreted from its situation. 'From the existentialist standpoint a neoplatonic, other-worldly "Church" is not possible, for it is precisely "time" that must be filled full; nor is a credalized or codified formulation of the "teachings" sufficient. . . . This suggests that an existentialist doctrine of the Church would be anti-authoritarian and anti-legalistic, but positively it stresses "apostleship" bearing witness and engagement in the world. . . . Existentialism is bringing about a sifting of Christendom from the perspective of the human situation, which implies, in its Christian forms, a return to the biblical categories. . . . Existentialism appeals from authoritarian formulae of whatever kind to the vitalities of faith, appropriated through personal decision and confession, and attested through vocation and creative engagement in the world.'[1] Such contributions of philosophical thought ought not to be hastily dismissed as destroying the substance of faith or pandering to fashion. It cannot be denied that this thought is related to Biblical categories, but it probably can really develop only where the Church already exists. If these categories are used in an attempt to build the Church and to explain the paradoxes of divided Christendom, then they may easily become dynamite, as they have done in Germany in the theology of Bultmann.

(e) THE TORONTO DOCUMENT

We have already discussed how the World Council of Churches understood its own function, which was defined at Amsterdam. Later this was frequently misunderstood and misinterpreted. Therefore the Central Committee of the World Council had before it at its conference at Toronto in July 1950 a document entitled 'The Church, the Churches and the World Council of Churches'. This was a statement of the ecclesiological importance of the World Council which the Toronto Conference commended for study and comment in the churches.[2] According to this declaration, the World Council of Churches is an attempt to tackle the problem of inter-church relationships in a new way, which has no historical precedent. For this reason its purpose and its nature could easily be misunderstood.

---

[1] Hopper, *Existentialism*, ibid., 75.
[2] Text in *ER* III, Oct. 1950, p. 47 ff.

And it was difficult to give a precise definition, because the churches themselves had refrained from giving detailed and precise definitions of the nature of the Church. Thus if the Council were to define itself it would have to take account of all the various ecclesiologies of its member churches. 'The main problem is how one can formulate the ecclesiological implications of a body in which so many different conceptions of the Church are represented, without using the categories or language of one particular conception of the Church.'

The document proceeds to state a number of negative propositions in a section headed 'What the World Council of Churches is not' and then follows this up with positive 'assumptions underlying the World Council of Churches'.

1. First of all, it is stated that the World Council is neither a 'Super-Church'[1] or 'World Church' nor the *Una Sancta* of which the Creeds speak. This is proved by the fact that the Council 'cannot legislate or act for its member Churches'; it is not a body that can take decisions, though the term 'member Churches' might suggest such an idea.

2. The purpose of the World Council of Churches is not to negotiate unions between Churches; this should be done by the Churches themselves. It is to bring the Churches into contact with one another and to promote the discussion of questions of Church unity. 'By its very existence and its activities the Council bears witness to the necessity of a clear manifestation of the oneness of the Church.'

3. The Council 'should not be based on any one particular conception of the Church'. It does not prejudge the ecclesiological problem. 'There is room in the World Council for the ecclesiology of every Church which is ready to participate in the ecumenical conversation and which takes its stand on the Basis of the Council, which is "a fellowship of Churches which accept Our Lord Jesus Christ as God and Saviour".'

4. 'Membership in the World Council of Churches does not imply that a church treats its own conception of the Church as merely relative.' The Council is criticized as well as praised for its alleged inherent Latitudinarianism. The Council opposes this view. It is a misunderstanding to suppose the Oecumenical Movement defends the equality of all Christian doctrines and conceptions of the Church and hence is not concerned with the question of truth. 'This mis-

[1] Cf. W. A. Visser't Hooft, 'The Super-Church and the Ecumenical Movement,' *ER* X (1958), 365–385.

understanding is due to the fact that ecumenism has in the minds of these persons become identified with certain particular theories about unity, which have indeed played a role in ecumenical history, but which do not represent the common view of the movement as a whole, and have never been officially endorsed by the World Council.'

5. 'Membership in the World Council does not imply the acceptance of a specific doctrine concerning the nature of Church unity.' The Council has room for the most diverse conceptions of Church unity, for those who insist on unity of doctrine or sacramental unity or on certain fundamental articles of faith and order as well as for those who acknowledge only a spiritual fellowship without visible unity. 'None of these conceptions can be called the ecumenical theory.' Nevertheless, the document does not seem to regard all conceptions of unity as equally valid, for it guards especially against the view of a spiritualized invisible Church. In this context the document cites, surprisingly enough, a sentence from the encyclical *Mystici corporis* as a term of reference: 'The World Council does not imagine a Church which one cannot see or touch, which would be only spiritual, in which numerous Christian bodies, though divided in matters of faith, would nevertheless be united through an invisible link.' According to the Toronto Document the error envisaged by the encyclical did not apply to the World Council.

The 'positive assumptions' examine especially 'the ecclesiological implications of membership' in the Council.

1. Christ is the divine Head of His Body, the Church. Relations between the Churches could have no substance or promise unless they started with the common submission to the Headship of Christ as the Head of His Church. 'The fact of Christ's Headship over His people compels all those who acknowledge Him to enter into real and close relationships with each other—even though they differ in many important points.'

2. Since the member Churches believe on the basis of the New Testament that the Church of Christ is one, 'it is a matter of simple Christian duty for each church to do its utmost for the manifestation of the Church in its oneness.'

3. The Church of Christ is not completely identical with one's own Church. 'The membership of the Church of Christ is more inclusive than the membership of their own Church body.' All Christian Churches, including the Church of Rome, 'recognize that there are Church members "extra muros", that these belong "aliquo modo" to

the Church', which is expressed 'in the fact that with very few exceptions the Christian Churches accept the baptism administered by other Churches as valid.' The question was, what consequences were to be drawn from this teaching? 'The underlying assumption of the ecumenical movement is that each Church has a positive task to fulfil in this realm. That task is to seek fellowship with all those who, while not members of the same visible body, belong together as members of the mystical body. And the ecumenical movement is the place where this search and discovery take place.'

4. It follows from this that it is necessary to discuss the relation of other Churches to the Holy Catholic Church professed in the Creeds. 'Nevertheless, membership does not imply that each Church must regard the other member Churches as Churches in the true and full sense of the word.' There was place in the World Council both for such a recognition and for its refusal. But even though the recognition of other Churches as Churches in the true and full sense of the word is not demanded, it is yet desirable that

5. 'The member Churches of the World Council recognize in other Churches elements of the true Church ... in the hope that these elements of truth will lead to the recognition of the full truth and to unity based on the full truth.' Such elements of the true Church—*vestigia ecclesiae*—are the preaching of the Word, the expounding of Scripture and the administration of the Sacraments. 'These elements are more than pale shadows of the life of the true Church. They are a fact of real promise and provide an opportunity to strive by frank and brotherly intercourse for the realization of a fuller unity.' These 'traces' should not be despised; they were hopeful signs pointing towards real unity. They were 'not dead remnants of the past but powerful means by which God works'. Yet, in the view of the compilers of the Document, questions 'must be raised about the validity and purity of teaching and sacramental life.'

6. The member Churches of the Council were willing to work together for a common witness to their common Lord before the world. This, too, was a manifestation of the Church.

7. A practical implication of common membership was that the member Churches should recognize their solidarity by assisting each other in cases of need and by refraining 'from such actions as are incompatible with brotherly relationships'.

8. 'The member Churches enter into spiritual relationships through which they seek to learn from each other and to give help to each other in order that the Body of Christ may be built up and that the

life of the Churches may be renewed.' It was 'the common teaching of the Churches that the Church as the temple of God is at the same time a building which has been built and a building which is being built. The Church has, therefore, aspects which belong to its very structure and essence and cannot be changed. But it has other aspects, which are subject to change'.

The declaration ends with the affirmation that 'A very real unity has been discovered in ecumenical meetings. . . . It exists and we receive it again and again as an unmerited gift from the Lord'.

It is not easy to pass judgement on this Toronto Document. For it uses terms that are by no means theologically clear. It begins with such terms as 'Church', 'Churches' and 'Council of Churches'. 'We are using the term *church* in a sense of which we have no agreed definition, and the *Council* is . . . a religious phenomenon that fits into no previously used categories.'[1]

The Document asserts that Christ is the divine Head of His Body, and the World Council is defined as 'a fellowship of Churches which accept Our Lord Jesus Christ as God and Saviour'. But Tomkins states that 'all the churches do not see the same consequences flowing from that acceptance, which drives me to admit that the Council as such must be committed to the view that faith in Christ can be legitimately attributed to those who hold widely differing views as to what that faith necessarily implies'.[2]

In what sense, he asks, can this faith be ascribed, e.g. to the Society of Friends, if it is believed 'that to worship Him as God necessarily involves Sacraments of initiation and communion which Quakers deny? . . . We disagree about what His Lordship involves'.[3] Hence disagreement begins even at the basis of the World Council, the faith in Jesus Christ, because the Christian communities represented in it are by no means agreed who Jesus Christ is. It has rightly been stated that this Toronto Document does not start from the doctrine of the God-man Jesus Christ and is not in harmony with 'ancient Christology, above all with the Council of Chalcedon'.[4]

Nevertheless, we welcome the fact that the Oecumene becomes increasingly conscious of Christology, and we would not consider this as an attempt to escape from the theological dilemma, as was

[1] O. Tomkins, 'The Church, the Churches and the Council', in *ER* IV (1951/2), 259.

[2] ibid., 260.

[3] ibid.

[4] 'Das Glaubensbewusstsein der "Ökumenischen Christenheit" ' *Der Grosse Herder*, vol. X, 1452/3.

done by H. Lilje.[1] It is true, this only 'moves back the crucial problem of the oecumenical movement by one step'. But it will not 'disappear', even if 'the different ways taken by the Churches would be re-traced' by 'realizing what a different conception they have of Christ'.[2]

With regard to this, the subject of the next Assembly of the World Council at Evanston in 1954, 'Jesus Christ, the crucified Lord, the only Hope of the World', should contribute to clarify the situation unless, as has been feared, 'the pre-decision of the American denominations have already involved the Assembly in a heavily a-dogmatic policy'.[3]

Is there no danger that the image of Christ, too, will be affected by the extreme eschatological view of the Church represented at Lund especially by Schlink in his idea of the 'pilgrim people'? Here Lilje has rightly spoken of a 'forward flight', 'for this view does not eliminate the problem of the present differences but only points to the hope of a future perfection'.[4]

In this context the words of K. Hartenstein deserve attention: 'Only within this framework of the history of salvation, steadfastly maintained in prospect and retrospect by the Old and New Testaments and centred in the decisive event of salvation, the coming of the Redeemer, can we speak of a genuine *parousia* as the end of history in time, in the old aeon, and the new "history of God" with His flock and the world, in the new aeon.'[5] The Church should be seen only within the comprehensive framework of salvation. What is at stake is the reality of an event, the true Incarnation of the Second Person of the Godhead. This, however, can be understood only if we go back to the old Christology of the first Councils.

This shortened oecumenical Christology with its eschatological Christ has its consequences also with regard to the unity of the Church. We have already mentioned the 'eschatological dialectic' which refers the question of the visible presentation of the unity of the Church to a future eschatological date. The Toronto Document preserves an attitude of detachment towards very different ideas of Christian unity: 'There are those who conceive unity wholly or largely as a full consensus in the realm of doctrine, others who

---

[1] 'Der gegenwärtige Stand der Ökumenischen Bewegung', *ThLZ* 78 (1953), col. 70.
[2] ibid.
[3] *HK* VII (1952/3), 91.
[4] 'Der gegenwärtige Stand . . . ', loc. cit. col. 70.
[5] 'Comments on the First Report of the Advisory Commission on the Theme of the Second Assembly', *ER* IV (1951/2), 169–71.

conceive of it primarily as sacramental communion based on common church order, others who consider both indispensable, others who would only require unity in certain fundamentals of faith and order, again others who conceive the one Church exclusively as a universal spiritual fellowship or hold that visible unity is inessential or even undesirable.' 'The whole point of the ecumenical conversation is precisely that all these conceptions enter into dynamic relations with each other.'[1] Surely one ought to have learned from the history of the Oecumenical Movement, in which all these forms of Church unity have been discussed. Is unity here still considered as a question of truth which, according to III, 4 cannot be left out, or does not this detachment really affirm the perpetuation of paradoxes? An attempt is made to avoid this danger by distinguishing between Churches 'in the full and true sense of the word' and those which are not such (IV, 4). In all churches elements of truth are to be recognized and acknowledged (IV, 5), and it is hoped that this recognition will lead to full truth and unity'. The document mentions the 'Holy Catholic Church which the Creeds profess' (IV, 4), but says nothing more definite about it. Yet these theologians speak of *vestigia ecclesiae*, traces of the true and one Church which are to be found in the 'churches'.

The Toronto Document uses the term 'churches in the full and true sense' and, on the other hand, speaks of churches which are not such. The World Council refrains from pronouncing judgement on where the full and true Church is and where it is not. It only states that there is a place in the World Council 'both for those churches which recognize other Churches as Churches in the full and true sense, and for those which do not'. The member Churches are left free to hold their subjective views. But where is the objective standard? This question goes beyond the terms of reference of the Toronto Document—which would not pre-judge a definite ecclesiology—yet is an implied question to the churches.

(f) LUND

The Third Conference on Faith and Order would have to show whether the preparatory work of the theological commissions showed signs of progress in the Oecumenical Movement. This Conference was held at Lund (Sweden) from 15th to 28th August 1952. The old oecumenical pioneers went there with certain misgivings, but also with high hopes. It was generally felt that the

[1] *ER*, loc. cit.

method of comparative theological statistics that had been followed so far had proved ineffective. The first section of Amsterdam had expressed the situation as one of 'differences in our agreement and agreement in differences'. 'Can we go on for ever and ever, round and round in the same circle, explaining ourselves to one another?' asked L. Hodgson.[1]

Lausanne and Edinburgh had, indeed, brought 'much growth in mutual understanding', but now 'the next step' would really have to be discussed. Of what kind would this have to be? The comparative method had brought many paradoxes to light. Hodgson cites, for example, statements of the Baptist Union of Great Britain and Ireland. In one and the same essay it is said that the Church is 'a new creation, gathered by the will of Christ', and then a few lines further on, that it is 'the response of believing men, membership constituted by personal allegiance'.[2]

Surely, a paradoxical view within the same denomination, and what paradoxes would not come to light if the whole Oecumene were to be questioned on the subject! Would it be possible to achieve a synthesis between the Catholic and the Protestant conception of the Church? 'Catholic sacramentalism and Quaker religion seem at opposite ends of the Christian world.'[3]

Hodgson, however, is very optimistic: 'Yet I have sometimes wondered whether there might not be a place for both in a united church.'[4] Starting from the thesis *Deus non alligatur sacramentis*, he thinks that the Quakers might perhaps have a special task in the Church to bear witness to this truth, for organic unity should not mean organization but organism. We see from this how the old Anglican Branch Theory still survives, though the 'next step' is not to be expected from these quarters.

O. Tomkins, too, speaks of the paradoxes which are at the basis of the Oecumenical Movement. He sees a paradox above all in the fact that 'we all believe that the Church, which is the Body and Bride of Christ, is something more than our own particular church tradition, and yet we all know that we can only live daily in the Body of Christ by living faithfully in our own churches'. The World Council of Churches is 'a Council of denominations, whilst its very creation has destroyed the justification of denominations'.[5] Tomkins holds

---

[1] *The Task of the Third World Conference on Faith and Order*, 1, 13.
[2] ibid., 7.
[3] ibid., 9.
[4] ibid.
[5] 'Implications of the Ecumenical Movement', *ER* V (1952/3), 16.

that the end of a purely comparative ecclesiology has been reached. In this comparative method lurks the danger of being tempted constantly to justify one's own position. Such language as this, is readily liable to misunderstanding, for it may suggest some kind of World Council *mystique* which evades, instead of transcending, the realities of our division, or that our 'denominations' have no validity or necessity'.

According to him, the Oecumenical Movement faces a dilemma: 'We claim that we have unity in Christ; we cannot show that we have unity in His Body, the Church,' whereas 'nothing in the biblical conception of the Church, nor in the lives of the primitive Christians, will allow us to affirm for ever that we have unity in Christ and deny that we have unity in the Church.'[1] This is how the situation appeared at the beginning of the Lund Conference. How did it look at the end of the Conference? Had the third attempt of Faith and Order been successful? Had the member Churches come nearer to the unity of the Church?

The central theme at Lund was the relation between Christ and the Churches. In 'A Word to the Churches' it is stated that it has clearly been seen that there could be no real advance towards unity 'if we only compare our several conceptions of the nature of the Church and the traditions in which they are embodied. But once again it has been proved true that as we seek to draw closer to Christ we come closer to one another. We need, therefore, to penetrate behind our divisions to a deeper and richer understanding of the mystery of the God-given union of Christ with His Church'.[2] The second chapter of the Report deals with this subject, 'CHRIST AND THE CHURCH'.

'Christ is never without His Church; the Church is never without Christ. Both belong inseparably together, the King and His people, the keystone and the temple, the Head and the Body. . . . On the ground of the apostolic witness to Jesus Christ, the Lord of the Church, and in obedience to Him, we seek to penetrate behind the divisions of the Church on earth to our common faith in the one Lord. From the unity of Christ we seek to understand the unity of the Church on earth.'[3] Thus the Church has to be seen in the light of the death and resurrection of Christ. Its nature must be understood in the sense of a twofold movement: called from the world and sent

[1] ibid., 25.
[2] Tomkins, *The Third World Conference on Faith and Order*, 15.
[3] ibid., 18.

into the world. By this movement the Church is ever being built up into Jesus Christ, its Head.

This Church must be deemed to be 'the new creation' to which it is already given to participate in the new life of the risen Christ; Christ dwells in the midst of His Church through the indwelling of His Spirit. Thus the new age is already present and 'the Church on earth is already given to participate in the power of the resurrection'.[1] Christ gives it a share in His work of Atonement. But the Church still lives between the first and the final coming of Christ. It is at the same time 'a community of forgiven sinners eagerly expecting and patiently watching for the final consummation of its redemption. It continues to be a pilgrim people in a strange land, so that all its life and work on earth is incomplete.'[2] 'To these convictions about the Church we are led by our faith in Jesus Christ and by our shared acceptance of the authority of the Holy Scriptures. We cannot build the one Church by cleverly fitting together our divided inheritances. We can grow together towards fullness and unity in Christ only by being conformed to Him who is the Head of the Body and Lord of His people. And He manifests His fullness, however brokenly, in the gifts He has given to us even in our separations.'[3]

Therefore, continues the Report, the churches must place themselves under His judgement and be obedient to Him, being prepared to be changed. 'Some of us who have been assured that we possess the true order and the true sacraments will find ourselves called to give its rightful place to the preaching of the Living Word. Some who have neglected the sacraments will be confronted by Him who humbled Himself in Baptism and broke bread and shared the cup to make us partakers of His passion and death. Those who have sought to show forth the glory of the Church as the Body and Bride of Christ must stand under the judgement of His simplicity and servant-hood.

'Churches which have valued little His prayer that the oneness of His people be made manifest to men will be summoned to make His prayer their own. . . .

'Those who are ever looking backward and have accumulated much precious ecclesiastical baggage will perhaps be shown that pilgrims must travel light and that, if we are to share at last in the great Supper, we must let go much that we treasure. Churches

[1] ibid., 20.
[2] ibid., 19 f.
[3] ibid., 20.

settled and self-assured will have to hear again the Lord's heart-broken concern for the sheep without a shepherd and know that to be His Church is to share in His world-embracing missions.'[1] Finally, the Conference recommends that 'the doctrine of the Church be treated in close relation both to the doctrine of Christ and to the doctrine of the Holy Spirit. We believe that this must occupy a primary place in the future work of this movement.'[2]

The third chapter treats the question of CONTINUITY AND UNITY. The starting-point is the 'People of God', but it is stressed that attention must be given also to the other New Testament designations of the Church all of which emphasize the unity of the Church, above all to the Church as the Body of Christ. Here, too, the in-dwelling of the Holy Spirit is mentioned, which fashions the faithful into a *communio sanctorum*, 'a company of the sanctified—forgiven, justified by faith, and born anew in Christ'. Again, the question of the relation between Christ and the Church is given priority. 'There are different emphases among us as to the differing modes of par-ticipation of the members in the Head. The former view stresses the fullness of Christ as something already received by the Church, though not always consciously apprehended, the latter the manifesta-tion of this same fullness at the Coming of the Lord in glory. In the present age, however, it is in the Church under the Cross that the fullness of Christ is realized.' This difference in emphasis affects the different opinions upon the nature of continuity. 'All agree not only upon the continuity assured by the constant action of the risen Lord through the Holy Spirit, but also upon the value of some form of continuity in history.'[3] 'Disagreement arises on the question whether some particular form of ministerial order is essential to the con-tinuity of the Church.'[4] The New Testament statements on Church order can be understood in different ways. 'It is clear that here is an obstinate difference, held with deep conviction and in a good conscience, which cannot readily be resolved.'[5] The doctrine of the ministry must be tackled 'in the light of a profound christological and eschatological approach to the doctrine of the Church'.[6] In the discussion of 'Discontinuity' the concepts of 'schism', 'apostasy' and 'heresy' are examined by the Report, which is of the opinion that these terms for division 'cannot be regarded as fully satisfactory'; 'the need is felt to discover words which as far as possible reflect the

[1] ibid., 21.
[2] ibid., 22.
[3] ibid., 25.
[4] ibid.
[5] ibid., 26.
[6] ibid., 26 f.

living nature of the Church'.[1] 'Of recent years it has been widely maintained that our breaches as Christian denominations are rather breaches within than from the Church.'[2] Hence, in the following discussions the term 'diversity' is preferred. All the communions represented agree in 'the original simple New Testament affirmation', in the confession of 'faith in Jesus Christ as Lord and Saviour'. Yet 'this common faith allows for certain differences of interpretation and practice'.[3] A special section is devoted to 'the unity we have and the unity we seek'. Collaboration in the Oecumenical Movement is a practical proof that the unity given by God in Christ already exists. On the other hand, 'we differ, however, in our understanding of the relation of our unity in Christ to the visible Holy, Catholic and Apostolic Church. We are agreed that there are not two churches, one visible and the other invisible, but one Church which must find visible expression on earth; but we differ in our belief as to whether certain doctrinal, sacramental and ministerial forms are of the essence of the Church itself. In consequence, we differ in our understanding of the character of the unity of the Church on earth for which we hope, though none of us looks forward to an institution with a rigid uniformity of governmental structure and all of us look forward to a time when all Christians can have unrestricted communion in sacrament and fellowship with each other. Yet our differences in the doctrinal and sacramental content of our faith and of our hope do not prevent us from being one in the act of believing and of hoping. For our faith and our hope are in the crucified and risen Jesus Christ, who is already working in us the purpose of His perfect will, and is already gathering up every fragment of obedient endeavour into the consummation of that purpose.'[4]

Summing up, the essence of the unity to be desired is again defined as 'a visible fellowship in which all members, acknowledging Jesus Christ as living Lord and Saviour, shall recognize each other as belonging fully to His Body, to the end that the world may believe'.[5] Some hold that the unity of the Church as the existence of the Body of Christ must be organic. 'A covenant relationship realized to the full would bind the Churches together into the organic unity of the Body of Christ, because it would be a relationship *in Christo*, the indwelling *Creator Spiritus* unifying the distinct members.' Others believe that this use of the term 'covenant' is far

[1] ibid., 27.
[2] ibid., 28.
[3] ibid., 30 f.

[4] ibid., 33 f.
[5] ibid., 37.

removed from Biblical usage. 'They would emphasize the finality of the "covenant" once made by God through Christ, and would urge that the task of Christian unity is to make effective our common response to that covenant.'[1]

Chapter IV deals with WAYS OF WORSHIP. The preamble states that 'Worship, no less than Faith and Order, is essential to the being of the Church'.[2]

The aim is not to list traditional oppositions, but to attempt 'to open the way for further discussion and explanations'. Differences of opinion cover the following questions:

1. The relation of Word and Sacrament; but this should never be more than a matter of emphasis.

2. The different emphases given to the place in worship of things that can be touched and seen. This use of material things should be carefully studied in the light of common agreement. Through the Holy Spirit God in some sense redeems the whole creation.

3. The opposed concepts of 'liturgical' and 'non-liturgical'. Both should have their place.

4. The importance of the ministry in matters of worship. Most Churches hold that 'our Lord has called forth in His Church a stated ministry. To this ministry alone the leadership of certain acts of worship is restricted. This raises for us the question of the basis of this restriction'.[3] 'We recognize that questions regarding the character of the ministry, priestly and prophetic, continue to be grave obstacles to unity. Behind them lie fundamental problems concerning the nature of grace and the Person and work of Christ. . . . Fruitful discussion here may well render less intractable the differences in defining the meaning of apostolic ministry and validity.'[4]

5. The view that Christ as High Priest unites the offering of His Body, the Church, with His own sacrifice. 'A measure of understanding' has been reached 'on the problem of the sacrificial element in Holy Communion'. Holy Scripture warrants the use of sacrificial language.

Some members of the Conference regretted, however, 'that the discussion of the Eucharist has concentrated on this sacrificial aspect. In their opinion the main issue is the real bodily presence of the crucified and risen Lord and our receiving His body and blood.'[5]

6. The conception of the Communion of Saints. Members were

---

[1] ibid., 38.
[2] ibid., 39.
[3] ibid., 41.
[4] ibid., 42.
[5] ibid., 43.

agreed on its existence. Deep divergences appeared especially in the position of the Blessed Virgin in Christian worship, and the Report referred to the relevant essays in the *Ways of Worship* volume. The Report rightly observes that 'these issues can be discussed properly only in the context of the doctrine of grace and of the work of Christ and of the Holy Spirit'.[1] The practice of prayer for the departed, too, would have to be referred to the doctrine of grace.

The Report then offers 'suggestions towards a new line of approach'; for certain differences in ways of worship could not be reduced to dogmatic differences alone. The Church was *in via*, and therefore involved in the historical situation. Here the non-theological factors played an important part. The Report concentrates on the social and psychological factors in the shaping of worship. Here, it is thought, much could be done to eliminate oppositions.

Chapter V deals with INTERCOMMUNION. The lack of sacramental unity probably made it clearer than anything else to the Oecumene how far it still was from the desired unity of the Church. Hence the Lund Conference considered it its urgent task to examine the questions concerning 'fellowship at the Lord's Table'. Now there are Churches, like the Orthodox, for which the question of Inter-communion simply does not exist, because it presupposes unity in the life and doctrine of the Church. Other churches, however, are able to envisage sacramental fellowship without complete organic union.'[2] Nevertheless, the Report warns against premature unions of this nature, to which 'non-theological factors' might lead, for 'the difficulties arise from profoundly held differences of conviction about the nature of the Church and of the sacraments. These cause grief and perplexity to us all.'[3]

First, much importance is attached to a clear definition of the concept of 'Intercommunion'. The Report distinguishes:

1. *Full Communion* between churches of the same confessional family.

2. *Intercommunion and Intercelebration:* 'Where two Churches not of the same confessional family by agreement allow communicant members freely to communicate at the altars of each, and where there is freedom of ministers to officiate sacramentally in either church, e.g. Lutheran and Reformed Churches in France.'[4]

3. *Intercommunion:* Here the freedom of ministers to celebrate is absent. The Intercommunion between Churches of the Anglican communion and Old Catholics is given as an example.

[1] ibid., 44.
[2] ibid., 49.
[3] ibid., 51.
[4] ibid., 52.

4. *Open Communion:* One Church invites members of other Churches to receive communion.

5. *Mutual Open Communion:* Two or more Churches on principle invite each other's members to receive communion.

6. *Limited Open Communion:* Admission in cases of emergency or in other special circumstances.

7. *Closed Communion:* Where a Church limits participation in the Lord's Supper to its own members.

Most Churches represented 'without for a moment losing sight of the ultimate goal of full unity, believe that there already exists among the members of the World Council of Churches such a fundamental unity as to justify, or indeed require, joint participation at the Lord's Table'.[1] The foundation of this is the recognition of 'elements of the true Church' (cf. Toronto Document IV, 5). According to this view Intercommunion may precede reunion.

Others, however, make 'fuller agreement in doctrine, a mutually acceptable ministry, or organic unity of Church life' the condition for Intercommunion. The Report refers to 'certain Lutheran Churches, maintaining that fellowship in the Lord's Supper depends upon the unity of the Church, and that such unity only exists where there is agreement in the proclamation of the Gospel', especially in the doctrine of the Real Presence.

Nevertheless, 'with the exception of the Greek Orthodox Church, none of the member Churches of the World Council so strictly interprets its responsibility for the ordering of the Lord's Table as to deny the Sacrament to members of other Churches in cases of urgent need'.[2]

The question of Intercommunion became topical especially at the Oecumenical gatherings. Where a clergyman celebrates, he does so, according to the Report, 'as a minister of the Church Universal'. Yet his authority is derived only through the church to which he belongs. 'A Conference, gathered together in the name of Christ, even though it may be regarded as a temporary and local expression of the Church, does not claim the right to ordain or authorize its own ministry to celebrate the Sacrament.'[3]

These discussions show the differences within the Oecumene on the question of authority in the ministry.

Chapter VI, WHERE DO WE STAND?, tries once more to define

[1] ibid., 54.
[2] ibid., 55.
[3] ibid., 57.

the position of the Oecumenical Movement. 'We confess our faith in the One, Holy, Catholic and Apostolic Church which is God's gift for the salvation of the world . . . . The Church . . . persists in continuity in history by the power of the Word of God and the presence of the Holy Spirit.'[1]

Members of the Oecumene are convinced that there is 'an underlying unity of life in Christ'. 'In seeking Him we find one another.'[2]

There is 'an encouraging degree of common ground', hence there is no reason for pessimism. 'Nevertheless we have now reached a point at which our divergences stubbornly resist easy solution.'[3]

Members of the Oecumenical Movement 'are faced with the dilemma of a proper confessional loyalty and obedience to the richer unity of the One Church to which Christ points'.[4] Then the Report makes an observation which, as we shall see later, is relevant for ecclesiology: 'By the final revelation of God in Jesus Christ at a particular point in history, the Church lives, but it is within the continuous movement of history that it bears witness to this Gospel and applies it to human need. The thought forms and language through which the Church proclaims the one Gospel are therefore subject to the limitations and changes of history'.[5] Now, no one age can fully express the truth of God's revelation. This does not mean that the Church should subordinate its message to the relativities of history, 'but the language and thought forms coined in history must be constantly corrected by the content of the Gospel'.[6] One must distinguish between the binding confession of the Truth itself and certain terminologies which are perhaps partly products of a particular age.

Further, the work of the theologians is carried out in a certain intellectual climate, which is also subject to far-reaching changes. 'Our understanding of the Scriptures to which the Reformers made their primary appeal has greatly advanced.'[7]

'We have all received patterns of thought not only from the Gospel but also from the structure of society.'[8]

All these chapters were read at Lund in plenary session and 'received *nemine contradicente*'. That means they were not *accepted*. The delegates representing the Orthodox Churches under the jurisdiction of the Oecumenical Patriarchate had taken part in the Conference by

[1] ibid., 60.
[2] ibid.
[3] ibid.
[4] ibid., 61.
[5] ibid.
[6] ibid.
[7] ibid., 62.
[8] ibid.

expounding the Orthodox view, 'but took no part in the voting upon the reception of the Report'.[1]

At Lund a special committee considered the constitution, task and organization of the Commission on Faith and Order and submitted it to the Central Committee of the World Council for final acceptance. According to this the tasks of the Commission are described as follows:

1. To proclaim the essential oneness of the Church of Christ and to keep prominently before the World Council and the churches the obligation to manifest this unity and its urgency for the work of evangelism.

2. To study questions of faith, order and worship with the relevant social, cultural, political, racial and other factors in their bearing on the unity of the Church.

3. To study the theological implications of the existence of the Oecumenical Movement.

4. To study matters in the present relationships of the Churches to one another which cause difficulties and need theological clarification.

5. To provide information concerning actual steps taken by the Churches towards reunion.[2]

All activities of the Commission were to be guided by the four principles of Faith and Order:

1. To draw churches out of their isolation so as to meet each other and come to understand their agreements as well as their differences.

2. The Conferences are to be attended by official delegates of the churches.

3. All churches that acknowledge Our Lord Jesus Christ as God and Saviour are to be invited.

4. The Faith and Order Movement is not to formulate schemes for re-union; it is only to be a handmaid helping the Churches by removing misunderstandings and obstacles, and by issuing reports which are to be submitted to the churches for consideration.

World Conferences on Faith and Order are to be held only 'when main subjects are ready for submission to the Churches, and when, on recommendation of the Commission on Faith and Order, the Central Committee so decides'.

The Commission is to consist of 85 members appointed by the

[1] ibid., 298.
[2] Cf. ibid., 359 f.

Assembly of the World Council. The Commission itself is to nominate up to fifteen further members for appointment by the Central Committee. 'In making appointments care shall be taken to secure adequate geographical and confessional representation of Churches.'[1] This is the geographical and confessional distribution according to the list compiled at Lund:

The United States and Canada 25, Europe 26, the United Kingdom 16, Asia and Africa 16, Australasia 1, South America 1.

Fourteen Lutherans, 12 Presbyterians and Reformed, 11 Anglicans, 9 Orthodox, 9 Methodists, 7 Baptists, 7 United, 7 Others, 4 Congregationalists, 3 Disciples, 2 Quakers. To these will be added the fifteen members to be appointed by the Central Committee.

This Commission was to nominate a special Working Committee of twenty-two members which should normally meet every year. The Chairman was the Archbishop of Uppsala, Y. T. Brilioth, the Vice-President Dean C. T. Craig (Methodist), and the Secretary J. R. Nelson (Baptist).

Opinions on the Lund Conference differ widely. While Schlink would place Lund on a par with the councils of the ancient Church[2] and holds it to be only a theoretical question which councils are preferred, Lilje speaks of a theological dilemma of the Oecumene. If its aim is a growing unity of organization, then Lund cannot be said to have brought this any nearer.[3]

It is generally admitted that, even at Lund, Faith and Order did not go beyond the statistical, comparative method, and hence had come to an impasse.[4] While Schlink asserts that the present-day oecumenical conferences are more truly Catholic than the old Councils, van Dusen, the President of the Union Theological Seminary in New York, denies Lund the designation 'oecumenical', because, according to him, the oecumenical will was dead and the preparatory material showed how much members wanted to keep to themselves. The attitude of the Orthodox implied particularly strong criticism of the Conference. The Orthodox Church of Greece was altogether absent, and the other Orthodox representatives announced at Lund the decision of the Patriarch of Constantinople that 'any participation by the Orthodox Church in the discussions and

[1] ibid., 361.

[2] *Evangelische Welt*, August 16; cf. *HK* VI (1952), 584.

[3] 'Der gegenwärtige Stand der Oekumenischen Bewegung: Kritische Ergebnisse der dritten Weltkonferenz für Glauben und Kirchenverfassung in Lund', *ThLZ*, 78 (1953), 69.

[4] Cf. Torrance, 'Wohin führt Lund?', loc. cit., 506.

operations of this Commission (on Faith and Order) should be avoided, inasmuch as this Commission has for its aim the union (of Churches) by means of dogmatic discussions between delegates of Churches separated from one another by the deepest issues ... Our Orthodox Church should also inform the heterodox about the content of her faith and teaching.'[1]

At Lund, too, the Orthodox asserted several times in friendly but definite terms that 'the aim of the Oecumenical Movement could mean for the Orthodox Church really only the return to this Church which, after all, was in possession of the only saving truth. The Metropolitan Athenagoras who lives in exile in London expressed this comparatively plainly; but his other co-religionists who took part in the work of the Conference with accustomed learning and fraternal charity really made it no less clear.'[2] Thus it can be said that the strongest criticism came from the Oecumene itself; on the one hand from the Anglo-American activists for whom all this theological labour is too slow and who urge unity, on the other from the representatives of a systematic theology, most strongly defended by the Orthodox Church which sees in the comparative method of Faith and Order attempts at a compromise.

With regard to the objective problems, the increasing interest in Christology is generally considered a positive result of the Lund Conference.[3] But this seems to us of existential rather than doctrinal value. One seeks union with Christ and places oneself under His judgement. This leads to statements which are certainly significant, for the Church is seen in closest connexion with the work of Christ. Only in this way can it be called 'the new creation' which 'has a share in the life of the risen Christ and His Spirit, in the office of atonement, in His fullness'. The Church itself is the Body of Christ, hence the faithful are a communion of saints. The Creator Spirit works in the Church even to the sanctification and redemption of visible elements.

Yet this oecumenical Christology is defective. The members of the Lund Conference could not even agree on the Christological basis of the World Council—faith 'in Jesus Christ as *God and Saviour*'. The enfeebled formula—which by now has become a statement of faith in the Oecumene—Jesus Christ *Lord and Saviour*—is used again

---

[1] *ER* V (1952/3), 167 f.

[2] Lilje, loc. cit., col. 68 f.

[3] Cf. A. C. Outler, 'A Way forward from Lund', *ER* V (1952/3), 60; Boyer, 'The Conclusions Reached by the Conference at Lund', *Unitas* IV (1952), 193.

and again; the Christological statement is watered down because it is thought that this formula leaves room for a different view of the Person and work of Jesus Christ. Hence Bishop Lilje has rightly criticized this oecumenical trend towards Christology. He feels that this way, though it may undoubtedly lead to essential truths, yet, on the other side, 'cannot really furnish a direct solution, but at the moment only puts the crucial problem of the Oecumenical Movement one step back'.[1]

According to Lilje, Christology and ecclesiology are indeed closely related to each other, but it is doubtful whether it may be hoped 'that the different ways in which the churches have walked can be retraced by the fact that they realize what different views they hold about Christ.'[2]

In our view this retracing is very important, if not decisive, for the question of the reunion of the churches. But what is this 'deepened Christology' in the Oecumene today? Now as before it fails to be guided by the Christology of the old Councils, especially by the Chalcedon definition of Christ as the God-Man.

Instead, the oecumenical theologians link Christology to eschatology. Schlink's essay on the Church as 'The Pilgrim People of God'[3] determined the programme of Lund. Indeed, the Report constantly refers to the Church as 'the People of God'.

Now Schlink sees Christ chiefly as the Lord who will return at the end of time. Attention should be directed to Him, because He will heal the divisions of the Church when He comes again. 'We shall have to learn . . . to free our eyes from the past, and look steadily forward to the Lord who is coming again.'[4] 'The only thing which remains is to look to the coming Redeemer and to cry in longing for the coming of His Kingdom.'[5]

The Church is *on the way* towards this last day which already casts its light on present history. In this eschatological light the questions which now separate the churches appear as unimportant. The Last Day will solve the problems of Christendom, therefore, as the Report says, we must 'travel light', leaving behind much ecclesiastical baggage. Lilje agrees with the *Herder-Korrespondenz* in calling this attempt at an eschatological solution an attempt to escape, 'a forward flight'. 'For in this case the problem of present

[1] Lilje, op. cit. 70.
[2] ibid.
[3] *ER* V (1952/3), 27–36.
[4] ibid., 30.
[5] ibid., 29.

differences is not solved but only referred to the hope of a future perfection.'[1]

He also calls an escape the suggestion of A. C. Outler who proposes an oecumenical commission of studies to work out an 'oecumenical history' of the Church. According to him the time has come for an oecumenical study 'of the total historical experience of the Christian community'.[2] Hitherto the traditional history of the Church and of doctrine has been 'more apologetic and partisan than synoptical and ecumenical'.[3] Hence there was a need for an oecumenical account of the pilgrimage of God's People which would put on record how and where Christendom had transcended the denominational frontiers by common action. 'It should be clear', observes Lilje, 'that this way which is indeed congenial to Anglo-Saxon empirical thought may result in far-reaching practical understanding, but cannot solve the problem itself. Hence it is not surprising that the leading thinkers of the Oecumenical Movement, looking back on Lund, should once more state this dilemma and present it quite soberly.'[4]

The *Herder-Korrespondenz* notes that in this presentation of the relation between Christ and the Church, Schlink 'strangely disregarded the presence of Christ and His share in the pilgrimage of the Church',[5] hence it becomes clear that the concepts of 'God's People' or the 'Body of Christ' alone are not sufficient to define the Church. The report of the Youth Group to the Lund Conference said quite plainly: 'We suggest a renewed emphasis on the study of the Bible, in a serious attempt to discern the true Biblical basis of the Church. Very much attention has been paid to the conception of the Church as the Body of Christ, but such living New Testament pictures as the Bride of Christ, Temple of Christ, New Israel, Royal Priesthood, and others also demand our attention. All these figures enrich the conception of the Church and consideration of all of them seems to us to be necessary for a true understanding of the New Testament Church.'[6]

The Report of the Lund Conference stated that the Church was still situated between the First and the Second Advent of Christ, that it was a community of sinners who had been forgiven and who ardently awaited the ultimate perfection of their redemption. Here seemed to be a possibility for the Lutherans to join in. Schlink's

[1] *ThLZ* 70 (1945) loc. cit.
[2] *ER* V (1952/3), 60.
[3] ibid.
[4] *ThLZ* 71 (1946) loc. cit.
[5] *HK* VI (1952/3), 583.
[6] Lund, 308.

view was too evidently an escape into eschatology. Bishop Lilje attempts to turn to the dialectical doctrine of justification held by the Reformers. He observes that Lutherans, in harmony with all Christendom, confess their faith in the *Una Sancta Ecclesia*. Now this can only mean that this one, holy Christian Church is confessed as existing. To the eyes of faith it is a reality which exists here and now. The question then arises whether this unity of the Church that exists in faith will also have to be visible in the concrete. 'We must answer: Yes, but not necessarily in invariably successful organizing activities; it can also happen in the grateful recognition of a fact perceived by faith. Here we have an exact parallel with the doctrine of justification. A man who has met Jesus Christ in faith is justified, not, however, in the sense of a perfectionist moralism but as the *peccator justificatus*. He knows by faith that he is justified, though what becomes visible in his Christian state is by no means the picture of perfection. In the same way the Oecumenical Movement must not strive for an ecclesiological perfectionism.'[1] Lilje then makes the strange statement: 'The visible union of the Church that can be realized on earth is not simply a New Testament promise that applies to this present age.'[2] Now is not the only difference between this—shall we say genuinely Lutheran?—attempt and Schlink's eschatologism one of emphasis? If the latter held a dialectical eschatology, Lilje teaches an eschatological dialectic.

Surely, here we have simply another attempt to escape from the theological dilemma of the Oecumene, a flight into the unworldliness of the Protestant faith.[3] Hence the Report of the Conference rightly says that the conception of the doctrine of grace is decisive for ecclesiological questions; but this applies not only to questions of worship but to all departments of ecclesiology.

In this context we are also concerned with the question of continuity. The Report said all too tentatively that members were agreed on the value of a certain kind of continuity *in history*. The oecumenical preference goes rather to the first part of the clause: the continuous action of the risen Christ through the Holy Spirit guarantees the continuity. The missing continuity of ministry and sacraments would be replaced by the continuity of Christian experi-

---

[1] *ThLZ* 72 (1947) loc. cit

[2] ibid.

[3] Cf. also Schlink, 'The Pilgrim People': 'We cannot be satisfied to find unity of the churches merely in the common belief in unity. Such limitation would mean a docetic conception of the Church and an indefensible "spiritualism".' (p. 34).

ence. This unity of experience is a key to the understanding of the
Oecumene. The unity of the Church 'is an experienced fact', as had
already been stated at Edinburgh in 1937. But where is it experienced? According to Schlink, on the one hand in our suffering and
persecuted brethren, on the other in the message of the young
churches, 'Forgetting the things which are behind, and stretching
forward to the things which are before' (Phil. iii, 13). Hence unity
with Christ, taking the place of historical tradition, is experienced
today, not least in the fact of the Oecumene. Hodgson has explained
it thus when introducing the reports of the theological commissions
at Lund: in the Catholic conception of the Church the divine action
is given primary importance. Christ continues His redemptive action
on earth through the ministry: 'The church is not constituted by the
response of faith made by its members: The Church is constituted
by Christ, revealed in Word and Sacrament through creed and
ministry; it is the divinely given framework enduring through the
ages within which successive generations of believers can make the
response of faith.'[1] But this strong emphasis on the divine action
contains two possibilities of corruption. If exaggerated to the
complete denial of the importance of the human factor, it would
lead to substituting worship for morality. And if it were then held
that man's duty consisted in the correct execution of the cult this
would result in a false, magical sense of the sacramental *ex opere
operato*. Protestants no less than Catholics and Orthodox believe in
the divine initiative: 'But because the Reformation came to reform
the Church at a time when it was suffering from both these forms of
corruption, it came to emphasize the importance of the response of
faith, to remind us that without this on the human side the Church
cannot be its true self.'[2] This view is characteristic of the Congregationalist conception of the Church: 'Congregationalists admit to
church membership only those who have attained sufficient maturity
and responsibility to profess faith in Jesus Christ as Saviour and
Lord. . . . Some Congregationalists, though not the majority, regard
Baptism as admitting to church membership; but all are agreed that
its privilege and responsibilities cannot be fully entered upon without
a personal profession of faith.'[3] Hence in a statement accepted by
the International Congregational Council at Wallesley, Boston, in
June 1949, the Church was defined as '. . . a covenant fellowship,

[1] *ER* V (1952/3), 8.
[2] ibid.
[3] *The Nature of the Church*, 181.

binding the members to God and to one another through Christ, the Head of the Church'.[1]

The Methodists regard continuity with the Church of past centuries as a 'continuity of Christian experience, the fellowship in the gift of the one Spirit; in the continuity of the allegiance to one Lord, the continued proclamation of the message, the continued acceptance of the mission.[2] ... This is our doctrine of apostolic succession. It is our conviction, therefore, that the continuity of the Church does not depend on, and it is not necessarily secured by, an official succession of ministers, whether bishops or presbyters, from apostolic times, but rather by fidelity to apostolic truth. ... The apparent discontinuity of office has sometimes been due to a re-assertion of the true and essential continuity of experience, allegiance, message and mission.'[3]

Hodgson, and with him probably a large section of the Oecumenical Movement, considers both these views as differences of emphasis, hence the One Church must have room for both. Now here it must be asked whether it is Christ's will that the Church should be a body constituted by ministry and sacraments and perpetuated throughout history, or simply a fellowship of those who believe in Him. It is true, in oecumenical questions the words either-or should be used sparingly. But since we are here concerned with the fullness of Jesus Christ which the Church has already received, this question must at first be formulated as an either-or. If the question were put in a different way it would lead to the thesis of the 'breach *within* the Church', the view of 'separation for the sake of truth': 'There are divisions in the Church which were caused not by sin and impenitence, but by the will to obey the truth of the Gospel.'[4] This, Lilje suggests, was the point of departure of the Reformation, which still has its importance today, and therefore it would be a simplification to speak merely of 'sinful divisions'. But does not this whole thesis of difference and division instead of schism and heresy come very close to the old Branch Theory?

The 'organizational' result of Lund has been extensively discussed by the *Herder-Korrespondenz*, and conclusions for the further development of the Oecumene have been suggested on this basis. According to this view, the essential result of Lund can be properly appreciated

[1] Cf. *The Nature of the Church*, 183.
[2] ibid., 207.
[3] ibid., 208.
[4] Lilje, *ThLZ* 71 (1946) loc. cit.

only if the efforts of Visser't Hooft and van Dusen are given their full weight. These aim at 'subjecting the Faith and Order Movement to Geneva and to the "free trade in charismata" of the American sects'. This aim was served by a proposal prepared by 't Hooft and put before the Lund Conference by the Anglicans, according to which the Faith and Order Movement was to be reduced to a relatively small commission of the World Council, consisting of about a hundred members. The *Herder-Korrespondenz* thinks that this formal simplification of the activity of Faith and Order, 'where everything depends on the choice of personalities', undoubtedly 'serves a unification of the plannings of the World Council', 'the balance having increasingly inclined to the "super-dogmatical" union policy of Geneva, the seat of the Secretariat of the World Council'.[1] The meaning of this proposal with regard to ecclesiastical policy becomes evident if it be remembered that the majority of the American denominations opposed the 'Continental theology' called by van Dusen 'the stronghold of particularism and prejudice'. The Americans want equality for the sects. At Evanston the Free Church tradition would have forty per cent of the seats because of the great number of its followers, and this would mean that 'Christian Europe would not in composition and structure be representative of the Christian world'. An examination of the list of members of the Faith and Order Commission drawn up at Lund would reveal that 'the predominance of "Continental theology" complained of by the Americans had been broken'. Thus the *Herder-Korrespondenz* states that the result of Lund was important from the point of view of Church policy rather than in terms of doctrinal progress. 'The essential thing was the decision to prepare this branch of the Oecumenical Movement for the course followed at Geneva; this anticipated the decisions of the future without making them manifest.' The future will show whether this prognosis of the *Herder-Korrespondenz* has been correct; but as far as the situation can be judged these views seem to be justified.

Despite all relativism, paradoxes and 'theological dilemmas', the theological result of Lund may be considered to have been positive in the sense that there has been progress as compared with Lausanne and Edinburgh. For the members of the Conference had the courage to approach central questions of ecclesiology. They expressed at least the desire to place themselves under the judgement of Christ and to obey Him. Certain points raise hopes for a further fruitful

[1] cf. *HK* VII (1952), 39–42.

development of the one true Church. For in future the doctrine of the Church is to be treated in close connexion with the doctrine of Christ and the Holy Spirit; it has been recognized that the fundamental problems of grace and of the Person of Christ underlie the theological differences in some ecclesiological questions (and thus it is admitted that the question of grace had not been solved at Edinburgh); the non-theological factors in doctrinal differences are perceived, and, above all, Holy Scripture is consulted without preconceived ideas. Yet the words of the Conference remain true: 'We have now reached a point at which our divergences stubbornly resist easy solution.' But where is the legitimate solution of the dilemma stated by the Conference 'of a proper confessional loyalty and obedience to the richer unity of the one Church to which Christ points'? Must it not be asked what is meant by 'proper' and where is the One Church to which Christ points? If one is 'agreed that there are not two Churches, one visible and the other invisible', and yet speaks of the clergyman as the 'minister of the Church Universal' when administering Holy Communion, who nevertheless holds his authority only from the Church to which he belongs—is all this not rather equivocal? Or should it be the secret intention of the Oecumene to consider itself as *the* One Church though this is explicitly denied? The statement that the Conference might be considered as the temporary and local form of the Church sounds suspicious. Is it not perhaps intended to arrive at the fullness of Christ by addition and synthesis, based on the doctrine of the *vestigia ecclesiae*?

(g) EVANSTON

The second plenary conference of the WCC took place at Evanston (U.S.A.) from August 15th to 31st. Its subject was 'Christ, the Hope of the World'. The earlier version, proposed by the Central Committee in 1950, was 'Jesus Christ as Lord is the only hope of both the Church and the World'.[1] In the following years this title was changed six times. An advisory commission of twenty-five theologians and laymen worked out a first report at Rolle (Switzerland) in 1951, a second at Bossey in 1952, and a third in 1953, which was placed before the delegates at Evanston. The subject, then, was a theology of hope, an eschatology, and it was obvious that continental and American theologians were bound once more to differ seriously on this question. In this connection the essays written in *Christian Century* in the United States as a preparation for Evanston are of

[1] Central Committee Minutes 1950, p. 23.

particular interest. We read there: 'The word eschatology is itself strange to all but a fraction of American churchmen. Even in the seminaries, it has not in recent generations assumed great importance —at least to anything like the degree which is current in Europe and in the "younger" churches. Fundamentalists preach it with vigour and abandon, often literalizing apocalyptic hopes. But on this issue, despite the return to orthodoxy, and partly in reaction against fundamentalism, the American theological scene is still prevailingly "liberal".' It is openly admitted that 'Our popular American substitute for biblical eschatology has been to a large extent the belief in progress.'[1] But even apart from this particular question of eschatology, before Evanston many theologians were afraid that, owing to the climate of American opinion, doctrinal problems would not be handled with sufficient seriousness and practical questions would take the first place. In his lecture before Section One. O. S. Tomkins' mentioned a malicious caricature which had appeared in a Church periodical, showing a group of theologians splitting hairs in a lecture room while outside, before the window, a refugee lies wounded and unattended. E. G. Homringhausen, discussing Bishop Berggrav's ideas on American Christianity in *Christian Century*, writes on this point: 'We must bear in mind that our large churches are the free churches. The Baptists and the Disciples of Christ have always repudiated creeds . . . They have their statements of faith which are not officially approved as having an authority alongside the Scriptures. Again, our theology of the Spirit and our tradition of dissent must be taken into account. Dissenters revolted against cold credalism which made Christianity into a formal set of propositions instead of a personal commitment to Jesus Christ. And while these free churches today grant the place of theology, they will never surrender to a propositional Christianity.'[2]

Returning to the subject of Evanston, the first report emphasized almost exclusively the Second Coming of Christ at the end of time: 'It is especially of His Lordship over the future that the Assembly is called to speak.'[3] Without doubt this document emphasizes the apocalyptic element. Protests multiplied not only from the Central Committee but also from the member churches of the WCC. Thereupon the advisory commission produced a second report: 'The first thing to be said is that in Christ the New Age has already come.

[1] T. O. Wedel in *Christian Century*, 28th October 1953 (LXX/43).
[2] *Christian Century*, 7th October 1953.
[3] Central Committee Minutes 1951, 72.

The next thing to be said is that the new life in Christ awaits fulfilment at the end of history. Both of these affirmations are essential to the Christian gospel, and they must be steadily maintained together. Neither one apart from the other can tell the full truth.'[1] So now more stress was laid on the earthly aspects of the hope in Christ.

However, the proper balance was established only by the third report, after some members of the Central Committee had criticized (at their meeting at Lucknow in January 1953) the Second Report for placing still too much emphasis on the Second Coming of Christ to the detriment of the presence of Christ in the world today.

The principal theme, 'Christ, the Hope of the World', was supplemented by six subsidiary themes to which the WCC attaches particular importance. They were: 'The Mission of the Church to Those Outside her Life'; 'Christians in the Struggle for World Community'; 'The Responsible Society in a World Perspective'; 'The Church Amid Racial and Ethnic Tensions'; 'The Christian in his Vocation'; 'Our Oneness in Christ and our Disunity as Churches'. It would, indeed, be interesting to discuss these themes which are all treated under the aspect of hope and from which Roman Catholic theologians, too, might receive many profitable suggestions. Nevertheless, in view of the subject of this book we shall confine our attention to the report of the section on Faith and Order.

To take first the text of the Theological Committee of the WCC on 'Christ, the Hope of the World'.[2] Part I treats of 'Christ our Hope'. In section C we read: 'In Christ and His community we are already sons of God and heirs of glory'. On the other hand, one paragraph is devoted to 'The Kingdom that is to come'. Part II treats of 'Christ and his People': 'We must now go on to speak of that people which He has called into being to be the bearer of hope, the sign and witness of God's mighty acts, the means of His working, and the field wherein His glory is to be revealed . . . His kingdom is inaugurated on earth, to be consummated hereafter'. Catholics will welcome this inclusion of the Church in the theme of hope, as well as the fact that the Church is seen so much in the christological context. 'The Church is the sign of that which He is doing and will yet do.' However, there is something equivocal about the statement that 'The Church stands upon the Rock and the gates of hell do not prevail against it', since the Scriptural passage in question speaks clearly of the Petrine office. While trying to escape this difficulty the oecumenical theologians

[1] ER V, 1, Oct. 1952, 82.
[2] ER VI (1954), 430–464.

again understand the unity of the Church eschatologically (Section C) in the sense suggested by Schlink at Lund. In the same way the unity of the Church is formulated so as to correspond with the seventh chapter of the Confessio Augustana: 'Where the one Christ is at work, where the apostolic witness to Him is truly set forth in word and sacrament, there is the one Church.' There is no question of the ministry; Bishop Newbigin did not gain his point. 'We are not at one concerning the form which the corporate unity of the Church should take. Our discussions have not yet led us to a common conviction as to the way which we can take all together towards that end.'

Criticisms of this text at Evanston made the following points: it was lacking in suggesting the 'joyful' character of the expectation of Christ. It did not emphasize sufficiently that the Holy Spirit is working in the Church and the world even now. The theme of the cosmic creation and redemption was not developed very well. The relations between present and eschatological hope were insufficiently worked out.

The Catholic theologian G. H. Tavard, who is well known in America, has criticized this 'theology of hope' in an unpublished essay from which we reproduce the following paragraphs:

'From the standpoint of the object of hope, the WCC's commission has produced a document which expresses, in terms that a Protestant can understand, a largely Catholic doctrine. It is true enough that the same document applies that doctrine to the notion of the Church in a way which is not compatible with Catholic tradition. It is also a fact that a disproportion in the arrangement of matter (the third chapter alone has the same length as the first two put together) risks promoting more interest in the use-value of hope (third chapter) than in its truth-value (1st chapter). Yet one must be fair. In spite of these imperfections the work on the doctrine of hope itself has been well done and is to be welcomed by Catholics.

We nevertheless sense a basic flaw in the document, which seemingly proceeds from a defective theological method. In a word, we would express our criticism thus: hope is described in a one-sidedly objectivistic way, whilst the subjective experience of hope is overlooked. From a Catholic standpoint this is very serious. As the wholeness of the Mystical Body is present to its members, likewise the totality of the supernatural order is present in grace and, accordingly, in its subjective apprehension in faith, hope and love. This entails an important methodological consequence: in the concrete one cannot fully know the object of hope apart from its experience by the

Christian soul, and vice versa. Like faith and charity, hope transcends somehow the dividedness—though not the distinction—of subject and object. Only in that existential correlation does it reach the fullness of its catholicity, for catholicity means the presence of the whole to the parts. Hope in Christ is the Christian hope of Catholic tradition insofar as it is infused and accepted as infused. Its infusion into the soul elevates us beyond all human, too human visions of the future and expectations of a better life: it makes a Pelagianism of hope unthinkable. Its acceptance places everything human in subservience to God's initiative: it condemns a fatalism of hope.

Had they attempted this approach, the theologians of the WCC would have been led to crucial issues which were evidently beyond the scope of the projected assembly. Among other items, the relations between hope and justification, and between hope and the sacramental order, could not have been eschewed. One may presume that on none of these a working agreement would have been reached. We cannot therefore blame the commission for avoiding dead ends. Yet we must regret that as a result of their limitation to a mere description of the objects of hope, they failed to see the exact insertion of hope in the theology of the Church (Ch. 2). This is not to be found first of all in the behaviour of Christians whose sum total would form, empirically speaking, the Church, the 'pilgrim people of God' *en route* for a better homeland. In the totality of our experience of hope, we know that the Church is already constituted, in the cosmos, as that part of the cosmos which is here and now transfigured into the spiritual world where all things will be changed. In the sacraments we have a foretaste of the parousiac sublimation of the creaturely order. Hope is the projection into our consciousness of our contact, through the sacraments of the Church, with the messianic status of things.

Thus, a complete theology of hope leads to a Catholic theology of the Church. Furthermore, as the Catholic mystics and theologians point out, hope is present in the soul under her aspect and function of memory. A study of this would have introduced to unperceived vistas on the theology of time and on the Christian status of the human person, which succeeds itself in a kind of ontological memory.

Such an outline would have related hope to many aspects of the Christian message, in an analogy of the faith which is largely unknown to Protestant theology.'

In our view Tavard has seen the decisive point. For the clarification of the Catholic view the question of the *how* of hope seems decisive. How does the Christian hope? Catholics may perhaps retain a thought that appears in chapter 2 of the Bossey report, according to which 'the true balance of the Christian outlook' is achieved in the Lord's Supper, with its equilibrium between present and future. For the Catholic hope is a sacramental reality of the Church, which produces in us the unity with the crucified and risen Christ: 'We cling to the hope we have in view, the anchorage of our souls. Sure and immovable, it reaches that inner sanctuary beyond the veil, which Jesus Christ, our escort, has entered already, a high priest, now, eternally, with the priesthood of Melchisedech.' (Heb. vi, 18–20). Scripture *and* Eucharist together will lead to the true perspective, as once happened at Emmaus after the short-sighted disappointment of the despairing disciples. For the unity of the Church is understood most deeply through the Sacrament of the Eucharist.

The Report of Section One

This report falls into three parts: 1. Our Oneness with Christ; 2. Our Disunity as Churches; 3. The Action of Faith. Part One first speaks of the unifying work of Christ: 'The New Testament conceives of the unity of the church not as sociological but as having its essential reality in Christ Himself and in His indissoluble unity with His people.' Then the Church is described in the New Testament images of the Body, the Bride, the People, the Temple and the Flock. It is important that Christ is not only called the Redeemer but also the Lord. 'The Church's unity is grounded in ... His passion and death, where sin was finally conquered and the power of divisiveness defeated; in His resurrection, where He manifested the new man unto whom we all grow (Eph. iv, 11ff), in whom all human divisions are done away (Gal. iii, 28); in His ascension and heavenly reign, by which all history is brought under His authority; in His outpouring of the Holy Spirit on the whole Church at Pentecost, which gives to each subsequent baptismal rite its deepest significance; and in His promise to come again as the triumphant and glorious king.' Here again the mention of the Ascension and heavenly reign of Christ appear to be of great significance. Further, the unity of the Church is seen as a growth 'from its unity, as given, to its unity, as fully manifested' (Eph. iv, 3, 13). Here the ancient Protestant thesis of man as both just and a sinner (*simul justus et peccator*) is applied to the Church. Later the Report speaks of the gifts of Christ to His Church, of apostles, prophets, evangelists, pastors and teachers, 'that the unity of the body may be continually built up'. Holy Scripture, the preaching of the Word, Baptism, the Lord's Supper and prayer are mentioned as further gifts of unity, which assure us of the presence among us of the undivided Christ, who infuses his life into us despite our divisions.

In his Introduction to the Report of Section I[1] Günther Jakob rightly observes: 'In modern Protestantism the theology of Ephesians had been widely neglected and forgotten. Now this has been remedied, for the conception of the Church as the "new humanity" founded by Christ such as it appears in Ephesians has been placed quite definitely at the centre of the consideration of the Church. In the last years commentaries on Ephesians have appeared in Germany, too (by Hans Asmussen and Heinrich Schlier), but their theological content has not yet been sufficiently assimilated.'

A good distinction between diversity and division is made in the section on 'Our Disunity as Churches' described thus: 'When diversity disrupts the manifest unity of the body, then it changes its quality and becomes sinful division.' The disunity is caused by our sin. It makes a patchwork of Redemption and contradicts the message of Atonement. 'We ask each other whether we do not sin when we deny the sole lordship of Christ over the Church by claiming the vineyard for our own, by possessing our "church" for ourselves, by regarding our theology, order, history, nationality, etc. as our own "valued treasures", thus involving ourselves more and more in the sin of separation.' Of the churches it is said that in certain circumstances they may be confronted with decision involving obedience even unto death. 'They may then have to be prepared to offer up some of their accustomed, inherited forms of life in uniting with other churches without complete certainty as to all that will emerge from the step of faith.'

The third part, 'The Action of Faith', treats of the World Council of Churches. 'All of us', runs a passage, 'as members of churches believe that we have been entrusted by God with certain elements of the one Church of Christ which we cannot forfeit.'

The Orthodox considered this Report entirely unsatisfactory so that their delegates regarded it as indispensable to put an axiomatic declaration before the Plenary Session. Since this brings out quite clearly the 'Catholic' point of view we will reproduce it as it stands:

'As delegates of the Orthodox Church participating at this As-

---

[1] *Christus—die Hoffnung der Welt. Ein Bericht uber die zweite Weltkirchenkonferenz Evanston* 1954. Editors, H. Grüber and G. Brennecke, 326.

sembly of the World Council of Churches, we submit the following statement concerning the report of Section I.

'1. We have studied the document with considerable interest. It falls into three parts: the first contains an able exposition of the New Testament doctrine of the Church. The organic character of the Church and her indissoluble unity with Christ are adequately stressed in the document. We feel that this at least provides fruitful ground for further theological elaboration. The second and third parts of the document deal with the divided state of Christendom and suggest practical steps toward union. It is our conviction that it does not follow logically and consistently from the first part and indeed if we do actually accept the New Testament doctrine of the Church we should come to quite different practical conclusions which have been familiar to us Orthodox for centuries. The whole approach to the problem of reunion is entirely unacceptable from the standpoint of the Orthodox Church.

'2. The Orthodox conception of church unity implies a twofold agreement:

'(a) The whole of the Christian Faith should be regarded as one indivisible unity. It is not enough to accept just certain particular doctrines, basic as they may be in themselves, e.g. that Christ is God and Saviour. It is compelling that all doctrines as formulated by the Ecumenical Councils, as well as the totality of the teaching of the early, undivided Church, should be accepted. One cannot be satisfied with formulas which are isolated from the life and experience of the Church. They must be assessed and understood within the context of the Church's life. From the Orthodox viewpoint, re-union of Christendom with which the World Council of Churches is concerned can be achieved solely on the basis of the total, dogmatic Faith of the early, undivided Church without either subtraction or alteration. We cannot accept a rigid distinction between essential and non-essential doctrines, and there is no room for comprehensiveness in the Faith. On the other hand, the Orthodox Church cannot accept that the Holy Spirit speaks to us only through the Bible. The Holy Spirit abides and witnesses through the totality of the Church's life and experience. The Bible is given to use within the context of Apostolic Tradition in which in turn we possess the authentic interpretation and explication of the Word of God. Loyalty to Apostolic Tradition safeguards the reality and continuity of church unity.

'(b) It is through the Apostolic Ministry that the mystery of Pentecost is perpetuated in the Church. The Episcopal Succession from the

Apostles constitutes an historical reality in the life and structure of the Church and one of the pre-suppositions of her unity through the ages. The unity of the Church is preserved through the unity of the Episcopate. The Church is one Body whose historical continuity and unity is also safeguarded by the common faith arising spontaneously out of the fullness (*pleroma*) of the Church.

'3. Thus when we are considering the problem of Church unity we cannot envisage it in any other way than as the complete restoration of the total faith and the total episcopal structure of the Church which is basic to the sacramental life of the Church. We would not pass judgement upon those of the separated communions. However, it is our conviction that in these communions certain basic elements are lacking which constitute the reality of the fullness of the Church. We believe that the return of the communions to the Faith of the ancient, united, and indivisible Church of the Seven Ecumenical Councils, namely to the pure and unchanged and common heritage of the forefathers of all divided Christians, shall alone produce the desired reunion of all separated Christians. For, only the unity and the fellowship of Christians in a common Faith shall have as a necessary result their fellowship in the sacraments and their indissoluble unity in love, as members of one and the same body of the one Church of Christ.

'4. The "perfect unity" of Christians must not be interpreted exclusively as a realization at the Second Coming of Christ. We must acknowledge that even at the present age the Holy Spirit dwelling in the Church continues to breathe in the world, guiding all Christians to unity. The unity of the Church must not be understood only eschatologically, but as a present reality which is to receive its consummation in the Last Day.

'5. It is suggested in the report of the section that the road which the Church must take in restoring unity is that of repentance. We recognize that there have been and there are imperfections and failures within the life and witness of Christian believers, but we reject the notion that the Church herself, being the Body of Christ and the repository of revealed Truth and the "whole operation of the Holy Spirit," could be affected by human sin. Therefore, we cannot speak of the repentance of the Church which is intrinsically holy and unerring. For, "Christ loved the Church and gave Himself for it, that He might sanctify it and cleanse it in the washing of water and the word, that He might present it to Himself as a glorious Church, not having spot or wrinkle or blemish or any such thing, but that it should be holy and without blemish" (Eph. v, 26–27).

'Thus the Lord, the only Holy One, sanctified His Church for ever and ordained that her task be the "edification of the saints and the building of the body of Christ." Her holiness is not vitiated by the sins and failures of her members. They cannot in any way lessen or exhaust the inexhaustible holiness of the divine life which from the Head of the Church is diffused throughout all the body.

'6. In conclusion, we are bound to declare our profound conviction that the Holy Orthodox Church alone has preserved in full and intact "the faith once delivered unto the saints". It is not because of our human merit, but because it pleases God to preserve "his treasure in earthen vessels, that the excellency of the power may be of God". (2 Cor. iv, 7)'

[Evanston Report, p. 92 ff.]

Günther Jakob says in his Introduction: 'Despite their basic opposition the orthodox representatives took part in the common work in a spirit of true fraternal charity. Yet their declaration reveals a fundamental dissension, which should damp any oecumenical enthusiasm. But all those Christian communions which stem from the Reformation will have to see in it a call to meditate on their own position.' So Georges Florovsky also said in his address to the Plenary Session: 'It can be objected at this point that all that has just been said amounts to a recognition that the Ecumenical Movement has reached a dead end and that no further discussion can be profitable or lead anywhere. In fact, it only means that some *new ways* should be discovered, if only we earnestly believe that Unity is God's Will and not just a human project'.[1] In his view the Oecumenical Movement had so far been only 'in space', it would now have to be supplemented by an 'Ecumenism in time'.

'It is but fair to say that we have not yet entered deeply enough into the labours of preceeding generations, of our father and forefathers in God. We are too much imprisoned in our own age. But all Christian convictions are subject to an ultimate test by paradosis, by Tradition. It is in the process of our common return to that Tradition, which had been continuous, even in the midst of conflicts and splits, if often in a disguised and obscure manner, that we, the "divided Christians", will meet each other on a safer ground than ever before.'[2]

[1] Florovsky, G., 'The Challenge of Disunity,' *Sobornost*, The Journal of the Fellowship of S. Alban and S. Sergius. Series 3, No. 16—Winter 1954-5. An address delivered to the Evanston Assembly of the World Council of Churches in August 1954, 173.

[2] ibid, 174.

For, he said, history had its place within the *Heilsgeschichte*.

The declarations of the Orthodox made a deep impression at Evanston. At the same time they bear witness to the possibility of taking part in the oecumenical dialogue even if one has to insist on a claim to absolute truth. Here we Catholics could learn a good deal from the Orthodox.

2. PRACTICAL ATTEMPTS AT UNION

Between 1937 and 1951 several different confessions and denominations[1] came together in a 'union'. We would select three characteristic examples of such attempts to unite which also illustrate the whole problematic position of the World Council.

1. THE UNITED STATES. On 28th November 1950 twenty-nine Protestant denominations united at Cleveland (Ohio) under the name 'National Council of the Churches of Christ in the USA'. All Protestant communions of the USA except the Southern Baptists and the Missouri Lutherans belong officially to this National Council. The dogmatic basis is faith in 'Jesus Christ as Lord and Saviour' as stated in the preamble. This National Council replaces the Federal Council of Churches that had been founded in 1908. However, this cannot be called a union in the strict sense, and attempts at reaching such a union are continued by Congregationalist circles. Theologically more important is the Conference of Greenwich (Connecticut), which was held from 14th to 16th December 1949. There seven Free Churches discussed the plan of a federative organic union. These were the General Council of the Congregational Christian Churches, the International Convention of the Disciples of Christ, the Evangelical and Reformed Church, the Presbyterian Church, the Methodist Episcopal Church, the African Methodist Episcopal Zion Church (negroes) and the Northern Province of the Moravian Brethren. This Union was designated as the United Free Liberal Church with synodal structure. According to the manifesto of the Conference of Greenwich the time had come for the Churches of America to formulate a plan for an organic unity. This plan was published in *Christian Century* of 11th January 1950 by its Editor, C. C. Morrison. It proposed to amalgamate those denominations which subscribed to the fundamental principle of voluntary association without any institutional or personal authority. This association would also comprise the Baptists who had not been represented at Greenwich, and who until then had found it difficult to join in. Beside the principle of independence, these in the widest sense 'congregationalist' groups were to accept also that of responsibility or 'connectionalism', on the basis of the existing status of their congregational independence. The draft asserts naively that it does

[1] On these terms cf. O. Tomkins in *The Church in the Purpose of God*, 148f.

not embody any dogmatic system, nevertheless it provides for a
'basis of unity', even though this is given the last place. This unity
is founded on the 'mutual recognition of ministry and sacraments'.

The *Herder-Korrespondenz*, discussing this Morrison plan,[1] rightly
observes that it deserves more attention 'since it best reflects the
main characteristic of American Oecumenicity and reveals the real
difficulty of a lasting unity of the Oecumenical Council'. It has
already been noted that the Congregationalist denominations were
urging an organic union. At the Conference at Cincinnati on 23rd
January 1951 the Methodist Bishop Lee Holt proposed the draft
constitution for discussion. The line of Greenwich was to be
continued. A divine imperative, so it said, demanded unity against
the demonic powers, and this was to be sought under the guidance
of the Holy Spirit, while respecting freedom of conscience. According to Morrison, Richard and Holt, the results of the Oecumenical
Movement had so far been disappointing. They considered that the
next step would have to be to achieve organic unity. It was assumed
that this unity could be established on the basis of a strongly de-
dogmatized Trinitarian formula, which evidently contradicted the
so-called 'Christological' basis of the Oecumenical Council ('Jesus
Christ as God and Saviour'). It involved an elastic scheme within
which the denominations that belonged to the union could gradually
grow together. Its structural simplicity and doctrinal indifference
distinguish it from the Church of South India scheme, which included also the Church of England, whose episcopal succession
and orders provided the foundation.

For American theology is less interested in doctrinal questions
than in the practical realization of the Kingdom of God in this world.
In his essay 'American Theology and Church',[2] Professor H. H.
Wolf has attempted to characterize the theological background of
the American Churches by the three catchwords of Puritanism,
Liberalism and Fundamentalism. For the Puritan Pilgrim Fathers
who landed in America in 1620, faith meant the practical shaping of
their life, while 'the eschatological content of the Kingdom of God
was progressively lost and the Kingdom of God was objectified'. By
liberalism Wolf means that 'which is common to the different
currents of American theology: the lack of connexion with revelation seen as an event in the historical act of the Incarnation of

[1] Vols. IV and V, 1949 and 1949/50.
[2] In the Oecumenical Study Department series *Theological Currents from 1900 to
1950*.

Jesus Christ'. In contrast with this, fundamentalism clings to the reality of the revelation, but 'by a massive doctrine of verbal inspiration'. The fact is that leading theologians like Richard and Reinhold Niebuhr, Konrad Bergendorff, Paul Tillich, to mention only some representatives of the 'new orthodoxy', severely criticize the liberal current. Yet the American Free Churches of Anglo-Saxon character are more or less hypnotized by the 'Social Gospel' theology. Their idea of the unity of the Church can scarcely be shared by Continental churches and theologians unless these, too, are caught in the current of liberalism.

2. EVANGELICAL CHURCH IN GERMANY. The continental struggle for the union of Churches has probably become most evident in the constitutional controversies of the *Evangelische Kirche in Deutschland*, and especially in the attitude of German Lutheranism to it. The National Socialist persecution had brought the denominations together in their common opposition to the Nazi errors reflected in the attempt of a nationally based union of 'German Christians'. The Confessional Synod of Barmen in 1934, which was the work of Asmussen and K. Barth, united Lutherans with Reformed and United Evangelicals in a 'confession that was a protest of the churches against the machinations of Reich-Bishop Müller'.[1] What was the theological basis of this confession? It subjected the denominations to the sole dominion of Jesus Christ over His Church. This confession of the rights of Christ was a protest against any ordering of the Church from below that was not based on Scripture and the Creed.

Thus a peculiarly Protestant emphasis was placed on 'pure doctrine'. But what did this mean in the doctrinal disputes of the denominations? Was a Church to be proved authentic by better theological arguments and a better theology? In the third thesis of the Barmen document the Church is called 'the congregation of brethren'. This was an equivocal conception, for the presence of Christ in this congregation was not described with any precision and left room, for example, for both Lutheran and Reformed views on the Eucharistic presence, a division evidenced by the fact that no communion services were celebrated in common. In his discussion of the Barmen document, Barth stated that at that time the Church was not asked to make its confession with reference to the Eucharist but to the First Commandment. Here, too, we now see more clearly that this view was a fearful error, not only with regard to the historical

[1] Text in *HK* I (1946), 136 f.

7

situation of the Church but also doctrinally, since it was based on the assumption that we could have communion with Christ without receiving it in the way He Himself gives it to us in His sacrament. Christians can understand and keep the First Commandment, too, only through the Incarnation: the Lord is given us bodily in the Eucharist, and it is of vital concern to the Church how this gift is made and how it is received. Neither at Barmen nor later did a common communion service take place; the Lutherans saw to it that no union was to be created at Barmen at all for whence could this synod have taken its canonical credentials? The Barmen theological declaration was submitted to the Churches for 'working out responsible explanations from the point of view of their confessions'. Thus J. P. Michael rightly asks whether 'the consensus of the truth of the bodily present Lord is not something different from a consensus achieved for an end of ecclesiastical policy or fraternal agreement, at the cost of the fullness of the truth and the full unanimous communion with the Lord? Apart from the fear of Prussian dictatorial feats, the Lutheran Veto is also caused by the question of truth.'

There is no doubt that Barmen was an important stage on the way to oecumenical unity. But the Oecumene as such should regard it as a warning. W. Zimmermann says truly: 'Theoretically it would for example, have been quite possible for certain Evangelical Free Churches such as the Methodists to join the Barmen declaration. It would never have meant that the common confession involved the assembled churches in any consequences for their beliefs or their organization. It remains a quite different matter whether in times of distress churches express themselves in common on questions of faith and life and thus speak from an ultimate union that defies earthly organization . . . or whether externally constituted churches strive for external union and amalgamation on the basis of a common doctrine.'[1]

At the Synod of Eisenach, 27th July 1948, the Evangelical Church of Germany tried for the third time to unite after the earlier attempts of the *Deutscher Evangelischer Kirchenbund* in 1922 and the *Deutsche Evangelische Kirche* in 1933. The Church assembly of the *EKD* had asked the Council of the *EKD* at the conference at Treysa of 5th and 6th June 1948 to draft a constitution. This was submitted to the individual churches of the *Länder* and provinces in the spring of

[1] 'Die Einigung des deutschen Luthertums. Erwägungen zur lutherischen General-synode in Eisenach' In *Die Zeichen der Zeit*, II, 249.

1948. In this draft the *EKD* affirms that it is based on the creeds of the Church (art. 1, 2) and confirms the 'decisions made by the confessional synod of Barmen'. It considers that 'the theological declaration of 31st May 1934 repudiates the false doctrine which destroys the Church, according to the demands of Scripture and Creed which bind the Church also in the future' (1, 4).[1] Articles 5, 3 and 4 mentioned the sharing of pulpits and of the Lord's Supper: 'Evangelical Christians may not be excluded from Holy Communion in a congregation because they belong to another confession recognized in the Evangelical Church in Germany.' This first draft of the *Grundordnung* was attacked by the Lutherans.[2] The second draft, proposed at Kassel on 9th March, brought out more clearly the federal character of the *EKD* and took account of the Lutheran warning against understanding Barmen as a confession of union. The regulations on the sharing of pulpits and the Lord's Supper were also examined. This led to the third draft, in which the theological declaration of Barmen was eliminated and only a limited sacramental communion admitted.[3] This *Grundordnung* of the *EKD* was decided on at Eisenach.[4] But did this mean any progress on the way to Church unity, if we have in view not only questions of Church policy but also of theology? The constitution of Eisenach is clearly provisional, and this was openly admitted. Bishop Wurm called it a half-way house. The subsequent discussions were concerned especially with the question whether a union abolished a denomination, and the importance to be assigned to the confessions in forming a church. The Lutherans refused time and again to consent to a 'levelling' of the denominations. Since the truth of the Gospel had entered history the confessions must be taken seriously.[5] They pointed repeatedly to the *Altpreussische Union*, a child of Schleiermacher's theology, in which doctrinal differences were regarded as non-essential. 'Actually the *Altpreussische Union* has no creed but consists of power groups.'[6] It does not stand by the principle of confession, hence it grants eucharistic communion without doctrinal unity. This contradicts Chapter 7 of the Augsburg

[1] Text in *HK* II (1947/8), 263 f.

[2] Cf. (1948) e.g. the declaration of the Konvent Lutherischer Pastoren im Rheinland, *ELKZ* II (1948), 121 f. 'A union of Churches cannot legislate on sharing of pulpits and the Lord's Supper for the churches belonging to it; where this is done, there the desire to be more than a union of churches can clearly be recognized'.

[3] Cf. *HK* II (1947/8), 397 f.

[4] Cf. *HK* III (1948/9), 402.

[5] Cf. Kimme, 'Grundfragen einer Theologie der Ökumene', *ELKZ* V (1951), 297.

[6] Kimme, 'Union und Konfession', *ELKZ* IV (1950), 113 ff.

Confession. According to the Lutherans this credal foundation raises insuperable obstacles, separating their own from the church of the Reformed: 'Lutheran and Reformed Churches can never be in communion with each other,'[1] because the doctrine of 'the Gospel alone' and, on the other side, that of 'Gospel and Law' are incompatible.[2] 'In Lutheran theology we cannot add a religious to a profane sphere.'[3] 'According to Luther's view, we must consider existence under two aspects, one temporal, the other religious.'[4] The President of the Synod of the *EKD*, W. Heinemann, attempted to compose the differences. He denies that the controversies between Lutherans and Reformed preclude a union of their Churches[5] and assumes that a 'minimum creed' should be a sufficient basis of unity, if this minimum creed were also a fundamental creed. On these basic principles Lutherans and Reformed are in agreement; even if, (according to Heinemann) among the Lutherans themselves doctrinal unity is lacking. 'The unity of the Church does not rest on—total—unity of doctrine.' The Lutherans objected violently. 'It would, indeed, be very nice if President Heinemann were right in his assertion. . . . But we must state in all sincerity that Lutheran and Reformed theologies differ in every point, even to the very heart of Christology . . . and at last give up the phantom of a super-union Church.'[6] 'We have all one and the same Gospel, but we have not all understood it in one and the same way.'[7] 'The *wholeness* of the belief of the Lutheran confession is different from the whole of the Reformed. Church communion depends decisively on the consensus of doctrine with regard to the nature of the Church.[8]' This is the Lutheran attitude to the *EKD* and beyond it to the whole Oecu-

[1] Kimme, 'Grundfragen . . . , *ELKZ* V (1951), 295.

[2] It is true, on the Lutheran side, too, there are movements to regard Gospel and Law no longer in the old tradition as mutually exclusive contraries, as is shown by H. Asmussen's and R. Prenter's addresses to the Conference of the Lutheran Weltbund at Hanover in 1952. Cf. also 'Umrisse lutherischer Theologie' by M. Schmidt, *ELKZ* VI (1950), 410 f.

[3] R. Bring, 'Lutherische Theologie angesichts der Ökumenischen Arbeit'. In *Luthertum*, Heft 1, 36.

[4] ibid., 29.

[5] 'Müssen wir heute lutherisch oder reformiert sein?', *ELKZ* IV (1950), 337 ff.

[6] F. Hübner, 'We cannot do otherwise, we must be Lutheran Church, only thus can we serve the true unity of the Church', *ELKZ* IV (1950), 339.

[7] Nygren, 'Eine theologische Grundlage des Ökumenischen Denkens nach lutherischer Auffassung', *ELKZ* II (1948), 199 f.

[8] Kimme, 'Union und Konfession—Schlusswort'. *ELKZ* IV (1950), 340. Cf. also the conference of the Theologische Arbeitsgemeinschaft Wittenberg January 30, 1950. 'Only the doctrinal unity of the denominations establishes Church unity', *ELKZ* IV (1950), 123.

menical Movement. The Lutherans oppose a 'double truth in the Church', which might well end in the view that Truth transcends history. In this way the historic confessions would become relative and be understood as a mere 'event' within the whole Truth, because it would only 'point' to the total Truth that is above the individual communions. Hence it is rightly said: 'The truth and unity of the Church have entered history. In the life and doctrines of the Church, too, there is no "truth in itself", transcending separate truths, but truth is indissolubly related to existence. This . . . means obedience to the law that the revealed truth and unity are historical.'[1]

These are also the difficulties of the Lutherans with regard to the Oecumenical Movement. They feared especially at Amsterdam that the World Council would not pay attention to this confessional principle. This fear led to the union of the Lutheran Churches in Germany in the *VELKD* (*Vereinigte Evangelisch-Lutherische Kirche Deutschlands*) which took place on 31st December 1948. 'If the confession is necessary, the association in the *VELKD* is also necessary.'[2] Since there is no consensus of doctrine in the *EKD*, 'there is *de iure*, no Church, but only a union of churches',[3] but the question whether it is possible to speak of the *VELKD* as of 'the Church that has just come into being', as was done by Bishop Meiser,[4] must be examined also from other points of view. Nevertheless, the existence of the *EKD* is a heavy burden for Lutheranism, as is proved by the protest against the Lutheran *Weltbund* that has been registered by the Lutheran Free Churches in Germany, the Missourians in the United States and the Evangelical-Lutheran Church in Australia.[5]

This account, however, should not suggest the conclusion that Lutheranism is opposed to the Oecumenical Movement. When the Movement began Lutherans had serious doubts, because they saw the influence of liberal theology in it, especially in Life and Work, and because the desire for compromise was all too obvious. But later it became increasingly clear that 'the content of the Oecumene can also be interpreted differently', namely as 'a conversation in which the deeper understanding and more profound interpretation of the common Gospel on the part of one church can be received as

[1] *ELKZ* V (1951), 294.
[2] G. Schlüter, 'Union und Konfession, einst und jetzt', *ELKZ* II (1948), 21.
[3] *ELKZ* IV (1950), 114.
[4] *ELKZ* III (1949), 49.
[5] Cf. *HK* VI (1952), 574.

a gratefully acknowledged gift on the part of the others.'[1] But the Lutherans regard themselves as the 'Gospel conscience of the churches and denominations',[2] as 'the centre of the confessions' to which 'is entrusted the truth of the Gospel'. Nevertheless, it must here be asked whether this emphasis on historical truth on the part of the Lutherans is not merely a pretext for saving their own confession. For this principle of historicity is no longer observed if Lutheran teaching subjects the unity of the Church to a one-sided principle of faith. By stressing historical truth Lutheranism certainly warns those who succumb to the illusion that the unity of the Church can be built up from below. But does it not also mean hiding behind the *faith in unity* against which Asmussen had warned? In fact, there are many questionable points in the Lutheran theologians' idea of their own church. They affirm that Lutheranism possesses the truth of the Gospel, but that this Gospel can be understood only through the creed of the Reformation, i.e. by the principle of justification; yet they show that this creed itself is not at all so Scriptural as is always alleged and that Scripture itself is 'many-sided', that its concepts have different meanings according to the different Biblical books and that 'this realization destroys the illusion that we can derive from Scripture a set of normative ideas and thus arrive at a decisive concept and form of Scripture'.[3] Despite these contradictions, however, the struggle for the Evangelical Church of Germany will help us to understand the oecumenical problem as such, which is very intricate, differing according to the standpoint of the various churches participating in the Movement.

3. SOUTH INDIA. In the third place we would mention yet another practical effort to achieve the unity of the Church, which concerns the Anglican communion. Anglicanism is no unified Church system; its representatives regard it as a *via media* between 'Catholic' and 'Evangelical' types. Two factors are by and large responsible for the structure of the Church of England: 'a sense of Incarnation, and a scholarly feeling for historical tradition'. The Church of England's contribution to the unity of the Churches was formulated by the theologians of the Oxford Movement in their Branch Theory. According to them, none of the existing churches could be regarded as *the* Church, hence they aimed at a synthesis of

[1] R. Bring, 'Lutherische Theologie . . .', loc. cit., 19.
[2] Kimme, 'Grundfragen . . .', loc. cit., 297.
[3] ibid., 14.

the churches which, in their view, were indeed separated in practice but one in origin as well as in the reality of the Apostolic Succession, that is to say in the divinely appointed ministry. 'Diversity in unity' was the watchword Anglicanism bestowed on the young Oecumenical Movement. In the *Lambeth Quadrilateral* of 1920 the Church of England formulated an Oecumenical minimum programme according to which ecclesiastical unity was to depend on four points:

'1. The Holy Scriptures of the Old and New Testaments as the revealed Word of God.

'2. The Nicene Creed as the sufficient statement of the Christian faith.

'3. The two Sacraments—Baptism and the Supper of the Lord—ministered with unfailing use of Christ's words of institution and the elements ordained by Him.

'4. The Historic Episcopate, locally adapted in the methods of its administration to the varying needs of the nations and peoples called of God into the unity of His Church.'

These principles were put to a practical test by the United Church of South India. In 1947, after a long preparation, the Church of England in that region was united with several Free Churches. The various communions had been brought together by the missionary need to proclaim the Gospel with one voice. The union does not rest on a 'federal basis' but is an 'organic union'.[1] Representatives of this new Union Church consider that it is premature to speak of a doctrine of the Church of South India, especially since this Church 'has the idea of development written into its very constitution'.[2] There would be time enough to draw up a confession in the sense of the documents of the Reformation when heresies actually invade the church. The basis of the churches of South India was not 'a confession. Its basis is the faith that the word "Church" *ought* to mean the whole company of Christ's people in any place gathered in one visible fellowship.'[3] It is further based on a regional foundation, i.e. only Christians who live in the region of this Church can become its members. 'The Church of South India is ... formed by a combination of different elements, each bringing its contribution to the whole, and not by the absorption of any one by any other. It is, therefore, also a comprehensive Church; and its members, firmly holding the fundamentals of the faith and order of the Church

---

[1] Cf. P. D. Davanandan, *The Ecumenical Movement and the Younger Churches* . . . , 331.
[2] A. M. Hollis, 'The Church of South India', Flew, *The Nature of the Church*, 221.
[3] ibid., 221 f.

universal, are allowed wide freedom of opinion in all other matters.'[1] Since the Church of South India consists also of churches which believe that they possess the historical succession of the consecration of bishops and of ordination, the Constitution provides 'that the episcopal succession is preserved and carried forward, but that all the existing ministers whether episcopally ordained or not are accepted as equally ministers of the Church, that for a period of thirty years, ministers not episcopally ordained may be received into its ministry.'[2] The Constitution holds that it is essential for full unity 'that all members of the Church should be willing and able to receive communion equally in all of its Churches. . . . But it is convinced that this can only take place on the basis of freedom of opinion on debatable matters and respect for even large differences of opinion and practice.'[3] No authority or majority of the Church should ever be allowed to make light of anyone's conscience. We see here the attempt to establish the unity of the Church on the principles of development, comprehensiveness and tolerance. The Lambeth Conference of 1948 had to discuss these presuppositions, especially the questions of ministry and communion. 'The most critical issue was that of the status of the Bishops, Presbyters and Deacons consecrated or ordained in the Church of South India or after the inauguration of that Church. On that issue there was a frankly acknowledged division. A majority was prepared to accept them as truly Bishops, Presbyters and Deacons of the Church of Christ. A substantial minority was not ready as yet to pass any definite judgement.'[4]

Another critical issue was the question of communion. Today Anglicans have full sacramental communion with the Old Catholics and sacramental relations with the Church of Sweden. The conditions of this are expressed in the following clause: 'Sacramental communion demands from neither side the acceptance of all doctrinal views, sacramental piety and liturgical practices of the other side. It means that neither side doubts that the other preserves the main elements of the Christian faith.'[5] It is understandable that the Anglo-Catholic section of the Church of England could not follow this lead, since it also wants to keep open the door to Rome; at Lambeth this section was called 'a substantial minority'. In the question of the validity of

[1] Const. II, 2, loc. cit., 225.
[2] Flew, loc. cit., 225 f.
[3] ibid.
[4] Angus Dun, *First Thoughts on Amsterdam and Lambeth* 1948 . . . , 444.
[5] In S. Neill, 'Die Anglikanischen Kirchen'. Vortrag in der Theologenschaft der Universität Basel. *Theol. Zeitschrift*, VIII, No. 3, 202.

the ministry Anglo-Catholics stressed especially that this did not depend on a guarantee concerning the 'form and manner' of ordination but: 'It remains true that form and manner alone are not sufficient to guarantee the character of ministry. That can be substantiated only by the faith and character of the Church itself.'[1] These are exactly the same reasons for which Rome declared Anglican Orders to be invalid.[2] The Lambeth Conference shelved the question of the Union of South India. While counselling moderation it once more explained its view on how Church unity was to be achieved: 'Here we desire to set before our people a view of what, if it be the will of God, may come to pass. As Anglicans we believe that God has entrusted to us in our Communion not only the Catholic faith, but a special service to render to the whole Church. Reunion of any part of our Communion with other denominations in its own area must make the resulting Church no longer simply Anglican, but something more comprehensive. There would be in every country . . . a united Church, Catholic and Evangelical, but no longer in the limiting sense of the word Anglican. The Anglican Communion would be merged in a much larger Communion of National and Regional Churches, in full communion with one another. . . . It is well to keep this vision before us; but we are still far from its attainment, and until this larger Communion begins to take firmer shape, it would be only a weakening of the present strength and service of the Anglican Communion if parts of it were severed from it prematurely. . . . In our Resolutions, we recommend that, in further schemes for reunion, care should be taken to see that they do not, unless for a brief time, put any member of our family of Churches out of communion with it and that they are not put into force unless after consultation with the rest of our family.'[3]

The Church of England has been called the 'Oecumene in miniature', because it is the meeting-place of two oecumenical currents and thus serves to illustrate the present difficulties in the Oecumene. The Church of England contains two main sections, Anglo-Catholics and Evangelicals, while the Nonconformists (Presbyterians, Methodists, Congregationalists and Baptists) are outside. At the suggestion of Archbishop Fisher they all have recently explained their position

[1] Rawlinson, Lambeth 1948, in *ER* II (1949).

[2] Cf. Apostolicae curae (September 18, 1896), in *Acta Leonis XIII*, XIV, 258 ff. Letter to Cardinal Richard. November 1896 (ibid., 305).

[3] *The Lambeth Conference 1948*, p. 22 f.

in three separate studies.[1] They all agree that the chief concern today is catholicity, which ought no longer to be claimed only by Rome. The 'Protestants' support the thesis that the churches continue to develop in their growing understanding of the Gospel towards the fullness of Christ, which will be perfected only in the Parousia. We live in the expectation of this fullness which needs the diverse ways in which all nations and races experience the faith. A very important factor in these essays is the controversy concerning the formal background, especially the discussion of the doctrine of grace. Here the Anglo-Catholics affirm that the Lutheran conception of grace identifies (in Neoplatonist fashion) the spiritual with the non-material, thus sacrificing the bodily factor of the Redemption. The Evangelicals admit this: the formula *sola fide* 'served to justify the exclusive prerogative of all that is interior and spiritual in the Gospel to the detriment of all that gives form and body to it. The organic constitution of the Church, the validity of its services, sacraments, liturgy, spiritual and ecclesiastical discipline, even the dogma itself was declared to be secondary or even invalid.'[2] But it is doubtful whether they will draw the consequences from this admission. Congregationalism with its principles of 'covenant fellowship' and 'spiritual authority'[3] has a great influence on the Church of England, so that the Anglican, E. Aubrey, has already spoken of the 'turning from W. Temple to 't Hooft'.[4] 'Once this turning has been accomplished it will no longer be possible to speak of a central position of the Anglican Church. . . . For if a theologian directs his attention solely to the Last Things, the historical plane has for him only the importance of an image of the divine sphere. The Incarnation is an idea, no longer a reality established somewhere, e.g. in the Sacrament' (Winterhager).[5] The Anglo-Catholics will be hard put to it to defend this sacramental realism. It remains to be seen whether this will bring them nearer to Rome.

These examples will show the magnitude of the Oecumenical problem and the futility of subscribing to an abstract idea of 'unity'.

---

[1] *Catholicity. A Study in the Conflict of Christian Tradition in the West* (1947); *The Fullness of Christ, The Church's Growth into Catholicity* (1950); *The Catholicity of Protestantism* (1950).
[2] Cf. *HK* VI (1951), 315.
[3] Cf. Flew, *The Nature . . .* , 185.
[4] Cf. *HK* VI (1952), 449.
[5] Cf. ibid.

3. ROME AND THE OECUMENICAL MOVEMENT

So far we have been trying to describe the nature of the Oecumenical Movement and of the Oecumene by tracing their historical development. Now we must describe the relation of the Oecumenical Movement to the Roman Catholic Church, and conversely Rome's attitude to the Oecumene.

When preparing the World Conferences of Stockholm and Lausanne the oecumenical 'pioneers' were hoping that Rome would participate in them. The steps taken for this purpose by the representatives of the Movement as well as Rome's answer have been fully described in Pribilla's book *Um kirchliche Einheit. Stockholm, Lausanne, Rom*.[1] Now the Life and Work Movement tended to regard dogma as relative and was itself strongly influenced by liberal Protestant thought, while the Lausanne Conference experimented vaguely with the branch theory. So it was clear that Rome's attitude would be negative. It was strongly expressed in Pius XI's encyclical *Mortalium animos* of 6th January 1928.[2] The Pope places the first oecumenical experiments within the whole contemporary situation, regarding the efforts to achieve religious unity as an imitation of the political methods by which the nations hope to reach political unity. These efforts are based on the false view that all religions are equally good and praiseworthy. The authority of John xvii, 21 is adduced in support of these attempts to reach unity among all Christians, demanding the unity in love mentioned in John xiii, 35. Pius XI calls those who attempt this *Panchristiani* 'Pan-Christians' and warns against them. For they refer to these words of Christ as if they expressed a desire or a prayer that was yet waiting for its fulfilment. According to this view the Church has never yet been 'one', except perhaps between the time of the apostles and the first oecumenical councils, for it consisted of various parts and particular churches which all had equal rights. Hence the necessity of completely disregarding all differences of opinion and controversial points. The other doctrines would have to be fashioned into a common rule of faith, which would then form the foundation of fraternal unity. This being the

[1] Pp. 123 f.; 202–40; cf. especially the exchange of letters between Robert Gardiner and Cardinal Gasparri.

[2] *AAS* XX (1928), 5–15. English translation, C.T.S., Do. III.

situation, it was evident that the Apostolic See could not take part in these oecumenical conferences, in any way whatever, and that no individual Catholic could be allowed to support these efforts. However sublime the motive of the charity of Christ, it was a duty to warn against contact with those who did not profess the teaching of Christ in its unsullied purity (2 John, 11).

Charity rests on the foundation of pure, untarnished faith. To deny the unity of the sacrament and of the rule of faith paves the way to indifferentism and modernism. The only way to the unity of the Church is the return of all separated Christians to the *one*, true, visible Church of Christ. The Pope then goes on to expound the unchangeable principles of the unity of the Church which necessarily follow from its very nature. The encyclical ends with a call to all separated Christians to return to their father's house: 'Thus may they all return to their common father who has long ago forgotten the wrong they have done to the Apostolic See and who will receive them with a loving heart. . . . O that we might be able . . . once more to embrace all our sons in fatherly love: O that God our Saviour, "who will have all men to be saved and to come to the knowledge of the truth" (1 Tim. ii, 4) would hear us, as we so earnestly implore Him, and bring back all that have gone astray to the unity of the Church. . . . You see how much we have this question at heart.'

Reading this encyclical today, after so many years of oecumenical effort, we should clearly distinguish its first part from its second. We have heard from oecumenical theologians criticisms of these oecumenical beginnings which come near to the judgement of the Pope. The first beginnings of the Movement were too optimistic and idealistic. 'There was too great an expectation of sensational results, and the situation as it was in reality was not sufficiently appreciated; thus inevitable disillusion followed.'[1] Van de Pol observes that this first part of the encyclical indeed described the Utopian and illusory expectations of the Oecumenical Movement in its first beginning, 'yet expresses no word of appreciation of this attempt which indeed deserved it.' But, he rightly continues, 'at present the outline it presented is out of date, since for some time now the Ecumenical Movement no longer resembles the portrait of its youth. During the quarter of a century of its existence it has already made a number of most important discoveries. It is to be hoped, however, that further results will be linked up with what has been reached already,

[1] Van de Pol, *The Christian Dilemma*, 225.

and that every new generation will not have to start afresh with the same difficulties, as if nothing had yet been accomplished.' Hence we may say that the encyclical's remarks on the Oecumenical Movement have a relative and transitory character, whereas its teaching on the nature of the Church is always binding and valid. Only with such a reservation can we agree with the view of Skydsgaard who writes: 'The exclusive study of the *Mortalium animos* would not be sufficient to obtain a really clear conclusion, as it is directed against the ecumenical movement in its first inadequate and groping attempts, an inadequacy which is now also felt by many leading theologians in the other churches. That encyclical is definitely in opposition to the ecumenical movement which found its expression at Stockholm in 1925 and may not be—and actually is not, even in the Roman Church—taken as covering everything which the Roman Catholic Church has to say in this matter.'[1]

In the discussions at Lausanne little was said about the Roman Catholic Church. Only Bishop Manning explained the attitude of the Conference towards it during the discussion on the Confession of Faith in the full session of 6th August 1927. He was applauded on all sides when he said:

'First, we all deeply regret that the Roman Catholic Church did not feel able to accept the invitation which was extended to her to send representatives to the World Conference.

'Secondly, although the Roman Catholic Church has not felt she could send representatives, we want her to know that our feeling towards her is one of love and fellowship, and that it is our desire to take fully into account her place and her great witness in this world for Christ.

'Thirdly, while the Christian Communions, Catholic and Protestant, which are represented here can, and we pray that they may, make true progress towards reunion, we recognize that Christian unity cannot be attained until its includes our brethren of the Roman Catholic Church. What we who are gathered here seek is not a unity of Protestants alone, or of Catholics alone. This might only accentuate differences, and perpetuate divisions. We seek a unity which shall include all Christian Communions throughout the world, both Catholic and Protestant, which confess Our Lord Jesus Christ as Saviour, Lord and God.

'Fourthly, may I not venture to say that there goes out from this

---

[1] 'The Roman Catholic Church and the Ecumenical Movement' in *The Universal Church in God's Design*, 158.

gathering the hope that our Roman Catholic brethren, clergy and people, will send up their prayers along with ours that in this Conference we may be guided by Him who prayed that we all may be one, and that by His Spirit we may all be led into that peace and unity which are agreeable to His will.'[1]

The representatives of the Oecumenical Movement were repeatedly told by Rome that the Holy Father was praying for them, and the Pope told the deputation which visited the Vatican in 1929 that he did not in the least disapprove of the Conference for those not in communion with the See of Peter. Pribilla rightly remarks that the members of the Lausanne Conference were completely ignorant of the Catholic doctrine of the nature of the Church. The Catholic teaching on the visible and the invisible Church, on the necessity of the Church for salvation and on extraordinary means of salvation, on the objective truth of revelation and on invincible ignorance, on the Church militant and the Church triumphant were 'to the Protestants altogether a *terra incognita*'.[2]

It was said over and over again at the Oecumenical Conferences that the absence of Rome was grievously felt. 'It has always been a source of grief to us that we have not the fellowship and the assistance of our Roman Catholic brethren in our enterprise and labours. We rejoice to know that we have your sympathy, and we join with you in prayer that the union of all Christians in one visible Church may by God's gracious mercy be accomplished to His glory and the salvation of men.'[3] Thus wrote the President of the Edinburgh Conference—in the name of the Conference—to the Prior of Amay-sur-Meuse.

During the preparations for the first Conference of the World Council of Churches at Amsterdam in 1948, it was hoped that Rome would at least send unofficial observers, and the necessary steps were taken for this purpose.[4] But on 5th June 1948 the Holy Office issued a *Monitum*[5] which called to mind the prohibition of can. 1325, § 3 in the *CIC*, according to which laymen as well as clerics are forbidden to take part in official religious conversations with non-Catholics without permission from the Holy See. This prohibition applied particularly to so-called 'Oecumenical' gatherings. The

---

[1] H. N. Bate, *Faith and Order*, 204 f.

[2] Pribilla, 171.

[3] Hodgson, loc. cit., 40.

[4] Cf. Visser't Hooft in *ER* I (1948/9), 197–201.

[5] *AAS* XL (1948), 257.

Monitum warned especially against a *communicatio in sacris* (Cf. *CIC*, can. 1278, 731, § 2).

This decree of the Holy Office caused a great stir throughout the world. In oecumenical circles it was thought that this meant the end of all Oecumenical Movements. The *Monitum* called forth indignant comments for exceeding its aim and intention, especially in evangelical circles. But this document was not meant to condemn the oecumenical work as such. Only a certain 'wild growth which had shown itself on the periphery of the Una Sancta movement and had recently penetrated to its very centre' was to be cut out.[1] Rome wanted to retain control of the Oecumenical Movement as far as it concerned the Catholic Church; the work of the Una Sancta was to be given an 'hierarchical superstructure'. This produced violent attacks from K. Barth at Amsterdam, who wrote to P. Daniélou: 'None of the churches assembled at Amsterdam has confronted the others with the claim to be the one infallible Church, holding a monopoly of the means of grace, hence to have answered by its very existence the question we all have at heart. This fundamental rule of our gathering and work would only have been disturbed if representatives of your Church had been present. They could not have taken their place by our side, but only (visibly or invisibly) on some throne high above our heads. But there is no room for the rich among the poor, for the sated among the hungry, or for those comfortably at the goal among the wanderers. To demand both is too much for us, I mean to take seriously your claim to superiority and yet to desire your company. . . . At Amsterdam we asked for the Kingdom and the work of God. But you would have given us to understand that we had to be converted to the human kingdom and the human work of your Church. . . . Your absence has saved us from a scandal and a temptation.'[2] Barth thinks that the absence of Rome and Moscow preserved the Oecumene from partners 'with whom we could here not even form an imperfect congregation, because, though for different reasons, they will not *move away from the Church and towards Christ*; and without this movement Christians of different origin and kind simply cannot talk to one another, listen to each other, let alone come together. And this places us perhaps in a favourable situation, that Rome and Moscow seem to be agreed

---

[1] Cf. the comments of Vatican Radio of June 6, 1948.

[2] K. Barth, Daniélou, R. Niebuhr, 'Amsterdamer Fragen und Antworten'. *Theologische Existenz heute*, No. 15; 19 f.

on this, that they will not have anything to do with us.'[1] The intention of these bitter words is obvious.

The Pastoral Letter of the Dutch Episcopate on the occasion of the Conference of the World Council at Amsterdam reflected the attitude of the Mother Church to the Oecumene in a special way. The bishops emphasized that they had followed the discussions of the Conference with keen attention, because it had originated in 'the great and earnest desire for the unity willed by Christ'. 'And how could we carelessly disregard a serious desire for unity, seeing that we are called by the Holy Spirit, under the guidance of Peter's successor, to preserve and spread the Church in her unity? Nor can we be indifferent to the question whether this Congress takes a step forward or a step back: forward, if the Conference leans to a stronger desire for the Mother Church and for the unity that exists in her; back, if many are content with a unity that is still far removed from that unity brought by Christ Himself.' On this road, however, there were many prejudices that had to be overcome. The estrangement had become such that the voice and language of Holy Church could no longer be heard and understood by the separated brethren. A return could take place only from complete conviction, and this would not be possible unless God gave His grace, enlightening men's understanding and moving their will. Therefore the bishops called upon all the faithful to unite with them in fervent prayer: 'Pray during these days for all those who take part in this Conference and for the many other non-Catholic Christians who ardently desire unity, who truly follow Christ and live in His love and who, though separated from the flock of Christ, yet look towards the Church, even though often unconsciously, as the only port of salvation. Pray especially for those men who act as leaders of the non-Catholic Christians and thus carry a heavy responsibility, because the simple faithful depend on their attitude and cannot gain the right understanding by their own efforts.' Above all, the faithful should not forget that their example was as necessary as their prayer. In former times the un-Christian life of many Catholics had contributed to defection from the Church, nor had all Catholics been guided by charity when defending the unity of the Church, hence they had not been without guilt in the estrangement between Catholic and non-Catholic Christians. Such an attitude was certainly not in the spirit of Mother Church. 'Hence we Catholics bear a heavy responsibility in these times. Since many who acknowledge Christ have shown a

[1] ibid., 7.

very real desire for unity it is very important that our life should be wholly permeated by the spirit of Christ and that we should desire nothing but Jesus Christ and the spread of His kingdom in all our actions and in every department of our lives.' Surely this pastoral letter is a great testimony of the oecumenical spirit and as such deserves our closest attention.

It was felt everywhere that the *Monitum* could not be the last word on the question of the relations between Rome and the separated brethren. Thus, on 20th December 1949, was issued an *Instructio* of the Holy Office to the local ordinaries entitled *De motione oecumenica*.[1] This pronouncement made two main points. First, in oecumenical meetings between Catholics and non-Catholics the former must not give the impression that the truths of revelation were still to be discovered by their common efforts in a higher synthesis of Catholic and evangelical doctrine. Second, it stresses that the division of Christendom is to be considered a grave disorder which Christians should strive to remove by their faith in Jesus Christ. 'Even though the Catholic Church takes no part in "oecumenical" conferences and similar events, it nevertheless emerges from several Papal pronouncements that she has never ceased, nor will she cease in the future, to follow with a lively interest and further with her incessant prayer all efforts that seek to attain this end which is so near to the heart of Christ, namely that all who believe in Him "may be made perfect in one" ' (John xvii, 23).[2]

On the Oecumenical Movement the *Instructio* observes: 'Now in many countries various external events but also a change in the minds of men through the prayers of the faithful under the influence of the grace of the Holy Spirit have brought it about that there has grown day by day the desire in the souls of those separated from the Church to restore the unity of all who believe in Christ the Lord.'[3] Thus, the highest ecclesiastical authority states that the Holy Spirit is working in the Oecumene. Hence this development 'is for the

---

[1] *AAS* XLII (1950), 142–7.

[2] 'Ecclesia catholica, et si congressibus ceterisque conventibus "oecumenicis" non intervenit, numquam tamen destitit, ut ex pluribus documentis Pontificis colligitur, neque umquam in posterum desistet intensissimis studiis prosequi assiduisque ad Deum precibus fovere omnes conatus ad illud obtinendum, quod tantopere Christo Domino cordi est, videlicet ut omnes, qui credunt in Ipsum, "sint consummati in unum" (John, 23)'. loc. cit., 142.

[3] 'Jam vero in pluribus orbis partibus, quum ex variis externis eventibus et animorum mutationibus fidelium orationibus, afflante quidem Spiritus Sancti gratia, in multorum animis ab Ecclesia catholica dissidentium desiderium in dies excrevit ut ad unitatem omnium redeatur, qui in Christum Dominum credunt' (ibid.).

8

children of the true Church a cause of holy joy in the Lord and at the same time a spur to offer help to all who sincerely seek the truth and through their prayer to obtain light and fortitude for them'.[1] The bishops especially are urged to give this help: 'They must not only supervise this whole work carefully and efficiently, but also prudently promote and direct it, so that on the one hand those who seek the truth and the true Church may be helped, and on the other the faithful may be preserved from the dangers which easily follow from activity in this "Movement".'[2] This danger is seen particularly in the temptation to give up Catholic principles, and whoever has an intimate knowledge of reunion work will be forced to admit that the *Instructio* speaks from experience. It also warns insistently against the danger of indifferentism. The heterodox may well be told that by returning to the Church they will lose nothing of the good things God's grace has so far worked in their souls, but that all this will only be fulfilled and perfected by their return. But things must not be presented in such a way as to give the impression as if their conversion would give the Church something essential she had so far been lacking. The *Instructio* also contains the important statement that in Oecumenical conversations 'the Catholic and the non-Catholic partners speak as equals (*par cum pari*) with each other about questions of faith and morals', each of them expounding the teaching of his faith as his own personal view. Nevertheless, such conversations require the previous approval of ecclesiastical authority. The Lord's Prayer, too, may be recited in common in such 'mixed gatherings'. The *Instructio* concludes: 'The highly important work of "reunion" of all Christians in the one true faith and the one true Church must increasingly become one of the most prominent tasks of the Christian ministry and a principal subject of ardent prayer.'

Thus oecumenical work has been elevated to a concern of the Church ('the above-mentioned "reunion" belongs before all to the tasks and duties of the Church').[3] The bishops are called to action and 'the Pope himself takes the lead in the great oecumenical task

---

[1] 'filiis Ecclesiae verae causa sanctae in Domino laetitiae simulque invitamentum ad praestandum omnibus sincere veritatem quaerentibus auxilium, ipsis lucem et fortitudinem effusa prece a Deo sollicitando'.

[2] 'ipsi igitur non solum diligenter et efficaciter universae huic actioni invigilare debent, verum etiam prudenter eam promovere et dirigere, tum ut adjuventur qui veritatem veramque Ecclesiam exquirunt, tum ut arceantur a fidelibus pericula, quae actionem ipsius "Motionis" facile consequuntur'.

[3] 'praefata "reunio" ad Ecclesiae munus et officium potissimum pertinet'.

of gathering Christendom, the task of the Good Shepherd who gave His life for the unity of His flock'.[1] This, says the *Herder-Korrespondenz*, is 'a turning point of Church history, for the time being only an experiment, but one with consequences, which creates a new situation for Catholics as well as for Christians in general'.

The reception of this *Instructio* in the Protestant world was generally reserved. It was welcomed especially in England. Visser't Hooft, in an official reaction, considered it an advance, but regretted that through being directed and supervised by the hierarchy the conversations would 'lose that informal and spontaneous character which was particularly valuable. The pioneers would now have less freedom. . . . Christians outside the Roman communion must now continue to pray that the Roman Catholic Church might be guided towards a less narrow and more profound conception of Christian unity.'[2]

Bishop W. Stählin observes that a different understanding of Christian unity will have to be accepted. 'It is part of the responsibility with which these conversations are conducted that we should know about this difference and not attempt to hide it from each other.'[3] The remarks of the *Instructio* about the Church not being essentially enriched by the conversion of Protestants gave offence to many non-Catholics. But M. Schmaus has pointed out that the two sides speak in different styles. In line with Roman tradition the *Instructio* is written, as it were, in a metaphysical style; whereas the Protestant Christian is used to a—so to speak—historical style. 'The *Instructio* is concerned with the metaphysical nature of truth, which is undivided and unchangeable. In this interpretation the Roman Catholic Church has the whole truth, not a partial truth. But this, as has recently been emphasized by Professor Karl Rahner, S.J., is different from the question whether this unchangeable and indivisible truth is known and lived most deeply in the Roman Catholic

---

[1] *HK* IV (1949/50), 325 f.

[2] *HK* IV (1949/50), 327. M. Schmaus said about this ecclesiastical supervision: 'It becomes understandable that the Church should reserve to itself a supervision of such conversations if it is recognized as a community whose members are the Catholics meeting the Protestant believers for discussion. The former speak not for themselves but as members of the Church to which the revelation of Christ has been entrusted. Hence the Church itself is engaged in such conversations. It would only be consistent if the relevant authorities of the Protestant Churches, too, gave their members directions for religious conversations with Catholics, because the Protestant Church, too, is represented by its faithful and hence their Church speaks where they speak'. (*Süddeutsche Zeitung* No. 126/50, special issue of Kyrios-Verlag: 'Der Vatikan und die Oekumenische Bewegung'. Interpretation of the Papal decrees on the Una Sancta Movement.

[3] Cf. *HK* IV (1949/50), 328.

Church, whether it is most clearly formulated there . . .'.[1] Summing up, we may say that the *Instructio* is a clear and not at all negative directive on Oecumenical rapprochement. It has relieved Catholic oecumenical theologians from the pressure of uncertainty from which their work had frequently suffered. They now know that their labours are safe and they are encouraged to seek for a mutual understanding on an unequivocal basis.

The Roman Catholic attitude to the oecumenical question is also being increasingly understood by Protestants. 'The attitude of the Roman Catholic Church must be explained in terms of far deeper and more essential motives, as is now being realized much more widely than previously. When Rome contends that the unity of the Church is not a goal lying ahead, but something which *has* already been made manifest in the Roman Catholic Church itself, because this alone is the Holy Catholic Church, and thus alone the Church of Jesus Christ, and when it further contends that true reunion can only take the form of a reintegration or reincorporation into this unity, this is not, on her part, the expression of some kind of spiritual imperialism, but the expression of a particular conception of the nature of the Church and its unity.'[2] If one wanted to study the nature of Catholicism, it would be futile to concentrate only on the official documents, but one would rather have to examine the living theological and ecclesiastical tradition, since this expresses the whole religious life of the Roman Catholic Church. According to Skydsgaard, the problem cannot be solved once and for all, since it could not be maintained that the Oecumenical Movement would have no consequences whatever for the Church of Rome. Further, Skydsgaard regards it as essential to consider the differences in the Roman Catholic Church's attitude to the separated Christians. Its relation to the Greek Orthodox and the Anglicans differs from that to the Lutherans and Reformed and to all the other larger or smaller denominations. This is expressed even in the way Rome addresses the separated Christians.[3] While the Easterns are frequently addressed as *Ecclesia orientalis* the Protestant communions are never referred to as 'churches'. In my view this is doctrinally important, especially in the case of the Orientals.

Peter Brunner, too, speaks of a 'dogmatic motive' preventing the

[1] ibid., 3.

[2] Skydsgaard 'The Roman Catholic Church and Ecumenical Movement', loc. cit., 157.

[3] Cf. Congar, 'Sur les termes' employés dans les documents catholiques officiels récents pour désigner les dissidents', in *Chrétiens désunis*, 381–3, ENG. TRANS.

Roman Catholic Church from participating in oecumenical activities.[1]

If we consider these ultimate principles it would have to be asked 'whether a Church which takes itself seriously can actually act in a different manner'. For every other attitude would contain an element of uncertainty. But where the answer to the question of salvation was involved, the Church was compelled to consider nothing else but the absolute certainty of the message of salvation, its knowledge and its mediation. 'We ought to be grateful to the Roman Catholic Church that, by her attitude, she forces all those involved in the oecumenical work to face these questions in all seriousness. It should, above all, be a matter for gratitude that, not least owing to the abstention of the Roman Catholic Church, the question of how to judge heresy cannot cease to be asked within the Oecumene.'[2] And, despite the unchanged doctrinal frontiers, a change in the fundamental attitude between the Roman Catholic and the Evangelical Church is to be observed. P. Brunner finds the reasons for this in the 'elimination, on principle, of neo-Protestant modernism from the evangelical Church' and in the fact that research has shown 'that the transition from the views laid down in the New Testament to the early Catholic Church can in no way be described only as a defection.'[3] Emil Brunner, opposing these recent insights, considers the early Catholic development of the Church a defection from the nature of the *Ecclesia* of the New Testament, but even he must admit that the Roman Church should not solely be seen under negative aspects: 'Who could deny that the Roman Church, too, lives by the Gospel of Christ, that, despite all changes, she, too, contains effective elements of the primitive Christian *Ecclesia* ... which, however, were discarded in the post-Reformation period in a too thorough-going reaction.'[4]

On the relation of the World Council of Churches to Rome opinions are divided. Some see in the Roman Catholic Church a constant exhortation to the World Council. Others deny this. O. Tomkins even speaks of the World Council being indebted to Rome: 'The World Council is in debt to Rome. Rome stands today

---

[1] 'Die römisch-katholische Kirche und die ökumenische Arbeit', in: *Die Ordnung Gottes und die Unordnung der Welt*, 29–44. These views of Skydsgaard and Brunner are supported also by E. Schlink, 'The Church and the Churches'. *ER* I (1948/9), 150–68. On the relation of the Lutherans to Rome cf. H. Asmussen, 'Ganzheit und Mitte des Glaubens', *WuW* 5 (1950), 167 ff., *ELKZ* VI (1952), 338.

[2] Brunner, loc. cit., 30 f.

[3] ibid., 33.

[4] *Das Missverständnis der Kirche*, 100.

as a perpetual commentary upon our work which we cannot ignore. For some she is only a warning against what they must not become; for others she is a perpetual temptation to escape from our intolerable tensions into unity at least of a kind. . . . But for us all, in all the contradictions in which we see her, she is a perpetual reminder to the Council that to speak of unity in Christ is not to speak of an abstract ideal but of something which must be expressed in history and in flesh and blood. Whether as warning or encouragement, whether as an offence or as a model (and in many of us, always as something of both), Rome stands over against all our tentative efforts, a unity embodied and therefore impossible to ignore.'[1] If we consider these words it must be admitted that Rome could do nothing other than stand apart. But the Roman Catholic Church has to face the question why it is that there is such agreement in the Oecumene to reject the unity presented by her. 'We are clearly united in not accepting the form of unity which she offers.'[2] Surely here appear again the deepest differences of our separation. Nevertheless, we shall also have to ask whether the Church really demonstrates convincingly the reality of Jesus Christ and the Holy Spirit present in her, whether her unity, catholicity, holiness and apostolicity are really shown forth by the pronouncements of her hierarchy and the attitude of the faithful.

So far we have been trying to set out the tendencies and aims of the Oecumenical Movement by tracing its historical development. We would now treat the subject systematically and ask where the struggle for the Church within the Oecumene offers points of departure for a fruitful conversation. For our theology is faced with new tasks, having to present the nature of the Church in a way that will lead our separated brethren to regard this Church no longer as the 'rock of offence' (Isa. viii, 14) but as the *signum levatum* (Isa. xi, 12),[3] as the fullness of Christ; or *must* the Church be the rock of 'offence' on which self-willed separations are broken? We have said that here theology is given new tasks. This, however, should not be understood in the sense that a so-called oecumenical theology could solve the problem of the unity of the Church. The question of this unity is a *Church* question, and theology can answer it only in so far as it is the theology of the Church. Hence certain members of the Oecumene deceive themselves when they hope to make capital from

---

[1] 'The Church, the Churches and the Council', *ER* IV (1951/2), 267.
[2] ibid.
[3] Cf., Denz, 1794.

an opposition between 'progressive, broadminded lay people and priests on the one hand and Vatican and other conventional circles, blinded or at least without sufficient understanding, on the other'.[1] It is a well-known fact that certain circles in the Oecumene are on the look-out for Catholic theologians who would let themselves be tempted to contradict Rome, and whose theology could then be used against Rome. On the other hand, there may also be Roman Catholic theologians who support the World Council of Churches because it gives them an opportunity to voice their opposition to Rome.[2] Such hopes are based on a misunderstanding of Roman Catholic theology and cannot lead any further. But we cannot overlook the fact that the Oecumenical Movement poses new questions for Roman Catholic theology and that certain problems, especially of ecclesiology, have to be considered anew in obedience to the revelation of Christ, which the Holy Spirit leads the Church to understand ever more abundantly.

[1] van de Pol, *The Christian Dilemma*, 233.
[2] Cf. Marc Boegner in *Le Semeur* No. 49, 170.

II. Systematic Part

UNITY

The following discussions will be guided by 'unity' as one of the notes of the Church, first formulated at the Council of Constantinople A.D. 381 and retained throughout Church history: the Church is *one*, holy, Catholic and apostolic. These notes of the Church are recognized also by most Protestant theologians, even though in a sense differing from the one the Catholic Church attaches to them. Luther spoke of seven notes of the Church: 'The Word of God, baptism, holy communion, the power of the keys, the office of preaching, prayer with public praise and thanksgiving, the cross and passion.'[1]

According to the Augsburg Confession two of these seven notes mediate grace more than the others; they are the word and the sacraments.[2] Some evangelical theologians distinguish between characteristics and qualities (*Kennzeichen und Eigenschaften*) of the Church. While the qualities, *una, sancta, catholica et apostolica* belong only to the *ecclesia proprie dicta*, i.e. the invisible Church,[3] the visible Church is recognized by the characteristics, which are the right preaching of the word and the proper administration of the sacraments.[4]

Even here a profound difference between the Catholic and Protestant conceptions of the Church becomes evident. According to the Catholic view the Church exists objectively in space and time, while in the Protestant view it is realized only when revealed in a special function. Article VII of the Augsburg Confession teaches that 'it suffices for a true union of the Christian Churches that the Gospel should be preached in concord and according to a pure understanding and that the sacraments should be administered according to the divine word. It is not necessary for the true unity of the Christian Church that uniform ceremonies instituted by men should be observed everywhere.' Interest is centred in the function of preaching and the administration of the sacraments. The Schwabach Articles contain a significant difference. According to them 'there is no doubt that one holy Christian Church exists and remains to the end of the world, as Christ says at the end of St Matthew's Gospel: Behold I am with you even to the consummation of the

---

[1] *Von den Konziliis und Kirchen* (1539).

[2] The Reformed, the followers of Zwingli spoke of three notes: the true preaching of the word, the orderly administration of the sacraments and ecclesiastical discipline (the power of the keys).

[3] Cf. Luthardt, *Kompendium der Dogmatik*, 326.

[4] Conf. August. VII.

world. This Church is nothing else but the faithful in Christ who keep the above-mentioned articles, believe and teach them and are persecuted and martyred for them in this world'.[1]

'Here the concept of the Church is defined not only by the preaching of the Gospel and the use of the sacraments, but also by articles confessing the Trinity, the divinity of Christ, the work of the incarnate Lord, death, original sin, etc.'[2]

The difference in the conception of the Church is further emphasized when Schlink points to the attempt of Stahl to supplement the Augsburg Confession. In the above-mentioned article VII 'the organic aspect of the Church, i.e. office and government, is ignored. Only the spiritual powers and their free activity are included in the notion of the Church, not the institutional edifice that is designed to carry them. Only the divine factor is emphasized, the effect of the Holy Spirit on souls, the Word of God and the sacraments, not, however, the medium of the human factor, the external order and organization through which the word is to be kept and preached in its purity.'[3] We certainly should not overlook the fact, as Catholics often do, that article VII must be read in conjunction with articles V and XIV. But we shall have to question Schlink's statements when he writes: 'This (fixed ecclesiastical) activity and its outcome in the constitution cannot be included in the conception of the Church side by side with the word and the sacrament; it is a human activity that must always be subjected to and judged by the word. Even though the constitution of the Church has legitimately developed in history from a divine origin it cannot be regarded as a divine "institution", as something established by God and thus placed before the congregation as something "higher".'[2] The opposition between Catholic and Protestant concepts of the Church is clearly shown by this controversy. (Cf. the discussions in the 'Digression' on 'The Church and the Law', pp. 203ff.) The Catholic identifies the qualities of the Church with its characteristics and these with its notes, while Protestants attribute the qualities to the invisible, the characteristics to the visible aspect of the Church. We would not enlarge on this difference between the Catholic and Protestant conceptions in this context; for it will be the leitmotive when treating of unity as one of the notes of the Church.

[1] *Die Bekenntnisschriften der Evangelisch-Lutherischen Kirche*, 61.
[2] Schlink, *Theologie der lutherischen Bekenntnisschriften*, 275.
[3] *Kirchenverfassung*, 2, p. 43 f.
[4] Schlink, loc. cit., 276.

1. THE CHURCH AND THE CHURCHES

The historical presentation of the Oecumenical Movement has shown it to be primarily a struggle for the unity of the Church. This has led to two mutually contradictory affirmations:

1. The Church of Jesus Christ is by nature the *one* Church; its unity is to be understood as an essential unity such as it is affirmed by the New Testament and by the Christian faith. It is the unity of a body, based on the oneness of Jesus Christ. Yet, on the other hand, it is a fact of experience that,

2. the Church of Jesus Christ is divided into a multitude of denominations. Hence it must be asked whether this historical experience of multiplicity abolishes the essential unity of the Church and how the confession of faith can be made to agree with empirical reality.

This question could simply be answered by affirming that the essential unity of the Church is shown by its complete identity of doctrine, faith, constitution and life. But as the New Testament proves that the unity of the Church is not uniformity, there remains a difference between the essential concept and its historical realization. Hence the question ought to be formulated thus: Within what limits are differences still compatible with the essential, God-given unity of the Church? Contemporary Protestant theologians have made various attempts to answer this question. There are those who hold that the unity of the Church is spiritual and invisible, and that it is not impaired by empirical divisions.[1] Some have even tried to justify the divisions, especially those who start from a sociological concept of the Church. According to them, the one Church is composed of ecclesiastical groups and denominations.[2] Others again consider the Church in its functions rather than in its essence, emphasizing its social and ethical aspects.[3]

[1] '. . . it makes no difference to this oneness, that as a fact of history members of the Sacred Society have come to be grouped in separate organizations. It makes no difference that these different organizations severally emphasize different aspects of Christian truth or that they are organized under different forms of government. Below all such distinctions there remains the "unity created by the spirit". That is a unity which is not even threatened by such divisions.' (C. A. A. Scott, *The Church: Its Worship and Sacraments*. London, 1927, 18). Cf. Nelson, *The Realm of Redemption:* 'Unity is an essential attribute of the invisibility of the church: but in its visible state the church must not consider diversity to be the same as disunity' (190).

[2] Cf. Paul Tillich, *The Interpretation of History*, New York, 1936, 220.

[3] Cf. S. Mathews, *The Church and the Christian*, New York, 1938, 12.

Those who hold such opinions regard the Church 'from below'. According to them it is built up by the religious action of its members; it is not an historical divinely instituted organism but a social contract based on individual freedom of belief and a democratic mentality. This view cannot be held to dominate the Oecumene today, even though the well-represented sects and many adherents of the non-conformist tradition subscribe to it. Theological liberalism is still alive in world Protestantism.

On the other hand, theological and ecclesiastical differences are accepted or even welcomed, because they are held to preserve the Church from smugness and stagnation.[1]

Representatives of the Branch Theory, too, which is so popular in the so-called Catholic tradition, especially among Anglicans, refuse to regard divisions within the Church as opposed to its essential unity, though they do not believe in the essential invisibility of the Church. They confess its historicity, but seek to justify the existing divisions, at least those of the three great types of Orthodoxy, Roman Catholicism and Anglicanism as 'branches' of the One Church. The Oecumenical Movement, however, has not adopted this point of view, and it would, indeed, be impossible to accommodate the whole 'left wing' in it.[2]

This conception, too, emphasizes the sociological aspect of the Church. It is opposed by another thesis, held today by certain Protestant theologians. According to them, the divisions attack the essence of the Church, and as long as they persist the whole Church is in a state of division.[3] At present the Oecumene seems to tend to this view, as is evidenced by the repeated confession of guilt of all Churches, even though, on the other hand, they hold on to the essential unity in Christ which they feel to exist and only to require visible expression.

Now here we encounter once more the problem of the opposition

---

[1] Cf. W. Elert, *Der christliche Glaube*, Berlin, 1940, 534. 'His view is: let us continue in division, that faith, or at least theology, may abound . . . . The danger of Elert's position is that it is easily perverted, being changed from a defence against theological stagnation to a pragmatic rationalization of divisions based upon issues which are not strictly theological'. (Nelson, op. cit., 192)

[2] This theory, observes W. A. Visser't Hooft, 'stands for a conception of tolerance which owes its origins, not to the Bible, but to modern humanitarianism. Its weakness is that it isolates the question of unity from the question of truth'. (*The Church and its Function in Society*, London, 1937, 92; Nelson, op. cit. 193). Cf. also A. C. Headlam, *The Doctrine of the Church and Christian Reunion*, London, 1920, 215 ; K. Barth, *Die Kirche und die Kirchen*, 27.

[3] Headlam, op. cit., 223 ; O. C. Quick, *The Christian Sacraments*, London, 1932, 147.

between theological and empirical evidence. Attempts are made to escape from this dilemma by dynamically relating the most diverse views of the unity of the Church, such as were proposed in the Oecumenical Movement. While the theologians of the old churches emphasize a 'vertical' unity and continuity with the Church of all ages and its creeds, the 'young' churches aim especially at a 'horizontal' unity, a synthesis of the various experiences of faith given to all Christians.[1]

The idea of the 'Covenant' is thought to provide this view with the basis of a Biblical ecclesiological concept. The existing divisions are to be overcome by a kind of federalism, represented by this idea. Indeed, in the Oecumene the Anglican branch theory has now been superseded by the conception of the 'Covenant', which, as has been seen, is realized in the Union of South India. The Covenant idea originated in the United States in the seventeenth century and was propagated by the Puritans and Independents who had emigrated from England; it is therefore typically Congregationalist.[2] Here the Oecumenical Movement sees its ideal of the unity of the Church in process of realization. Yet this thesis of 'Oecumenical collectivity' is not stated without misgivings. For it must be admitted that the Biblical idea of the Church knows nothing of such a collectivity and that, for this reason the necessary doctrinal requirements for constituting the unity of the Church are missing.[3] More or less consciously, the theologians of the Oecumene remember the One Church of the New Testament and of tradition, which gives the lie to this method of addition. The Toronto statement speaks several times of *the* Church, and characteristics of it may be found in various affirmations. Thus it is said that the Church is one because it is called thus in the New Testament, and that there is a membership of this Church which is not wholly identical with membership of one's own 'church'.

This is the Holy Catholic Church confessed in the Creeds, the Church of the full truth. The 'churches' are not within this full truth, but are led towards it through the elements of *the* Church contained in them. The Church is the temple of God, 'an edifice that

[1] Cf. G. S. Shaw and E. Hagman, 'An Approach to the Work of Reunion through Common Devotional Understanding'. In *Ways of Worhip*, 340.

[2] Cf. Flew, *The Nature of the Church*, 105, 177, 183, 185.

[3] We cannot believe that Lutherans, for example, would take to the covenant idea, for after 1525 Luther argued from the ministry as opposed to the congregation. The covenant idea in its congregationalist form cannot be harmonized with articles V and XXVII of the Augsburg Confession.

has once been built and is still being built further'. It is the Body of Christ, His *pleroma*, His bride. And there are characteristics of the Church 'that belong to its fundamental structure and its essence in such a way that they cannot be changed'. Here we must ask where is this Church that is described in such a way? Is all this only an ideal, or is it an historical reality? For the invisibility of the Church in a Platonic sense is denied. Hence the Church that is thus described ought to be found somewhere. This is the decisive question facing the Oecumene.

It is a favourite view in the Oecumenical Movement that the Church should be seen as an organism, not as an organization.[1] An organism is something living and dynamic, and the New Testament applies to the Church such organic images as body, bride and people. An organization, on the other hand, is easily thought of as rigid, objective and impersonal. Hence Protestants consider that to see the Church as such is an illegitimate objectification. Recently the Catholic conception has been most passionately rejected by E. Brunner.[2] According to him the *Ecclesia* of the New Testament is not an objective institution, but a community of persons, a people, an assembly, in fact the congregation of Christ. This conception has deep roots and far-reaching consequences. If the Church is a living organism as *opposed* to any kind of institution, its unity cannot be seen in any particular characteristic. Rather, as it is perpetually becoming a dynamic 'event' (*sich ereignet*), its unity will be recognized by the functions manifested in this process.

Here again the 'Catholic' differs from the 'Evangelical' type of faith as distinguished at Amsterdam. While the 'Catholic' tradition emphasized a vertical unity, assured through the centuries by an external continuity of spirit, faith and practice,[3] the 'Evangelical' party denied or depreciated the importance of external and historical factors in this unity; they wanted horizontal unity. Ecclesiastical organization must either be reduced to a minimum necessary for manifesting the unity[4] or the unity is seen as wholly spiritual,[5] or again the institutional factor is affirmed solely for practical purposes of security, e.g. to ensure the preaching of the pure Gospel.[6]

---

[1] 'The Church's unity is not that of an organization, but of an organism' (Nelson, op. cit., 203).

[2] *Das Missverständnis der Kirche*, 12 f., 17 ff., 73 and passim

[3] Cf. the Anglican view in N. Flew, op cit., 142.

[4] The conception of the Churches of Christ, cf. Flew, op. cit., 220.

[5] e.g. by the Congregationalists, Flew, op. cit., 184.

[6] Thus in Lutheranism; 'The Lutheran Church does not claim that its present

This view rests on the conception of the Church as *congregatio fidelium*, a community constituted by the intrinsically supernatural and invisible grace and the act of faith of those who have received it.

It must be admitted that the exponents of this idea have grasped an essential aspect of the Church. Without the divine grace that redeems men in Christ there can be no Church, and without the answer of faith there is no justification. Indeed, it corresponds to our observation and experience that the Church is a community formed by its members, that is to say the faithful. The Reformers attached such importance to this common act of faith that they considered it the constituent element of the one, holy Christian community.[1] Luther for example was anxious to distinguish the Christian Church from any kind of earthly community founded on birthright or power; it was to be based solely on faith in Christ. Congar has observed on this point: 'Taken literally, this was nothing but traditional and Catholic teaching; the patristic and theological tradition had, practically unanimously, 'defined' the Church as *Societas fidelium*, or else as *communio, congregatio, collegium, coetus, universitas, collectio, aggregatio, unitas . . . fidelium*.'[2] But however identical the expressions, the words of the Fathers mean something other than those of Luther. Hence we must ask by what influences Luther was led to understand the *Ecclesia* so exclusively as a *congregatio fidelium*. In our view the answer to this question will also explain why the Oecumenical Movement regards the Church as an organism as opposed to an organization.

---

organization is that of the New Testament but it strives always for an organization which will express its nature and be adequate to its needs.' Flew, op. cit., 266. 'The principle of organization must be the best means of serving the divine message, which is the creative factor in the Church.' Aulén, 'The Church in the Light of the New Testament', in *The Universal Church in God's Design*, 29.

[1] 'Of all the great teachers of Christendom Martin Luther alone saw most clearly the difference between the *Ekklesia* of the New Testament and the institution of the Church and reacted most passionately against the "*quid pro quo*" of the identification of both. He therefore disliked the very word "Church"; he called it a "blind, vague word" (Luther *WA*, L, 625). In his translation of the Bible he rendered the New Testament word *Ekklesia* by "congregation", and in his catechetical writings he paraphrased the *credo ecclesiam* by "Christendom" or "Christian assembly" (*WA*, XXX, 189). He felt that the New Testament *Ekklesia* is precisely no it, no thing, no institution, but a unity of persons, a people, an assembly, and, being well versed in the New Testament he knew and emphasized that it often speaks of *Ekklesia* without using this word; these equivalent terms are always personal: the Israel of God, the seed of Abraham, the elect priestly race, the special people and so forth. The word *Ekklesia* itself means assembly, people of God'. (E. Brunner, *Das Missverständnis*, 17).

[2] Littérairement parlant, il n'y avait rien là que de traditionnel et de catholique: d'une façon moralement unanime, la tradition patristique et théologique avait défini l'Eglise ; *Societas fidelium*; ou encore *communio* etc. *Vraie et fausse Réforme*, 385 f.

9

2. SALVATION AND MEANS OF SALVATION

Theologically Luther was in the Augustinian tradition.[1] Now according to E. Gilson, Augustinian thought may be described as a *métaphysique de la conversion*. Congar interprets it as a dialectic of conversion always leading from image to reality, from without to within, from external elements to interior reality.[2] According to St Augustine the Church is the *communio sacramentorum*, but just as the sacrament consists of the external sacramental sign and the inner reality of grace, so the Church of the sacraments and the hierarchical power is wholly ordered (*ordonnée*) towards the Church as *communio sanctorum*. 'The whole mystery of the Church, together with all the gifts of God, is drawn into a movement of "interiorization".'[3] The liturgy and the sacraments, indeed the whole Church are to be realized in men, in the spiritual life, in the faith and charity of the human soul itself. Congar observes that this implies a certain dualism, for there is on the one hand the reality of salvation, which is totally spiritual and eschatological, and on the other the means of salvation which can be perceived and exist on earth. This duality may be exaggerated, as frequently happens in Protestantism, so that it is asked whether the Church is salvation and communion with God in Christ *or* a means of salvation and an institution through which salvation is obtained. The Catholic answer is that the Church is both and that the two factors are connected with each other. But we must admit that they are not entirely identical. A man can be within the *communio sacramentorum* without being truly in the communion of saints, and it is not impossible to have a share in salvation without practising the acts of the *communio sacramentorum*. The absolute order of salvation which depends on an act of God who is in heaven is not perfectly identical with the relative order of the

---

[1] It is not easy to see exactly what ideas have inspired Luther's theology. 'Scholars in both camps are equally divided on the extent to which Luther himself and his opponents had succumbed to humanist and Ockhamist influences' (M. Lackman, 'Unsere apostolische Verantwortung'. *Quatember, Evangelische Jahresbriefe* 1952/3, 227). Nevertheless, it cannot be overlooked that Luther's conception of the Church was fed by Augustinian ideas. In the subsequent discussions we follow Congar, *Vraie et fausse Réforme*, 386 ff.

[2] ibid., 224.

[3] 'Tout le mystère de l'Église, comme l'ensemble des dons de Dieu, est entrainé dans un mouvement d'intériorisation'. ibid., 225.

Church's means of grace. This is the real ecclesiological problem. We shall see later how this becomes apparent in the questions of the *vestigia ecclesiae* and of membership. Here we are concerned with the connexion between these two aspects. Congar[1] says that the Reformers interpreted this Augustinian view with its stress on the interior in connexion with the saint's polemics against Donatists and Pelagians; especially among the latter the communion of saints is supposed to appear as a *communio praedestinatorum, electorum*. Several texts of St Augustine indicate, indeed, that the Church as *communio sanctorum* is identical with the *sancta ecclesia in praedestinatis*.[2]

According to Congar, some Augustinian die-hards later isolated these texts and used them as a basis for an ecclesiology. In this way they arrived at separating the purely spiritual communion with Christ from the visible Church.[3] Thus, instead of the Catholic sequence: Incarnate Word—Church/Institution—Christian life—Church/Community, Protestants have that of: Heavenly Christ—Christian life—Church/Community.[4] It was fatal that Luther combined these Augustinian ideas with the Neoplatonist ideas of Ockham, according to which all external things are regarded as the 'flesh' hostile to God. If, as in the case of the Church, a community is formed in the earthly and external sphere, it can escape the sinfulness of the flesh only by believing in and confessing Christ. Thus the external elements of Christianity are mere signs, but not causes. The only cause is faith, i.e. ultimately the Holy Spirit or the Word, hence an act of God. Everything is constituted, valued and judged by faith and the Word.[5] These, then, are the true differences between Catholicism and Protestantism: in Catholicism we have the sacramental reality, *incarnatio continuata*, in Protestantism the reality of lived Christianity. In the former, the Church has principally the character of an historical fact, an objective reality, independent at first of the personal faith of its members. In the latter the Church is an event,[6] ever realized anew by a certain attitude of the faithful.

---

[1] ibid., 385 f.

[2] Cf. F. Hofmann, *Der Kirchenbegriff des heiligen Augustinus*, Munich, 1933, 239 ff.

[3] Congar, loc. cit., 370.

[4] ibid., 442.

[5] Cf. ibid., 406.

[6] 'The congregation is the *event*—taking place in this last time—which consists in gathering together (*congregatio*) those men and women (*fidelium*) whom the living Lord Jesus Christ chooses and calls to be witnesses to the victory He has already won and heralds of its future universal manifestation'. K. Barth, 'The Church—The Living Congregation of the Living Lord Jesus Christ', in *The Universal Church in God's Design*, 71 f.

The oecumenical idea of an organism seems to be based on this line of thought; for these views are rife wherever the Church is seen as a communion of the faithful rather than as an institution. Now this raises certain questions. First of all, it is an undeniable fact that the communion of the faithful is an essential aspect of the Church which may not be neglected. Nevertheless, it seems that Catholics have often been in danger of disregarding it for the sake of the institutional aspect. Now how has the Church been regarded as far as its visible, institutional side is concerned? The Catholic mind likes to 'ontologize', it understands the 'thing that has happened' (*die geschehene Sache*) as an actual reality that can be experienced in the concrete and proved historically. Protestantism, on the other hand, places faith as the distinctive symbol before the bracket in which the visible elements are enclosed. Things become true through faith. We are, of course, concerned with the constitution of the Church, and what has just been said cannot be applied, for example, to the conception of the Sacraments in the confessional writings. These vigorously emphasize the objectivity of the sacrament and its independence of the faith of both minister and recipient. Thus Article VIII of the Augsburg Confession says: 'Though the Christian Church actually is nothing else but the assembly of all the faithful and saints, nevertheless, because in this life there remain many false Christians and hypocrites, even sinners, among the faithful, the sacraments are yet effective, though the priests who distribute them are not pious,' as Christ Himself says: 'The Pharisees sit in Moses' seat, etc.'[1] The Reformers do not see the Church from the perspective of the sacraments, e.g. the Eucharist. The formula *communio sanctorum* which derives from the Apostles' Creed and is originally in the neuter, means in the Middle Ages a participation partly in the sacraments, partly in the merits of the saints; in St Thomas it means both. In Luther this changes into the communion of mutual participation and surrender that exists in the *congregatio sanctorum* (assembly, congregation, Christian people).[2] Surely Catholics ought to ask themselves whether the elements do not become real also in this way. Reality in the Catholic sense may be regarded as something existing by itself, without human co-operation and thus as too objective and external. This would be the conception of a divine reality of perfect mercy and grace which man would have merely to accept. However much Catholics believe in an embodiment of grace—we shall discuss

[1] *Die Bekenntnisschriften der Evangelisch-Lutherischen Kirche*, 62.
[2] ibid., 62, note 3.

this in connexion with the role of the Holy Spirit in the constitution of the Church—the subjective element of faith may yet not be overlooked. The Church is based not only on the objectively transmitted deposit of faith but also on the act of faith of the believers.

Thus we have on the one hand the order of salvation, of invisible grace, on the other the order of the means of salvation through visible elements. The ecclesiological and oecumenical problem as such concerns the nature of the bond that unites both orders. The theologians of the Oecumene prefer to revert to the invisible order of salvation and to base the unity of the Church on this. This does not mean that they simply believe this to be invisible, for they aim precisely at the visible expression of unity. But the reality of this spiritual salvation constitutes the unity, in which the means of salvation play only a subordinate role. For the order of grace extends farther than any historical unity. For this reason they are content with the common faith in Christ as God and Saviour as a basis of unity. But they like to link the idea of the unity of grace with the eschatological aspect of salvation. Since Protestants consider grace as essentially uncreated (cf. the Edinburgh Resolution), they frequently regard it as a transitory help of God which does not effect a permanent change in the soul. Even when they speak of a 'new creation', this does not mean that nature is essentially transformed and assumed into super-nature. This view is linked to their concept of justification, which is largely understood as an attitude of God towards man. Thus there is a chasm between God and creature, grace and element, the invisible and the visible world. A reconciliation and unity is achieved only in the eschatological perfection when faith becomes vision. If visible things are not *a priori* devalued by a negative nominalist point of view, they are at least considered relative. For the Catholic theologian, on the other hand, the visible unity of the Church is perfectly realized only if three conditions are fulfilled: (1) agreement in the same objective content of the faith; (2) membership in an hierarchically organized Body of the Church; and (3) a share in the communion of the same sacraments, especially of the Eucharist.

Hence the visibility of the Church is subject to these conditions.

Of what kind is this formal visibility of the Church? It might be said that the visible, historically concrete form of the Church is of the same kind as other sociological forms that can be perceived by the senses. Bellarmine's statement that the Church is as visible as the republic of Venice points in this direction.[1] We know that this definition of the Church was opposed to the spiritualizing definition of the Reformers, expressed in Article VII of the Augsburg Confession. Here, however, we have to raise an objection. The visibility of the Church is something different from the visibility of a state. The fact that the visible Church is constituted by the elements of faith, hierarchy and sacrament as means of grace will indicate the right point of view. For these elements are intrinsically spiritual. The Church of the New Covenant was founded by Christ and by the mission of the Holy Spirit at Pentecost. Thus it was assigned its place in the new order of redemption; but this 'place' is not the same as the sphere which the first article of the Creed calls creation. The Church as the assembly of the redeemed is a new creation. For this reason Protestant theologians have frequently defined the Church exclusively in terms of the third article of the Creed and linked it to the Spirit in such a way that its formal visibility, too, was defined by the reality of the Spirit. Hence we would not simply assert that Protestantism owes to Idealist philosophy its emphasis on a certain invisibility. The ecclesiological problem of the visibility of the Church is its development in the sphere of the new creation of the Spirit. Both the first and the third articles of the Creed must be taken into account, if the Protestant inclination to spiritualize the Church as well as certain Catholic tendencies to objectify it are to be excluded. The new reality has been created by the same God confessed as the Creator in the first article. The creation of the Spirit is also the creation of the Father; both meet in the incarnate Word of God. The Church cannot be seen merely as a created object. It is an object of faith, for it is both visible and invisible. This fact is truly expressed if the Church is seen under sacramental categories and is called the great primary Sacrament.[2] Thus we may say that the Church is both

---

[1] *De conc. et eccl.* III, ii.

[2] Cf. O. Semmelroth, *Die Kirche als Ursakrament*, Frankfurt, 1953; Eichmann-Mörsdorf, *Kirchenrecht* I[7], 27; Y. Congar, *Esquisses du mystère de l'Église*, Paris, 1941; H. de Lubac, *Catholicisme*, Paris, 1938; E. Mersch. *La théologie du corps mystique*, Paris, 1946 (Eng. trans. *The Theology of the Spiritual body*, St. Louis, 1951).—This idea has been profitably applied to the oecumenical question by J. Gribomont, O.S.B. ('Du sacrement de l'Église et des ses réalisations imparfaites', *Irénikon* XXII (1949), 345–67). His starting-point is the distinction between *res* and *sacramentum*. Grace, as *res*, demands to express itself in the visible order, and, conversely, the external rites are there to be simply and effectively carried out and to realize what they mean. The Church is incarnate in a world of ignorance and sin; only its full revelation will identify the reality of grace with the visible sacrament. In the period of expectation both elements may arrive at being in a state of tension, either because the *res* does not achieve the manifestation which will develop it, or because sin deprives the *sacra-*

the spiritual reality of salvation and historical reality. But the term 'historical' ought not to be understood exclusively as a chronological and historical continuation, for here we are concerned with the history of salvation which is subject to conditions different from those of profane history. This also means that the eschatological character of the Church must be included in the question of its properties and notes. We shall later return to this point.

What sort of a bond is there between the two aspects of the Church as the community of salvation and the means of salvation? Most oecumenical theologians hold the connexion between the invisible and the visible elements of the Church to be one of 'manifestation'. The invisible unity of the Church, which is always essentially present, is to become manifest in the visible, historical unity. Now Catholic doctrine expounds the manner of this manifestation quite clearly. It is contained in the three conditions mentioned above; if these are realized the maximum of manifestation is attained. But this concept of manifestation does not completely describe the nature of the bond we have mentioned. The relation between the visible and the invisible elements is a causal relation. The means of salvation, the elements, are related to grace and salvation as cause to effect.[1] True, this applies only to the earthly condition of the Church, and it does not apply in the sense that salvation could be attained only by way of the means of grace. It must be kept in mind that the order of salvation and the means of salvation are not wholly identical. As we said before, men may submit to the demands of visible unity without possessing sanctifying grace and, conversely, may obtain salvation yet not belong to the visible communion of the Church. But it cannot be denied that in the normal order of things the fulfilment of the three conditions is the surest way to salvation. If Catholic tradition insists on this, it does so not because the Church wants power and dominion, as non-Catholics so often assert—though certain abuses of power on the

---

mentum of its healing effect. Theology has taken account of this tension and worked out a twofold doctrine: that of the substitution of desire, which takes effect when the reception of a sacrament is prevented or delayed by *force majeure*; and the other of the 'character', *res et sacramentum*, which concerns the objective and certain supernatural efficacy of the sacrament in the case of a badly disposed subject. This could also be applied to the Church as sacrament. There are members of the Church *in re* and *in sacramento*. In the earthly condition of the Church a man who is not a member of the Church *in sacramento* may nevertheless be one *in re*.

[1] Cf. 'La charité, effet et cause de l'unité' in *Vers l'Unité chrétienne*, No. 55, July-August 1953.

part of members of the Church might suggest this idea—but because the Church cares for the salvation of souls. In this earthly condition the possession of sanctifying grace is a precarious matter because of the possibility of sin,[1] and men need the external and visible means to help them not to lose salvation.[2]

*   *   *

DIGRESSION:

The Unity of the Church according to J. A. Möhler

No other modern Catholic theologian seems to have treated this problem of the two aspects of the Church and their relation to each other as lucidly as J. A. Möhler. His work is particularly important for us since the solution of the problem was by no means clear to him from the beginning but developed in the course of his writings. Möhler began his search for a right conception of the Church with his lectures on Canon Law in 1824. The notion of unity on which they are based[3] takes its terms of reference from the legal, external side of the Church and is 'in line with the post-Tridentine theology that begins with Bellarmine' (137). According to Möhler, the objective unity of the Church consists in a certain doctrinal concept, a cult and a constitution fixed in its fundamental features. The unity of the community is identical with this unity of its constitution. 'Here Möhler regards only the external and visible factors as constituting the Church's unity. . . . The Church is viewed as an advocate appointed to mediate the salvation of individual believers. Hence it follows that there is a distinction between the Church as the sum total of the objective means of salvation and the Church as the totality of the members to whom salvation is mediated subjectively.'[4]

---

[1] Cf. 'Du caractère collectif de l'espérance chrétienne' in C.-J, Dumont, O.P., *Les Voies de l'Unité Chrétienne, Doctrine et Spiritualité*. Paris, 1954, 184 ff.

[2] 'Quae quidem, si extremum illud quod vult, causaeque proximae sanctitatem efficientes spectentur, profecto est (Ecclesia) spiritualis; si vero eos consideres, quibus cohaeret, resque ipsas quae ad spiritualia dona perducunt, externa est necessarioque conspicua. Docendi munus accepere Apostoli per cognoscenda visu audituque signa . . . .' 'Fides ex auditu, auditus autem per verbum Christi' (Rom. x, 17) (*Satis cognitum*, ed. Herder, p. 233). 'At the beginning of the Christian era God endowed the Church with the necessary means so that, overcoming countless dangers, she might fill not only the whole earth, but also the kingdom of heaven' (*Mystici corporis* 20, C.T.S. edn.).

[3] Described by J. R. Geiselmann, 'Einheit und Liebe. Ihr Gestaltwandel in Möhlers Theologie der Kirche' in H. Tüchle, *Die Eine Kirche. Zum Gedenken J. A. Möhlers*. Paderborn 1939, 137 ff.

[4] Geiselmann, loc. cit., 147.

Later, in his publications in the *Theologische Quartalsschrift*, the mystical aspect of the Church is stressed more strongly. In the post-Tridentine notion of the Church Möhler senses the danger of a certain naturalism: 'God created the hierarchy, and now the Church is more than sufficiently equipped with all it needs until the end of the world.'[1] Hence he stresses the importance of the Holy Spirit in the constitution of the Church. 'Here the opposition to the external conception of the Church based on the hierarchy is so strong that the Church's ministry, especially its teaching office, is endangered.'[2] Purity of doctrine is not ensured by physical succession but by the presence of the Holy Spirit. 'There have been times when the Sorbonne could rightly say that a council should not be attended only by bishops, because they could not be expected to possess either the necessary knowledge or sufficient interest in the matter; in such a case the hierarchy was no longer the organ by which the old tradition was kept alive.'[3] In such a conception of the Church its unity is understood as an invisible communion of faith and love, the decisive factors being the working of the Holy Spirit and interior sanctity.[4] But this conception of unity was not Möhler's last word. In his early work *Die Einheit in der Kirche oder das Prinzip des Katholischen im Geiste der Kirchenväter der ersten drei Jahrhunderte* (Mainz, 1825), he sought to reconcile the contradiction in an organological notion of the Church. The basic theme of this work is the idea of a dialectic operating from within outwards and also from below upwards. The one divine Spirit is the cause of the one spirit of the faithful (cf. 8). The unity of the Church 'is effected through a life that is directly and always moved by the divine Spirit and preserved and transmitted by the mutual love of the faithful' (17). The common faith and the love that unites all is a revelation of the divine power of the Holy Spirit (ibid.). Since doctrine is a gift of this Spirit, Möhler emphasizes here again that not each one of the bishops 'need always and for ever have been in possession of the authentic apostolic

---

[1] *Theol. Quartalsschrift* 1824, 105; Geiselmann loc. cit., 149
[2] ibid., 150.
[3] *Theol. Quartalsschrift* 1823, 499.
[4] These ideas of Möhler recall St. Augustine's conception of the Church. In this context, F. Hofmann's discussions on the 'invisible basis of the Church' in his *Der Kirchenbegriff des heiligen Augustinus*, Munich, 1933, could be read with profit. 'For St. Augustine the *sancta mater ecclesia* is not a merely objective, impersonal entity, it is not the sacramental apparatus by which it functions outwardly, nor the ecclesiastical hierarchy which serves it, nor the visible, empirical Church in so far as it includes sinners and saints; it is the *sponsa Christi sine macula et ruga* which we have met before as the invisible essence of the Church' (265).

doctrine, simply because he was placed in an apostolic succession through which this property was transmitted to him as it were by magic. This would be a very materialistic view' (17). 'It would be a very one-sided view if the Church were to be defined merely as an institution or association founded to preserve and transmit the Christian faith; it is rather a product of this faith, an effect of the love alive in the faithful through the Holy Spirit' (129). This, however, does not mean that Möhler defended an invisible Church. 'The idea of an invisible Church . . . is contrary to Christianity' (130). He disliked the term 'institute' because 'with the notion of an institute is inseparably linked the idea of a mechanism' (132). For this reason he describes the Church as an organism,[1] in which the power of the Holy Spirit forms its visible body. This early work develops most clearly the idea of an organism, which guides the author towards a true conception of the Church's diversity in unity. The Church must leave sufficient room for the development of the particular individualities and the peculiarities of its members (cf. 85 f.), for this rich variety of gifts is a fundamental characteristic of its life. Where there is life there is not uniformity but variety. Möhler sees the organic development of this individuality revealed 'partly with regard to Christian theory, partly in the Christian life in the narrower sense, partly in matters of external worship' (85). Hence 'unity can also contain true contrasts' (113). He distinguishes contrast from contradiction, which latter is not compatible with the organic life of the Church. Heresy is a contradiction of the Church.

Within this idea of an organism Möhler also places the constitution of the Church, thus connecting organism with organization. The organs of the Church are formed by the one mystical principle of the Spirit who is active in the Church. 'The bishop represents the visible union of the faithful in a certain place, their love for each other as embodied in a person . . . , the love of Christians that has attained consciousness as well as the means to continue in it' (137). The Primacy had 'long been doubtful' to him—he writes: 'I was even determined to deny it, for the organic union of all the parts in a whole . . . seemed to be achieved by the unity of the episcopate'

---

[1] Here, too, we find a kinship with Augustinian thought: 'St. Augustine understands by the life-giving *matter* . . . not in the first place the Church as the sacramental institute of salvation but as the living organism of it . . . . Hence the active factor in the saving activity of the Church is not the ecclesiastical organization, but the invisible *unitas caritatis*, the *communio sanctorum* . . . . Fundamentally St. Augustine's conception of the *ecclesia mater* is as personal and spiritual as his doctrine of the nature of the Church' (Hofmann, loc. cit., 267).

(117)—but now he realized that it was 'the reflexion of the unity of the whole Church that had become a person' (173). Thus Möhler's 'unity in the Church' is a completely Spirit-centred conception of the Church in which the divine element predominates. Geiselmann rightly remarks that this idea of unity in Möhler's earliest work was dominated by the ideas of the German romantic movement.[1] But he did not stop at this organological view of the Church. We agree with Geiselmann that he later turned towards a trans-subjective conception. He no longer considered faith, for example, as merely a datum of consciousness, but penetrated to the objective preaching of the word by the Church, faith being 'the reflexion of the Christ-given teaching in the heart of man'.[2] The teaching of Christ has an objective content freely accepted by men. Later, indeed, 'human freedom' becomes 'one of the starting-points which help to create his new conception of the Church'.[3] The Church is a 'moral body'.[4]

In his *Athanasius* and especially in his *Symbolik* Möhler turns from the Spirit-centred to the Christocentric idea of the Church. Geiselmann rightly remarks that 'the Spirit Church of his early romantic work could hardly integrate the centre of our salvation, Christ and His redemptive work. . . . This and the Spirit Church were left unrelated side by side'.[5] Turning to Christology, Möhler finds a new category to describe the nature of the Church, which does justice to both its divine and its human aspects; this is the category of the Incarnation. Thus Möhler moves right away from his dialectic of inward and outward. The external aspect of the Church is now no longer only the presentation of the interior, which had been the basis of the organological concept of the Church, but it is causally related to the interior. The invisible Church emerges from the visible Church.[6] Divine truth, for example confronts man externally in the teaching and instruction of the Church 'that the germ within should develop'.[7] Now the Church is not only a communion of love but also an authority with the right to make demands on man. Thus its unity is founded on truth. This does not mean that later Möhler gave up his organological conception of the Church; but he deepened it by basing it on Christological categories. The organs of the Church

[1] loc. cit., 175.
[2] Geiselmann, loc. cit., 181.
[3] ibid., 185.
[4] *Symbolik*[2], 386.
[5] Geiselmann, loc. cit., 186.
[6] Cf. *Symbolik*[2], 398 f.
[7] Cf. Geiselmann, loc. cit., 191.

are not only forms of a mystical principle of the Spirit, but, being 'extensions of the incarnate Christ',[1] they are essentially juridical. The law makes for unity.

'What would the Universal Church do without the organ, and the organ if no one were obliged to obey it?'[2] The Church is a visible institution, hence it demands a visible head, the primacy,[3] to guarantee the unity by exercising its rights over the bishops and the faithful.

Hence Mohler was concerned to preserve the external, historical Christ and His external, historical revelation. But, having laid this basis in the concept of the 'incarnational' (das Inkarnatorische), he developed all the more richly the conception of the Church as a unity. For him it is and remains an organism. Even in his Symbolik he stresses that the 'interior' takes precedence.[4] 'We are not living members of the external Church until we belong to the interior one'; 'that which is offered us from outside must have been reproduced in us and by us, the objective element must have become subjective before we are entitled to regard ourselves as true members of the Christian Church'.[5] Möhler then assembles his elements for a synthesis, the highest principle of which is not 'either-or' but 'as-well-as'. In his later doctrine the Church is both; Church of the Spirit as well as institution, visible as well as invisible, because it is constituted by the Holy Spirit and the incarnate Christ. The Church's principle of unity is both organological and authoritative; external and internal elements mutually affect each other. The heart of his synthesis and thus the fundamental category of his ecclesiology is the idea, more, the reality, of the Incarnation.

*   *   *

We have discussed Möhler's ecclesiology in such detail because many of the present oecumenical questions as well as their answers can be found in the theological development of Möhler's conception of the Church. It would be very desirable for oecumenical theologians to study Möhler's ecclesiology, in which all has grown organically. True, much of what he says should also give Catholics food for thought. The incarnational category is familiar to modern Catholic ecclesiology. Möhler made it the crown of his work, but only after

[1] 'The Church is the permanent copy of Christ, the original Image' (Symbolik[2], 315)
[2] Symbolik[2], 370.
[3] ibid., 369.
[4] ibid., 403.
[5] ibid., 403.

using the other building materials of the pneumatological and organological concepts. This ought not to be overlooked; for the idea of the Incarnation should not be used without qualifications.

Present-day oecumenical debate is centred in the question whether the Church is a community of salvation or a means of it, an organism or an institution. The conception of the Church as an organism is linked to the New Testament idea of it as the Body of Christ. For this Biblical conception reflects most adequately the organic aspect of the Church: the organic union of the members with the Head and with each other. Now 'body' is an image concept, not in the sense of a metaphor, but neither in that of a *corpus physicum*. In the First Epistle to the Corinthians the idea of the body is always joined to the two supplementary notions of ἕν and πνεῦμα: τὸ σῶμα ἕν ἐστιν ... καὶ γὰρ ἐν ἑνὶ πνεύματι ἡμεῖς πάντες εἰς ἕν σῶμα ἐβαπτίσθημεν (1 Cor. xii, 12–13; cf. also Eph. iv, 4). Hence the mystical Body of Christ should be understood in the context of this triad. This is the Scriptural foundation of what is said of the Church in the third article of the Creed, in which it is co-ordinated to the *pneuma*. The Church is a personal Body with a personal Spirit. What, then, is the relation between Body and Spirit? We have seen that the oecumenical theologians combine the two ideas of the Church as the Body of Christ and as an organism. It is the principle of an organism that the exterior should be transformed and fashioned by the interior or soul.[1] Hence a strict dialectic of interior and exterior. 'The nature of the Church is not determined by any form of organization.'[2] If it is called a body, this means that the Church 'is to be the agency for the visible expression of the soul or spirit'.[3] Hence body means a manifestation of the soul. But a body can exist also as a soulless corpse, hence 'no outward forms can guarantee the Church's presence. An institution may become a corpse from which the true spirit of Christ has departed'.[4]

[1] Cf. C. T. Craig, 'The Church in the New Testament', *The Universal Church in God's Design*, p. 41.

[2] ibid., 39.

[3] ibid., 40.

[4] ibid., 41. This thought has been theologically developed by M. Keller-Hüschemenger ('Umfang und Grenzen der Kirche als Leib Christi', *ELKZ* 4 (1950), 66 f. He opposes above all the principle of identity on which he believes the Roman conception of the Church to be based: the Body of Christ is identical with the real Church. According to him, this fails to conform with the hidden character of the revelation of Christ. The Body of Christ is not identical with the Church, but can be grasped only in such a way that 'in, with and under its really visible body as a community of persons it may also be the wholly present Body of Christ'. And this means a hidden presence.

Here must be made clear what St Paul meant when he called the Church the Body of Christ.[1] The concept of the body in the genuine Pauline Letters is certainly akin to the Hellenistic image of the organism.[2] But E. Käsemann has decisively corrected the equation of the Body of Christ with the idea of an organism. For he has shown that this latter idea ultimately does justice neither to the thought in 1 Cor. xii, 14 nor to the relation of the Body of Christ to Pauline anthropology and the Sacrament nor to Christology.[3] In this context we are especially concerned with the inner relationship between the σῶμα Χριστοῦ and the eucharistic Body of Christ. Since Rawlinson drew attention to the sacramental significance of the term Body of Christ[4] suggested by 1 Cor. x, 17, this idea has found favour with some evangelical theologians. 'Between the use of the phrase "Body of Christ" as a description of the Church and the use of the same phrase as a description of the sacramental "loaf" of the Eucharist it is permissible to suspect a connexion; and the rite, surely, precedes the doctrine.'[5] Thus the concept should not be understood sociologically (social life, community), but it means: 'Corporality, visible, concrete reality, unity . . . of a "bodily" kind.'[6] The concept σῶμα Χριστοῦ evidently means that the crucified and exalted Lord makes use of a human community to spread His word and sacrament on earth.[7] We would sum up in the words of Käsemann: 'The Lord's Supper as Agape constitutes at the same time the Agape-Aion or the σῶμα Χριστοῦ that is identical with it.'[8] According to these exegetical

---

[1] Cf. L. Cerfaux, La théologie de l'Église suivant saint Paul, Coll. Unam. Sanctam 10, Paris, 1942; L. Malevez, L'Église Corps du Christ. Sens et provenance de l'expression chez saint Paul, Paris, 1944. By this image St. Paul means to show the visible, organic and hierarchical character of the Church as well as its mysterious union of life with its Head, the glorified Christ.

[2] 'It cannot be denied that the idea of the organism is really present in St Paul, in Rom. xii, 4, as well as in 1 Cor. xii 14–21. Here Greek Stoic material also found elsewhere in St. Paul is actually used, when the body is considered in the multiplicity of its members, and the members in their various activities', (Käsemann, Leib und Leib Christi, 160).

[3] ibid., 161 f.

[4] 'Corpus Christi' in Mysterium Christi (1930), 225 ff.

[5] ibid., 227. Cf. O. Michel, Das Zeugnis des Neuen Testamentes von der Gemeinde Göttingen, 1941, 52. Like Michel, we would question the latter statement about worship and doctrine; but this does not concern the question under discussion.

[6] Rawlinson, loc. cit., 231, Michel, 53.

[7] Michel, loc. cit., 58.

[8] Cf. also: 'Das Abendmahl im Neuen Testament', in Abendmahlsgemeinschaft, 1937, 60 f. 'The Body of Christ is the goal to which I am led by the Sacrament of the Lord's Supper, by which I share in this Body—the exegesis of 1 Cor. x ends in this statement, which is confirmed by 1 Cor. xi' (81). O. Dilschneider reaches the same conclusion:

findings an external, sacramental form may very well effect the presence of the *pneuma*. In the Church we are confronted with the pneumatic reality in its historical appearance.[1] Luther seems to have neglected this sacramental significance of the term. But if the sacramental character of the Body of Christ is underestimated, the importance of the formal visibility of the Church suffers as well. The mystical Body of Christ, the invisible *communio sanctorum*, is no longer identical with the visible Church; but in this view the mystical Body is the 'true Church' constituted by 'true believers' who, being incorporated in Christ by faith, are therefore His members, and thus this mystical Body is opposed to the visible Church. Subsequently the invisibility of the mystical Body was still further emphasized on the grounds that the members of Christ ought to be as invisible as their Head. The ultimate consequence of this speculation on invisibility is the complete exclusion of the Church's hierarchy, headed by the Pope, from the mystical Body of Christ; thus the body is turned, almost ironically, into a soul.[2]

This sacramental conception of the Body of Christ makes it clear that the saved community is intimately united to the institution and that each is causally related to the other.[3] Thus there is not only a dynamism between within and without, but also a movement from without to within. E. Brunner completely disregards the Biblical data when he tries to play off the pneumatic unity against the sacramental unity[4] so that when 'the sacramental salvation becomes the main thing, the *Ekklesia* changes from a *Koinonia pneumatos*, a

---

'The Supper establishes the congregation as the Body of Christ'. *Gegenwart Christi* II, 310.

[1] Cf. V. Warnach, *Die Kirche im Epheserbrief*, 1949, 10 f.

[2] Cf. D. C. Lialine, 'Une étape en ecclésiologie'. *Irénikon* XIX (1946), 136; W. Wagner, 'Die Kirche als Corpus Christi Mysticum beim jungen Luther'. *ZkTh* 61 (1937), 29–98. Lialine notes that the erroneous conceptions of the Corpus Christi Mysticum of Wyclif, Hus, Luther, Calvin, Quesnel and the Jansenists, condemned by the Church, all resemble each other (cf. Denz. 584, 588, 627–32, 1422–28, 1515). P. Tromp, S. J. explains the fundamental speculation on which these doctrines are based (*Corpus Christi quod est Ecclesia*. I. Introductio generalis, Roma 1937, 156): 'quorum omnium erratum est in propositione minori eiusdem syllogismi: Ecclesia teste Apostolo est Corpus Christi; atque Corpus Christi est tali vel tali modo intelligendum: sequitur aspectus peculiaris v.g. coniunctio justorum cum Christo Capite; unio sanctorum inde ab Abel: Coetus praedestinatorum in praescientia divina . . . Ergo.'

[3] 'La forme théologique de la liaison serait double en ecclésiologie thomiste: L'Église-institution est la forme même d'existence du Corps mystique et de la vie nouvelle dans le Christ; l'Église-institution est le sacrement, le ministère, bref, l'instrument de réalisation du Corps mystique' (Lialine, loc. cit., 135).

[4] *Das Missverständnis*, 75.

personal unity, into an objective unity, a collective'.[1] Käsemann, on the other hand, considers that the pneumatic reality in man is established chiefly by the Sacrament.[2] We shall return to this question when discussing the Holy Spirit and the Church. Here we would only say that the concept of the organism as it is widely held in Protestantism and in the Oecumene today fails to do justice to the Biblical view of the Body of Christ. Hence Schlink's criticism of the essays by Aulén, Craig and Florovsky is on the right lines when he says: 'The conception of the Body of Christ is still worked out too much in terms of organism.'[3]

How far this criticism applies to Florovsky we would not presume to say. For he thinks that 'perhaps an "organism" is the best modern rendering of the term "soma" as used by St Paul'.[4] For an Orthodox theologian, however, the relation between the mystical and the eucharistic Body of Christ should be sufficiently obvious to exclude the problems the word organism raises for Protestants. Hence this term sounds also very different when Pius XII calls the Church 'organic' in his encyclical *Mystici Corporis*. Since the Church is constituted by the sacraments, especially the Eucharist, its structure is sacramental; that is to say spiritual, invisible salvation is profoundly related to the visible means of salvation. These are no mere manifestations, but efficient causes. In the Oecumene, too, the importance of the visible means is increasingly felt, because it is recognized that one cannot speak of the complete unity of the Church as long as there is no full eucharistic unity. Thus 'covenant fellowship' is rather a questionable term by which to express unity, for it does not really convey the Scriptural meaning of the Body of Christ.

But perhaps the aspect of the Church as a community of supernatural grace might correspond to the New Testament concept of κοινωνία (1 Cor. x, 16; 2 Cor. xiii, 13; Phil. ii, 1; Acts ii, 42). Could this term even simply mean what contemporary oecumenical theologians call fellowship 'in the sense of association with other persons'?[5] The first opinion might be suggested by the fact that the concept of *koinonia* is sometimes called κοινωνία τοῦ πνεύματος (cf. 2 Cor. xiii, 13; Phil. ii, 1). Would that not be E. Brunner's pneumatic community of persons? Recent research of Protestant theologians has led to a different result. They have reached the

---

[1] ibid., 76.
[2] *Leib und Leib Christi*, 126 ff.
[3] 'The Church and the Churches', *ER* I (1949), 158.
[4] 'The Church, Her Nature and Task', in *The Universal Church in God's Design*, 49.
[5] Nelson, op. cit., 53.

conclusion that in St Paul *koinonia* never means 'the fixed covenant of believing brethren but the participation in an objective value granted to the individual, or which he grants to a brother in an objective fact',[1] hence that it 'describes not so much a subjective human relationship as an objective fact'.[2] *Koinonia*, therefore, means 'participation' in objective realities.[3] St Paul speaks expressly of κοινωνία τοῦ αἵματος and τοῦ σώματος τοῦ Χριστοῦ (1 Cor. x, 16), ὅτι εἷς ἄρτος, ἐν σῶμα οἱ πολλοί ἐσμεν (x, 17).

Thus the pneumatic community of persons is founded on sacramental communion, which constitutes the organism of the Church with its union of opposites.

Thus, the conception of the Church as a community of salvation is not opposed to that of an institution; these are two aspects of the same thing. But the bond that unites them is causal in both directions, because the movement goes from within to without and vice versa. God has disposed matters in such a way that external things work salvation. The unity of the Church results from its share in both spheres.

The Orthodox prefer to describe the Church in terms of *koinonia*. They understand it as a type of the *koinonia* of the apostles, as a confederation of churches which are united in the same faith and the common love of our Lord Jesus Christ. Contemporary Russian theologians include this concept in the notion of *sobornost*, which corresponds to the English 'togetherness'. But *sobornost* as a term for the unity of the Church is a dynamic—we might also say a mystical—concept. Unity is established by charity. C. Lialine has connected this idea with the 'dialectical solidarity' in the Oecumene, which he considers 'a wholly new and valuable phenomenon in the Christian world'.[4] Now Dejaifve thinks that this concept of *sobornost* is more than mere kind feeling and fellowship, that, rightly understood (he refers to Bulgakoff), it is quite compatible with the hierarchical principle, even with the principle of a supreme personal

---

[1] Lohmeyer, *Philipper-Kommentar*, 1930, 17.

[2] E. Käsemann, *Leib und Leib Christi*, 174 f.

[3] Käsemann enumerates the following: Christ (1 Cor. i, 9; Phil. iii, 10) Spirit (2 Cor. xiii, 13; Phil. ii, 1); Faith (Philem. 6); Gospel (Phil. i, 5); Ministry (2 Cor. viii, 4), loc. cit., 175. The importance of participation was worked out especially by J. Y. Campbell, 'Koinonia and its Cognates in the New Testament', *Journal of Biblical Literature*, LI, 352-80. H. Seesemann, *Der Begriff Koinonia im Neuen Testament* (1933); F. Hauck in *ThWB* III, 804 f.

[4] 'Nouvelles précisions sur le Conseil Oecuménique des Églises', *Irénikon* XXIV (1951) 51, 53.

authority such as the primacy of jurisdiction in the Church of Rome.[1] If this be the case, the concept of *sobornost* might provide a link between the Catholic and the Protestant views of the Church. It could bring the true elements in the Covenant idea to fruition; but it might also be an appeal to the Roman Church not to regard the unity of the Church too exclusively from the juridical point of view. For *sobornost* assigns to the hierarchy the place that belongs to it and which does not place it above the Church. The hierarchy becomes a form of organization within the living organism of the Church.[2] As far as Roman Catholic ecclesiology is concerned, this means that greater importance is given to the independence of bishops. Leo XIII has emphasized this idea in his encyclical *Satis cognitum*.[3] The Pope writes that the authority of St Peter and his successors is indeed the fullest and highest, but it ought not to be assumed that it is the only one. The bishops, who are the successors of the apostles, inherit their ordinary power. Hence they are not to be regarded merely as vicars of the Roman Popes, *quia potestatem gerunt sibi propriam*. It is correct to speak of churches in the plural, because these have their own particular standing within the universal Church. The episcopal office traces its origin to a divine institution.[4] But the bishop is a member of the whole episcopate: *apostolorum successor est*. And, as the Vatican Council says, the primacy is *principium et visibile fundamentum* of this unity.[5] In fact, the prooemium of the *Constitutio dogmatica prima de ecclesia Christi* is extremely important for the proper understanding of the primacy. The Pope is here seen from the point of view of the bishops, as had been done already by Cyprian in his *De catholicae ecclesiae unitate*. Thus the individual churches are given great prominence. In the view of our separated brethren the idea of the primacy always involves a claim to absolute government which destroys the organism of the Church. Unfortu-

---

[1] 'Sobornost ou Papauté? La notion de l'Église dans l'orthodoxie contemporaine'. *Nouv. Rev. Théol.* 74 (1952), 358 ff. English translation in *Eastern Churches Quarterly* 10 (1953–4), pp. 28, 75, 111, 168.

[2] Many Catholics, by the way, do not pay sufficient attention to the fact that beside and before the infallibility of the Pope there is an infallibility of the Church, which the Pope represents in questions of vital concern to Christendom. The Vatican Council, which defined (but did not teach for the first time) the infallible doctrinal authority of the Pope is still a very recent event; this may account for the fact that this dogma is more alive in the consciousness of Christians as well as others than that of the infallibility of the Church as the indestructible creation of God in this world' (Rademacher, *Die Wiedervereinigung*, 68 f.).

[3] Also Pius XII in *Mystici corporis*.

[4] Cf. *CIC* c. 329, § 1.

[5] Denz, 1821.

nately this opinion is strengthened by the way in which the primacy is presented in the theological manuals. St Bernard was right, and he expressed a theological truth when addressing this exhortation to Pope Eugene III: 'Consider above all that the Holy Roman Church which you govern by the authority of God, is the Mother of the churches, not their mistress, and that you are not the master of the bishops but their brother and one with them.'[1] The term *ecclesiae* (in the plural!) is perfectly legitimate also in the Church of Rome, and it ought to show our separated brethren that their concern for the Church as an organism has its home in the Roman Catholic Church. The Mother Church is not committed to uniformity, whether in spirit or in form, a fact witnessed by the variety of theological opinions and the multitude of devotions and rites. There is no papal absolutism. 'The definition of 1870 has changed nothing in the organic idea of the Church, especially as regards the collegial structure of the ecclesiastical hierarchy.'[2]

---

[1] 'Consideres ante omnia sanctam Romanam Ecclesiam, cui Deo auctore praees, ecclesiarum matrem esse, non dominam, te vero non dominum episcoporum, sed fratrem unumque cum ipsis'. *De consideratione* IV, 7.

[2] Dejaifve, loc. cit., 466. On the ominous *La tradizione sono io* of Pius IX cf. Karrer, *Um die Einheit der Christen*, Frankfurt, 1953, 63 f. On the whole subject cf. W. Soloviev, *Monarchia Sancti Petri*, especially the chapter on 'Papacy and Papism' 173 ff.

3. CHURCH AND ESCHATOLOGY

The question of the Church, which is an essentially supernatural phenomenon, implies the further question whether the unity of the Church can be realized in history, or whether it is of a wholly eschatological character. This question has recently been much canvassed in the Oecumene. Humanly speaking, the paradox of the God-given unity and the verifiable fact of the many divisions seems impossible to solve in this earthly time. Hence the members of Lund looked 'forward', to the Parousia of the Lord, who was to heal the schisms of the Church at His coming. Even now, however, the Church was seen in this eschatological light, so that the questions that separated the various communions seemed unimportant in view of the return of the Lord. The subject of the Second Conference of the World Council of Churches at Evanston in 1954, 'Christ the Hope of the World', was also a subject directing attention to eschatological facts, since the term hope implies the expectation of the future. But even apart from this typically oecumenical question, ecclesiology cannot neglect the doctrine of the *eschata*.

Eschatology is generally regarded as the doctrine of the Last Things, death, judgement, heaven and hell. These are essentially determined by the Parousia of Christ. They refer to eternity, and the Christian meets them in an attitude of expectancy, whether this be positive or negative. Protestant theology of the last decades has presented this doctrine of the *eschata* in a different way. The actual problem of eschatology is the fact that in a certain sense the Last Things are already present, for eternity encounters time just as God encounters man. Hence eschatology is related both to the present and to the future. The tension between these two, time and eternity, divine and human things, constitutes the problem of eschatology.

Protestant theologians have tried to solve this problem in different ways. In ecclesiology it is the problem of the relation between the Church and the Kingdom of God. During the so-called *zeitgeschichtliche Epoche*, which Braun assigns to the period from 1892 (the year of the publication of J. Weiss' book *Die Predigt Jesu vom Reiche Gottes*) to 1913 (the date of the *Geschichte der Leben-Jesu-Forschung* by Albert Schweitzer)[1] the eschatological passages of the New Testament, which liberal Protestantism (Ritschl, Harnack, Sabatier) had rele-

---

[1] *Neues Licht auf die Kirche*, 104.

gated to oblivion, were re-discovered, but declared unimportant. The historicism of this epoch considered eschatology an illusion: Jesus had used this rhetorical form of speech, which was made necessary by the circumstances of the time. 'Consistent eschatology' (*konsequente Eschatologie*) was a reaction to this. It was taught particularly by A. Schweitzer and M. Werner,[1] according to whom the expectation of the early return of Christ is the principal content of Holy Scripture. Hence Jesus had advised His disciples to adopt a mode of life suited only to the short time before the final catastrophe, but which became the foundation of a new culture when this catastrophe failed to materialize. Agreeing with Holmström,[2] F. M. Braun observes that 'this conception meant more or less a return to the attitude of Ritschl' and to liberalism.[3] Recently syntheses have been attempted by H. D. Wendland,[4] K. L. Schmid,[5] W. Michaelis,[6] A. Fridrichsen,[7] F. J. Leenhardt,[8] O. Cullmann[9] and W. A. Visser't Hooft.[10] Braun calls them representatives of a 'new consensus', who seek the truth in the harmony of both concepts. It would go beyond the scope of this book to examine the attempts of these scholars to resolve the tension between time and eternity, Church and Kingdom of God. F. M. Braun draws the final conclusion that 'so far there has been no single comprehensive theory that has done complete justice to the data of the Bible',[11] but the way towards one was open, since the problem was clearly seen.

Protestant ecclesiology can best be understood by considering the representatives of *Formgeschichte* and *Dialectical Theology*, because they speak with the authentic voice of Protestantism and exercise the greatest influence in the Oecumene of today. In their system teleo-

[1] *Die Entstehung des christlichen Dogmas*, Berne, 1931.

[2] *Das eschatologische Denken der Gegenwart*, German trans. Gütersloh, 1931.

[3] Cf. especially the replies of Cullmann, 'Neutestamentliche Eschatologie und Entstehung des Dogmas.' *Kirchenblatt für die reformierte Schweiz* 98 (1942), 62–73. Foi criticism cf. also Schmaus, *Dogmatik*,[4] IV, 29–41.

[4] *Die Eschatologie des Reiches Gottes bei Jesus*, Gütersloh, 1931.

[5] 'Das Kirchenproblem in Urchristentum.' *Theol. Blätter* VI (1927), 293–302; *Die Kirche des Urchristentums. Festgabe für A. Deissmann*; Tübingen, 1927, 259–319; Art. βασιλεία *ThWBNT* I, 573–595; Art. ἐκκλησία ibid. III, 502–539; 'Le ministère et les ministères dans le Nouveau Testament.' *RHPR* XVII (1937), 313–36; 'Relations et contrastes'. ibid. XVIII (1938), 145–73.

[6] *Täufer, Jesus, Urgemeinde*. Gütersloh, 1928; *Der Herr verzieht nicht die Verheissung. Reich Gottes und Geist Gottes nach dem Neuen Testament*, Basel, 1930.

[7] 'Église et sacrement dans le Nouveau Testament,' in *RHPR* XVII (1937), 337–56.

[8] *Etude sur l'Église dans le Nouveau Test.*, Geneva, 1940.

[9] *Königsherrschaft Christi und Kirche im Neuen Testament*, Zurich, 194.

[10] *Misère et grandeur de l'Église*, Geneva, 1943.

[11] *Neues Licht auf die Kirche*, 93.

logical eschatology becomes axiological. Eschatology is no longer merely the doctrine of a chronological event, but of a qualitative decision. If these theologians say that Christianity or the Church is eschatological, they make a fundamental statement on the nature of the Church. For to them eschatology is above all the category by which the distinctive quality of Christianity can be grasped. Most of them do not subscribe to a linear notion of time but consider time and eternity as concepts of value. In this way they normally tend to depreciate time. History, like all created things, is little esteemed; only eternity is properly real. Hence they equate Christianity with eschatology.

In his exposition of the Epistle to the Romans, Karl Barth takes eschatology to be the situation in which man recognizes his limitation and awaits the Kingdom of God. Eschatology is a human attitude transcending the notion of time,[1] hence it is expressed in concepts of absolute transcendence. God transcends history absolutely as Creator, Saviour and King.[2]

For Bultmann eschatology is a decision of man. According to him, the general judgement is 'not a future cosmic event, but the fact that Jesus has come into the world and has called it to faith'.[3] Bultmann wants to clarify the Christian conception of being. Because God's grace forgives sin, man is released from the past and from the world. For his sin consists in this that he wants to safeguard himself and 'therefore grasps what is at his disposal and clings to what passes and is always already past'.[4] Faith means precisely to be open to the God-given future. Man's decision of radical surrender to God means 'to be freed from all that is at one's disposal in the world, hence the attitude of detachment from the world (*Entweltlichung*)'. Now, according to Bultmann this *Entweltlichung* is eschatological. All 'that is in the world is relegated to the indifference of something unimportant in itself'.[5] For him the congregation, or Church, is 'not an historical phenomenon in the sense of being itself part of world history, but of being realized in history'.[6] Historicity becomes a form of human life. Here the Lutheran *pro me* receives its ultimate meaning. Bultmann understands the New Testament expres-

[1] 4th edition, 481. Cf. Luthardt, *Dogmatik*, 430.
[2] Cf. Nelson, op. cit., 231.
[3] *Neues Testament und Mythologie. Kerygma und Mythos*. Ed. H. W. Bartsch, 1951, vol. I, 30.
[4] loc. cit., 29.
[5] Schniewind, *Antwort an R. Bultmann*, loc. cit., 101.
[6] Bultmann, loc. cit., 42.

sion *en Christo* as an eschatological event in the sense that the Christian is transferred into an unworldly existence.[1] He sacrifices the incarnate Christ: 'I turn away from all historical encounters and turn towards the unique encounter with Christ who is preached, and who meets me in the kerygma and touches me in my historical situation. It seems to me that the paradox or *scandalon* of Christian eschatology in which the *eschaton* enters history can be preserved in no other way.'[2]

Bultmann's critics have stressed that he interprets the term eschatology metaphysically,[3] spiritualizing and approximating it to a purely axiological meaning.[4] 'What Bultmann calls eschatology has nothing to do with the eschatology of the New Testament.'[5] We would not here comment on Bultmann's theology as a whole. We will, however, emphasize that his work brings out the Protestant conception of being. It matters little that, in his interpretation of the Christian event of salvation (*das christliche Heilsgeschehen*) Bultmann uses the categories of Heidegger. For he says himself that Heidegger's *Existenzphilosophie* would be unthinkable without Kierkegaard and Luther. It is difficult for Protestantism to resolve the tension between time and eternity, history and grace in a way consonant with revelation; for its conception of being is unworldly, dialectic, hidden in the sense of an eschatological existence in which God's grace is always in the future. Protestant theologians refuse to admit that this world has a significance of its own, whether, like Künneth, they see eschatology *sub specie resurrectionis*, or, like P. Althaus, spiritualize and idealize eschatology by placing it outside time and space[6] (though in his later works he sees history in a more favourable light), or, like C. Stange, following the authentic Lutheran tradition, assigns the outward life to the law and the inward life to the Gospel.[7] The break with history becomes most evident in dialectical theology. E. Brunner writes that 'from the existential point of view the temporal is insignificant, spirit is unrelated to time; thought and sense within time is nonsense.'[8]

We have said before that in the sphere of ecclesiology this whole

---

[1] ibid., 130.
[2] On J. Schniewind's theses, ibid., 134.
[3] Cullmann, *Christus und die Zeit*[1], 80.
[4] Oepke, *Entmythologisierung des Christentums. Kerygma und Mythos*, vol. II, 175.
[5] Künneth, *Theologie der Auferstehung*, 200.
[6] *Heilsgeschichte und Eschatologie*, 1924.
[7] *Das Ende aller Dinge*, 1930.
[8] F. M. Braun, *Neues Licht auf die Kirche*, 115.

problem is seen as concerning the *Church* and the *Kingdom of God.* How are these related to each other?

According to one view, the Church is *identified* with the Kingdom of God. At Lausanne this was represented above all by the Orthodox.[1] Among Protestants, the liberals consider the Kingdom of God as present on earth, basing themselves especially on Mark i, 15. Modern Protestants suspect that the doctrine of the Roman Catholic Church identifies the Church with the Kingdom of God.[2]

Another thesis, which may well be considered to be the general Protestant view, *distinguishes* between the Church and the Kingdom.[3] There are, however, differences of opinion among the proponents of this distinction. Some of them arrived at it by way of a sociological conception of the Church, represented e.g. by Schleiermacher.[4] The Kingdom of God was regarded as an eschatological and apocalyptic, the Church only as a human and sociological entity. In this way, however, the two could not be brought together. Later a solution of the problem was approached more closely by emphasizing the charismatic and pneumatic presence of the Kingdom (cf. Matth. xii, 28; Luke xvii, 20 f.; Rom. xiv, 17; Gal. v, 22) and the eschatological basis of the Church. Nevertheless, the principal question remained: How are the Church and the Kingdom of God related to each other? Several answers were given. G. Gloege tried to define the Church as the organ of the Kingdom of God,[5] without, however, making any more definite statement about this organ. Karl Barth, who strongly emphasizes the difference between the Church and the Kingdom,[6] understands the Church as the Kingdom of God in time.[7] For the 'New Consensus' the Church is situated within the Kingdom, the frontiers of history are enlarged. But the Kingdom is also within the Church, for that which transcends history is actualized in history.[8] Through Jesus Christ the Kingdom is introduced into the present age. According to Origen, Christ Himself is the

---

[1] 'The Kingdom of Christ is not merely the reign of grace in the hearts of men; it is the organized and visible Church,' Bate, Lausanne, 155.

[2] Cf. Michel, *Das Zeugnis des Neuen Testamentes*, 30.

[3] Cf. H. J. Wotherspoon, in Bate, 157.

[4] 'The Christian Church is formed by the association of individual re-born men towards an orderly working upon and with one another.' *Der christliche Glaube*, § 115.

[5] *Reich Gottes und Kirche*, 1929, 257; cf. K. L. Schmidt, *RHPR* XVIII (1938), 154. 'The Church is God's organ for His Kingdom. She is not herself the eschaton, but she is directed towards it and in this sense eschatological.' Visser't Hooft, *Misère et grandeur de l'Église*, 14.

[6] Cf. *Credo*, 128 f.

[7] ibid., 123.

[8] Braun, *Neues Licht*, 150.

auto-basileia, a concept taken up by K. L. Schmidt.[1] Christ, who is the Kingdom, gives those who belong to Him a share in it.[2] This thesis was also defended by the authors of the preparatory material drawn up for the Lund Conference: 'Theologians of many different communions now recognize that the future Reign of God, the coming Kingdom, was regarded by Jesus as in some sense present. . . . The "reign" is embodied in him.'[3] But it seems to me that the concentration on the historical figure of Jesus Christ contains the danger of a Christological contraction (*Engführung*). For it might mean that once, indeed, the Kingdom shone forth in history, but that it disappeared again, or at least became completely hidden, with the Ascension, and has now to be waited for until the end of time in the Parousia. In this view the Kingdom of God would only be a point-like 'event' that happens, wherever Christ approaches man through the kerygma, hence a totally hidden, invisible entity that can be experienced only in faith.[4] Surely what is at stake here is the concept of the whole Christ who consists of Head and members and who continues to exist mystically here on earth even after the Resurrection of Jesus Christ. Before Lund, the Oecumene seemed to be moving towards this insight, at least as far as the theological commission of Faith and Order was concerned: 'The Church is eschatological as the people of God on pilgrimage towards the future Reign of God. It is the Church Militant (*in via*) on the march towards the Church Triumphant in the world to come. At the same time the Church is sacramental in the sense that in and through human words and bodily acts . . . the Kingdom of God which is to come is also present here and now. The eschatological and sacramental character of the Church are thus quite inseparable. . . . The Kingdom of God "broke into" the world at the first coming of Christ in holiness. It will "break right through" at His second coming in glory. The new creation is already present in those who are in Christ; at the same time it is yet to come for all believers.'[5]

Unfortunately at Lund this new trend seems to have been obscured again by the ideas of Schlink.

At present the concept of 'realized eschatology' is used to express the fact that the Kingdom of God is a present as well as a future reality. This is increasingly gaining ground in the Oecumene and is

---

[1] *RHPR* XVIII (1938), 151 5.
[2] Cf. R. N. Flew, *The Nature*, 74.
[3] *The Church*, 44 f.
[4] Thus e.g. Némégoz, in Braun, *Neues Licht*, 126 f.
[5] *The Church*, 45 f., 58.

developed in this country especially by H. C. Dodd.[1] History has been fulfilled in a series of events, that is to say in the life, death and resurrection of Jesus Christ. Here the *eschata* were experienced; in the coming of Jesus eschatological hope found its true fulfilment. Hence eschatology has already been realized in Christ. Nelson states that English-speaking Protestantism 'in particular' gave 'a warm reception to Dodd's interpretation of eschatology'.[2] Other theologians, however, thought that it emphasized the present at the expense of the future.[3] Indeed, Dodd invited criticism when considering e.g. the Last Judgement merely 'as a mythological and symbolic statement of Christian teleology'.[4]

It seems that all these attempts to concentrate the presence of the Kingdom of God in the historical person of Jesus Christ betray a characteristic of Protestant thought, which tends to regard the history of salvation (*Heilsgeschichte*) as completed with Jesus Christ and the apostles. Now is the time of 'realized eschatology', because the fact of the Cross is *eph' hapax* behind us.[5]

We see how difficult it is for Protestantism to maintain the balance between present and future, between history and eternity. Its basic tendency is to depreciate the historical and the concrete; God's sovereignty is thought to be safeguarded by reducing the importance of creatures. When discussing the question whether the Church is an organism or an organization we had found what now becomes once more evident: time, and thus the formal visibility of the Church, have no meaning of their own. The Church is merely the sphere where the divine manifests itself.[6] Protestantism lacks the category of the Incarnation in which both divine and human things can be grasped in their indissoluble—though unconfused—unity. Because the Word was made flesh, eternity has invaded time and already broken through it, even though the manifestation of final glory is still to come. 'Father, ... the glory which thou hast given me, I have given to them' (John xvii, 22).

[1] In *The Kingdom of God and History*, vol. III, London, 1938, 23.

[2] *The Realm*, 220.

[3] Cf. ibid., 221, n. 42.

[4] *History and the Gospel*, 1937, 168–71.

[5] Cf. T. Strothmann, *Irénikon* xxv (1952), 250.

[6] Compare Bishop Leslie Newbigin's decisive criticism of this theology of the 'event' of the Reformers and Karl Barth: 'The obvious defect of this conception ... is that it gives no real place to the continuing life of the Church as one fellowship binding the generations together in Christ. It makes of the Church practically a series of totally disconnected events.... There seems to be no place in the picture for a continuing historical institution. The eschatological has completely pushed out the historical' (*The Household of God*, 50).

In the Oecumene the eschatological situation of the Church is frequently expressed by the term 'God's people'. 'The Church is a community of forgiven sinners eagerly expecting and patiently watching for the final consummation of its redemption. It continues to be a pilgrim people in a strange land. . . . At the end of its pilgrimage Jesus Christ . . . will come again to meet His Church in order to complete His work of redemption and judgement.'[1] The concept of God's people expresses especially the connexion of the Church with the Old Covenant. The Church of Jesus Christ appears in the continuity with Israel. But in applying the concept of 'people' to the Church it should not be overlooked that the conditions for God's people have changed in the New Covenant. The Old Testament Church was wholly under the promise: its members died 'not having received the promises, but beholding them afar off and saluting them and confessing that they are pilgrims and strangers on the earth' (Heb. xi, 13; cf. xi, 14–16, 33, 39 f.). But the promises of the Old Covenant are fulfilled in the New (Eph. iii, 6; cf. Acts iii, 18; xiii, 23; Rom. i, 1 ff.; xv, 8; 2 Cor. i, 20). The old order of salvation was a covenant, but God left Israel when it turned away from Him. Christ is being awaited, and the Spirit of God comes to it only at times and unexpectedly. 'The order is essentially prophetic'.[2] In the new order, things are different. What had been unexpected and transitory in the Old Covenant, now becomes certain expectation (cf. Matt. xvi, 18), the promises are to be fulfilled. Thus 'the order of the Church is no longer prophetic, but apostolic'.[3] Hence the eschatology of the Old Covenant differs from that of the New,[4] and so the concept of God's people must be transformed if it is to be applied to the Church of the New Covenant. 'The Church is the reality of something that has come, which only consummates and perfects itself: she is the Body of Christ, the Spouse of Christ.'[5] Hence it was rightly said at Lund that if the starting-point for considering the unity of the Church was to be the concept of the people of God, this would have to be related to the other designations of the Church in the New Testament, all of which emphasize its unity. 'This new people of God is described in the New Testament as the Body of Christ . . . as a "people belonging to God",

---

[1] Tomkins, *Lund*, 19 f.

[2] 'Le régime est essentiellement prophétique.' Congar, *Vraie et fausse Réforme*, 79.

[3] 'Le régime de l'Église n'est plus prophétique, mais apostolique,' ibid.

[4] Cf. O. Cullmann, *Christus und die Zeit*, 70 f.

[5] 'L'Église est la réalité d'une chose advenue qui achève seulement de se plénifier: elle est Corps du Christ, épouse du Christ.' Congar, loc. cit., 80.

who share in common the gifts of the One Spirit.'[1] It seems that Schlink has neglected this. Pure eschatology misunderstands the conditions of the new order of salvation, and Protestantism seems to prefer taking its stand on this Old Testament prophetism. The prophetical conception is familiar to it, as will be seen later when we discuss its view of the ministry. Luther himself was certainly a prophetic type, and the concern of the Reformers was largely the same as that of the Old Testament prophets, namely the re-divinization of the world.[2] But this ought not to have led them to overlook the new, apostolic status of the Church. For the Incarnation has established a 'numinous' world, which has nothing to do with polytheism.[3]

But this does not imply a weakening of the eschatological character of the Church, of which Catholic doctrine is accused by Protestant theologians time and again. The Roman Catholic Church does not identify the Church with the Kingdom. She knows that the Church has sinful members and that the day of consummation has not yet come. The Church is in an intermediate state, an *entre-deux* as Congar expresses it.[4] This is a period of time which both separates and unites two points, that is to say Pentecost and the Parousia. It is traditional Catholic teaching that the Church is the pilgrim people of God. The twin concepts *in re* and *in spe* are at the centre especially of the Augustinian tradition. We may also refer to St Bonaventure's *Liber vitae* with its analogical pair *in via* and *in patria*. These theologians have understood the Johannine triad of *veritas, via* and *vita* to mean that we have, indeed, *veritas* and *vita*, but only in the state of *via*, of the way. The *heilsgeschichtliche* situation of the *conditio humani generis* must be taken into account also in the conception of the Church. The Church is situated between *pneuma* and *sarx*, i.e. between the synagogue and the Kingdom: the synagogue, which had been all expectation and promise, and the Kingdom, which will be the perfect reality. This is the eschatological situation of the Church, which contains the reality of the principle as well as the first appearance of the effective substance.[5] The Church is a reality that has come into being but is not yet perfected. Its essence is

---

[1] Tomkins, *Lund*, 23.

[2] On the relations of the Old Testament prophets and the role of the Reformers cf. Congar, loc. cit., 201 ff.

[3] Cf. on this K. Rahner, 'Die ewige Bedeutung der Menschheit Jesu für unser Gottesverhältnis,' in *Geist und Leben* 26 (1953), 284.

[4] *Vraie et fausse Réforme*, 170.

[5] ibid., 470.

development, transition from the substance of the first Adam to the wholeness of the second. From this point of view Congar has drawn attention to the dangers confronting the Church.[1] There is, first, the danger of Pharisaism. This is inclined to forget that religion is ultimately concerned with men; it prefers instead to concentrate on 'things', turning means into ends and regarding temporary arrangements as final. The other temptation is that of wanting to be the synagogue. Any change in the forms through which God realizes His work is rejected. The institution becomes formalistic, and the forms become rigid because they are made absolute. Congar says drastically but aptly: 'The body of the Church has grown, but its skin has not; hence it is in danger of breaking.'[2] It is undoubtedly a danger for the Church to make its home in this world and to become worldly, so that its members cease to regard themselves as strangers and pilgrims. But the eschatological situation of the Church admits neither of worldliness, nor, on the other hand, of an unwordliness such as Bultmann demands. For this would be an attack on the Incarnation. Since the Son of God has become man, history must be taken seriously; the temporal is not meaningless, the pure light of the Incarnation must not be broken.

With regard to the unity of the Church this means that it can be, and has been, realized on earth in the true Church. But this unity is an object of faith: *Credo unam ecclesiam*. However much men can 'see' the one Church, they must also believe in it. They must believe in its divine side just as they must believe that Jesus of Nazareth was the Son of God.

The French Dominican C.-J. Dumont has recently tried to elucidate the concept of eschatology in the Oecumene and to find the corresponding term for it in Catholic theology.[3] He starts from the twofold aspect of the Church and its unity. There is, on the one hand, the spiritual aspect, realized in the common participation in sanctifying grace, while, on the other hand, there are the visible elements of the Church. Now man so receives sanctifying grace that it develops into glory without substantially changing its nature, while the visible elements that constitute the Church here below will disappear in the next world. Inspired by the Eastern Church and modern Catholic theology, Dumont considers that this eternal

[1] ibid., 153 ff.
[2] 'Le corps de l'Église a grandi, mais pas sa peau. Alors, cela risque de craqué,' loc. cit., 171.
[3] *Vers l'Unité chrétienne*, No. 48, 1952.

manifestation of the realities of salvation in different modes but in the same substance corresponds to the concept 'eschatological'. 'In this sense we can say of the Church that she is an eschatological reality, for she is not only wholly directed towards the future coming of the Kingdom but actually represents its first-fruits even now, since the mystical Body of Christ which she is here, is the same as it will be in eternity, after the Parousia, except in its mode of being: in faith, in struggle, in growth while she is *in via*; in vision, in victory, in perfection when she will be *in patria*.'[1] In this sense Dumont also speaks of an eschatological aspect of the unity of the Church. We think, however, that his discussion of John xvii, 21 in this connexion might easily be misunderstood. For he concludes from this prayer of our Lord that He leads us towards a spiritual form of unity (*vers une forme spirituelle de l'unité*), because He presents His own unity with the Father as the type of the unity of His disciples, and because He did not make the visible unity of all believers the object of a formal promise, as e.g. the forgiveness of sins (John xx, 22, 23) and the primacy (Matth. xvi, 18). Now it is quite true that there is a unity of all men in the state of grace, which is the basis of Dumont's argumentation, and this unity can no more be perceived than grace itself. For God's grace is not tied to human mediation. All ecclesiology must certainly take this into consideration. There exists a direct intervention of the heavenly Christ through the Holy Spirit, for, as has been shown before, the invisible salvation is not absolutely restricted to the visible elements. 'Not everything comes from the visible apostolic apparatus.'[2] Congar points out that at the very beginning the Church had a St Paul, who was not one of the Twelve, and who received his mission not from Christ in the flesh but from Christ in glory, a fact he stresses particularly in his Epistle to the Galatians. The Schoolmen always taught that there is a *sacramentum tantum*, a rite without spiritual substance, and that God's omnipotence is not tied to the sacraments, that He can create the reality of salvation even without the visible signs of the Church. The work of the Holy Spirit cannot be identified with that of the ecclesiastical apparatus: 'This, we might say, is the portion of Protestantism: that element of the Christian revelation which, disregarded by an ecclesiology which too rigidly identified the work of the Holy Spirit with the operations of the ecclesiastical apparatus,

---

[1] Dumont, 'Zur Ökumenischen Eschatologie,' *HK* VIII (1954), 46.
[2] 'Tout ne vient pas de l'appareil apostolique visible.' Congar, *Vraie et fausse Réforme*, 481.

has in some measure justified the reaction of the Protestant Reformers.'[1] But, Congar continues, this element of the free act of God must not be constituted into a law and used as an acid 'to dissolve the very structure of God's work, the surest foundation He has created for bringing us the salvation and life won by Jesus Christ: His Church, which continues His corporal presence and action till He comes again'.[2] The encyclical *Mystici Corporis* adds to the juridical ties 'a further principle of unity arising from those three virtues which knit us most closely with God: Christian faith, hope and charity'.[3] These are the realities of grace, *virtutes supernaturales*. Sanctifying grace (but also the visible elements, above all the sacraments) has certainly an eschatological character in Dumont's sense. But can it be conceived as so spiritual and invisible as he does? Is not all grace *gratia Christi*, because He is the Mediator between God and man? Now Christ is both, God and Man.

Surely grace must therefore also have a bodily dimension, and Christian salvation must be governed by the fundamental law of the Incarnation and itself have an incarnational structure.[4] Hence salvation, though spiritual, is yet also ecclesiological. It must, however, be asked how this is to be reconciled with the abnormal cases in which a man is given grace without the intervention of visible ecclesiastical factors. In the case of non-Catholic Christians at least one such factor is always present, namely the sacrament of baptism. But what about those who are saved without being baptized?

It seems questionable whether Dumont's concept of the 'eschatological' is really that of oecumenical theology. He himself relates it to the conceptions of the Eastern Church, but our previous exposition of the oecumenical and Protestant views of eschatology could scarcely lead to such a result. But we see how the discussion of the nature of the Church gains in depth if we include the 'abnormal'

[1] 'C'est, pourait-on dire, la part du Protestantisme: l'élément de la révélation chrétienne qui, méconnu par une ecclésiologie qui identifiait trop l'oeuvre du Saint-Esprit et les opérations de l'appareil ecclésial, a en quelque mesure justifié la réaction des réformateurs protestants.' ibid., 482.

[2] 'Pour corroder et dissoudre la structure même de l'oeuvre de Dieu, ce qu'il a fait de plus certain pour porter jusqu'à nous le salut et la vie acquise en Jésus-Christ: son Église, qui prolonge sa présence et son action corporelle jusqu'à ce qu'il revienne,' ibid.

[3] *CTS*, ed. n. 70.

[4] Cf. Karl Rahner, 'Persönliche und sakramentale Frömmigkeit' in *Geist und Leben* 25 (1952), 412 ff. M. Schmaus, *Katholische Dogmatik*[4], III, 2: 'The theology of the ancient and of the Eastern Church does not consider grace and sacrament in isolation from each other. On the contrary, existence in grace is understood as sacramental existence,' 2, 3, 6, 7 and passim.

situation, on which French theologians build a theology of the relative. We believe that these considerations will provide us with a basis from which to approach the question of membership and of the *vestigia Ecclesiae*.

4. THE FRONTIERS OF THE CHURCH

(a) MEMBERSHIP

The nature of the Church and its unity can in a certain sense still be discussed theoretically. But it becomes an existential question if considered from the point of view of membership. Who is truly a member of the Church, of the Body of Christ, a participant in God's saving grace, and who is not? What are the conditions of membership? The answer to these questions will reveal the gravity of the oecumenical problem. What is at stake is salvation itself. Hence this problem must be treated very carefully.

In general we may say that the question of membership will be answered according to one's basic conception of the Church. Nevertheless, it cannot be denied that Protestant theologians have separated these two questions of the nature of the Church and of membership and have not paid much attention to the latter.[1] Nowadays the problem of membership has again come to the fore in the Oecumene, yet we would venture to say not quite so much as it deserves. For this problem, too, appeared in a new light when the different confessions and denominations were led out of their isolation into an oecumenical breadth of vision. If the Toronto Statement declares that the member churches of the Oecumenical Council need not recognize other 'churches' as churches in the true and full sense of the word, this must surely imply that other Christians need not be regarded as true and full members of the Church. This question became topical in Germany during the struggle of the Church under National Socialism. Were the 'German Christians' members of the Church? Why not? What were the terms of reference?

If the different opinions are to be brought to a common denominator, this means that very liberal and tolerant views will have to be combined with narrow ones. Perhaps it will emerge from these different standpoints that 'the calling of God through the Spirit by the revealing of His Word, and the response of the individual in

---

[1] Lutheran apologetics distinguish between living and dead members of the Church. 'We also confess and affirm that the hypocrites and wicked may also be members of the Church, in an external community of name and ministry. . . .' As the gloss in the decree of Gratian takes the word Church in the large sense (*large*), the wicked are members of the Church in a wider sense, 'only in name, not in works' (*Die Bekenntnisschriften der Evangelisch-Lutherischen Kirche*, 235 f.).

faith'[1] are the two elements constituting membership. In the course of this study it has become clear that these terms may conceal very different conceptions; hence to us they seem much too vague to constitute an ultimate standard of membership. God's action through the Spirit and the Word can be understood in such a spiritualistic sense and the individual answer of faith leaves so much room for ambiguity that it becomes possible to say with C. E. Raven: 'Those that are led by the Spirit of God, be they Jew, Turk, infidel, or heretic, are within its membership; all mankind belongs to it if having eyes they see, if their lives display the fruits of the Spirit, if they have love one toward another,'[2] or with certain Baptists: 'The one test of membership is the conscious experience of rebirth.'[3] As we have seen before, this question is complicated especially by the distinction between an inner and an outer sphere, between the invisible action of God and the visible acts of the Church that establish membership. One thing can certainly be said: the theologians of the Oecumene are agreed in principle that baptism is the surest sign of membership. Precisely this point of membership the Oecumene seems most anxious to discuss with the Roman Catholic Church. It was emphatically stated at Toronto that according to Roman Catholic doctrine, too, there are members belonging to the Church *aliquo modo* and *extra muros*; surely this must mean that certain Oecumenical Christians are asking themselves how far non-Roman individual Christians or even non-Roman Christian communions as such belong to the Church. The Catholic answer is not quite so simple and should not be given without qualifications, as is sometimes done when it is asserted that a person who does not belong to the visible Roman Catholic Church is not a member of the mystical Body, hence cannot obtain salvation. Let us then examine the teaching of Pius XII's encyclical *Mystici Corporis*[4] on the nature of the Church with regard to the conditions of membership.

In it the Pope considers the Church particularly as the mystical Body of Jesus Christ. Being this Body, the Church is unique, indivisible and visible, and the encyclical is particularly concerned with this external, palpable reality. 'It is therefore an aberration from divine truth to represent the Church as something intangible and

---

[1] Nelson, *The Realm*, 171.

[2] *Jesus and the Gospel of Love*, 1931, 447.

[3] Cf. Nelson, op. cit., 170.

[4] *AAS*, XXXV (1943), 193 ff.

invisible, as a mere "pneumatic" entity.'[1] This stress on visibility also removes the error of regarding this entity as 'joining together by an invisible link a number of communities of Christians in spite of their difference in faith'.[2] Hence the holy, catholic and apostolic Roman Church is the only true Church, as had already been taught by the *Constitutio de fide catholica* of the Vatican Council.[3] Now this statement restricts the Church to the *Ecclesia militans*.

Who is a member of this Church?

The encyclical says emphatically: 'By baptism those who have been born to this mortal life are regenerated from the death of sin and made members of the Church',[4] Hence baptism constitutes membership. However, several other conditions are enumerated: 'Only those are to be accounted really members of the Church who have been regenerated in the waters of Baptism and profess the true faith, and have not cut themselves off from the structure of the Body by their own unhappy act or been severed therefrom, for very grave crimes, by the legitimate authority.'[5] 'It follows that those who are divided from one another in faith or government cannot be living in the one Body so described, and by its one divine Spirit.'[6] Thus, apart from baptism, the further condition of membership is, positively, the true faith and unity under the primacy, and negatively freedom from excommunication. Hence excommunication destroys membership. The sinner remains a member, whereas schism, heresy and apostasy 'are such of their very nature that they sever a man from the Body of the Church'.[7] Members completely severed from the body are separated from the life of the organism: 'For He (the Spirit of Christ) refuses to dwell by sanctifying grace in members that are completely severed from the Body.'[8] But the true love of

[1] 'A divina veritate ii aberrant, qui Ecclesiam ita effingunt, ut neque attingi neque videri possit, sique tantum "pneumaticum" aliquid,' ibid., 199; CTS edition, 14.

[2] 'Christianorum communitates, licet fide a se invicem seiuncta, inter se tamen haud adspectabili nexu coniungantur,' ibid., 200; CTS 14.

[3] 199; Cf. also *'Humani generis'*, *AAS* XLII (1952), 571.

[4] 'Per lustralis aquae lavacrum . . . qui sunt mortali vitae huic nati, ex peccati morte renascuntur et Ecclesiae constituuntur membra,' ibid., 201; CTS 18.

[5] 'In ecclesiae autem membris reapse ii soli annumerandi sunt, qui regenerationis lavacrum receperunt veramque fidem profitentur, neque a corporis compage semetipsos misere separarunt, vel ob gravissima admissa a legitima auctoritate seiuncti sunt,' ibid., 202; CTS 21.

[6] 'Qui fide vel regimine invicem dividuntur, in uno eiusmodi Corpore, atque uno eius divino Spiritu vivere nequeunt,' ibid., 203; CTS ibid.

[7] 'Suapse natura hominem ab Ecclesiae Corpore separent,' ibid., CTS 22.

[8] 'membra tamen, a corpore omnino abscissa, renuit (Christi Spiritus) sanctitatis gratia inhabitare,' ibid., 220;

the Church requires 'that in other human beings not yet united with us in the Body of the Church we should see brethren of Christ according to the flesh, called with us to the same eternal salvation'.[1] The Pope says that it is his pastoral care and that he desires nothing better than that also those 'who do not belong to the visible structure of the Catholic Church'[2] should have life abundantly, for at the moment they are in a state 'in which they cannot be secure of their own eternal salvation; for, though they may be related to the mystical Body of the Redeemer by some unconscious yearning and desire, yet they are deprived of those many great heavenly gifts and aids which can be enjoyed only in the Catholic Church'.[3]

Therefore they should enter Catholic unity, 'not as strangers, but as those who are coming to their own father's home'.[4] We see that these passages from the encyclical are not univocal in their teaching on membership. On the one hand a man becomes a member by baptism and is ordered towards the mystical Body of Christ at least by the *votum Ecclesiae*, on the other he is separated from the Church by heresy, schism and apostasy. How can these statements be reconciled?

Here begins the work of the theologians, which is not easy, because the encyclical speaks about the Church and membership in metaphorical terms. It is the task of the theologians to translate this figurative language into theological terminology, which, however, needs a different approach and can never result in an exact equivalent.

The interpretation of the membership visualized by the encyclical has not been unanimous; it has been said that canonists and dogmatic theologians have given contradictory interpretations. The canonists have a secure basis from which to start in canon 87 of the *CIC*: 'By baptism a human being becomes a person (*persona*) in the Church of Christ with all the rights and duties of a Christian, unless, as regards the rights, there is an obstacle impeding the bond of ecclesiastical communion, or a censure imposed by the Church.'[5] It

---

[1] 'ut alios homines nobiscum nondum in Ecclesiae corpore coniunctos, fratres agnoscamus Christi secundum carnem, una nobiscum ad aeternam salutem evocatos,' ibid., 240, CTS 95.

[2] 'Qui ad adspectabilem non pertinent Catholicae Ecclesiae compagem,' ibid., 242; CTS 102.

[3] 'In quo de sempiterna cuiusque propria salute securi esse non possunt; quando-quidem, etiamsi inscio quodam desiderio ac voto ad mysticum Redemptoris Corpus ordinentur, tot tamen tantisque coelestibus muneribus adjumentisque carent, quibus in Catholica solummodo Ecclesia frui licet,' ibid., 243; CTS 102.

[4] 'Non tamquam alienam, sed propriam paternamque domum adituros,' ibid.

[5] Baptismate homo constituitur in Ecclesia Christi persona cum omnibus Christian-

seems striking at first that the Codex here speaks of *persona*, not of *membrum*, which might have been suggested by the sources of can. 87. But, in keeping with the peculiarity of Canon Law the lawgiver changes from figurative language to conceptual theological terminology. The juridical term *persona* used by the Codex describes two orders: the order of being, in which the person *is* with his juridical power either in active or passive form, and the order of action, which is based on the order of being and in which the person is active according to his active or passive potency.[1]

From these two orders Mörsdorf deduces constitutional and active spheres of membership. Baptism is essential for constitutional membership: a man comes into the Church not by his own activity but by a 'birth from above'.[2] The sources of the Codex are the well-known utterances of Leo IV,[3] Eugenius IV,[4] Benedict XIV[5] and Pius IX.[6] Because of the indelible character of baptism constitutional membership is indestructible, hence cannot be lost in any way whatever. Mörsdorf compares it with membership of a family. A child is born into a family; it may renounce it or be expelled from it, yet nothing can dissolve the blood relationship which binds the child to his family.[7] Mörsdorf considers that the constitutional, indelible membership is expressed in the encyclical where the Pope mentions the sacramental birth of the children of the Mother Church through baptism and where he calls the separated members not strangers but men who return to their father's house.[8] Hence heretics and schismatics belong to the Church within the sphere of this constitutional membership.

This view has been criticized by Karl Rahner.[9] He thinks that the Canon and its sources refer to the normal case of baptism, i.e. baptism in the Catholic Church, and especially infant baptism. Moreover, the encyclical says exactly the opposite 'if it declares of

---

orum juribus et officiis, nisi, ad jura quod attinet, obstet obex, ecclesiasticae communionis vinculum impediens, vel lata ab Ecclesia censura.'

[1] Cf. Mörsdorf, 'Die Kirchengliedschaft im Lichte der kirchlichen Rechtsordnung,' in *Theologie und Seelsorge* I (1944), 116 f.

[2] ibid., 118.

[3] Cf. Denz., 324.

[4] Cf. ibid., 696.

[5] cit. in Gaspari-Serédi, *Codicis Juris Canonici Fontes* (Rome, 1923–35) II, 394, 197.

[6] ibid., 510, 856.

[7] *Die Kirchengliedschaft*, 119.

[8] ibid., 130.

[9] 'Die Zugehörigkeit zur Kirche nach der Lehre der Enzyklika Pius XII. "*Mystici corporis Christi*",' in *ZkTh* 69 (1947), 129–88.

schism, heresy and apostasy that their effect is: *hominem ab Ecclesiae corpore separari*'.[1] According to Rahner the argument from Canon Law is too abrupt in reasoning directly from the fact of being subject to the Church's jurisdiction to the membership of the person so subject. One who is passively subject to the legal claims of the community is not necessarily also a member of it. The only effect of baptism which certainly occurs at every baptism is the *character sacramentalis*. Rahner admits that it includes a disposition towards Church membership 'in so far as the character, being *signum configurativum*, *distinctivum* and *dispositivum* is the presupposition and root of all the effects of baptism'.[2] But the other effects of baptism are not given together with the character, and the same holds good for membership of the Church. The canonistic view places the cleavage between membership and non-membership at baptism, and thus the dividing line 'runs along the plane of inner personal being, that is between those who are justified and those who are not'.[3] This dividing line ought rather to be drawn on the visible, historical and juridical plane, hence also on the plane of the sacramental sign. But in this case it is incomprehensible 'why baptism should rank above union with the Church's unity of faith and law as far as Church membership is concerned'.[4] Rahner considers the thesis of constitutional membership of the Church impossible especially because, if all baptized Christians belonged to the Church, 'the communion of the Church would be constituted also by those groups of baptized persons who have associated in other Christian denominational communions. Thus the Church would be the sum of Christian confessions, a view which the magisterium of the Church rejects explicitly and emphatically.'[5]

Now what is the answer to this?

1. It can on no account be assumed that the Canon and its sources refer only to the normal case of baptism. The verbal terms of a law are normally very exact, and it cannot be supposed that just in this case of a fundamental decree on the foundation of the ecclesiastical legal personality the legislator should have been lacking in precision.

2. The encyclical also declares the excommunicated person to be separated from the Body of the Church. Rahner restricts this to the *excommunicatus vitandus*. According to him, it had until then been a matter of controversy whether such a person still belonged to the

---

[1] ibid., 142.
[2] ibid., 143.
[3] ibid., 144.
[4] ibid.
[5] ibid., 133 f.

Church; the encyclical had now decided authoritatively that an *excommunicatus vitandus* was deprived of Church membership. No essential objection could be made on the grounds of can. 2257. For there was a difference between *excommunicatus vitandus* and *toleratus*, because the latter was still in possession of ecclesiastical dignities and offices, and thus 'of course must still possess Church membership'.[1] This distinction seems unjustified. Even an *excommunicatus vitandus* could, for example, be elected Pope. Thus someone who, according to Rahner, is not a member could from the moment of his acceptance of the election hold the highest ecclesiastical authority. The rite of excommunication in the *Pontificale Romanum* also speaks of a separation from the Body of the Church. As is shown by the formula of reconciliation the actual ban of the Church is a real exclusion. But exclusion from what? From the *communio fidelium*. Hence it is said in the reconciliation: 'I restore you to the bosom of Holy Mother Church and to the fellowship and communion of all Christendom, from which you have been separated by the sentence of excommunication, and I re-admit you to the sacraments of the Church.'[2] The expression *exclusio a communione fidelium* seems important to us. This exclusion which takes place in every excommunication is not identical with exclusion from Church membership, as is clearly shown by the legal position of the *excommunicatus toleratus*. But there is no essential difference between the *excommunicatus toleratus* and the *excommunicatus vitandus*. It seems that the separation of heretics and schismatics has also to be placed within this sphere of removal from the communion of the faithful. It is true, the heretic is separated from the Church, but not from the sphere of constitutional membership. The term *separari* used in the encyclical must refer to another plane.

3. Rahner would first have to prove that a passive object of the legal claim of a community is not for this reason also a member of this community. Of course, a non-member can be a passive object of the claim of a community in the same sense that a non-member can, by reason of a private tenancy agreement, be the object of a claim of a community to payment of rent. But it is quite a different

---

[1] ibid., 148 f.

[2] 'Restituo te in gremium sanctae matris ecclesiae et ad consortium et communionem totius Christianitatis, a quibus fueras per excommunicationis sententia eliminatus; et restituo te participationi ecclesiasticorum Sacramentorum.' *Pontificale Romanum*, Summorum Pontificum jussu editum; a Benedicto XIV et Leone XIII recognitum et castigatum, Turin, 1941.

matter to be bound by the laws of a community without belonging to it. Where does such a situation exist?[1]

4. If the essence of the sacramental character consists in that threefold distinctive mark, then this character includes membership, which consists precisely in this *configuratio* and *distinctio*.

5. The looser membership of the Church of the non-baptized just man is surely essentially different from the looser membership of the baptized non-Catholic. This is more than a difference in degree. According to the view of canonists the Church membership of the baptized non-Catholic is definitely on the plane of the sacramental sign, for baptism can be apprehended historically as well as juridically.

6. Even though the Church cannot be equated with baptism, and though she is also a community, this does not mean that dissident communities would also be cells of the Church. Besides, there remains the visible unity of the Church through the unity of faith and jurisdiction, even though apostate members do not submit to the bond of faith and to the jurisdiction to which they ought to be subject. Hence Rahner's objections are not convincing.

Now how does Mörsdorf seek to solve the difficulties that have appeared? Besides constitutional membership he also speaks of active membership—according to the order of a person's activity—both in the inner and the outer spheres. In the active order the community of the Church strives to realize God's kingdom by accepting God's saving gifts. If this active membership is realized in the inner sphere it remains secret and invisible; if in the outer sphere, it is, or can become, publicly known and concerns the well-being of the community as such. Now Mörsdorf says that there is also an inmost sphere of membership 'to which the law may indeed lead, but which it may not enter: the sphere of the invisible action of the Spirit of God who is the soul of the mystical Body of Christ and thus the most intimate principle of the unity of the Church. Before this forum of the Spirit of God it is finally decided whether, in the order of action, a constitutional member of the Church is to be considered active or passive'.[2] It is quite possible that a member who is passively active in the external sphere may be actively active in the inmost sphere, and vice versa. [3]According to Mörsdorf, active

---

[1] Cf. W. Onclin, Considerationes de iurium subiectivorum in Ecclesia fundamento ac natura: Eph. iur. can. 8 (1952), 9–23.

[2] *Die Kirchengliedschaft*, 128.

[3] ibid., 129.

members are such as are in undiminished possession of their essential rights of membership. In the case of the passive members the general rights of membership have been fundamentally severed. Nevertheless, even the passive members do not cease to be constitutional members of the Church.[1] The final decision on activity or passivity, however, is made before the forum of the Spirit of God.

Comparing this notion of membership with the encyclical, Mörsdorf comes to the conclusion that 'the definition of membership given in the encyclical is concerned with the actively-active membership, and first and foremost with that of the external sphere'. As has been said, the encyclical is interested only in the visibility of the Church. Hence the concept of membership is seen from this point of view. The sphere of active membership is suggested by *reapse*; this includes the idea of completeness, leaving room for an inchoate, diminished, partially or totally invisible, anomalous, but nevertheless real membership.[2]

This, however, as Mörsdorf rightly states, does not mean that constitutional membership, irrevocably conferred by the valid reception of baptism, could or should be denied.

The encyclical does not mention the Spirit of God in this context. This is not surprising, since it envisages only the external sphere. In this connexion its expression *omnino abscissum* should also be given due consideration. For this term refers to members in whose case the last uniting bond of the Holy Spirit has been severed. Summing up, we may say that heretics, schismatics, apostates and excommunicated Catholics belong to the Church but are not its members, according to the point of view from which the question is examined. Here the

---

[1] ibid. The three marks of membership are exactly defined in Eichmann-Mörsdorf, *Kirchenrecht* I[7], 183–90.

[2] Cf. M. Nothomb. P. B., 'L'Église et le Corps mystique du Christ,' *Irénikon* xxv (1952), 242. D. C. Lialine distinguishes degrees of membership in the mystical Body of Christ analogous to the various degrees in which Christ is the Head of all men according to St Thomas (*Summa Theol.*, III, qu. 8, a.3): '(a) Whoever is baptized, confesses the true faith and is not excommunicated, is visibly and actually a member of the mystical Body. (b) Though one of these three visible elements may be missing, a man is visibly and potentially a member of this Body if he is ordered towards it by 'an unconscious desire and longing'. (c) If all three visible elements are missing a man is invisibly and potentially a member of this Body if he is ordered towards it by 'an unconscious desire and longing'.' 'Une étape en ecclésiologie, Réflexions sur l'encyclique *Mystici Corporis*.' *Irénikon* xx (1947), 43 f.

Under the aspect of the Church as sacrament J. Gribomont distinguishes between a wholly invisible membership of the *res* of the Church depending on good faith and grace, and an imperfect visible membership. The latter is that of the Protestant. From this point of view an Orthodox Christian is nearer to the Church than a Protestant; loc. cit., 361.

decisive factor is the conception of the Church. We may start from that of a corporation, according to Bellarmine's well-known definition: 'The Church is an assembly of human beings bound together by the profession of the one and the same Christian faith and communion in the same sacraments, under the government of legimately appointed pastors, and particularly of the one Vicar of Christ on earth, the Roman Pontiff.'[1] In this case a person not united to the Church by the threefold *vinculum symbolicum, liturgicum et hierarchicum* does not belong to its corporate body.

Another conception is based on the character of the Church as an institution, and hence includes all those among its members who are irrevocably incorporated in it by sacramental baptism.[2] Mörsdorf takes both conceptions into account, as indeed the encyclical *Mystici Corporis* mentions the theological virtues as the foundation of unity together with the juridical ties. They must never be separated from each other, and neither must be made an absolute, for the question of membership is not solely concerned with the notion of visibility, though this must always be included.

The mystical Body of Christ can be considered from various points of view. This becomes evident if the teaching of the encyclical is compared with that of St Thomas Aquinas. The latter starts from Christ, the head of the Body formed by its members, which is the Church,[3] while Pius XII starts with the Roman Catholic Church as the mystical Body whose head is Christ. Some theologians have seen an opposition between St Thomas and Pius XII.[4] Nothomb observes that it is quite possible for the magisterium to correct old positions, as was done e.g. in the case of the Immaculate Conception.[5] Speaking of the mystical Body, St Thomas always starts with the *gratia capitis* which is communicated to the members by a vital influx. Basing himself on this *vis influendi*, St Thomas defines as members of the mystical Body those who receive the supernatural communication

[1] 'Ecclesia est coetus hominum unius et eiusdem fidei christianae professione et eorundem sacramentorum communione colligatus, sub regimine legitimorum pastorum ac praecipue unius Christi in terris vicarii, Romani Pontificis.' *De controversiis christianae fidei*. Lib. II, prima controversia *de ecclesia militante*, Lib. III, 2.

[2] Cf. N. Hilling, 'Die kirchliche Gliedschaft nach der Enzyklika *Mystici Corporis* und nach dem Codex Juris Canonici,' *Archiv. für katholisches Kirchenrecht*, 125 (1951), 127 f.

[3] Nothomb, op. cit., 228–32.

[4] e.g. Mitterer, *Geheimnisvoller Leib Christi nach Thomas von Aquin und nach Papst Pius XII*, Vienna, 1950.

[5] loc. cit 227.

of grace either *de facto* or *de jure*. Now this applies to all men, though in different ways; hence there are different degrees of membership. Thus the concept of member is not univocal, 'it is an analogical and proportional notion, capable of being realized in different degrees'.[1] From the point of view of grace there are members *in actu* and *in potentia*.[2] Our question regarding Church membership of heretics and schismatics concerns members *in actu*.

Following St Thomas, Journet subdivides these members *in actu* into two categories:

1. The faithful who possess at least *fides informis*.

2. The heretics (Journet uses this term in the old sense: heretics are always sinners, they are not simply dissidents), who have the baptismal character and perhaps also that of confirmation and orders, but who have consciously renounced their former membership of the Church through the sin of heresy. They belong to it only in contradiction or by a kind of fatality. Journet calls this membership an *appartenance de servitude*, a 'compulsory membership'.[3] Hence, as has been stated above, the heretic both does and does not belong to the Church. As far as depends on himself, *ex parte sua*, he is an infidel and not a member of Christ and the Church because he has voluntarily abandoned the true faith. On the other hand, however, as far as depends on Jesus Christ, *ex parte autem Christi*, he is a member of Christ and His Church because of his baptismal character. Cajetan observes[4] that in the view of St Thomas this is the *fides informis*, by which we begin to be members of Christ *secundum quid*, in a certain measure. But, Cajetan continues, this membership *secundum quid* admits of various degrees.

As regards the unity of the mystical Body, according to St Thomas external visibility is not essential for it as such, but it is so for the *ecclesia militans*. His conception of the Church is very comprehensive; the Church embraces heaven and earth and all time, from Abel to the end of the world.[5] Hence the Church as the mystical Body is not limited to the earthly, Roman Catholic Church.

Thus Nothomb comes to the following conclusion: 'For our

---

[1] 'C'est une notion analogique et proportionelle, susceptible de se réaliser à des étages différents.' C. Journet, *L'Église du Verbe Incarné. Essai de Théologie spéculative* II, 1058.

[2] Cf. *S.Th.* III, qu. 8, art. 3.

[3] *L'Église du Verbe Incarné* II, 1060.

[4] *De comparatione papae et concilii*; Journet, loc. cit., 1061.

[5] III, *Sent.*, D. 13, qu. 2, a. 3.

Doctor the concept of "body"—Mystical Body or Body of the Church—does not by itself imply visibility, as for Leo XIII (*Satis Cognitum*) and for Pius XII, as we shall see. If the "Body of the Church" must be visible, this is so because its earthly condition requires it, not because the Church is a body.'[1] The question is whether the image of the Body of Christ in the encyclical has the same meaning. We must keep in mind that the encyclical understands the Body of Christ in a figurative sense. Pius XII restricts the figure to the *ecclesia terrestris*. Nothomb poses the question whether this stress on its visibility is opposed to St Thomas. He denies it, because the importance of the supernatural *influxus* of the Holy Spirit is preserved also in the encyclical. 'By that deeper communication, intimate and altogether sublime, which We mentioned above when describing the dynamic influence of the Head upon His members, Christ our Lord bids the Church live by His own supernatural life, makes His divine power pervade the whole of His Body, and feeds and sustains each member according to the place which it occupies in the Body.' 'This Spirit of Christ is the invisible principle to which we must also attribute the union of all the parts of the Body with one another and with their exalted Head,' says the encyclical.[2] Nothomb rightly asks: 'Hence, if outside the visible limits of the Roman Church some man is found favoured with the presence of the Holy Spirit—undoubtedly produced in him by the touch of an intervention, whether sacramental or even extra-sacramental, of the Roman Church and in any case directing him towards her—why should we not assign to him, even according to the statements of the encyclical, the quality of a real and true, though incomplete and invisible member of the mystical Body and hence of the unique Church of Christ?'[3] As regards the visible *structure* of the Catholic Church (*ad adspectabilem catholicae Ecclesiae compagem*), the dissidents

---

[1] 'C'est que, pour notre Docteur, le concept "corps"—Corps Mystique ou Corps de l'Église—n'implique pas par lui-même et directement la visibilité, comme ce sera le cas pour Léon XIII dans l'encyclique *Satis Cognitum* et pour Pie XII, comme nous le verrons. Si le "Corps de l'Église" doit être visible, c'est parce que sa condition terrestre l'exige, et non parce que l'Église est un corps.' *L'Église*, loc. cit., 233.

[2] CTS 53, 55.

[3] 'Dès lors, si en dehors des limites visibles de l'Église Romaine, tel homme se trouve gratifié de cette présence du Saint-Esprit—produite sans doute en lui par le touchement d'une intervention, soit sacramentelle, soit même extra-sacramentelle, de l'Église Romaine, et en tout cas l'orientant vers elle—, pourquoi ne pas lui reconnaître, selon les données mêmes de l'Encyclique, la qualité de membre, réel et véritable, quoique incomplet et invisible, du Corps Mystique et donc de l'unique Église du Christ?' *L'Eglise*, loc. cit., 240.

do not belong to it, but, Nothomb concludes, not 'necessarily as regards the Church that is visible' (*ad adspectabilem Ecclesiam*).[1]

Since the encyclical also includes the souls in purgatory and in heaven in the mystical Body of Christ, a person can belong to this Body *actualiter* without being *actualiter* a member of the visible Roman Church. This view in no way defends the idea of an invisible Church. As *ecclesia militans* the Church is visible. But there are 'invisible members of this visible Church'.[2] Where are the dissidents to be included? In their case it will be best to speak, with Journet, Lialine, Congar, Chavasse and Nothomb, of a partially visible membership of the Church, but *virtualiter* or *en acte ébauché* (Journet), *in actu* by way of suggestion, as it were, since one or another of the three signs is missing. According to these authors the partially visible membership can be of three kinds:

1. Spiritual and living (*spirituelle et vivante*), e.g. in the case of the material heretic in the state of grace. He is an invisible member of the visible Church by grace, which produces in him a conscious or unconscious *votum* or *desiderium* (v. infra). This is the case if somebody positively rejects the Catholic Church in good faith because of an invincible error.

2. Material or enfeebled: the same without grace.

3. Material and rejected (*reniée*): those who, though baptized, have separated themselves in bad faith (*de mauvaise foi*).[3]

We see that the question of membership and of the frontiers of the Church cannot be answered in smooth, simplifying formulae.

(b) THE DOCTRINE OF THE VOTUM

The encyclical *Mystici corporis* speaks of those who, under the impulse of divine grace are 'related to the mystical Body of the Redeemer by some unconscious yearning and desire'.[4] What is this

---

[1] 'nécessairement à l'Église qui est visible,' ibid.

[2] Cf. A. Liégé, 'L'appartenance à l'Église et l'Encyclique *Mystici corporis Christi*,' *Rev. des Sc. Phil. et Théol.* (Oct. 1948), 355; Journet, *L'Église du Verbe Incarné*, 1941, I, 47f. II, 953, 1065; Taymans S. J., 'L'Encyclique *Humani generis* et la théologie,' art. cit. *Nouv. Rev. Théol.*, 73 (1951), 19; De Montcheuil, *Aspects de l'Église*, Paris, 1949, 138; Marchal, P. B., *L'invisible présence de l'Église*, Algiers, 1950, 10, 11, 14, 45–49; L. Richard, 'Une thèse fondamentale de l'oecuménisme: le baptême, incorporation visible à l'Église', *Nouv. Rev. Théol.*, 74 (1952), 491; W. van de Pol in 'Extra ecclesiam nulla salus', *Jaarboek 1951 Werkgenootschap v. Kath. Theol. in Nederland*, gedachtwisseling, bl. 26.

[3] Nothomb, loc. cit., 243. The question of membership has also recently been treated by Cardinal Julius Döpfner, under the title 'Die alleinseligmachende Kirche'. Cf. *Una Sancta* 10 (1955), No. 2.

[4] CTS 102.

desire or *votum*? Nothomb observes that traditional teaching has always understood it in the sense of a real disposition, the fruit of an authentic divine grace, which produces a real union. Now, if this is ontologically real and objective,[1] we must speak of a real membership even though imperfect and incomplete. Is this *votum* something quite subjective and interior? If this be the case, Karl Rahner asks why it should still be necessary for salvation to be mediated through the visible Church, seeing that a man can also receive God's grace outside the sacramental medium of the visibly 'historical' Church in a purely interior and spiritual personal decision.[2] We have met this question before, in the context of the eschatological view of the Church and the incarnational structure of grace. Rahner is particularly concerned with this structure, which is to be found in all his more recent theological writings. Hence he also looks for a quasi-sacramental visibility of the *votum ecclesiae* which he thinks he has found in the concept of 'God's people'. He sees all mankind as destined to be the people of God. According to him, this is a true reality based on the incarnation of the Word of God, not simply an abstract idea of something that ought to be. The historical reality of the people of God precedes the Church as a legal and social entity, but can become concrete on the juridical and social plane. In the people of God the Church exists in germ. And 'where, and in so far as the personal will to be God's people is there, a reality is grasped which is actually meant to become concrete on the legal and social plane'.[3] Here we are faced with the main problem of the doctrine of the *votum*, namely whether this does not place baptized and non-baptized non-Catholics more or less on an equal level. God's grace in the heretic of good faith has not a 'somehow' sacramental structure, for this structure belongs to it in the full and real sense. If the doctrine of the *votum* were understood differently, it might surely lead to eliminating the reality of baptism. Actually it can be applied lawfully and traditionally only to the unbaptized just. Rahner would like to support the doctrine of the *votum* with the concept of being. There is certainly something to be said for this, but it has its place rather in the doctrine of the *vestigia*. If the encyclical speaks of a *votum* which directs dissidents to the mystical Body, it envisages first of all not any extraordinary ways of grace but certain phenomena in the oecumenical sphere which show a desire for the fullness of truth

[1] Cf. Journet, op. cit. II, 1065 f.
[2] 'Die Zugehörigkeit zur Kirche,' *ZkTh* 69 (1947), 182.
[3] ibid., 185.

and the visible Church. The *Instructio 'De motione oecumenica'* states that this desire exists *afflante Spiritus Sancti gratia*. Hence we are inclined to say that such a *votum* can be found in the Oecumenical Movement, which seems to have an unquenchable desire for the one Church and thus for its divinely willed visibility.

Under the influence of this Movement Protestantism has developed an oecumenical faith, which may be regarded as a *votum ecclesiae* in the sense of the encyclical. Its positive characteristics are: (1) the recognition and confession of the division of Christendom as sin and guilt; (2) the surrender of a narrow individualist denominationalism, and the beginning of a new oecumenical solidarity which finds its living expression in oecumenical discussion; (3) a struggle for truth and a great desire for the unity of the Church. A theology of revelation is increasingly gaining ground, as the theology of the believing individual and the relativism of the old *religions-geschichtliche Schule* lose their hold. Theologians go back to the Bible and begin to consider tradition; old positions are subjected to objective criticism, and admitted to be in need of revision; (4) the faith of the Reformers with its centre of justification by grace alone has changed into the doctrine of the One Church as the centre of the Gospel. There is a growing consciousness that 'to be in Christ' means also 'to be in the Church'. (5) Thus there is a desire for knowledge and life in the fullness of Christ, expressed especially in the liturgical revival of certain confessions. This is connected with (6), a growing rejection of spiritualism and thus of the teaching of the Reformers on the invisibility of the Church and its means of grace.

All this, however, is not yet a common possession of the Oecumene. There is a difference between the Conferences of Faith and Order and those of the World Council of Churches. The *Herder-Korrespondenz* has had reason to speak also of a *votum contra ecclesiam* in the Oecumene, expressed, for example, in the obstinate refusal to recognize the unity of the Roman Church as binding and in the polemics against the primacy or Mariology. Nor can it be considered a *votum ecclesiae* to delay clearing up the Christological basis of the World Council and to permit old Christological heresies. In view of these facts the *votum ecclesiae* cannot be affirmed for the separated Christians, as has sometimes been done, without modification;[1] nevertheless, the above statements on the oecumenical faith may be considered positively, as a *votum ecclesiae*. In the near future it will probably be the special task of Catholic oecumenical theologians to

[1] Cf. *HK* VIII (1953), 32.

investigate this *desiderium dissidentium* for the day of unity, as says the *Instructio*, and to pursue the *votum ecclesiae* also in the individual denominations.

(c) VESTIGIA ECCLESIAE

There is, however, an even more important problem for a comprehensive ecclesiology, that of the *vestigia ecclesiae*, the remaining traces of the one true Church in the communities separated from the Mother Church. In the past, the frontiers of the Church have been defined too negatively by considering only what the separated Christians were lacking. Now, in his allocution of 9th January 1927, Pope Pius XI said of the separated Eastern Churches: 'Those parts that have separated from an auriferous rock themselves contain gold.' This statement provides a guiding principle for a positive oecumenical theology which ought to search for the 'gold content' in the separated Christian communions and to use the knowledge thus gained for furthering the reunion of Christendom. For we desire to know and acknowledge what signs of real Church life there are in the communions separated from Roman Catholic unity.[1]

At Toronto much attention has been given to these *vestigia ecclesiae*, the 'elements of truth in the individual churches', such as the preaching of the Word of God, the exposition of Holy Scripture and the administration of the sacraments. But as the Toronto Statement declares that they do not necessarily imply the validity and purity of doctrine and of sacramental life, these elements cannot furnish the right basis for a theology of the *vestigia*. If preaching, exposition and administration are not in accordance with revelation, then we shall indeed have to do only with 'dead relics'. For the problem of the Church is concerned with the reality that is at the root of all her functions. Hence it will be best first to ask what the Reformers meant by these *vestigia*. This may lead to fruitful conversations with oecumenical Christians.

Luther does not use the term *vestigia* itself, but has similar expressions; he speaks for instance of the *reliquiae* which God preserves.[2] Asking whether there are people in the Roman Church who are within the Church he answers in the affirmative, because the Papacy

---

[1] Cf. Congar, 'A propos des "vestigia ecclesiae"' in *Vers l'Unité chrétienne*, No. 39 (1952), 3; G. Thils, *Histoire doctrinale du mouvement oecuménique*, Louvain, 1955. Cf. the discussions of the historical problem of the doctrine of the *vestigia* in this book (183–7). Thils refers to his earlier work, *Les notes de l'Église dans l'apologétique catholique depuis la Réforme*, 1927.

[2] Lectures on the Book of Genesis, *WA* 42, 299.

has baptism, the Word, the Sacrament (Eucharist), the power of the keys, the Creed, the *vox evangelii*, the Lord's Prayer, the ministry, and the names of God and Christ. 'All these are things which we would call traces or elements of the Church, understanding by the latter the ecclesiastical institution,' as Congar says.[1]

But here we must remember that Luther assigns to these elements a meaning other than ours. According to him they are realized only by faith, and thus their proper content is diminished; the objective being is turned into an event that takes place. It is clear that the problem of the *vestigia* is seen differently from the Protestant and the Catholic angles. Because Luther's conception of the Church is that of *communio* he calls these elements signs, which in themselves need not be lies but which may be abused by men.

In Calvin's view the Papacy retains marks or signs of the Church which may, indeed, be abused, but which remain substantially notes of the Church.[2] But in this sense Calvin mentions only baptism. Hence there are in the Papal Church Christians and individual churches possessing the signs of the true Church. Congar asks our Protestant friends to tell us what, in Calvin's view, is the relation between the notes of the Church and the Church itself, and between the particular churches which Calvin recognizes in the Papacy and the Church itself.[3]

J. Hamer has made a similar study of the *vestigia* in the teaching of the Reformers.[4] He seeks to elucidate their meaning by distinguishing them on the one hand from the *points fondamentaux* of Calvin and his followers[5] and on the other from the *signa* or *notae ecclesiae* of the *Apologia* of Melanchthon.[6] He clearly shows from the Augsburg Confession, the *Apologia* of Melanchthon and the *Confession de foi* of Calvin, that the use of the term *vestigia ecclesiae* in the Toronto Document excludes any possibility of understanding it in the sense of the *signa* or *notae ecclesiae*.

Signa ecclesiae are the signs of the true Church which, according to the Protestant view, is present wherever the Gospel is preached in

---

[1] 'Ce sont là autant de choses que nous appellerions vestiges ou éléments de l'Église, entendant par là de l'institution ecclésiale.' *Vers l'Unité chrétienne*, No. 39 (1952), 5.

[2] Cf. commentary on Acts xxiii, 7; *Institutio Christiana* (Lat. ed. 1559, French ed. 1560), IV, 2, 11 and 12; Letter to Sadolet, éd. '*Je sers*', 71; *Confession de la foi de La Rochelle*, a. 28.

[3] *Vers l'Unité chrétienne*, No. 39 (1952), 5.

[4] 'Le baptême et l'Église. A propos des "vestigia ecclesiae" ', *Irénikon*, xxv, 142–64; 263–75.

[5] Cf. 143 ff.

[6] Cf. 146.

its purity and the sacraments are administered correctly. In Protestant usage the term *vestigia ecclesiae* has a derogatory sense, which is obvious in the Confession of Calvin: 'The relation of the Church, such as the Confession envisages it, to the Roman Church is therefore that of the true Church to a small trace of a Church.'[1] So it can be said both of the Protestant and the Catholic notion of the *vestigia* that it contains a *nuance péjorative*. But this should not prevent us from considering the *vestigia* in the non-Catholic communions from the Catholic point of view. For the Catholic the question of the *vestigia* concerns the order of being. The being can, indeed, be diminished, but not altogether destroyed. Thils defines the *vestigia ecclesiae* as 'certain authentic Christian values belonging to the Church which appear in non-Roman denominations because of the structure of these communions'[2]. These *vestigia ecclesiae* are not just any data of the Christian religion but are of a specifically ecclesiastical nature. One could speak of invisible and visible ecclesiastical elements, such as the presence of the Holy Spirit and the uninterrupted apostolic succession (e.g. in the Eastern Churches) respectively. Further, a distinction might be made between essential and accidental elements. The true Church can never be without the essential elements, and they do not admit of a more or less. The accidental factor concerns the mode in which each of these individual elements is actually realized. Here there may be different degrees and modes due to history. For there exists a possibility of development and progress as well as of decadence and regression.[3] Even though whole Christian communities may be separated from the Church, they will nevertheless retain some of its properties in varying proportions and modes.

Take for example the means of grace whose objective existence makes the Church an institution. These means of grace are varied; in their essence and totality they are to be found only in the Church of Christ and the apostles. They resemble a bundle from which parts may be separated. And one or other of these parts may exist like relics in another denomination, where it performs the same task as in the Catholic Church: it effects and mediates grace. Thus the Orthodox Churches, the Jansenists of Utrecht and the Old Catholics retain a valid priesthood which guarantees the validity of their Eucharist because they have the apostolic succession, even though they are

[1] 'Le rapport de l'Église, telle que la Confession la voit, à l'Église romaine est donc celui de la vraie église, à une petite trace d'Église.' loc. cit., 147.

[2] loc. cit., 187.

[3] Cf. J.–C. Dumont, *Approaches to Christian Unity*, 1959.

separated from the centre. Hence we may probably argue that all those Churches not in communion with the Petrine see are indeed outside the Catholic Church, 'but nevertheless the elements, some external and perceptible, others purely spiritual, which constitute this community and make it and it alone the Church of Jesus Christ, can be shared in different degrees.'[1]

With regard to an oecumenical attitude towards the separated Christian communions the doctrine of the *vestigia* offers a good foundation, of which Cardinal Döpfner writes: 'We want to be just not only to individual non-Catholics but also to other Christian denominations. Certainly, we must clearly recognize the errors which developed through their separation from the Mother Church. But we should not overlook that, through the sacred inheritance they have taken over, these communions accomplish for many the task of the Church according to God's plan. Hence we are sincerely happy if for example the evangelical Church leads its members to Christ by means of a vigorous and successful pastoral care, and we would consider it wrong to prevent this activity. This would only promote Godlessness and the disappearance of the Christian life. I would also mention Cardinal Newman, who even after his conversion held the Church of England in great respect and esteemed it as an opponent of errors even graver than its own.'[2] Now what are these elements of the true Church that can be found in the separated Christian communions?

1. *Jesus Christ*

Jesus Christ cannot be separated from His Church. Where He is there is the Church, and where the true Church is there is Christ. Hence the oecumenical Christians strive to find Christ more intimately, and by growing into Christ they hope to further the growth of the unity of the Church. Theologically this relation between Christ and the Church is expressed by the fact that Christology and ecclesiology are inseparable, indeed that all ecclesiology is also Christology and vice versa.[3] Now this implies that errors in Christology will have their repercussions in ecclesiology.

In our historical survey of the Oecumenical Movement we have repeatedly encountered Christological problems. They began even at the basis of the World Council of Churches which was to be

---

[1] ibid., 138.

[2] In Sartory, *Die katholische Kirche und die getrennten Christen*, (1957), 98.

[3] Cf. K. L. Schmidt, art. ἐκκλεσία *ThWzNT* III, 515, 21; Dilschneider, *Gegenwart Christi*, II, 252.

'faith in Christ as God and Saviour'. We have seen that the National Council of the Churches of Christ in the USA (the 'churches' united in it are members of the World Council) deliberately chose another formula as their foundation of faith: 'Jesus Christ as "Lord and Saviour".' Even leading theologians of the World Council like E. Schlink say of this 'basis of faith' that it is not necessarily an expression of the common faith in Christ, since it could also be understood in an anti-Trinitarian, i.e. modalistic or Patripassianist sense.[1] But we need not go as far as the Oecumene to find a contradictory Christology. We have already mentioned the words of F. Hübner, who said that the *dissensus* between Lutheran and Reformed theology goes to the very heart of Christology.

O. Dilschneider has attempted to determine the place of Christology in the age of the Reformation,[2] and we propose to follow his, in our view important, findings in our discussion. The Fathers of the first Christian centuries were concerned to elucidate the Person of Christ; they examined the *physis* of the God-Man, because there were Monophysites, Diophysites and exponents of a Logos-Christology. The Christology of the first five centuries places the emphasis on ontology; the work of Christ is of secondary importance, i.e. it is included in the ontological statement, for—and we would stress this more strongly than Dilschneider—a Monophysite or Nestorian Christology endangers the salvation of men. *Quod non assumpsit, non redemit*. With Luther and the other theologians of the Reformation, following in the footsteps of Anselm of Canterbury's *Cur Deus homo*, the work of Christ becomes the centre of Christology.

'Now soteriological Christology begins to take the place of the ontological Christology of Scholasticism.'[3] The statements of Melanchthon in the introduction of his *Loci* of 1521 are typical: 'To know Christ means to know His benefits, not, as is taught elsewhere, to contemplate His natures and the modes of His incarnation. What use would be the knowledge of His history if you did not know for what purpose Christ took flesh and was nailed to the Cross? Does St Paul in his Epistle to the Romans philosophize about the mysteries of the Trinity or the mode of the Incarnation? ... No, the apostle makes the law, sin and grace the centre of his teaching.' Luther's theology is determined by the soteriological point of view. The *Christus pro nobis* is the principal theme; Christ is seen wholly

---

[1] 'The Church and the Churches,' *ER* I (1949), 151.
[2] *Gegenwart Christi* I, 252.
[3] ibid., 256.

in the perspective of His redemptive work. To know Christ means to know the benefits He confers on us. Thus the question of the old Church, centred in the Person of Christ, was changed to the question: What do I gain from Christ? This question dominates Protestant theology even today, whether we think of Karl Barth, Vogel or Bultmann. Asmussen says that the evangelical Churches have apostatized from the old Christian doctrine: 'The evangelical Church drifted towards a development in which the old doctrine of the Person and work of Christ was almost lost. The Catholic Church has been spared this development.'[1] This shift of emphasis from the Person to the work of Christ made it difficult for Protestantism to pass from the second to the third article of the Creed. As Dilschneider says, we are concerned with a 'change of form' (*Gestaltwandel*) from Christ Jesus to the Lord in the form of the Holy Spirit, and thus to Christ in the Church. The Fathers spoke of the *totus Christus* who comprises the Head and its members. This unity was seen as being so close that, after the manner of a *communicatio idiomatum*, statements on Christ were applied to His visible Body, the Church. Such a conception was necessarily alien to a purely soteriological Christ-ology: '(The theology of the Reformers) was quite incapable of a Christological presentation of the Church as the Body of Christ, because all its theological concepts were shaped by a soteriological Christology'.[2] It is true that theologians speak today of an incarnation of Christ in the Church, of an 'extension of the incarnation',[3] or of a 'continuation of the incarnation'[4] but it makes a great difference whether these words are used by a Quaker[5] or by an Old Catholic.[6] For the 'Catholic' (in the sense of Amsterdam), the *incarnatio continuata* means that Christ continues His redemptive work on earth through the Church, or, more precisely, through its ministry and sacraments. The Catholic calls this incarnation of Christ in 'elements' 'created grace', because he is taught by the Council of Chalcedon that there is a legitimate connexion between divine and human things. The Protestant knows nothing of this. Hence he knows hardly any transformation of the Logos into creatureliness after the Ascension, and expressions like *incarnatio continuata* are

[1] *Warum noch lutherische Kirche?*, Stuttgart, 1949, 59.

[2] Dilschneider, loc. cit., II, 225.

[3] Flew, *The Nature*, 219.

[4] ibid., 268, 286.

[5] H. Haymann, *Worship and the Common Life*, Cambridge, 1944, 98.

[6] Cf. Flew, loc. cit., 155.

understood as 'a figure of speech'[1] or 'as a figurative statement that the Church seeks to make known by word and deed the redemptive significance of the Incarnation'.[2] It is valid only for 'the inner being of the Church',[3] but not for its formal visibility. Hence Nelson rightly says: 'If the Church is the extension of the Incarnation, we must revise our belief concerning the nature of the Incarnation.'[4]

For Protestants hold that this incarnation of Christ in the Church endangers the uniqueness of His Person and His redemptive work. In this case the Church would 'supplement' the incarnation of Christ, and this would mean that Christ was imperfect. Above all else, however, they fear that the doctrine of a perpetual incarnation of Christ in the Church would imply a deification of the Church.[5] According to them, the idea of extension is ruled out by the sinfulness of the Church.

* * *

DIGRESSION:

The Category of the Incarnational

We must leave our main subject for a moment to clarify the concepts used and to define the category of the incarnational with greater precision. Does the concept of the *incarnatio continuata* really lead to the identification of divine and human realities, the Person of Jesus Christ and the Church? A good Catholic ecclesiology will give a clear answer to this question. Going back to the reality of Christ does not mean deifying the Church, since Christ, too, was true God and true Man. It is an essential element of the Church that she is *ecclesia ex hominibus*. If the Church is Christ living on in the world, the formula of Chalcedon, two natures in one Person, can easily be applied to her.[6] The relation between Christ and the Church has been understood as a kind of parallelism by such prominent Catholic theologians as Möhler, Tyskiewicz, Perrone, Feckes, Sertillanges, Scheeben and Franzelin, as well as by Leo XIII in the encyclical

---

[1] Flew, op. cit., 286.

[2] ibid., 321.

[3] E. Lewis, *A Philosophy of the Christian Revelation*, London, 1948, 321.

[4] Nelson, op. cit., 97.

[5] Cf. R. Niebuhr, *The Nature and Destiny of Man*, New York, 1941.

[6] On the following cf. Congar, 'Dogme christologique et Ecclésiologie. Vérité et limites d'un parallèle' in Grillmeier-Bacht, *Das Konzil von Chalkedon* III, 239–86.

Satis cognitum. They speak of a theandric, divine-human structure of the Church.

The element of truth in this 'parallelism' is obvious. The Church belongs to God's economy of salvation, to His redemptive dealings with mankind. History shows one single plan of salvation. Hence the continuity with the incarnate Word may well establish a certain structural similarity with this Word. For it would hardly be possible to speak of the Church as the Body of Christ if its structure had nothing in common with Him. Nevertheless, 'parallelism' is not the right way towards a solution of our problem. For this rests on a romantic view of the Church. The unity between Christ and the Church cannot be understood in the sense of a natural organism. The humanity of Jesus was united with God according to its being (*secundum esse*). In the case of the humanity of Christ this union with God was brought about hypostatically, whereas the relation between Christ and the Church is a dynamic unity. The Church is an instrument of God in her human reality, which has its own proper value. Where this is overlooked, we are threatened with the danger of an ecclesial monophysitism, i.e. with a deification of the Church. There are certain acts in the Church which can derive only from a divine principle: these are the administration of the sacraments, the solemn exposition of the deposit of faith, the infallible *magisterium*. Besides these, however, there are many functions the material cause of which is the human side of the Church, and which are therefore subject to relativity, change and historical conditions. Congar draws attention to the fact that in religious instruction this human side is often passed over, and that therefore many of the faithful think for example, that papal encyclicals are 'infallible'.[1] Hence in the case of the Church we cannot speak of a divine nature or a divine personality in the strict sense. A direct *comunicatio idiomatum* between Christ and the Church is therefore impossible, nor can we speak of the Church as a continued incarnation of Christ without a precise definition of what this means. The relation between Christ and the Church is not a parallelism but an analogy, and in the case of the latter the unlikeness is always greater than the likeness.

But even the divine reality in the Church (*depositum fidei*, sacraments, ministry) is actualized in history, that is to say the divine elements appear in the state of their historical realization. Divine structures are joined to historical, i.e. relative, structures, and this has certain implications for the three constitutive elements.

[1] loc. cit., 247.

A. Dogma

The deposit of faith (1 Tim. vi, 20; 2 Tim. i, 12–14) is a divine reality, which God has given His Church through Christ. No human speculation can invent any truth of faith, which is the revelation of Christ, preached by the apostles at the very beginning of the Christian community. St Paul exhorts the Romans to obey 'that form of doctrine into which you have been delivered' (vi, 17). This deposit of faith consists of Scripture and the tradition transmitted by the apostles. Now what is the position of the Church with regard to this revealed deposit of faith? Modern theologians call the *magisterium* of the Church the *regula proxima fidei*, the proximate rule of faith, whereas Scripture and tradition are termed the *regula remota*, the remote rule of faith. This conception differs fundamentally from that of Protestants; Evangelical Christians cannot understand that for us Scripture is only *regula remota*; an explanation of this will also throw light on the nature of the Church.

1. The fact, object or deposit of faith is something given: *traditio passiva*; it is opposed to the transmitting activity, the preaching of the Church: *traditio activa*. The opposition of these two should be clearly understood.

2. The deposit of faith is governed by the inspiration of the Holy Spirit; it is the direct word of God; whereas the preaching is done only with the assistance of the Holy Spirit, *sub assistentia Spiritus Sancti*. This assistance of the Holy Spirit in the Church is something different from inspiration.

3. Hence the deposit of faith is the source of revelation. The preaching, that is the Church, is not the source of revelation but only *regula fidei*, a regulative norm which governs something that has already been constituted. The deposit of faith, that is Scripture and tradition, is the ultimate internal norm, while the preaching, hence the Church, is indeed also the ultimate, but only the external norm. The deposit of faith is an interior, constitutive principle; the preaching of the Church is certainly the proximate rule of faith, but an external and merely directive one (*mere directiva*).

The Vatican Council has endorsed this very important distinction by not including the Church in the causality of *fides divina*, divine faith. The sphere of Christ and the apostles differs essentially from that of the Church; there is a profound gulf between St Peter and the first Pope. The Pope can never be the bearer of revelation like the apostles; both Pope and bishops are only successors of the apostles, they act on an entirely different plane.

There is also another point. The doctrines of the Church contain an immutable divine truth. This is a clearly divine element. But this nucleus of immutable absolute truth is transmitted in human language. The Jesuit J. Ternus rightly says: 'The linguistic expression of a definition of faith such as that of Chalcedon is a creation of the Church of her time, and thus the divine revelation transmitted to the Church by the apostles is expressed in terms conditioned by this time. In contrast to the inspired divine Word of Scripture the human form of expression is here not formally the word of God, but the way in which the Church presents her decision as a binding rule of faith in her own name, by virtue of the teaching authority given to her.'[1]

Now it is quite true that the different doctrinal and confessional statements still divide the confessions in many ways; nevertheless, a new relation between the Catholic Church and evangelical Christians has developed because evangelicals have found a new relation to dogma. Exponents of a non-dogmatic Christianity can no longer be regarded as representative of the evangelical Church. Surely it is a great gain that separated churches today are teaching: 1. that dogma is rooted in the confession of Christ; 2. that it is the confession of the Church, i.e. that it does not originate in the formulae of an individual or a committee of theologians; 3. that dogma is opposed to erroneous teaching; 4. that on the Last Day salvation will be decided by dogma, hence the creed has eschatological validity, 5. That dogma has a binding authority for all believers.

Here we must carefully decide between dogma and theology. In this context the article of Edmund Schlink, 'Die Struktur der dogmatischen Aussage als ökumenisches Problem'[2] is of great importance. The author is in complete harmony with the Catholic Church when he rejects as a fundamental error 'an agreement on questions of common moral Christian action while eliminating doctrinal questions or even in principle declaring unity in dogmatic statements as irrelevant for unity in Christ.' We Catholics can further agree with Schlink in not regarding the postulated unity of dogmatic affirmations as uniformity in identical formulations. It is an eminent oecumenical task to consider in which different dogmatic statements the unity of doctrine can be recognized and acknowledged. We can only agree with Schlink on the necessity of philological and historical analysis; for 'the unity of dogmatic statements may be concealed under different

---

[1] 'Chalcedon und die protestantische Theologie'. In: Grillmeier-Bacht, *Das Konzil von Chalcedon* III (1954) 567.

[2] *Kerygma und Dogma* 3 (1957), 251-306.

terms'; it may even be 'hidden under apparently contrary affirma-tions'. It is equally important to take account of the anthropological conditions and of the place 'occupied by the various doctrinal state-ments in the context of the basic theological teachings'.

Hans Küng's book '*Rechtfertigung. Die Lehre Karl Barths und eine katholische Besinnung*' (Einsideln 1957) shows that misunder-standings are quite possible, but also that they can be cleared up. In his preface to the book Karl Barth writes: 'If the doctrine of the Catholic Church is really such as you develop it in the second part of the book, then I must certainly admit that my doctrine of justification agrees with yours.'

Our statement that unity of doctrine does not mean uniformity of formulations will perhaps surprise some Catholics who have not studied the early Christian Creeds. These, too, did not consist in identical formulae; but we must look out for the common truth in the different expressions. An evangelical Christian will probably be surprised to read this passage from the pen of a Catholic theologian: 'All human statements, including those in which faith expresses the divine truth of salvation, are human statements. This means: they never express a reality exhaustively ... True, we base ourselves on the Word of God which itself became "flesh" in human words, but what we say of the divine truths can never be altogether adequate. Our statements are not therefore false. They are "adequately true", in that they contain nothing false. If we were to call them "half-false", because they do not express everything pertaining to their subject, we would in the last resort abolish the absolute distinction between truth and error. But if, on the other hand, we were to regard such dogmas, because wholly true, as adequate to their subject, that is as exhausting it, we would wrongly identify human truth with God's simple and exhaustive knowledge of Himself and of all that has its origin in Him. If and because such dogmas are true—even though they are finite—there is yet an infinite qualitative difference between them and false statements, even though it may—perhaps often—be difficult to determine the dividing line between an inadequate and a false proposition in individual cases. Now our statements concerning the divine, infinite realities are finite and inadequate in the sense that they do, indeed, hit the mark but fail to cover their subject completely. For this reason every formula expressing the faith, though remaining true, may yet be superseded and, at least in principle, be replaced by another which says the same, but with certain additions and nuances. This means that it does not only not prevent, but actually opens up further prospects regarding facts, realities or truths which the earlier formula had not expressly envisaged. These new aspects will show the same reality in another light or in a hitherto neglected perspective.'[1]

This means for example that, as regards the doctrine of the Eucharist, the Aristotelian categories of substance and accident do not belong to faith in the sacramentally present Lord.[2] This mystery is defined as transubstantiation only *'aptissime'*, not *'unice'* (most suitably, not solely). It must, however, be admitted that such a method may also bring to light differences of meaning despite a similar terminology of the various denominations.

Another important point is Schlink's suggestion of the morphological examination of a dogmatic statement, in which its relation to the whole complex of a church's doctrine is to be investigated. Thus the Marian dogmas of the Catholic Church have also a profound Christological significance. As has been mentioned before, the doctrinal statements regarding the Blessed Virgin are bound up with the question of the being and proper reality of the creature. It has sometimes been said that the 'and' in Christ and the Church, Christ and Mary, Christ and the saints, faith and works etc. is a typically Catholic characteristic, whereas the specific hallmark of the Reformation is the 'alone': Christ alone, Scripture alone, faith alone and so forth. This opposition is not quite exact; for the 'and' is a basic form of the theological problem as such. For this 'and' does not at all mean an addition of equals, but a certain relationship between different persons or things. Both 'and' and 'alone' are qualified theologically. Creeds and doctrines have their background like all other theses; they reflect a quite definite problem, the elucidation of which is an oecumenical task. The discussion of this question makes it particularly clear how much the Church is *in via*, on the way, and, though being the infallible exponent of truth, is yet herself involved in the struggle for expression, for embodying truth in human language.

B. The Sacraments

This difference between divine essence and human forming (*Ausgestaltung*) in the deposit of faith is also present in the sacraments, the principal, though not the only vehicles of God's grace. Scripture bears witness to this fact by calling justification a birth from water and the Holy Spirit (John iii, 5 f.), by ascribing the

[1] Karl Rahner, *Schriften zur Theologie* I, (1954), 54.
[2] Cf. F. Selvaggi, 'Il concetto di sostanza nel Dogma Eucaristico in relazione alla fisica moderna'. *Gregorianum* 30 (1949) 7–45.

forgiveness of sins to being plunged into water (Acts ii, 38; viii, 16–18; Rom. vi, etc.) and by uniting eternal life to eating the flesh of Jesus Christ and drinking His blood (John vi, 52 ff.). Invisible reality even becomes visible in the sign. It is a dogma that the sacraments contain grace and communicate it to those who place no obstacle in its way.[1] The Church is deeply implicated in this external symbolism where her instrumental character becomes evident. But this instrument does not act blindly and impersonally. Since Christ established only the foundation for the external signs of the sacraments, the Council of Trent ascribed to the Church a certain power with regard to these signs. She cannot alter and may not touch their essential 'being such' (*das wesentliche So-Sein*). Nevertheless, she distributes the sacraments, which are therefore signs of her life; they are dramatic actions, established, it is true, by Christ Himself, but enjoying the breadth of application belonging to the sphere of signs; hence the Church may truly be said to have a certain power over the sacraments. Does she therefore also have power over grace? By no means, for Christ alone is the true Giver of the sacraments. This question shows clearly the close connexion between Christ and the Church, but shows also that they cannot be identified. The sacrament of penance reveals the intimate union between the spheres of God and the Church. It is of faith that 'as Christ Himself forgave sins, so He has also given His apostles and their successors the power to forgive sins.'[2] Here, too, appears the instrumental character of the Church. According to Matt. xviii, 15–18, Christ said to His disciples: 'If thy brother shall offend against thee, go and rebuke him between thee and him alone: if he hear thee, thou hast gained thy brother. But if he hear thee not, take with thee one or two more, that at the mouth of two witnesses or three every word may be established. And if he refuse to hear them, tell it unto the church: and if he refuse to hear the church also, let him be to thee as the Gentile and the publican. Verily I say unto you, What things soever ye shall bind on earth shall be bound in heaven: and what things soever ye shall loose on earth shall be loosed in heaven.' Binding and loosing signifies the exclusion from the community and the annulment or non-infliction of the exclusion. According to this Scriptural passage exclusion from the communion of the Church means also exclusion from the kingdom of God. After the Resurrection Christ delegated His own mission to the Twelve (John xx, 21) and endowed them with divine

[1] Denz., 847–51.
[2] ibid., 894.

authority: 'He breathed on them, and he said to them: Receive ye the Holy Ghost (i.e. the strength and power flowing from Christ). Whose sins you shall forgive, they are forgiven them: and whose sins you shall retain, they are retained' (John xx, 22 f.). The judgement of the Church becomes the judgement of God; expulsion from or reception into the community of the Church is valid before God. Does the Church then forgive sin? This is badly put. Re-admission is not formally identical with forgiveness of sin. On the other hand, however, it may nevertheless be said that the Church effects forgiveness, because re-admission to the Catholic communion of life results in sharing in the Holy Spirit who in His turn forgives sin. God alone can forgive sins; the Church cannot remit them directly. This problem has occupied theologians for centuries. Here it becomes evident that the co-operation and the separation of divine and human factors is the 'neuralgic spot' not only of ecclesiology, but of theology. The fact that God's judgement is present and effective in the judgement of the Church gives that judgement its fearful importance.

We see then that divine and human spheres are intimately related, and that both these elements are also interwoven in the structure of the Church, but we also realize that they must not be confused.

C. The Hierarchical Constitution of the Church

The Church is the hierarchically organized new people of God. The term hierarchy means holy origin and holy order. Christ called a group of disciples among whom the Twelve were the most prominent, and endowed them with sacred powers (Matt. xviii, 18; Mark xvi, 15; John xx, 21). Peter, the supreme Shepherd, is the head of this college of apostles (Matt. xvi, 13–19; John xxi, 15–17; Luke xxii, 31 f.). Just as Christ is the principle of life and order of the new people of God (John xv, 1–11), so the Church receives the power to consecrate and to govern. The pastoral power of Christ is incarnated in the divinely instituted orders of the papal primacy and the episcopate.[1] We will here discuss the primacy, again under the aspect of the divine and human elements in the Church.

The papal primacy as such is based on divine institution and represents a divine principle; as a truth of faith it may be formulated thus: Christ has appointed Peter head of the apostles and communicated this headship also to his successors. This is a mystery of

[1] Cf. Eichmann-Mörsdorf, *Kirchenrecht* I[7], 24 f.

faith. Here an important distinction must be made between physical and mystical person.[1] As physical persons the apostles have died and have physical successors. As mystical persons, however, the Twelve continue to live in their successors, whose physical number may increase or decrease, but whose mystical number remains: they are the Twelve. It is the same with St Peter. As the Head he does not die but continues to live in the Bishop of Rome. The Popes Linus, Cletus and Clement are dead and so are the others. It does not matter whether they have adorned or disgraced their see materially or spiritually, whether they were saints or sinners; Peter, their head, who cannot die mystically, continues to live in them. This mystery can be grasped only by divine faith. 'Perhaps it will be said that this conception (of the primacy of Peter) is above all the outcome of the work of Western theologians intent on the political rise of Papal Rome, that their legalistic mentality was prone to develop such views. We do not deny this. But, traced back to its origin, this notion is not linked to any changeable way of thinking dependent on historical circumstances. It is quite in the line of Patristic theology, which often emphasized the eternal character of our dogmas much more strongly than we do today.'[2]

Here again the difference between divine and human spheres becomes visible. The doctrinal aspect of the primacy must be distinguished from the historical one.[3] According to the former, the primacy is instituted by Christ and is the mystery of the mystical person; it must not be identified with certain temporary aspects of the historical Papacy. The question of the primacy is certainly the main point of controversy between the denominations, but Rousseau rightly observes that this is due perhaps not so much to its doctrinal aspect as to a confusion of this transcendent reality with other elements which, though quite legitimate, are nevertheless of human origin. This is certainly the case in the controversy with the Eastern Church.

*   *   *

Yet this 'neuralgic spot' of which we have spoken seems to lie even deeper. E. Brunner vigorously denies that his view of the Ecclesia as a pneumatic community of persons 'does not really take

---

[1] Cf. O. Rousseau, 'La notion théologique de la Papauté et l'Unité chrétienne,' in Irénikon XX (1947), 372–80.

[2] Rousseau, loc. cit., 376.

[3] 'The doctrine of the primacy is to be distinguished from the exercise of the primacy.' Schmaus, Katholische Dogmatik III, i, 98.

account of the incarnation of Jesus Christ in His Church', as his opponents affirm. According to him 'the New Testament Ecclesia is the incarnation of Jesus Christ precisely in so far as it is the body of Jesus Christ'.[1] But, he continues, 'we are told that if we take the incarnation seriously we must also justify the growth of the Church (*Kirchwerdung*) and recognize it as the necessary embodiment of the exalted Lord. This opinion, however, neglects the fact that, though He was certainly embodied in the Ecclesia, this embodiment . . . had not at that time the character it assumed later, namely that of an institution'.[2] This view misunderstands the nature of an institution. Brunner surprisingly defines it according to the Swiss Dictionary, where the institution is described as the most important form of social order. 'There is in the institution an explicit will to regulation, by which relations between men and objective or ideal data are ordered . . . ; if this is set down in writing, its highest form is the law.'[3] Now, apart from this over-simplified solution, Brunner's thesis will lead us to examine whether the historical incarnation is really the ultimate principle of the Church. How would it be, for instance, if we did not take the incarnation but, say, the resurrection as this ultimate principle? W. Künneth did this in his *Theologie der Auferstehung*. He writes, 'The incarnation frequently appears as the central Christian dogma which expresses the essence of Christianity even apart from the resurrection.'[4] 'This exclusive emphasis on the dogma of the incarnation, however, rests on an abstraction that is foreign to it. It not only contradicts primitive Christian teaching, but it cannot establish the dogma of the divinity of the Son. . . . The miracle of the incarnation depends on the miracle of the resurrection. . . . Now incarnation and resurrection must not be seen as equal poles of a sphere; their co-ordination means an unjustifiable shifting of emphasis. . . . The incarnation of the Son is neither the summit nor the completion of Christ's vocation, but the beginning of God's action that is directed towards the resurrection as its goal.'[5] Hence Künneth concludes: 'As soon as the Christological importance of Christ as *Kyrios* (*Kyriostum*) is recognized, the theologians engaged in elucidating New Testament thought are confronted with a new situation. They must tackle the New Testament problems . . . from

[1] *Das Missverständnis*, 84.

[2] ibid., 85.

[3] ibid., 119.

[4] *Theologie der Auferstehung*, 119.

[5] ibid., 121 f.

the key position of the resurrection.'[1] We will not discuss Künneth's conception of the Church in this connexion; for our purpose his way of posing the problem is rather a question of method. We have raised the problem, because Congar, too, says 'that the mystery of Catholic or traditional ecclesiology lies in the relation between the historical and the heavenly Christ.'[2]

This relation is indeed a mystery, and traditional theology ought not to take its clarification too lightly. If Künneth asserts that the ascended *Kyrios* is the corner stone and basis also of the conception of the Church, and if ecclesiology is faced with the question whether the Church started from heaven, from God, from the Holy Spirit, from the heavenly Christ *or* from the incarnate Word, from His incarnation in the womb of Mary, this question cannot lead us much further.

*   *   *

If Catholic theologians start from the glorified Christ, they will better be able to meet the one-sidedly soteriological aspect of the Protestants. Contemporary exegetes speak of the apostolic kerygma and the so-called kerygmatic formulae. It may be regarded as certain that the kerygmatic formulae contain the witness of the death and resurrection of Christ. But the centre and sum of the Gospel, too, can be determined from the apostolic kerygma. The Protestant Christian sees the sum of the Gospel in the doctrine of justification, which is thus raised into the formal principle of his faith. To us, however, it seems that the Catholic theologian Robert Grosche is nearer the mark in regarding the statement that Jesus is the *Kyrios* as the *Summa Evangelii* and the apostolic kerygma *par excellence*.[3] The evangelical theologian H. Asmussen is right in saying: 'it must be admitted that the Fathers of the Reformation have taken into account the message of the dominion of the risen King, in so far as this concerns the reign of the risen Lord in history.'[4]

[1] ibid., 124. In his review of G. Thils, *Théologie des réalités terrestres* II, *Théologie de l'histoire*, Paris, 1949, in *Theol. Revue*, 48 (1952), 172, Viktor Warnach has also drawn attention to the fact that Thils sees God's initiative too one-sidedly under the aspect of 'incarnation'. 'We may, indeed, understand the assertions of the author as springing from a justified opposition to the "docetism" and "eschatologism" of certain modern theologians, but we cannot make them our own. For however fundamental the incarnation of the Pneuma is for the economy of salvation, according to primitive Christian teaching the decisive moment must be seen in the Pascha, i.e. in the Lord's entering into glory, through death into the life of the resurrection. God's entry into time is not . . . the goal, but only the, indeed necessary, transitional phase, as it were the means for realizing the divine plan. . . . The katabasis must be followed by an anabasis.'

[2] *Vraie et fausse Réforme*, 474.

[3] *Catholica* 11 (1957) 125–1238.

[4] Asmussen-Sartory, *Gespräch zwischen den Konfessionen* (1959), 69.

Returning to faith in Jesus Christ as *vestigium ecclesiae* we have to admit that this faith does not mean the same for Catholics and Protestants, owing to the following tendencies of Protestantism:

1. Protestantism, as far as it follows Luther, devalues the importance of the humanity of Christ in the process of salvation.[1]

As has been said before, Luther's Christology is only concerned with soteriology, i.e. with the doctrine of redemption. It is interesting to ask which role he assigns to the humanity of Christ in this connexion. He strongly emphasized the unity of divinity and humanity in the one Person. His whole religious thought is permeated by the idea of the sole activity of God, hence of a movement from above to below. This principle is clearly expressed in his conception of the relation between faith and works, between the law and the gospel, and is also applied to Christ Himself. Thus the humanity of Christ is not really given a positive importance. In the Commentary on Galatians (1535) Luther states explicitly that Christ works only through His divinity, *humanitate nihil cooperante*.[2] The redemption is regarded only as the work of God in Christ, and Christ only in His divinity; it is a drama in which there is only one actor, God, who justifies; the humanity of Christ is but the stage on which this justification is enacted. In Christ God makes satisfaction to Himself.[3] Congar points out that the Formula of Concord of

---

[1] On the following cf. Congar, 'Regards et réflexions sur la christologie de Luther', in Grillmeier-Bacht, *Das Konzil von Chalkedon* III, 457–86.

[2] 'Theologicum opus est fidele opus. Sic homo theologicus est fidelis, item ratio recta, voluntas bona est fidelis ratio et voluntas, ut fides in universum sit divinitas in opere, persona et membris, ut unica causa iustificationis quae postea etiam tribuitur materiae propter formam, hoc est operi propter fidem. Ut regnum divinitatis traditur Christo homini non propter humanitatem sed divinitatem. Sola enim divinitas creavit omnia humanitate nihil cooperante. Sicut neque peccatum et mortem humanitas vicit sed hamus qui latebat sub vermiculo, in quem diabolus impegit, vicit et devoravit diabolum qui erat devoraturus vermiculum. Itaque sola fecit et humanitas propter divinitatem. Sic hic sola fides iustificat et facit omnia; et tamen operibus idem tribuitur propter fidem.' *WA* 40, 1, 417 f.; cit. by Congar, loc. cit., 467, note 38.

[3] 'Faith is also purely theocentric, because he sees only God in Christ' (E. Vogelsang, 'Die Anfänge von Luthers Christologie nach der ersten Psalmenvorlesung insbesondere in ihren exegetischen und systematischen Zusammenhängen mit Augustinus und der Scholastik dargestellt.' *Arbeiten zur Kirchengeschichte* 15, Berlin-Leipzig, 1929, 161);— 'For if Luther says: the Man Christ is King of the Church, he shifts the conception of the *humanitas Christi*. *Humanitas* in this sense is not that side in Christ which He shares with man, but the form in which the divinity appears in the humanity. . . . Hence not the man Christ, as separate from His divinity, is king, but the man Christ in whom the Godhead is incarnate.' (F. Huck, 'Die Entwicklung der Christologie Luthers von der Psalmen–zur Römerbriefvorlesung,' in *Theol. Stud. Krit.* 102-1930 = Lutherana VI, 61-142, 127);–'God and Christ are not placed side by side in competition, nor are they subordinated in such a way that the existence of Christ would be the necessary condition of the working of God's grace and thus restrict the omnipotence of the

1576 ascribes to the humanity of Christ, which is not separated from His Godhead, the merit and cause of our justification, but that such a formulation could hardly be found in Luther.[1]

This Lutheran conception differs essentially from that of Western theologians, who follow the Fathers in their exegesis of St John and St Paul: In his humanity the incarnate Word of God becomes the original, even though secondary, source of salvation. Christ is not simply the 'sphere' in which the saving will of God is active, but He Himself works salvation, also through His humanity. Thus the historical incarnation is effective, and this means that redemption does not work without contact with creation but inside creation, which is seen as important. Congar here poses the question whether Luther really had a precise and correct trinitarian theology. He denies it, since the Reformer was not in the least concerned with the mystery of the Trinity, but solely with 'God'. In fact, in Luther's theology Christ and the Holy Spirit are functions of the one 'God', who has revealed Himself only as the God of our salvation.

This soteriological Christology has its effect on the doctrine of the Church. The principle of God as the sole agent leaves no room (however relative) for creation and the visible creature. For Luther devalued the humanity of Christ only because he followed the *schema* of Nominalism (if we leave the religious intention out of account). All visible things have the quality of 'sinful flesh'; the true spiritual reality is confined to what is invisible. To the movement from above to below corresponds one from within to without, but never the other way round. Christ is the Head of His mystical Body. But how does Luther understand this Headship? In his later works he takes it less and less in the sense of a causality but increasingly as an exemplar, a pattern, though not only in the sense of a moral

---

latter. . . . Hence the problem Christocentric or theocentric does not exist for Luther. For him "Jesus has become neither a primary nor a secondary object of his devotion, but He has remained for Luther the revelation of the divine act of redemption" (Gogarten).' (H. Thimme, *Christi Bedeutung für Luthers Glauben. Unter Zugrundlegung des Römerbrief-, des Hebräerbrief-, des Galaterbriefkommentars von* 1531 *und der Disputationen*, Gütersloh, 1933, 148);—'All depends on the assertion that it is God Himself who in Christ overcomes the tyrants. It is at the same time evident that the Deity of Christ is not for Luther a bare metaphysical dogma, still less a "physical" doctrine; for in the work of redemption the actual agent is no other and no less than God's own Blessing, Righteousness, and Life' (G. Aulén, *Christus Victor*. Engl. translation, London, 1931, 124).

[1] ' La Formule de Concorde de 1576 attribue au Christ (en son humanité, qu'elle ne sépare pas de sa divinité, dans l'unité de sa Personne) un mérite et une causalité qui interviennent dans notre justification.' Congar, loc. cit., 466.

example but also of an ontological one. Nevertheless, Christ is *caput*, Head of the mystical Body only in the sense of an *exemplum*. The mystical Body is not the visible organism of the Church with its sacraments and ministry, but the sum total of persons to whom is imputed *fides*, the faith of Christ and the justice of Christ. Christ is the Head of His Body not as the source and cause, but as the first man in whom God has defeated evil and after whose example He defeats it ever again in the believer.

On the one hand Luther is a dualist, for he radically separates the divine from the created order and sharply opposes them to each other even in Christ. On the other, he is a monist, because he assigns salvation to the sole agency of God. So here we have a philosophical dualism and a religious monism (Congar). By following an essentially soteriological line, Luther's Christology assumes a monophysite colouring despite his emphasis on the reality of the two natures. This has also been noticed by Protestants and Orthodox such as K. Holl, E. Vogelsang, K. Barth, N. Berdyaev and Ludolf Müller.

2. Protestantism confines the incarnation to the Person of Christ, its *hapax*, and spiritualizes it. The reason for this is probably the Protestant attitude to physical life, to the realm of matter, which has been explained above. Today this spiritualizing tendency is opposed especially by the Protestant liturgical movement. This is discovering once more the importance and value of 'external' things, which according to the Augsburg Confession are counted among the *adiaphora*, i.e. signs which need not be objects of controversy. 'Emphasis on the "spiritual" in every form is, of necessity, somewhat mistrustful and hostile towards all liturgical form, because it is only prepared to admit what has been sensed and experienced in a wholly "inward" fashion. But, the other side asks, is it not consistent with the Incarnation, in which God's Word became flesh, that in our worship likewise salvation in Christ materializes in our physical comportment, in physical actions, in forms, colours and symbols?'[1] Obviously all these problems are concerned with the conception of grace. In order to solve them it would be important to study the nature of salvation, especially in the Old Testament. There religious values are closely connected with material things (cf. Os. ii, 16–24; Isa. xxxii, 16; Amos ix, 11–15). Messianic salvation as conceived by the prophets is directed above all to the physical order which is 'changed'. M. Schmaus rightly says: 'Transformation is the most

[1] 'Insights and Open Questions Concerning Ways of Worship,' *ER* IV (1951), 248.

important concept of the Christian faith.'[1] Now transformation attaches the greatest importance to the incarnation, so that it does not remain restricted to Jesus Christ, as if salvation were to be had only in the Word of God.[2] The Protestant liturgical movement may cause important changes in this matter.

3. A third tendency, which is closely connected with the first and which is evident especially among the followers of Barth, favours a Christological 'contraction' (*Engführung*). This school of thought moves wholly along the lines of a one-sided soteriological Christology. No one has more vehemently warned against seeing the Church as a continuation of the incarnation than Karl Barth. 'If this were so, then the reign of Jesus Christ at the right hand of the Father and hence the working of God's Providence would evidently have passed, as it were, into the direction and administration of Christendom.'[3]

Urs von Balthasar has recently attempted to find a link between Barth's *Kirchliche Dogmatik* and Catholic dogma.[4] In his interpretation of Barth's theology Balthasar limits himself to the group of themes centred round creation, redemption and incarnation, with special emphasis on the relation between nature and grace. Letting himself be guided by Barth, he shows the formal element in Catholicism to be the *analogia entis*, in Protestantism the *analogia fidei*. It is

---

[1] *Kath. Dogmatik* III, 2, 219.

[2] It seems to us that this spiritualizing tendency is due to Luther's conception of the Church and to art. 7 of the Augsburg Confession. It is interesting to read Bishop Leslie Newbigin's criticism of this Lutheran position. He speaks of an exaggerated intellectualization of the concept of 'faith' (*The Household of God*, 52). He starts with the question of how we are incorporated in Christ: 'I think it is true that if we answer the question: "How are we made incorporate in Christ?" *solely* in the words "by hearing and believing the Gospel", and apart from the context of a continuing fellowship through which the Gospel comes to us, we become inevitably involved in an over-intellectualized conception of faith. . . . But of course the unity of believers with Christ and with one another in Him is of a far deeper nature than intellectual agreement' (ibid., 53). The reason for this Lutheran conception is a false and un-Biblical dialectic of outward and inward, visible and invisible (56). The apostolic moment is overlooked: 'He sends His apostles forth to be His representatives and He promises His presence with them always. They are the beginnings of a real continuation of His redeeming work, an extension of the divine humanity—though in a different mode—through history. . . . But when the Church is defined *simply* (N. speaks of an over-simplification in Luther) as that which is continually (or perhaps one really should say repeatedly) created from above by the work of Christ in the word and sacraments, then a real distortion has taken place. . . . The word is preached and the sacraments are administered in and by the Church as well as to the Church, and Christ, the Head of the Body, acts in them, both through and for the Church' (57).

[3] *Amsterdamer Fragen und Antworten*, 5.

[4] *Karl Barth. Darstellung und Deutung seiner Theologie*, 1951.

doubtful, especially after the studies of G. Söhngen,[1] whether this is a genuine contradiction, for Söhngen reaches the conclusion that *analogia entis* and *analogia fidei* are not in opposition, but that the latter includes the former.[2] There is rather an opposition in *analogia fidei contra analogiam entis*, which he finds in the theology of the Reformers. If the order of creation is given its full weight a genuine opposition between the order of faith and the order of being is impossible. Barth seeks to resolve this supposed opposition by the 'perfect form of the analogy' (*die Vollgestalt der Analogie*), that is Jesus Christ. This in itself is a correct point of departure. But what is Barth's view of Christ? In order to introduce the *analogia entis* into the sphere of Christ, Barth understands Christ in a '*Prius* before creation and fall'. Balthasar states that Barth arrives at this *Prius* by using the idealistic concept of presupposition (*Voraussetzung*), i.e. through transcendental categories. But by using this category Barth fails to leave their own proper status to creation, covenant and the order of nature. Balthasar, too, poses the critical question whether 'the way in which Barth uses these categories does not presuppose theological tendencies of his own which show a dubious and one-sided conception of revelation, which then expresses itself in the use of precisely this philosophy.'[3] Barth's Christological starting-point is contracted, or, more clearly expressed: the incarnation of Christ is not fully developed because the natural order has no standing of its own. Balthasar rightly expresses 'very grave doubts' about what Barth calls the Church, i.e. 'the sphere in which sounds the Word of God which supports all things'.[4] According to Balthasar, Barth's tendency is 'universalist-socialist, sharply anti-institutional'.[5] In a kind of preview Balthasar only touches on the second group of questions (Church, sacraments and Christian life), which really ought to be included in any interpretation of Barth's theology,[6] even though the relevant volumes of his *Kirchliche Dogmatik* have not yet been published. There Balthasar says, very surprisingly after what has gone before, that because of Barth's views on the first group of questions 'the remaining differences of opinion are not such as to divide the Church'.[7] But one such remaining difference of opinion

---

[1] *Einheit in der Theologie*, 235–64.
[2] ibid., 245.
[3] *Karl Barth*, 253.
[4] ibid., 257.
[5] ibid., 258.
[6] As was done by J. Hamer in *Karl Barth. L'occasionalisme théologique*, Paris, 1949.
[7] ibid., 389.

is for example Mariology. This will show the mistake Barth has made in 'contracting' his Christology. Where such Christological contraction exists Catholics and Protestants are *not*, as Balthasar assumes, in the same sphere of faith in Jesus Christ because they have received the same baptism.[1]

The Mother of God is so important for Christology and Ecclesiology precisely because she is a testimony, a personal sign of the *Christus totus* and of an undiminished incarnation.[2] It was surely not by accident that at the councils of Ephesus and Chalcedon Christological truths were expressed in terms of Mary as *Theotokos*. Nor is it mere chance that heretics protest against her, because through her body she bears witness to the *gratia creata*, the new creation in the order of being, the covenant partnership of man with God and the beginning of the *eschata*. According to the consensus of the Fathers Mary is the type of the Church. She stands by the side of Christ as the Woman, the new Eve, the type of the Church, supplementing His humanity. The mystery of Christ's Body embraces Mary. For this reason the early Fathers complemented the Pauline Adam-Christ with the parallel of Eve-Mary, because they knew that the whole Christ is Christ and the Church in her bridal relationship to Him, as St Paul says in Eph. i, 23.[3] Hence H. Asmussen rightly stresses that 'Mary belongs in the Creed, just as the apostles and the prophets and Pilate. . . . And in any case Mariology is part of Christology.'[4] Indeed, Mariology is no special doctrine of Catholicism; Mary the *Theotokos* is, as was said at Edinburgh, at 'the centre and heart of the Oecumenical Movement'.[5]

It may now be asked whether this diminished Protestant view of Christ does not result in a diminished Presence of Christ in the order of being.

There are different modes of Christ's Presence. Besides His presence in faith and grace there is His sacramental presence, especially in the Eucharist. The presence of faith and grace realized by faith (Eph. iii, 17) is a *praesentia spiritualis* and a perfectly true and real presence. It forms the Church (*ist kirchenbildend*), because Christ is the head of the Church. But side by side with this there is the essential, substantial and bodily presence of Christ in His divine-

[1] ibid., 28.

[2] Cf. 'Sartory, Maria und die getrennten Brüder,' in *Una Sancta Rundbriefe* 9 (1954), No. 3, 10–20.

[3] On this subject cf. Sartory, 'Maria assumpta est.' *Gloira Dei* V, 233–43.

[4] 'Ist Christologie auch Mariologie?' *ELKZ* 5 (1951), No. 4.

[5] Cf. L. Hodgson, *The Second World Conference*, 153; the Mariological studies of Pepler, Parker and especially F. M. Thurian in *Ways of Worship*, 255–89 are also very instructive.

human nature.[1] This, too, forms the Church; indeed, according to the Biblical doctrine of the Body of Christ it does so in a pre-eminent manner. This dimension of the presence of Christ is lacking in the communities that are separated from the Mother Church. Considering these in their whole range from the Orthodox to the sects it must be said that Christ is incarnate in these 'churches' in a whole variety of degrees, for, as J. Hamer truly observes, in the eyes of the Orthodox it makes a difference whether an Old Catholic or a Calvinist celebrates the Lord's Supper. In the case of the latter this is only a rite displaying outwardly the institution of the Eucharist as Christ has taught it, 'but the guarantee of the reality of the sacrament is missing: the pastor who celebrates does not possess the power of the ministry'.[2] Here, too, we can speak of *vestigium ecclesiae*, but only with regard to the image and appearance. This external similarity is by no means worthless, but it cannot be considered *vestigium ecclesiae* in the sense of a fragment of the reality. 'Deprived of all objective consistency this is not a stone of an edifice, nor a fragment of a reality, but solely a psychological value which directs (perhaps para-doxically) towards the real plenitude.'[3] O. Karrer thinks that, in the case of the separated Christians, faith in the presence and com-munion of Christ in the Eucharist is 'Church forming' (*kirchenbildend*) on principle, and that the Lord's Supper, 'even though not cele-brated with complete ecclesiastical legitimacy, should, at least through the *votum sacramenti*, have a power surpassing the merely subjective state of mind'.[4] Certainly, some objective power is there, present at least in the sphere of faith. But can the *votum sacramenti* replace the sacrament itself in the case of the holy Eucharist?[5]

[1] Cf. Söhngen, *Die Einheit in der Theologie*, 338 f.

[2] 'Mais ce qui assure la réalité au sacrement fait ici défaut: le pasteur qui célèbre ne dispose pas du pouvoir ministériel.' *Le baptême*, 150.

[3] 'Dépouillé de tout consistance objective ce n'est pas une pierre d'un édifice, ce n'est pas un fragment de réalité, mais uniquement une valeur psychologique qui oriente (paradoxalement peut-être) vers la plénitude réelle.' ibid.

[4] *Um die Einheit der Christen*, 27.

[5] The connexion between baptism and the Eucharist noted by St Thomas Aquinas is important. St Thomas says that every man who has himself been baptized receives the Eucharist *in voto*. He distinguishes between the *res* and the *sacramentum*. The *res* of a sacrament (which in the case of the Eucharist is the unity of the mystical Body of Christ) can be received even before the reception of the sacrament, by the desire to receive the sacrament itself, just as baptism, too, can be received *voto*, by desire. As baptism is necessary for the beginning of the spiritual life, so the reception of the Eucharist is needed for its perfection. 'Yet it is not necessary to receive it actually, but it suffices to have it according to desire, even as the end is had in desire and intention' (*S.Th.* III, 73, 3). However, one word ought not to be overlooked in this context. For St Thomas says that baptized infants e.g. are directed towards the Eucharist *per ecclesiam*

We may consider faith in Jesus Christ and the presence thus realized as a genuine *vestigium ecclesiae*, though a very imperfect one, because we are concerned with the *totus Christus*, in whose fullness the separated Christians cannot share.

(ii) *The Action of the Holy Spirit*

'Where the Church is, there is the Spirit of God, and where the Spirit of God is there is the Church and the communion of grace.'[1] Hence the question of the Church and its unity is closely connected with that of the Holy Spirit, especially with His action.[2] This is clearly recognized also within the Oecumene, as is evidenced by the fact that the Church is generally held to have been founded when the Holy Spirit came down on the apostles at Pentecost.[3] There can be no doctrine of the Church without an account of the nature and work of the Holy Spirit. In modern Catholic theology this is clearly expressed especially by M. J. Scheeben whose comprehensive *Dogmatik* contains no special ecclesiology, but who develops the doctrine of the Church when treating of the Holy Spirit. Can we therefore conclude that a person is within the Church if God's Spirit dwells in him? If the question is thus formulated the answer will be that the Church is perfectly present where the action of the Holy Spirit finds its perfect fulfilment. Is this true of those Christians who are separated from the Mother Church?

The theological Commission on Faith and Order in the World Council of Churches asked the churches, in its report on the preparation for the Lund Conference, to examine the subject of 'Holy Spirit and Church'. The churches were asked to discuss how they understood the presence of the risen Christ in the Church in view of the New Testament doctrine of the Holy Spirit, with special reference to the New Testament statements on the gifts of the Holy Spirit (charismata) in their relation to the ministry. These questions raise many

---

through the Church (ibid.). Now the Church denies eucharistic communion to all who are not fully active members of the Church, hence to all non-Catholic Christians, whether they are in good faith or not (*CIC* c. 731, § 2). They can be admitted only after being reconciled to the Church. The general rights of membership are restricted by an obstacle of prohibition, i.e. by a purely factual circumstance, solely because such is the will of the Church (cf. Eichmann-Mörsdorf, *Kirchenrecht* I, 187). Because of the constitutional membership, there remains for the baptized Christian an ontological ordering towards the Eucharist and hence the possibility of partaking of the *res* of the sacrament by desire (*voto*). The sacrament itself, however, is prohibited.

[1] Irenaeus, *Contra haereses* 3.24.
[2] Cf. Schmaus, *Kath. Dogmatik*[2] III, 1, § 168.
[3] Details in Schmaus, 26–31.

problems which can undoubtedly be solved only by having recourse to the New Testament itself. But oecumenical conversations have made it abundantly clear that Holy Scripture can be interpreted very differently.

Protestantism tends to regard the interior and spiritual domain as the proper sphere of action of the Holy Spirit. No doubt this goes back to the idea of the invisible Church, the true Christians who cannot be perceived by the senses. This seems to be more than a mere shift of emphasis, for this interior sphere is often seen as opposed to an external, empirical manifestation. Apart from a generally spiritualizing tendency one reason for this view may be the Protestant doctrine of man, who is simultaneously *justus et peccator*. Now this means that grace does not touch man in his physical essence. Hence the action of the Holy Spirit points to that of grace and Jesus Christ, who willed to be present in His Church in a certain well-defined manner.

To the question where exactly is the presence of the Holy Spirit in the Church the Catholic answers: in the ministry, the sacraments, canon law, in the charismata and in the free invisible workings of grace. The Catholic does not forget that the Holy Spirit indwells in the individual souls of the faithful, but he knows that He first descended at Pentecost on a *community* and was received by individuals as members of this community, together with Mary and the apostles. In the young Church the Holy Spirit was given not only through baptism but through the laying on of hands (cf. Acts viii, 17; 1 Tim. iv, 14). The indwelling of the *pneuma* was therefore attached to external signs; God's Spirit could be experienced by Christians. Thus Wendland writes: 'The *pneuma* ... is strictly bound to history, it is in time as the Logos becomes flesh, hence the *pneuma* becomes history and time.'[1] The Spirit's becoming history has continued throughout the time of the Church under the same conditions as in the early Church. It seems that Protestantism does not quite know what to make of this embodiment of the Holy Spirit; here, too, its tendency is opposed to history. For if the Oecumene attributes the same value to an invisible continuity of the Holy Spirit as to an historical continuity (e.g. in the episcopate), this is due to a misconception of the way in which the Holy Spirit acts in the Church. It seems that the whole 'left wing' of the Oecumene tends to ascribe a docetic form to the action of the Holy Spirit, and, according to P. Brunner, this tendency has grown in Protestantism

[1] 'Das Wirken des Heiligen Geistes nach Paulus,' *ThLZ*. 77 (1952), col. 468.

in the last two hundred years. Brunner[1] connects this with the influence of the 'spiritual philosophy' of Idealism. In our view the roots go even deeper, to the genuine Protestant tendency to divorce the spiritual from the physical. Here Christological errors come to light: a Nestorian Christology leads to a docetic pneumatology. The sects within the Oecumene are particularly addicted to this docetic view of the Spirit.[2] Over and over again they claim the authority of the Holy Spirit which among some of them (to mention only the Quakers) is based on real proofs of His presence in the works of charismatic love.

In connexion with Eph. iv, 3–6 Asmussen speaks of objectivations of the Holy Spirit and of objectivated grace.[3] Following St Paul, he sees such objectivations in the sacraments and the ministry of the Church. We will begin by discussing the latter.

Church and Ministry

A Protestant, let us say a Lutheran, would be very surprised if he were told that there are neither ministry nor ministers in his denomination. We need only look at modern theological Protestant literature to realize how frequently the ministry is mentioned there. But the 'evangelical' type (in the terminology of Amsterdam) understands the ministry of the Church differently from the 'Catholic'. The Protestant view of it may be summarized thus:

1. The essence of the ministry is the preaching of the Gospel and the proper administration of the sacraments.[4] Hence the office is only a function; it does not establish a 'state'. Here, too, the point of departure is the 'event' of the atonement (2 Cor. v, 18).

2. A man is elected to the ministry by a charisma of the invisible Lord which is confirmed and accepted by the visible brethren of the congregation.[5] There is an ordination, but this does not confer divine grace but simply endorses the gift of grace on behalf of the congregation.

[1] 'The Realism of the Holy Spirit,' *ER* III (1950), 224. Cf. R. Paquier in *Ways of Worship* where he says of the Reformed Church that 'liberal idealism, which rests upon the disjunction of spirit and bodily nature ... has been the spiritual climate of two generations of Churchmen, and its traces survive tenaciously in our communities' (241 f.).

[2] On the sects in the Oecumene cf. Sartory 'Offener Brief an Pf. K. Lehmann,' *USR* 8, 3.

[3] *Der Brief des Paulus an die Epheser*, 104.

[4] Cf. E. Wolf, 'Das kirchliche Amt im Gericht der theologischen Existenz,' *Evangelische Theologie*, 11 (1951–2), 519.

[5] Cf. Vogel, *Gott in Christo*. Berlin, 1951, 898.

3. There is only one office, that of preaching, which at the same time entitles its holder to administer the sacraments.[1] 'It is Luther's merit clearly to have defined the spiritual ministry as a function of the Gospel. The Church of Christ lives solely by the one ministry which is effective through baptism, preaching and the Lord's Supper.'[2]

4. Through the universal priesthood all the faithful share in the ministry. 'Whoever has emerged from baptism can boast of being already consecrated priest, bishop and Pope.'[3] This, however, is not meant to abolish the particular ministry.[4] The sacerdotal theory, on the other hand, is held to endanger the unique Mediatorship of Christ.[5]

5. The external form and constitution of the ministry is neither laid down nor is it a matter of faith; the confessional writings leave it an open question. The office of preaching, the sacraments and the keys are the property of the *ecclesia perpetua mansura*, hence belong to *Jus divinum*. The 'orders' and traditions arising from this fall under *Jus humanum*.[6]

6. The apostolic succession is not needed for the authority of the office. According to Lutheran doctrine the *successio apostolica* must be considered from the point of view of the *viva vox apostolica*. If the purity of the apostolic word demands it, because the ministers teach false doctrine, the apostolic succession must be interrupted. 'The constitutive factor in the preservation of the Church is not the succession of episcopal consecration but the succession of the preached gospel.'[7]

Catholic doctrine is opposed to this Protestant view. Recently evangelical theologians have approached the former more closely by an unprejudiced exposition of Scripture, especially of the Pastoral Epistles and the First Epistle of Clement, i.e. the earliest Christian

---

[1] Cf. Confessio Belgica, art. 31.

[2] J. Behrens, 'Das geistliche Amt und die Laienämter der Kirche,' *ELKZ* VI (1952), 97.

[3] An den christlichen Adel deutscher Nation, l.c. Behrens, 98.

[4] Cf. W. Schnorr, 'Die Krisis des geistlichen Amtes,' *ELKZ* VI (1952), 177 f.

[5] Cf. M. G. G. Scherer, in Sasse, *Die Weltkonferenz*, 312. P. Althaus, *Die Christliche Wahrheit*, vol. II, 298.

[6] Cf. Wehrhahn, 'Die Grundlagenproblematik des deutschen evangelischen Kirchenrechtes, 1933–45.' *Theologische Rundschau*, 19, (1952) 255.

[7] *ELKZ* IV (1950), 322. Cf. *HK* VII (1952), 508 f.; on the apostolic succession as an oecumenical question cf. *ER* IV (1952), n. 2, 139–60; A. Volkmann, 'Evangelisch-katholische Gedanken zur Frage der Successio Apostolica.' *USR* 10 (1955), 42–55.

tradition.[1] On the office of St Peter the reader may consult the relevant book by O. Cullmann. Here, too, it can be seen how the Church and the ministry can be spiritualized. Protestantism is not consistent in its interpretation of the ministry. For a long time (four hundred years according to Asmussen)[2] little was heard of the charismatic and spiritual character of the ministry. 'It was regarded as an essentially formal function.'[3] Nowadays, theologians go back to the Reformers and place the ministry on the plane of the *ecclesia stricte dicta* (unless they try to interpret it by means of the sacrament), asserting its outer form to be irrelevant. Unfortunately for them, however, revelation speaks of the ministry in quite unmistakable terms. 'The Pastoral Epistles are quite incompatible with any form of congregationalism and consistorialism. They presuppose all too clearly a ministry based on a sacramental existence.'[4] Why is the order of the ministry, the laying on of hands and tradition so strongly emphasized only in the Pastorals? Because, writes O. Michel, they are 'strongly anti-Gnostic'.[5] Besides, each Scriptural passage can only be understood from its background. The idea of succession, for example, is familiar Old Testament practice which must be taken into account if we are to understand Matt. xvi, 18; 1 Tim. iv, 14 and 2 Tim. i, 6. It can serve no reasonable purpose always to play off Christ against Peter, the Eternal against the temporal Shepherd, God against man if an earthly representative existed even under the Old Covenant who, in the person of Moses, transmitted his pastoral staff to Joshua and through him to subsequent generations. Through the laying on of hands Joshua was appointed his successor (Num. xxvii, 18) who sat in the seat of Moses.[6] The ideas of E. Stauffer

---

[1] Cf. H. Schlier, 'Die Ordnung der Kirche nach den Pastoralbriefen', *Gogarten-Festschrift 'Glaube und Geschichte'*, Giessen, 1948, 54 ff. and H. Asmussen's works on the ministry which refer especially to the sacrament as its foundation. *ELKZ* V (1951), 362: 'If it were asserted, perhaps with reference to the First Epistle to the Corinthians, that the charisma came first and the ministry was only a product of a later age (Pastorals), the answer would be that the apostolate, which is undoubtedly founded on a command and has the character of an office, existed before the congregation'; P. Menoud, *L'Église et les ministères selon le Nouveau Testament*. Cah. théol. de l'act. prot. No. 22, Paris, 1948 especially pp. 49–61, where the episcopate is understood as an authority from above incarnated in a person. Almost the same in J. Colson, 'Aux origines du sacerdoce et de l'épiscopat', *Vie Spirituelle* (1949), 24–59. E. Kohlmeyer, 'Charisma oder Recht?' *Zeitschr. der Savigny-Stiftung*, Kan. Abt. 38 (1952), who states that in earliest Christian times the ministry was an office of the cult and finds in 1 Clem. a clerical state.

[2] 'Ganzheit und Mitte des Glaubens,' *WuW* 5 (1950), 169.
[3] ibid., 170.
[4] ibid.
[5] *Das Zeugnis des Neuen Testamentes von der Gemeinde*, 66.
[6] Cf. A. Ebneter, 'Die Petrusfrage,' *Orientierung* 17 (1953), 221 f.

which point in this direction[1] might open a way for Protestants to understand the Catholic idea of the ministry.

The Catholic View of the Church's Ministry

By Dr Otto Karrer, Lucerne[2]

The present subject makes many, even Catholic Christians, feel uncomfortable. The ministry is necessary—and one feels inclined to add: a necessary evil. But Christ has provided for it because it is necessary. It belongs to the Body of the Church, to its structure as a society. And we can love the Church as the community of all the faithful touched by the Spirit, and among them no doubt especially the 'good shepherds'. Perhaps even St. Augustine, the great bishop of the Church, felt like this, as is suggested by F. Hofmann in his book on St Augustine's conception of the Church.[3]

Such a view of the ministry is certainly not that of the Reformers, at least not the Lutheran conception, according to which it is not a divine ordinance, as the Catholics hold, but only a matter of human convenience. Even though the apostles had organized the Church somewhat on the lines of the Synagogue, the Reformers argued that, by emphasizing the Holy Spirit, brotherly love and the common witness, they had left enough room for adapting this organization to the human needs that varied according to time and place. Convinced that the increasing worldliness of the clergy left them no choice, the Reformers therefore confined themselves to what seemed essential, that is to say the message of Christ itself, while considering the apostolic order of the community as something that could reasonably be changed in accordance with the requirements of the times. Thus they saw themselves as knights of Christ destined to free the Gospel from the captivity of human usurpers.

1. Even this preliminary sketch will have shown that the ecclesiastical ministry is the most difficult problem of the Oecumene and that which will divide Christendom for a long time to come, because, according to the Catholic faith, it implies the apostolic succession and the primacy of the Petrine office.

---

[1] *Die Theologie des Neuen Testamentes*, 1947³, 14 ff.

[2] The Swiss Catholic theologian O. Karrer has clarified the relevant points of view involved in this question of the ministry in an article which has appeared in the periodical *Una Sancta* 14 (1959). I therefore insert it here.

[3] *Der Kirchenbegriff des hl. Augustinus*, Munich 1933, 257ff.

Nevertheless, even here there is some common ground: the religious meaning of the ministry for the community is not disputed. All acknowledge that there is not and cannot be an ecclesiastical ministry by itself and in its own right, but only in the service of the flock of Christ and of the individual Christians. It is service in the spirit of Christ, hence for the Kingship of God, for the purpose of man's encounter with God and for the free development of the spirit of sonship. This is the exact opposite of the widespread view, according to which the Catholic Church prevents a direct relationship with God, because the priest stands between God and the individual human being. In actual fact, seen from the theological point of view, the ministry exists precisely for leading every Christian directly to God—including Christian responsibility. In the words of Pius XI, it is the duty of priests 'so to educate the conscience of the faithful that they are able to find themselves the Christian solutions of the questions that arise in the various situations of life'[1]

We may even say more: Everything in the Church, preaching, sacraments and juridical order have been provided by Christ precisely for this, that God's grace should be brought to every one, that every man should find the essence of life in being Christ's disciple. The Church's ministry exists for the people, not the other way round. 'That is how we ought to be regarded' says St Paul, 'as Christ's servants, and stewards of God's mysteries' (1 Cor. iv, 1), that is to say not as tyrants, but as servants of a master. Catholic theologians emphasize this one meaning of the sacred ministry just as much as Karl Barth in his *Kirchliche Dogmatik*, so for example F. X. Arnold in his *Theologie der Seelsorge*, Yves Congar in *Esquisses du Mystère de l'Eglise* and *Théologie du Laicat* or K. H. Schelkle in his exegetical meditations on *Jungerschaft und Apostelamt*. True, the ecclesiastical ministry involves a responsible share in the office of the one Lord and High Priest, but in such a way that the faithful are aware of 'the good shepherd (in the words of St John), 'the impulse of the heart' (accord- to St Peter) and the 'Father' (in the words of St Paul), not of a power that stands on itself—also for this reason that all those who have received the grace of baptism and the faith have a share in the dignity and mission of Christ, according to a diversity of graces and grades of responsibility.

The ministry of the Church is something the priest receives in trust and for which he accepts responsibility—the one receiving ten pounds, the other five, the third one, entrusted to him for the time of

[1] Letter to Cardinal Segura, 'Laetus sane nuntius' (6th Nov. 1929).

the 'absence' of the Master, i.e. for earthly time. Despite the beautiful pictures of Fra Angelico there are no longer distinctions according to hierarchical rank in heaven; all this passes, love alone remains.

It is, however, another question in how far these ideal truths of the Gospel are reflected in this world or become dubious and give rise to misunderstandings, because the reality does not correspond to the idea. We are all human, and perhaps those with great natural or spiritual gifts are particularly exposed to the temptation of power. Our evangelical brothers know this—and not only with regard to us. Therefore Jesus has warned his disciples so clearly: 'You know that the princes of the Gentiles lord it over them and they that are the greater exercise power upon them. It shall not be so among you . . . The Son of Man is not come to be ministered unto but to minister and to give his life a redemption for many' (Matth. xx, 25–28). We should remember this and realize what exactly we mean if we speak of the Church's ministry.

2. In the spirit of Jesus, therefore, with the image of the great Shepherd before them the apostles have received the commission to 'feed the flock', according to the Biblical metaphor. Being, in the words of Ignatius of Antioch, themselves 'presidents of love', they appointed shepherds to guide the communities, *presbyterepiscopi* and deacons, to continue the work of the apostles as preachers of the Gospel and stewards of the mysteries of God and to transmit it in their turn to others.[1]

The laying on of hands, the sign of ordination, means that the person who ordains wills to transfer his power, and the accompanying prayer expresses the consciousness and the request that the Holy Spirit, the gift of the ascended Lord, operates through his human representative. St Paul tells his disciple Timothy to 'fan the flame of that special grace which God kindled in thee, when my hands were laid upon thee' (2 Tim. i, 6). Those who are in this way ordained by others are made bishops by the Holy Spirit (cf. Acts xx, 28). And what the man ordained by the apostles has received he is to transmit to 'men thou canst trust, men who will know how to teach it to others beside themselves' (2 Tim. ii, 2). Thus we see a continuing series of missions in the Holy Spirit leading from eternity into time.

But has Jesus really envisaged a Church enduring through the centuries? Because of some scriptural texts Albert Schweitzer and others thought that this must be denied. In their view, Jesus had expected His Second Coming for the Judgement very soon after his

---

[1] Ignatius of Antioch, *Romans*, introduction; Clement of Rome, *Corinthians* 43, 44.

death. But this view is no longer held. Because of Christ's undoubted statement that the Father had reserved the knowledge of this Day to Himself, the apostles counted on an intermediary period before the Last Day—otherwise their preaching and other activities, as recorded in Acts, would be quite inexplicable, as the evangelical theologian Bo Reicke states in his book on the faith and life of the early Christians.[1] The words of Jesus spoken before the High Priest (similarly elsewhere) 'You will see the Son of Man again, when he . . . comes on the clouds of heaven' (Matth. xxvi, 64) visualize the beginning of a new era of the Kingdom.[2] They refer obviously to the prophecy of Daniel, according to which the Kingdom of God, the Nation of the Saints represented by the Son of Man will, through the power of the risen Lord, overcome all opposition and remain until the (uncertain) end of the world.

Thus the apostolic Church set out on her journey, while the ecclesiastical powers were transferred to the successors of their first representatives. The exegetes are agreed that their functions concerned preaching, the liturgy and the ordering of the community. The worship of the primitive Church especially, the communion in the word and bread of life, is unthinkable without responsible holders of the apostolic office. This fact has been established by Ethelbert Stauffer and Werner Elert in agreement with Catholic liturgists.[3] The great importance of the laying on of hands by ordained exponents of authority 'in the presence of many witnesses' is clearly emphasized in Scripture even through its preparation by fasting, prayer and the invocation of the Holy Spirit. Hence today evangelical theologians are becoming increasingly convinced that a mere succession in the preaching of the Word without a sacramental commission handed on from one person to the other constitutes a revolutionary innovation of the Biblical structure of the Church which may be understandable as an emergency measure, but which cannot be considered legitimate in principle.

---

[1] *Glauben und Leben der Urgemeinde*, Zurich 1958, 43.

[2] See Mark ix, 1 and Luke ix, 27 explaining the term 'Son of Man' (Matth. xvi, 28) for the Hellenists. On the meaning and relationship of 'People of God', 'Servant' and 'Son of Man' see O. Cullmann, *Christologie des Neuen Testamentes*[2] 1958, 53ff, 154ff.

[3] *Abendmahl und Kirchengemeinschaft*, Berlin 1954; cf. H. D. Wendland, 'Gleichheit und Ungleichheit im Leibe Christi' in Asmussen-Stählin, *Die Katholizität der Kirche*, 1957, 205ff.

[4] W. Stählin, *Vom göttlichen Geheimnis*, 1936, 101; H. Dombois in Asmussen-Stählin, loc. cit. 169, 172.

3. In view of the late medieval corruption the Reformers thought to act in the spirit of Christ when they tried to organize the community from below, according to the sole principle of the universal priesthood, regretting, like the Confessio Augustana, that they had not a sufficient number of 'true bishops' at their disposal. It could surely not be in the spirit of Christ, they thought, to transmit 'mechanically' continuing and 'automatically' effective powers to, say, the second sons of noble families who frequently were not at all spiritually-minded. Hence even today world-Protestantism in general continues to cling to the view that there is no need for a 'continuous organization', that the 'succession in spirit', based on faith in the grace and glory of God, is a sufficient basis of Christian existence. This opinion has recently been re-affirmed by the Lutheran declaration on the Church Order of South India of 1951, and similarly by the statement of the *VELKD* of 1958 on the apostolic succession. But who explains the Word of Scripture? The Spirit? Certainly, but, according to St Paul, this is done by men solemnly appointed to this duty (cf. 2 Tim.). Scripture has been given to be preached, and, as Ernst Fincke says, 'Christian preaching is committed to persons who have a ministry, that is to say a solemnly accepted responsibility. Seen from this point of view the position of the Reformers is a defection from (Biblical) truth, because they have divorced doctrine from ministry. They believed that there was a succession of the confession as such, and that this succession was sufficient.'[1]

But even serious theologians like Heinrich Vogel, Hans von Campenhausen and Oscar Cullmann suspect such a formalistic, seemingly automatically effective succession to smack of magic. Karl Barth probably expresses the view of most Protestant theologians when he writes in the first volume of his *Kirchliche Dogmatik* in terms which may sound bold even to Evangelicals: 'The idea of succession current in the early Church could be right in itself (i.e. the knowledge of the presence of Christ with the Church), nor would there be an objection to the fact, only to the How—and even to the How we would not object in principle, neither to the summing up of the apostolate in Peter nor to the possibility of a primacy in the Church which, in that case, might even be that of the Roman community. The protest is directed only against this, that the authority is mechanically vested in successive bishops (or in the Roman bishop) over the head of the first, as if the succession could be other than pneumatic, or, when

---

[1] H. Asmussen in *Katholische Reformation*, Stuttgart 1958, 210f.

14

pneumatic, as if it could be tied to the profane fact of a list of bishops.'[1]

It would be a mistake to take no account of the historical motives which led the Reformers to claim a state of emergency; it would be wrong to tax men who did not want to separate themselves from the apostolic Church with conscious apostasy. Despite the passions we should honour their intentions; and if there is to be talk of collective guilt, this would concern in the first place the attitude of the papal and of most of the episcopal curias of the time, which tried to avoid necessary reforms. What had been necessary in the emergency might have been accepted as lawful for a time, until the apostolic order had been re-established. But after the reform of Trent the Mother Church has freed itself from the abuses opposed by the Reformers, while Protestantism with its many sects which emerged as a consequence of the re-ordering from below has had its own painful experiences. Besides, in the Una Sancta movement the latter has met both the 'Catholic' wing of the Oecumene (Anglicans and Eastern Churches) and Catholic theologians, and thus there are now more and more evangelical theologians, especially members of the 'Michaelsbruderschaft' and the 'Sammlung' and their friends who ask whether the apostolic order itself is not surrendered if the emergency order be raised into a permanent principle.

In the work of Wilhelm Stählin, Hans Asmussen and their friends on the catholicity of the Church (*Die Katholizität der Kirche*, 1957) this question is posed quite openly. The Reformed are beginning to take a similar line. The Neuenburg theologian Jean-Jacques von Allmen writes in his Introduction to the French edition of the Anglican Benedictine Gregory Dix's work on the ministry in the early Church: 'The full recognition of the pastoral office is the principal oecumenical problem of our time. To shirk this would mean to shirk unity. If we want to remain in touch with the Orthodox, the Roman Catholics and the Anglicans we must take the apostolic succession seriously. It has proved necessary for the preservation of the apostolic tradition and the order of worship. If the apostolic succession be denied the validity of ordination for the ministry is made doubtful.'[2]

Is the way blocked by insuperable obstacles? Most of them rest on misunderstandings. Once they have been removed the rest may safely be left to God.

---

[1] *Kirchliche Dogmatik* I/1, 105f.

[2] Cf. also J.-J. v. Allmen, *Diener sind wir. Auftrag und Existenz des Pfarrers*, Stuttgart 1958.

The question of the so-called 'automatic mechanism of succession' seems either due to a misunderstanding or to affect the sacraments themselves. Protestants in general are of the opinion that Catholic theology ascribes the effect of grace—in our case the transmission of spiritual authority—to the external matter or action in themselves. This they take to be the meaning of the so-called *opus operatum*. But, according to the Catholic faith as expounded at Trent, the Spirit of God works indeed through sensible, audible and visible signs, as through the Word of Scripture as *signum audibile*, so also through the *signum visible* of the baptismal water or of the eucharistic signs, the laying on of hands in confirmation, in the ordination of priests and the consecration of bishops. Nevertheless, these outward signs are effective only on condition that something interior be set in motion, the spiritual intention of minister and recipient, faith in the forgiveness of sins in baptism and penance, in communion with the sacrificed and present Lord in the Eucharist, in the responsibility undertaken in the name of the Spirit in confirmation and ordination. Those who administer the sacraments, in the present case those who ordain and consecrate, are always only servants of the divine Spirit; it is He, the Holy Spirit, who really consecrates. Hence the transmission of spiritual power rests not so much on the continuous succession of consecrating acts historically ascertainable on the horizontal plane, but on the gift of the Spirit descending from above, outside space and time, even though in the space-time dimension the consecrating agent will always be a man. In the Holy Spirit the heavenly Christ baptizes, consecrates, forgives and sends; the human instruments are always only more or less suitable or 'worthy'. Whether they be vessels of clay, silver or gold makes no difference to faith. And even if doubtful ordinations should occur or lawfully ordained men be—rightly or wrongly—deposed, even if Antipopes should mutually dispute their rights—the succession does not primarily depend on the spiritual state of a man but on the grace of the divine Spirit despite the changing, occasionally imperfect human acts. But as regards bishops' lists, on which Barth thinks consecration depends, these have no other significance in the life and consciousness of the Church than the genealogical tables in those of an old family. Their life does not depend on the list of their ancestors, though this is important as signifying a spiritual obligation. In the case of the Church such lists are a call to become disciples of the witnesses that have gone before, many of them venerable martyrs, reaching even to 'the glorious company of Apostles'.

4. The question, however, arises whether the power of any conse-crated minister, be he priest, bishop or Pope, is given 'unconditional-ly'? Can he 'dispose' of the apostolic inheritance or of heavenly gifts? Even oecumenically-minded evangelical theologians and laymen hold views on this subject to which we do not subscribe or which we at least cannot lawfully entertain. Karl Bernhard Ritter writes in his review of Richard Baumann's book *Fels der Welt* (Rock of the World): 'The apostolic ministry of the Catholic Church compels us to ask how it understands itself: whether its spiritual power is given once and for all and is therefore at the minister's disposal, or whether it knows it itself to be attached to the risen Lord and his Spirit. In this case its authority could be used only in the service of the Gospel and in the spirit of love and would always be prepared to be called back to the obedience of Christ.'[1] Catholic theologians cannot actually think differently on this subject. The ministry is a service of love. This, however, does not preclude the transmission of an authority with responsibility in the sense of de-voted service. No one can dispose of the Lord. Certain exaggerated and actually misleading expressions may have given rise to such ideas. In sermons at the celebration of the First Mass of a newly ordained priest one may for example sometimes be told that the priest 'has the power, denied even to the angels, to draw Christ down into the Sacrament'. Even Catholics often resent such language. But Catholic doctrine should not be judged by such blunders. The power 'to bind and to loose' is promised and given by God; but this does not mean that we can dispose of the divine gifts according to our own liking. We are bound to understand the ministry in the spirit of Christ. And if we were to think and act autocratically this would be guilt—possi-ble, indeed, among human beings, but wrong all the same. And every Christian in his own place is justified and called by the Spirit to oppose this wrong by testifying to the truth, as long as he does not act from selfish motives but in the spirit of truth and love.

This is valid also with regard to the Petrine office. The Church is built on the foundation which the Lord has laid, that is on Peter, the rock (Matth. xvi). In Luke xxii we read that his power does not rest on special human aptitude but on the prayer of Christ. In Matth. xviii he teaches that the Church is carried not only by Peter but also by the other Apostles, who form a fraternal Council, and in 1 Peter and Ephesians ii we are told that beside the apostolic ministers the whole people as a royal priesthood and especially the freely called witnesses

[1] *Deutsches Pfarrersblatt* 1957, 203f.

of the Spirit have a share in their responsibility. Jesus *prays* for Peter and the apostles and *promises* them his assistance. Prayer on the one hand, promise on the other show the tension between the divine Absolute and human relativity. The divine promise is absolute, the faithfulness of human service is relative, and we know from history and experience how very relative everything human is. But did Paul, for example, consider Peter's authority as abrogated when he opposed him at Antioch, or would the Council of Constance have been allowed to abolish the Petrine office itself when it deposed the quarrelling Antipopes for the sake of the unity of the Church? If authority ceased with human failure neither Peter nor anybody else could hold an office. This was known also to the theologians of the Augsburg Confession who wrote in their first draft that the ministry derived its power not from human virtue but from Christ's institution, 'even if it is carried out by bad men.'[1]

To whom is the promise given? Without doubt in the intention of Christ, and hence primarily, to the Church as the instrument of the kingdom of God in the world, and therefore in the second place to the Church's ministry and to its representatives, who are to be considered not so much for their own sakes but for the sake of the Church so that she can fulfil her mission. Anyone may be found wanting, and for this reason he needs the prayer of Christ and His saints, of 'the community of saints' as St Augustine wrote against the Donatists. The communion of saints together with the one Mediator (1 Tim. ii), the great High Priest of Hebrews, sustain the workmen of the Kingdom of God through their intercession; they also bear the human failings, for lastly all are in need of the mercy of God, as Pius XII expressed it in his last prayer.

More, the whole Church, not only the Petrine Office, is coresponsible for the preservation of the spirit of Christ. The bishops individually and as a college, but also the faithful people, the so-called laity with their representatives and those called by the Spirit are all responsible that authority should not degenerate into arbitrariness. Clement of Rome admonished the Corinthians in the name of the Roman community. Cyprian, as the classical exponent of episcopal power surely the last to abandon his responsibility, affirmed that he always consulted his community before important decisions.[2] Obviously both follow the apostolic example. The Acts of the Apostles

---

[1] T. Kolde, *Die älteste Redaktion des Augsburgischen Bekenntnisses*, Gütersloh 1906, 13.
[2] Cyprian, Ep. xiv, 4; more in Congar, *Jalons pour une théologie du laïcat*, Paris 1953, 76, 229, 329f, 335, 357.

afford a series of examples which show how the ideal of cooperation between ministry and community was realized: the apostles call the community together when the college of the Twelve is to be supplemented; Paul and Barnabas are sent on their mission by the community following a prophetic suggestion. Thus St. Paul administers Church discipline (1 Cor. v; 2 Cor. ii); thus the primitive Church elects the bishops and deacons that are to be ordained; and according to Clement of Rome the heads were appointed from the beginning with the assent of the congregation. The function of the sacred ministry corresponds to this co-responsibility of all the faithful which is expressed in ordination. If the medieval laity had not been so one-sidedly trained to obey the clergy, and if the majority of bishops had not shirked their part of the responsibility for the state of the Roman curia, the catastrophe of the Reformation would never have happened. This is an illustration of Möhler's principle of unity in multiplicity: 'Two extremes are possible in the life of the Church, and both are called egoism: if every one, or if one man wants to be all. Neither one nor every one must want to be all; only all can be all, and the unity of all can only be a whole.'[1]

There will never be a perfect insurance against the abuse of the holy thing, this would mean asking too much from the earthly Church which consists of human beings. But we can gather from the teaching of Scripture and the experiences of Church History what ought to be done in view of serious failure or threatening developments. There is the duty of fraternal admonition also of those of lower to those of higher rank; there is the freely spoken word of the 'prophets', in serious cases there is the sacred right and duty of opposition to tyrannical or dangerous behaviour of superiors. St Thomas Aquinas, surely an authority in the Catholic Church, praises St Paul for his opposition to the dangerous attitude of the First of the Apostles in the question of common meals between Jewish and Gentile Christians. 'The incident', St Thomas says, 'gives an example, 1. to the ecclesiastical superior: the example of humility, to be blamed by inferiors and subjects—2. to the subject: the example of zeal and frankness, that he may not be afraid to oppose the superior, especially if the trespass be public and threatens to endanger many'.[2]

Even though there may remain open questions regarding the past or the present—we should decidedly take our directives from the

---

[1] *Die Einheit in der Kirche*, ed. by J. R. Geiselmann, Cologne 1956, 237.
[2] Comm. ad Gal. 2, 111.

apostolic image of the Church which the present should reflect. If this be our attitude then both Catholic and Evangelical Christians, guided by their superiors and theologians, will find much food for thought. Looking to the common example and listening to each other, both Catholics and Protestants have come considerably nearer to each other during the last decades, and it is to be hoped that this process will be intensified through further conversations. Evangelicals have become conscious of the severe losses sustained by the Protestant world, when it gave up the authority of the apostolic ministry with its sacramental seal of ordination as opposed to the free witness of the spirit. The writings of Leslie Newbigin and Gregory Dix have not failed to make an impression. In the same way Catholics realize how much authentic Catholic truth was lost when, for fear of the 'Protestant spirit' we suffered genuine evangelical freedom and responsibility to be reduced to a degree unknown either in the primitive Church or in the age of the Fathers. We all need to learn what good there is on both sides. The situation of Christianity in the world of today is an urgent warning to divided Christendom, as says Heinz Schütte in his fine summary of oecumenic concerns: 'The existing rift (in Christendom) is the most serious obstacle to the Christianization of the world and our constantly increasing guilt. A Christian who is not concerned to remove the division and does not constantly pray for its healing must become anxious, and even frightened when he hears the words of St Augustine: 'He is lacking in the true love of God who does not love the unity of the Church.'[1]

*   *   *

The Reformers broke away from the apostolic succession established by revelation. Can their ministry be in any way a fragment of the reality of the true Church? And how are the official acts of 'evangelical' ministers to be regarded? Here it is not enough to point to the good faith and the subjective good will of giver and recipient. We have deliberately included the treatment of the ministry in the doctrine of the *vestigia ecclesiae*, because the doctrine of the *votum* is insufficient for dealing with this question of 'being'.

If Pope Leo XIII has declared Anglican ordinations invalid, how much more does this lack of validity apply to the whole 'evangelical' sphere. But lack of validity does not mean complete inefficacy. Hence we believe that a *vestigium ecclesiae* must be admitted also for the ministry.

   1. The evangelical ministry, too, contains a true spiritual reality

---

[1] *Um die Wiedervereinigung im Glauben.* Essen 1958; Preface.

based on the universal priesthood. If we insist on the fullness of Christ and understand the *totus Christus* as Christ and the Church, then the constitutive elements that make a man a member of the mystical Body continue to affect the actions of the baptized, even though not with their full power. 'Every baptized person has a share in the priestly, prophetic and royal activity of Christ.'[1] 'The Church has a priestly character. The deepest reason for this is that she is the Body of Christ. Christ is *the* priest. . . . The Church is a priestly community. Hence each individual member of the Church is able and obliged to perform priestly tasks. If the Church attributes to herself a priestly character, she does not establish another priesthood beside the priesthood of Christ.'[2] Now this universal priesthood is the basis of the particular one, which is transmitted through special ordination and to which alone are reserved the special offices of consecrating and blessing, because the priests are 'endowed with a special similarity to Christ and hence are enabled to symbolize Christ in a special way'.[3] To this consecrating power is added the sovereign pastoral power which is imparted by appointment to an office through the Pope or bishop.[4] The evangelical communions as well as all other Christian communities separated from the Mother Church have no particular priesthood, except the Orthodox who are within the apostolic succession. Though they are not united to the centre, they have nevertheless a valid and efficacious priesthood, which proves that this can exist even in separation from the centre. Congar speaks of a *succession sacramentelle du sacerdoce* and of certain acts of the teaching office which are not tied to actual jurisdiction (*magistère proprement dogmatique* as distinct from a *magistère directement pastoral*).[5] All others have the reality of the universal priesthood. Now to which order does this 'ministry' belong?

2. In the case of the separated Christians the ministry does not belong to the apostolic but to the prophetic order.[6] It cannot be

---

[1] Schmaus, *Kath. Dogmatik*,[4] IV, 1, 124.

[2] ibid., 571.

[3] ibid., 575.

[4] Cf. Mörsdorf, 'Abgrenzung und Zusammenspiel von Weihegewalt und Hirtengewalt.' *Die Kirche in der Zeit*, 4, fasc. 1, 17–22.

[5] 'A propos des "Vestigia ecclesiae" ' in *Vers l'Unité chrétienne*, No. 39 (1952), 4.

[6] We here distinguish the 'apostolic' from the 'prophetic' order in the sense in which J. L. Leuba has distinguished the 'institution' from the 'event'. (*L'institution et l'événement, les deux modes de l'oeuvre de Dieu selon le Nouveau Testament* in 'Bibliothèque Théologique', Neuchâtel-Paris, 1950.) In this important work Leuba attempts to prove from the New Testament that the two complementary aspects of the incarnation of God in Christ and in His Church are that Jesus, the apostles and the Church are institutionally integrated as well as events of God's direct presence. Among the apostles the Twelve,

doubted that the ministry has also a charismatic character, represented by the prophet, who is not ordained like the priest. What
Protestants today understand by ordination is actually within the
prophetic order. The orders of the prophet and of the apostle are
co-ordinated; for the Church is also founded on the prophet (cf.
Eph. ii, 20). His function is especially that of the preacher. However,
in the New Testament this prophetic order is guided by the apostolate: 'Prophecy, to be used according to the rule of faith' (Rom. xii,
6). For there is a danger of false prophets (Apoc. xi, 10). However
essential this service of the prophetic office may be for the Church,
and though we see in it the power of the evangelical ministry—a
true *signum ecclesiae*—we have yet to ask our separated brethren
several questions on this subject.

Enthusiasts at Corinth had misunderstood the Gospel and the
apostolate, considering the former as the personally received
message of their leaders who possessed the gift of the Spirit. They
wanted to identify the apostle with the recipient of the charismata
and even to substitute the one for the other. St Paul directs these
enthusiasts to the apostolic preaching of the Gospel (1 Cor. xv, 1).
He tells them to obey the *regula fidei*. He does not despise the gifts
of the Spirit, but they must conform to the apostolic rule of faith.
The *credere in Christum* presupposes the *credere apostolis*. Now what is

---

with Peter at their head, represent the institutional aspect: they are the authorized
witnesses. This authorization constitutes the apostolic order in the narrower sense. In
contrast with this the apostolate of St Paul has the character of an 'event'. He did not
receive his gospel from men 'nor did I learn it but by the revelation of Jesus Christ'
(Gal. i, 12). This would be the 'prophetic' order, the non-institutional, prophetic
office. Both these aspects of the ministry are complementary; for the Twelve recognized
the apostolate of Paul: 'They do not lay their hands on him nor ordain him, but rather
give him "the right hand of fellowship" (Gal. ii, 9)' (p. 63) and, on the other hand,
for St Paul 'the apostolate of the Twelve is an element of the Gospel (1 Cor. xv, 1)'
(p. 72). We might add that he is at pains to show that his experience agrees with that of
the older apostles (cf. 1 Cor. xv, 11). True, St Paul has received his apostolate outside
the hierarchy of the Church, but he only exercises it in agreement with the hierarchy.
A critical evaluation of Leuba's ideas is to be found in *HK* VI, 1951, 15 f.: 'This book
should encourage Catholic theologians to pay much more attention to the historical,
besides the institutionally juridical, side of ecclesiology. This will help them to find a
common language in which to speak to our separated brethren. Like them, we shall
learn once more to use the New Testament concept of the (non-institutional) prophetic
office within the Church. It will be the task of the institutional, hierarchical magisterium
to examine whether its utterances are in accordance with the faith (Rom. xii, 6; 1 Thess.
v, 20 f.), but this prophetic office will not simply be absorbed by the doctrinal office.
(Or, as J.-H. Dalmais, O.P., writes in *Vie Spirituelle* October 1950 on the subject of
this book: 'If here some Protestants may learn to re-discover the institutional concept,
some Catholics will also be well advised to develop a livelier consciousness of the
Lordship of Christ and the sovereign liberty of the Holy Spirit.' ibid., 16.)

the peculiar characteristic of the apostolate? It rests on the fact of being sent; the apostolic office of the Church guarantees the presence of Christ. As it comprises rights and duties it is transmitted by 'sending' and authorization. Now this raises the question how this admission to the ministry is carried out in the Protestant communities. Is it done by the invisible Christ and confirmed by the congregation? Who confers the *potestas*, and who guarantees the orthodoxy of the teaching of the 'prophets'? The answer will be: Holy Scripture. But surely the Oecumene itself supplies the clearest evidence how differently Scripture can be interpreted. The *regula constitutiva* (Scripture and *traditio passiva*) must be supplemented by a *regula directiva*, which is the teaching office of the Church. Where is this office in Protestantism? Here again one is afraid of identifying God and man. But we have clearly distinguished the teaching office as *regula directiva* from the *principia constitutiva*. Pope and bishops are not apostles; they are their successors, and, as far as revelation is concerned, occupy a different sphere, as has been pointed out before. We know, too, that the apostolic succession may not be understood in the sense of a mechanistic laying on of hands. But since the Protestants have broken away from this succession they lack the teaching office of the Church in its strictly doctrinal sense.

Now what is the position with regard to the office of the keys?

Its Biblical foundation is John xx, 22 f. and Matt. xvi, 18 and xviii, 18. Today Evangelicals recognize this in their attempt to re-establish confession. An essay by W. Spocka[1] makes an important contribution to this question. The author states that this office is concerned with a twofold key (of binding and loosing) of 'objective power' and reaches the conclusion: 'Where the binding key is no longer used ... there the loosing key can and may no longer be used either. In this case any officially pronounced absolution is devoid of justification and validity, because the New Testament foundation for such an absolution no longer exists. ... I have called this a monstrous thought, because we are now faced with the inescapable question whether the words of absolution, spoken by and in churches which no longer use the binding key, are really anything more than pious formulae. It must be asked whether it is not a disgraceful abuse of the all too lightly abandoned office of the keys still to use the old form of absolution ...   If the office is halved, this does not mean that its efficacy is halved but rather that

[1] *ELKZ* VII (1953), 145 f. 'Das Lehrstück vom Amt der Schlüssel als Frage der Kirche.'

the whole authority inherent in this office is destroyed.' If Protestants ask such questions merely from the point of view of exercising the ministry, our separated brethren must surely understand if the Mother Church confronts them with the same questions on the grounds of the data of revelation. The separated Christians lack the *fullness* of the ministry, and thus of the Holy Spirit objectivated in it. What remains is a trace, a particle, yet containing a spiritual reality which can find its perfection only in the sphere of the objectively true deposit of the faith, the objectively valid sacrament and the objective, God-given ministry. Hence the return to the Father's house is always a way to plenitude, to the *totus Christus*.

The Roman Catholic Church has been blamed time and again for not leaving room for the charismata. We may answer that, according to Catholic teaching, too, the charismata belong essentially to the Church. These are the words of the encyclical *Mystici Corporis*: 'But it must not be supposed that this co-ordinated, or organic, structure of the Body of the Church is confined exclusively to the grades of the hierarchy, or—as a contrary opinion holds—that it consists only of "charismatics", or persons endowed with miraculous powers; though these, be it said, will never be lacking in the Church. It is certainly true that those who possess the sacred power in this Body must be considered primary and principal members, since it is through them that the divine Redeemer himself has willed the functions of Christ as teacher, king, and priest to endure through the ages. But when the Fathers of the Church mention the ministries of this Body, its grades, professions, states, orders, and offices, they rightly have in mind not only persons in sacred orders, but also all those who have embraced the evangelical counsels and lead either an active life among men, or a hidden life in the cloister, or else contrive to combine the two, according to the institution to which they belong.'[1] 'Certainly our holy Mother shows herself without stain in the Sacraments with which she begets and nurtures her children; in the faith which she preserves ever inviolate; in the holy laws which she imposes on all and in the evangelical counsel by which she admonishes; and, finally, in the heavenly gifts and miraculous powers by which out of her inexhaustible fecundity she begets countless hosts of martyrs, virgins, and confessors.'[2] Here the charismata are even enumerated together with the three constitutive elements of the Church. No one will deny that such charismata may

[1] CTS edn. n. 17.
[2] ibid., 65.

be found among the separated Christians; they, too, are genuine *vestigia ecclesiae.*

The decisive point is that Protestant teaching divides the ministry into a sphere of *Jus divinum* and one of *Jus humanum*, thus abandoning its element of visibility. The motive for this may be the fear of giving the ministry a significance of its own. We, too, consider that it is a relative entity if compared with Christ and the apostolate. But it contains an absolute element, which is God's entry into time and humanity. 'This precisely is the problem, that God gives Himself into our hands with His gifts and graces. What is given is in the hands of man, and he must administer the gift. . . . The reference to a Body (Eph. iv) cannot possibly envisage something invisible. The forms are really not quite so insignificant as Protestantism would like to make them. . . . If we live by the Word that was made Flesh and created a Body for Itself in the Church, then we must be concerned with all the objectivations in which the gift of grace desires to take form. For the urge to form is the theme of the Epistle to the Ephesians.'[1] Spiritual and earthly spheres in the Church must not be divorced from one another so as to exclude each other; for this contradicts the nature of the incarnation. 'There are no "secular" offices in the Church from which a "spiritual" office would have to be distinguished. The Spirit-giving God has instituted them all and thus "tempered the body together" (1 Cor. xii, 11, 18, 24, 28).'[2] God's Spirit dwells in the Church—we may say, with the necessary modification, that He embodies Himself in her. But this eliminates the essential difference between God and man as little as in the case of the one Person of Christ. Pius XII has sharply rejected this tendency of identification in certain Catholic circles: 'Any explanation of this mystical union is to be rejected if it makes the faithful in any way pass beyond the order of created things and so trespass upon the divine sphere, that even one single attribute of the eternal God could be predicated of them in the proper sense.'[3]

So we see here, too, in dealing with the question of the ministry, that the actual, essential differences between the Mother Church and the members separated from her is a difference of *being*. To clarify this will prepare a way that leads from fragments to the fullness of being.

---

[1] Asmussen, *Der Brief des Paulus an die Epheser,* 106.

[2] Wendland, *Das Wirken,* 465.

[3] *Mystici Corporis,* CTS 78.

Church and Sacrament

The ministry, as Asmussen says, derives from a sacramental existence. Now this is a fundamental assertion of the sacramental being of the Church, through which alone the Protestant concept of function can be corrected. But what is sacramental being?

A fruitful oecumenical debate on the meaning of sacrament must be preceded by research on the method of the subject, since this will bring to light also the formal differences between the Catholic and Protestant views of the sacraments. There exists an important study of this question of method by O. Dilschneider,[1] which we will here briefly summarize. Dilschneider begins with the fact that the doctrine of the Reformers was based on a conception of the sacraments which was institutional, because their nature was examined by a method based on Scripture and confined to the exegesis of texts concerning the individual sacraments, whose institution by Jesus Christ was to be proved. This is a perfectly legitimate procedure which has also been followed by Catholic theologians. But, as Dilschneider states, this exclusive preoccupation with the exegetical problems of the texts of institution resulted in something like 'inbreeding', by which process the whole sacramental problem was over-simplified and gradually degenerated. (The author refers to the controversy on infant baptism in contemporary theology as proof of his thesis.) Without wanting to exclude this textual exegesis, Dilschneider starts from a different point. He places the science of the sacraments 'within the theology of revelation linked to theology as a whole'. This theology of revelation, the chief concern of the Berlin systematic theologian, is directed towards salvation and thus leads to Christ Himself. The sacrament is $\mu\nu\sigma\tau\acute{\eta}\varrho\iota o\nu$, and the essence of the New Testament mystery is 'Christ as the irruption of eternity into time, as the Logos entering the flesh.'[2] The incarnation is the essence of the mystery and the sacrament, which is *instrumentum incarnationis Christi*.

This, indeed, seems to be the Catholic view, and one might ask whether this incarnational redemptive conception is still representative of the genuinely Protestant idea of the sacraments. Thus even here the problem of the Catholic and the evangelical conception of the sacraments becomes evident.

We have raised the question of the nature of sacramental being. According to the teaching of the ancient Church (down to St

Gegenwart Christi II, 266–77.   [2] ibid., 279.

Augustine), 'in the sacramental action the Holy Spirit descended on the material elements which He sanctified, communicating to them His sanctifying power.'[1] Thus the sacraments are taken to be an enlargement of the existence of Christ, more exactly of His sacred Humanity, hence they point to the mystery of the Incarnation. The external sign of the sacrament 'is itself the taking shape of an invisible reality . . . the emanation of a hidden being.'[2] In Augustine's theology this unity was broken up in the course of his controversy with the Donatists, which led him to distinguish between the *sacramentum* and the *res sacramenti*. Grace is divided into a lower and a higher reality, dependent on the recipient's act of faith. This, however, does not alter Catholic doctrine, according to which 'the sacramental sign is the form in which grace is expressed.'[3] In their different ways the Reformers void the sacramental sign of its reality, watering it down into something symbolic. The *Apologie* defines the sacraments as 'rites which are ordained by God and to which the promise of grace is added.'[4]

At Lausanne J. Schoell gave a good description of the different doctrines of the nature of the sacraments (and of grace): 'According to the first (*scil*. Catholic) view the grace of the Sacrament is bestowed by the penetration of the divine essence into the human nature . . . from this point of view, the grace which is bestowed by the Sacrament is something new. . . . According to the other (Protestant) conception . . . it is the will of divine love manifested in Christ, which judges and saves the sinner.'[5] We see that this is an exact parallel to the different views on justification. We are almost tempted to speak of a forensic conception of the sacraments in certain Protestant circles. But the elements over which the sanctifying words are spoken receive an instrumental significance for salvation; they are integrated in the *nova creatio Spiritus Sancti*, since the *pneuma* exists in a sacramental mode.[6] We cannot, as Brunner has tried to do, regard *pneuma* and sacrament as opposites, because 'these so-called sacraments' are seen 'as the starting-point for the later institutional development',[7] which Brunner takes to be opposed to the primitive Christian 'pneumatic communion of persons'.

[1] Schmaus, *Kath. Dogmatik*[4] IV, 1, 7.
[2] ibid.
[3] ibid., 24.
[4] Cf. 'Ritus qui habent mandatum Dei et quibus addita est promissio gratiae.' Luthardt, *Dogmatik*, 241.
[5] Bate, 310.
[6] 'The *Pneuma* is sacramental in its essence,' Käsemann, *Leib und Leib Christi*, 128.
[7] *Das Missverständnis*, 66.

The sacraments are evidence of the presence of the Holy Spirit and of grace; they are *signa ecclesiae*. Hence, where a sacrament is validly administered and received there is an element of the Church, a *vestigium ecclesiae*. The individual sacraments 'build up the Church' in different degrees; among the dissidents those of baptism and matrimony have this power in an eminent degree, but, apart from the Eastern Church, confirmation, Eucharist and ordination are absent.

* * *

DIGRESSION:

The Church and the Law

The difference in the doctrine of the working of the Holy Spirit shows itself especially in the question of the nature of the Law in the Church. At the turn of the century Rudolf Sohm declared the nature of the Church to be opposed to Canon Law,[1] and in our own days Emil Brunner, following in Sohm's footsteps, asserted the juridical order of the Church to be a substitute for the missing fullness of the Holy Spirit. 'Canon Law is a substitute for the Spirit.'[2] We would not affirm this to be the general Protestant view—Protestants, from Holl to Harnack, have contradicted Sohm—but it is an extreme expression of a latent tendency of Protestant thought. It is true, the Protestant communities have a church law, but its function and nature are quite different from its position in the Catholic Church.

A. The Protestant View of the Law of the Church

To understand this view we must follow J. Heckel[3] and start with the concept of the Church. Here we gather the threads of the Protestant view of the Church as they have come to light in our previous discussions. Luther distinguished between the *ecclesia spiritualis, abscondita*[4] and the *ecclesia universalis*, between the Church of the true believers and saints and the Church in its empirical form. According to him this difference is essential.[5] Corresponding to this

---

[1] *Kirchenrecht*, 2 vols., Munich, 1923, reprint of the edn. of 1892, I, 1.

[2] *Das Missverständnis*, 51; cf. ibid. 89.

[3] *Initia iuris ecclesiastici Protestantium*, Munich, 1950.

[4] *Dictata super Psalterium, WA* III, 5.47, 5).

[5] This does not mean that one Church excludes the other. 'Both are indispensable to each other and can be conceived only together. The universal Church is the field of action of the spiritual Church, the spiritual Church is the life force of the Universal Church.' Heckel, loc. cit., 15.

division of the Church the Law, too, is divided into *Jus divinum* and *Jus humanum*. Now what are the respective spheres of these different laws? Divine law exists only in the *ecclesia abscondita*: '*Ecclesia (spiritualis) vivit jure divino*.'[1] Thus *Jus divinum* is relegated to the invisible realm. Hence its sphere of action is the *homo interior*, because he alone is directed towards the *ecclesia spiritualis*.

What is the position of the visible side of the Church, the primacy, the power of the keys, the councils, the external order, the ministry? As far as all this belongs to the *ecclesia universalis*, hence to the visible realm, it is not subject to *Jus divinum* but to *Jus humanum*. The latter is not 'secular' law in the sense of the civil power; it is a law *sui generis*,[2] but never divine law. The distinction corresponds exactly to the Protestant doctrine of justification. As this distinguishes between law and Gospel, so *Jus divinum* applies solely to the inner man and can be perceived only by the *intellectus fidei*, whereas *Jus humanum* concerns the *homo exterior*, can be perceived by human reason and has an educational value for the progress of *homo interior*.[3] This 'autonomous' law of the Church 'has no formal claim to validity'.[4] The external order of the Church which is served by its autonomous law 'does not bind primarily, for the sake of salvation, but secondarily, for the sake of order. We do not submit to it for the sake of faith, as if it were necessary for salvation, but for charity's sake, because the Church cannot live and act without order.'[5] According to Luther, 'the whole structure of the Church is interior, before God and invisible'.[6] Thus the *potestas ecclesiastica* is divided into a spiritual (invisible) and a non-spiritual (visible) part, according to the sphere in which the *potestas* operates. In the Protestant view, the power of the keys, for example, lies with the spiritual church and derives from divine law, whereas the external power of government belongs to the sphere of *ecclesia universalis* and derives from human law.[7]

This is the characteristic Protestant conception of the law of the Church. On this basis various theories have been developed, with certain nuances, whether for or against Sohm.[8]

Here the absence of the incarnational category becomes particu-

[1] Cf. ibid., 51.
[2] Cf. ibid., 53.
[3] ibid., 57.
[4] ibid., 64.
[5] P. Althaus, *Die christliche Wahrheit* II, 292.
[6] 'Omnis structura Ecclesiae est intus coram Deo invisibilis.' *WA* IV, 81, 13.
[7] Cf. Heckel, loc. cit., 32.
[8] Cf. H. Wehrhahn, 'Die Grundlagenproblematik des deutschen evangelischen Kirchenrechtes, 1933–45.' *Theol. Rundschau*, 19, 231–52.

larly noticeable. Protestants are unaware of the legitimate link between the divine and human spheres. It is surely significant that throughout his work Sohm speaks almost exclusively of Christ as God.

Some Protestant theologians, however, are anxious to revise this view, e.g. E. Kohlmeyer who is led by Matt. xviii, 15–20 and 1 Cor. v, 1–5 to affirm that there was a sacred law in the Jewish as well as in the Hellenistic tradition, and that this influenced the primitive Church.[1] 'The whole Jewish law was not constitutional or corporate or in any way human law, but theocratic law.'[2] Kohlmeyer opposes especially Sohm's theory, according to which there had been no law among the 'bearers of the spirit' (*Geistträger*), but only a free activity of the charismata and a free incorporation into the Body of Christ. 'It is a profound thought which, grasping impressively the incompatibility of formulated law and the free life of the spirit, makes this the basis of a new edifice of Church Law. However, according to the unanimous opinion of scholars our sources do not permit us to subscribe to this view.'[3] The New Testament Kingdom of God is not a social community but a sovereign society. The religious characteristic of the oldest Church law is its sacred juridical character 'which we may well say to be related to God, and which makes itself felt in a great variety of forms.'[4] This examination of the sources has led Kohlmeyer to discover 'a line of divine law' which was realized in the visible community.

A. Oepke emphasized that the New Testament community needed an external form 'not only because it also existed in time and space, but on principle. It knew itself to be the Israel of the last times, the legal successor and perfector of the ancient people of God that had broken the covenant.' 'Hence a certain Church law belongs from the beginning to the very nature of Christianity and the Church.'[5] 'St. Paul identifies ecclesiastical and spiritual authority. This is created by the Spirit, who establishes ecclesiastical order and founds law.'[6]

But, according to the Protestant view of the Church stated above, such assertions have no definite meaning in themselves. Here, too, we see that everything depends on the underlying principles.

---

[1] 'Charisma oder Recht? Vom Wesen des ältesten Kirchenrechtes.' *Zeitschrift der Savigny-Stiftung* 38 (1952), 1–36.

[2] ibid., 8. [3] ibid., 14.

[4] ibid., 16.

[5] 'Das Recht im Neuen Testament,' *ELKZ* 4 (1950), 360.

[6] H. Conzelmann, article 'Amt' in *R.G.G.*

Continuing the line of Kohlmeyer, E. Stauffer considers the question whether the Jewish elements are primary or secondary, constitutive or accessory, and whether they have been inherited or constitute an 'invasion' of Jewish legal concepts and practices that may have taken place only in the second or third century.[1] Stauffer thinks that they are an inheritance, seen in such concepts as *adelphoi*, *topos*, *kleros*, *diakonia*, *apostole*, *episkope* and *episkopos* as well as in the legal acts of selection and presentation.

In this research of Protestant scholars we miss, nevertheless, the dogmatic conclusion that should be drawn from its results. For this, however, the forensic concept of justification would have to be abandoned and to be replaced by incarnational categories that would lead to the fullness of Christ. A beginning of this could be noticed at the Conference of Treysa, where the New Testament scholar N. A. Dahl (Oslo) drew attention to the link between creation and redemption. According to him the Christian lives simultaneously in the old and the new aeon; but this does not mean that he is torn between the two, for Christ is the *Imago Dei*, the second Adam, the Mediator of creation, while the Church represents the new creation even on earth. There is 'something like a juridical order' in the Church. Dahl asks 'whether we may regard this in such a way that the powers of the coming aeon inchoatively affect the formation of the juridical life.'[2] K. L. Schmidt, too, referred to the doctrine of the *Imago Dei* at the Treysa Conference. In the light of this doctrine Christian power is 'not a demonized autonomy of itself but... is derived from God; only in union with this power is there a human law that is also a divine law.'[3]

B. The Catholic Doctrine[4]

The Church is the continuation of Christ. Canon Law belongs to its visible sphere and has a formal claim to validity. What is the foundation of this claim?

The Church is constituted by the Word and the Sacraments. Now both have a legal structure. Christ speaks with authority (John viii, 12–20; Matt. ix, 1–8; John xx, 30 f.). The Word is preached by the authority of the Lord (cf. the juridical term *apostolos* and the legal

---

[1] 'Jüdisches Erbe im urchristlichen Kirchenrecht.' *ThLZ* 77 (1952), 201 ff.
[2] *Die Treysa-Konferenz 1950 über das Thema Gerechtigkeit in biblischer Sicht*, Geneva, 1950, 32.
[3] ibid., 27.
[4] The substance of the following discussions was developed by K. Mörsdorf in a lecture, 'Geist und Sendung des kanonischen Rechtes,' *WS*, 1952.

symbolism of the laying on of hands). Christ demands obedience because He is the Lord. The juridical structure of the sacraments is evident especially in those that confer a character, i.e. baptism, confirmation and Holy Orders. The legal character appears especially in ordination, where it is related to jurisdiction. Now the Word and the Sacrament give the Church its supernatural foundation. But Canon Law has also a natural basis, since the Christian lives also in the order of creation. Thus natural law does not constitute a 'depravation' of sacred law, because the God of the first article of the Creed is the same as the God of the third. But the natural law can exist in the Church that is constituted by Word and Sacrament only in so far as it agrees with the order of these two, since it is not independent, but is limited by the supernatural foundation. The structure of the Church is hierarchical, because it was the will of the Lord that it should continue His saving work according to a certain order. Protestants, too, recognize the fact that within the Church there is a legal order established by the Gospel. The question is how this authority takes concrete form. There is evidence in Holy Scripture that external actions such as the laying on of hands are an instrumental cause in the communication of the Pneuma (cf. Acts viii, 9 ff.). It is a fundamental thesis of Catholic teaching that there is a *Jus divinum* in the visible sphere of the Church on which, for example, the *potestas suprema jurisdictionis* of the Pope is based.[1] But besides the *Jus divinum* Catholic doctrine also acknowledges a *Jus mere ecclesiasticum*.[2] After what has been said of the special nature of the incarnational sphere this distinction will easily be understood.

A dogmatic exposition of this Catholic teaching is given in H. Volk's essay on the action of the Holy Spirit.[3] He begins with His action in Christ, who is the *causa exemplaris* of Redemption. Volk understands the unity of the Divinity and humanity in Christ as *gratia unionis*, which is unction for the humanity.[4] This unction has two components: as setting apart for a work it is *consecratio*, as ordering towards God it is *sanctificatio*. Christ's offices of Teacher, Lord of Creation, Shepherd, King, Judge and Priest are contained in His anointing as *consecratio*. The character of these offices leads Volk to conclude: 'As an office this *consecratio* as an element in the

---

[1] Cf. *CIC*, c. 219.

[2] Cf. Eichmann-Mörsdorf, *Kirchenrecht* I⁷, 36.

[3] 'Das Wirken des Heiligen Geistes in den Gläubigen,' *Jahrbuch für Kontroverstheologie* 9 (1952), 13–34.

[4] ibid., 15. On the notion of unction in Christ cf. Isa. lxi, 1; Luke iv, 21; Acts iv, 27; x, 38.

bestowal of graces on Christ has a legal character. Through the *gratia capitis* Christ holds a position which cannot be described without using legal terms. By making Christ by His nature Son of God the *gratia unionis* gives Him rights in the world. . . . Grace itself contains office and law as elements.'[1] Now the action of the Holy Spirit in the Church and the faithful also receives its structure from Christ, for He sends the Holy Spirit. Scripture uses the same expressions for the communication of the Spirit to Christ and to the faithful. In the latter case, too, the action of the Spirit is regarded as an unction (2 Cor. i, 21 f.; 1 John ii, 20). 'This anointing is an image and participation of the anointing of Christ and, like this, the effect of the Spirit.'[2] Volk finds the consecration in the Biblical term 'sealing' (Eph. i, 13; iv, 30; 1 John ii, 27). 'Hence justifying grace confers the character of a state and with it an office.'[3] So Volk reaches the conclusion: 'Since one element of grace has a consecrating power, law, office and state are themselves pneumatic; they are modes of spiritual being, hence within the Church also in so far as she is from above and pneumatic, and so they are themselves from the beginning divinely instituted and pneumatic.' 'Office and law are theological realities belonging to the sphere of grace. Hence Canon Law is definitely and in the strictest sense a theological discipline. The Pneuma effects . . . law, hence in the Church law is pneumatic.'[4]

Protestants fight shy of thus embodying the Holy Spirit in creation. Here again they feel that such a teaching diminishes God's sovereignty. But surely their view would limit the action of the Holy Spirit. Here again a 'contracted' conception is the result of an absence of reality, the necessary result of leaving the Church, which is the 'pillar and ground of the truth' and of living only by a fragmentary reality.

*   *   *

iii. *Baptism*

We have seen that Church membership is established by the sacramental character of baptism.[5] This unites all the baptized with Christ and with each other, at least with regard to constitutional

[1] ibid., 17.
[2] ibid., 31.
[3] ibid., 33.
[4] ibid., 20.
[5] Cf. Schmaus, *Kath. Dogmatik*[4] IV, 1: 'The sacramental character is Church-creating.'

membership. Wherever baptism is validly administered there is the Church. For the Church itself is engaged in the act of baptism, even if administered within a dissident community. This is clear in the case of infant baptism, where the Church confesses the faith on behalf of the infant.[1] But this faith, which is the proper disposition for baptism, 'is not the thing that makes baptism as such effective'.[2] The new life mediated by baptism is 'an admission to the common life of the Church; the new life is realized only in unity with her. According to primitive Christian teaching there is no baptism outside the Church.'[3] The concept of a valid but inefficacious baptism taught by older theologians cannot be admitted in view of the statement of Pope Stephen I: 'But the name of Christ, said he (Stephen), profits much for faith and sanctification by baptism, so that whoever has been baptized, and wheresoever, in the name of Christ, at once receives the grace of Christ.'[4] Hence baptism may rightly be called an 'oecumenical sacrament'.[5] It is a true *vestigium ecclesiae* and expresses the presence of an ecclesiastical reality.

We call baptism a *vestigium ecclesiae*, because as the sacrament of 'embodying', of the reception into the Church, it is itself only part of the so-called *Ritus initiationis christianae*; for it points to the pouring out of the Spirit in confirmation,[6] in which the *Ritus initiationis* is completed. This in its turn is directed towards participation in the Eucharist which it requires for its perfection. Only this will provide an integral share in salvation, by which the honour and glory of God in Christ and in His own is revealed as perfectly as possible here and now. Baptism is only the beginning, after which the process of the forgiveness of sins, rebirth, justification and sanctification must be continued in order to reach its earthly fulfilment in the Eucharist.[7]

---

[1] Cf. J. Hamer, 'Le baptême et la foi,' *Irénikon*, XXIII (1950), 387–405, following St Augustine.

[2] Schlier, 'Zur kirchlichen Lehre von der Taufe,' *ThLZ* 72 (1947), 332.

[3] A. Fridrichsen, Kyrka och sacrament. Cf. Schrey in 'Verkündigung und Forschung', *Theologischer Jahresbericht*, 1951, 139.

[4] 'Sed in multum, inquit (Stephanus), proficit nomen Christi ad fidem et baptismi sanctificationem, ut quicumque et ubicumque in nomine Christi baptizatus fuerit, consequatur statim gratiam Christi.' Denz., 47: Firmilian, in whose letter to Cyprian this fragment of Stephen's letter is transmitted, explains: 'Nullo adversus haereticos zelo excitatur, concedens illis non modicam, sed maximam gratiae potestatem, ut dicat eos et asseveret per baptismi sacramentum sordes veteris hominis abluere, antiqua mortis peccata donare, regeneratione coelesti filios Dei facere, ad aeternam vitam divini lavacri sanctificatione reparare,' *CSEL* III, 2, 821; *ML* 3, 1169A.

[5] P. Brunner, 'The Realism of the Holy Spirit,' *ER* III (1950), 226.

[6] Cf. L. S. Thornton, *Confirmation, its Place in the Baptismal Mystery*, London 1954.

[7] Cf. F. Thijssen, Sakramente und Amt bei den nichtkatholischen Christen, *Una Sancta* 14 (May 1959), 82–108.

iv. *The Word of God*

Protestantism likes to call itself 'the Church of the Word'.[1] H. Diem has asserted only recently that 'the congregation is born through preaching'.[2] In this view the Word is regarded as a means of grace. 'The Church's most important means of grace is the preaching of the Word, which, being a witness to sin (law) and grace (gospel), is apt to effect the penitent obedience of faith in the measure as it is a true expression of the salvation in Christ that is clearly affirmed in, and is according to, Scripture.'[3] These ideas are quite in the tradition of Luther who held that the Word alone is capable of justifying man, whom it awakens to spiritual life, an event that takes place only in the inmost sphere of his being. Not all to whom the Word of God comes open their minds to it. 'Thus within the external community there is a small circle which alone deserves to be called Church, i.e. Church of Christ. These are the truly faithful, who have been won through the Word and been awakened to spiritual life. They alone can fitly be called "members of Christ", for they are incorporated in Christ by faith.'[4]

We see clearly that here the efficacy of God's Word is relegated to a purely interior sphere. This view of the Word and its pre-eminence could not fail to change the conception of the Church's means of grace. 'Whereas, according to medieval scholastic teaching the sacrament is the Church's principal means of grace, Luther instinc tively introduces the Gospel where he ought to mention the sacrament, or at least places the Word before the sacrament.'[5]

Catholic doctrine, guided by Scripture, regards the Word of God as a *dynamis*, a power of God, which effects what it announces (cf. Rom. i, 16). The Word of God becomes a powerful event in the life of man, it is God's creative deed which brings salvation to the sinner. Through the Word man becomes a new creation, and the men of this new creation become the Church. Thus the Word is a

---

[1] Cf. E. Brunner, 'Die Kirche als Lebensgemeinschaft,' in *Die Zeichen der Zeit* II, 381. V. Herntrich, 'Die Kirche Jesu Christi und das Wort Gottes,' *Bekennende Kirche* 35, p. 3.

[2] *Evangelische Theologie*, 1949, pt. 5, 193–211. Cf. R. Bring, 'Lutherische Theologie angesichts der Ökumenischen Arbeit,' *Luthertum*, pt. 1: 'The Church is constituted by an activity, i.e. the preaching of the Word and the administration of the sacraments' (34).

[3] Luthardt, *Kompendium der Dogmatik*, 339.

[4] K. Holl, *Gesammelte Aufsätze zur Kirchengeschichte*. 'Die Entstehung von Luthers Kirchenbegriff,' I, 295.

[5] ibid., 292.

constructive element of the Church,[1] because it bears witness to the incarnation of the Son of God. For this reason it contains the features of the God-Man and thus becomes a faithful mirror of the Church. But if the Church is *incarnatio continuata*, the Word of Christ is at the same time the Word of the Church; hence the Word has also an ecclesiological structure, and this means that the Church mediates it.

The Protestant definition of the Word of God is dominated by two tendencies. One is that of interiorizing and spiritualizing religion. This shows itself most clearly in the forensic view of justification.[2] 'Forensic justification is ultimately a verbal concept foreign to the Gospel.'[3] Dilschneider speaks of an idealistic withdrawal into the abstract and spiritual sphere.[4] He concludes that 'the pneumatic powers intrinsic in the words of the Bible have vanished. . . . This results from the exaggerated attachment to the Word of which contemporary Protestant theologians are so proud. This pride is unfortunately without foundation, for this attachment to the Word has come to be no more than a thin spiritualism, a Western emptying of what is meant when the Old and the New Testaments speak of the *dynamis* of God as the characteristic of the Word'.[5] This is indeed a momentous statement, asserting that a change in the understanding of God's Word causes the disappearance of pneumatic powers.[6] In this connexion a passage from the report of the theological commission on 'Forms of Worship' is relevant: 'The idealistic view that the Word belongs wholly to a non-material sphere of pure spirituality endangers not only the whole conception of the sacraments but even such essential Christian doctrines as creation and incarnation.'[7] Might we not even conclude that the

---

[1] 'The preaching of the Word has the power to form and preserve a community: it is an essential element in the structure of the visible Church. The preaching of the Word derives a juridical character from the fact that it is done in the power of the Lord.' Eichmann-Mörsdorf, *Kirchenrecht* I[7], 28.

[2] Cf. on this I. Dilschneider, *Gegenwart Christi*, vol. 2, pp. 255-7.

[3] loc. cit., 111.

[4] ibid., 230.

[5] ibid., 257.

[6] 'We have no right to justify evangelical piety and preaching simply by claiming the authority of the Word of God, for this is largely against us. And this means that Christ is against us. The Body of the Church is sick, as a human body is sick if it is lacking the necessary nutritive elements in its blood. As far as its preaching is concerned the "Christ-substance" of Protestant Christendom is lacking indispensable ingredients, a fact that hinders the development of a healthy life of faith and community in the New Testament sense.' Max Lackmann, *Zur Reformatorischen Rechtfertigungslehre*, Stuttgart, 1953, 79.

[7] ibid., 19.

Incarnation itself loses its efficacy in such an interpretation?[1] What are the reasons for this diminished efficacy?

The second tendency in defining the Word concerns its immediacy. For Protestantism tends to play off the Gospel and the Word against the ecclesiastic, or better the apostolic Body. The Gospel becomes efficacious in the inward man through the testimony of the Holy Spirit, and outwardly through the Bible or Christian preaching. Luther says: '*Non de evangelio scripto sed vocali loquor.*'[2] Because the divine and human spheres are divorced from each other they must not be mixed in the matter of salvation either. The divine sphere must remain completely free from all human intervention; hence it may not be related to ecclesiastical actions. Thus Protestants do not associate the Word of God with the Incarnate Word, but relate it solely to the heavenly Christ. This is quite clear especially in the case of Karl Barth.

Such a view opens the way to an exaggerated spirituality and immediacy. Protestantism goes past the historicity of the Word of God;[3] hence oral tradition is completely subordinated to Holy Scripture, indeed it tends to be regarded as negligible. Such a conception, however, abandons a fundamental characteristic of the mystery of Christ, which, as Söhngen has shown, is a *factum historicum*.[4] The Word of God comes to us in the form of the apostolic witness (*credere Christum* presupposes *credere apostolis*), and reaches man by way of historical tradition as *depositum fidei*. As Congar has shown, this tradition is not only a certain deposit of truths that are transmitted, but a sum total of realities handed on like a treasure.[5] '*id quod traditur, id quod traditum est.*' Thus tradition comprises the deposit of faith (and with it Holy Scripture), the sacraments in the narrower sense, the power of the ministry, the law of God, etc. The Holy Spirit who accompanies tradition ensures that these elements are alive and fruitful.[6] Hence the Word of God must not be transposed into a supra-historical transcendence and be made absolute. True, the Word of God forms the Church, but together with other elements, the most important of which in this

---

[1] 'Since the Lutheran Church teaches that through justification sins are forgiven but not taken away, the Word of God, through which we receive justification, may be suspected of not accomplishing what it says. This is a legitimate Catholic criticism which must be taken seriously.' H. Asmussen, *Warum noch lutherische Kirche?* 76.

[2] *WA* VII, 721.

[3] Cf. Newbigin, *The Household of God*, 49 ff.

[4] *Die Einheit in der Theologie*, 291 f.

[5] Cf. *Vraie et fausse Réforme*, 488.

[6] ibid., 489.

context is the apostolate. For the exegesis of Scripture is not left to the freedom (which may also be arbitrariness) of the individual, but the Church preaches and interprets the Word from which she herself receives her being. It is certainly right to see the Word as an act of God, a view that would correspond to what Catholic theology calls *revelatio activa*. But this act concerns the life of the people of God which is already in possession of its Christian structure and exist-ence;[1] an ecclesiology cannot be based on this act alone. Indeed, in Protestantism the place of the rejected ministry has evidently been taken by the professors.[2] Nowadays Protestants everywhere become painfully aware of the absence of an authoritative teaching office.

The essential need is to preserve the historical reality of the Word of God, for if it is deprived of this it loses a whole dimension of being. The Word and the sacraments claim the ministry as their servant.[3] But this means that the preaching of the Word must include the preacher, the Church as something already given, a fact which clearly emerges from Rom. x, 14 f.[4] This connexion (not subjection) of the Word with the preacher guarantees its historicity. But if the Word is more than mere communication, if it is a *dynamis* that creates salvation, its preacher must be endowed with authority and power. That this was so in the case of the apostles is proved by the very term *apostolos* which corresponds to the Old Testament *shaliach*. This means that the 'envoy' 'is legally charged with repre-senting the person or cause of another'.[5] The apostles are authorita-tively sent by Jesus in the sense of having authoritative and representative power.[6] There can be no doubt that this legal authorization was transmitted by the apostles through the laying on of hands. Thus the Word of God was situated in the historically

[1] Cf. ibid., 506.

[2] Cf. H. J. Iwand, 'In wessen Händen liegt das Sakrament?' in *Evangelische Theologie*, August 1951, pp. 86–92 (The teaching office is reserved to the university professors).

[3] Cf. G. Aulén, 'The Church in the Light of the New Testament,' in *The Universal Church in God's Design*, 27.

[4] The interior witness of the Spirit in 1 John ii, 20.27 is related to the external witness of the preacher (i, 1–4; iv, 14) and to the witness of the Church (ii, 22–4; iv, 1–3; v, 1.5 ff.). Cf. R. Schnackenburg, 'Glaube und Tradition,' *USR* 9 (1954), No. 1.

[5] Rengstorf in *ThWzNT* I, 422, 3.

[6] Cf. E. K. Kirk, *The Apostolic Ministry*, Essays on the History and the Doctrine of Episcopacy, London, 1947, 2, p. 228 ff.; Stauffer, 'Jüdisches Erbe im urchristlichen Kirchenrecht,' *ThLZ* 77 (1952), 203; A. Fridrichsen, *The Apostle and his Message*, Uppsala, 1947; H. v. Campenhausen, 'Der urchristliche Apostelbegriff,' *Studia Theo-logica* I (1948), 96 ff.; O. Cullmann, *Petrus*, 1952, 57 ff.; G. Söhngen, 'Uberlieferung und apostolische Verkündigung,' in *Episkopus. Studien über das Bischofsamt*. Regensburg, 1949.

definable sphere of the apostolic Church.[1] If this sphere is abandoned, the Word loses its pneumatic power.

No one will deny that the separated Christian communions 'have' the Word of God, especially in Holy Scripture, and that they preach it. But with them this Word is impoverished, hence it is a *vestigium ecclesiae* in a 'degraded, partial and impoverished state'.[2] Nevertheless, it is a fragment of reality; it is more than a mere psychological 'remnant'. And this constitutes the fragmentary reality of the one true Church.

*   *   *

We see how the doctrine of the *vestigia ecclesiae* leads us to the very centre of the oecumenical question and enables us to do justice to the Christianity and churchmanship of our separated brethren. Since we are concerned with *vestigia ecclesiae* and not with individual Christian values it is obvious that we may argue from the individuals to the ecclesiastical character of their communions. Has a dissident communion the character of a church or is it only the sum of believing individuals?

Here we must first clearly distinguish our position from the 'Branch Theory', according to which all confessions are branches of the Church and only their synthesis results in *the* one Church.

Despite this distinction, however, we are faced with the question whether these dissident communities do not share in a graduated ecclesiastical being (*kirchliches Sein*) similar to that of individuals. Catholic oecumenical theologians seem to have avoided this question like poison. As far as we can see, it has been discussed systematically only by J. Gribomont.[3]

In agreement with other theologians, Gribomont speaks of a visible but imperfect union of the dissidents with the Church. But the specific characteristic of this situation cannot remain restricted to individuals, for as soon as we meet external and visible signs of the Body of Christ we are confronted with 'the social problem'. For individuals derive their faith from a community, and this in turn derives it from the Church. This is true especially of baptism and the

[1] Cf. L. Newbigin's criticism of the Protestant definition of the Church: 'Does not this Protestant view err in isolating the word and the sacraments from their actual context in the on-going life of the Church? The word and sacraments are never isolated events. . . . These things do not come, so to say, naked. They come clothed in the forms of the Church' (*The Household of God*, 50 f.).

[2] J. Hamer: 'État dégradé, partiel et appauvri.'

[3] G. Thils, too, devotes a separate chapter to this question in his book *Histoire doctrinale du mouvement oecuménique* (Louvain, 1955).

Eucharist. 'In a word, the very elements which make the dissidents imperfect members of the Body do so by constituting them into communities.'[1] Y. Congar has objected to such a view: 'If the dissidents as individuals can be said to be members of the Catholic Church, this is done on the basis of their good faith, i.e. of a reality of the human order. But in the case of a group, an institution, a social body as such, which is not a person, it does not make sense to speak of good faith or any other moral act, at least not in the strict sense.'[2] Gribomont finds it easy to answer this objection, since the dissidents have more than an invisible, subjective good faith. We see that the doctrine of the *vestigia* opens new perspectives on this subject. Gribomont states that a sociological body, having no personal conscience, must be judged by its official acts. In the case of the dissident communities these acts contradict one another and cannot be posited simultaneously since some of them affirm, others deny the Church. The separated Christians are and remain schismatics or heretics.

Gribomont's speculation starts from the doctrine of the sacraments, which, as he points out, are internally connected with each other. The visible sacramental signs form a 'ladder' and belong essentially together. They do not simply make a sum but depend on one another organically. This inner connexion of the visible elements also has its effect on the dissident communities. 'The lower degrees which they pretend to have preserved in fact include the rest.'[3] They preserve one Catholic element and reject the other, hoping that by doing so they will preserve the former in greater purity, but failing to realize that all elements are organically connected. Gribomont concludes that the dissident communities therefore must have preserved, *de facto*, some of the character of the Church; for the individual sacraments are related to the basic sacrament, which is the Church. The sacraments that have been preserved retain a certain measure of their sanctity. Here the possible tension between *res* and *sacramentum* comes to the fore: there is, on the one hand, the possibility of desire taking the place of reality, and on the other the objective supernatural efficacy. If a community breaks away from Catholic unity, while preserving the external forms (*sacramentum*

[1] 'En un mot, les éléments mêmes qui constituent les dissidents en membres imparfaits du Corps, le font en les constituant communautés.' Gribomont, 'Du sacrement de l'Église et de ses réalisations imparfaites,' *Irénikon* XXII (1949), 358.

[2] *Chrétiens désunis*, French edn., p. 301.

[3] 'Les degrés inférieurs, qu'ils prétendent avoir conservés, impliquent en effet le reste.' Gribomont, loc. cit., 357.

tantum), it is, indeed, no longer a member of the Body of Christ on the plane of *res tantum*, but 'it retains a certain supernatural value, a kind of invisible consecration which distinguishes it from profane societies, demands its return to unity and produces its effect of grace in every individual member of good faith.'[1]

Gribomont observes that Western medieval theologians studied the individual sacraments in isolation from each other, and thus worked out the two categories of 'validity' and 'licitness'. The fact that a sacrament can be valid though illicit, contains the possibility of an imperfect realization. The idea that a sacrament may be realized only in an analogous and imperfect manner seems at first surprising. But this problem can be approached only after a careful study of the relation of the individual sacraments to the Church and to jurisdiction. Gribomont's ideas are worth considering. They seem to us to be so fruitful because here the problem is not seen under the aspect of the moral but of the 'ontic' order. It also seems to us important that he applies to ecclesiology certain Scriptural statements which are only too easily overlooked and which nevertheless make important assertions about the Church (cf. also the statements of the encyclical *Mystici Corporis* on the visible marks of membership of the Church): 'With the mouth confession is made unto salvation' (Rom, x, 10): 'He that believeth and is baptized' (Mk. xvi, 16); 'Except ye eat the Flesh of the Son of man' (Jn. vi. 53); 'He that despiseth you despiseth me' (Lk. x, 16). Only a view of the whole and of the organic connexion of the individual parts can do justice to the mystery of the Church.

The various non-Roman Christian communions cannot be denied a certain ecclesial character. They have nothing that the Church does not also possess in its essence. What makes the Church the true, recognizable Church of Jesus Christ is the constituting elements of it which tradition has summarized under the notes of holiness, unity, catholicity and apostolicity. The dissident communities can possess *partes potentiales*, i.e. parts presenting possibilities of these constitutive elements. According to Dumont they can share in these elements of the one true Church in various degrees.[2] One can say with Lialine that the potential members of the mystical Body of Christ constitute visible Christian communities which are very imperfect and do not absolutely transcend other human societies.

---

[1] Gribomont, 362.

[2] C.-J. Dumont, O.P., *Les voies de l'unité chrétienne. Doctrine et spiritualité*. Paris, 1954, 127.

Nevertheless, the sum total of them forms the 'potential mystical Body'.[1]

This raises the question what contribution the dissident communities make to the Church on their return to it. As we have already seen,[2] the *Instructio* of the Holy Office has rejected a form of expression according to which the Catholic Church does not yet possess the fullness of Christ in questions of Catholic doctrine but

---

[1] Cf. Lialine, 'Une étape en ecclésiologie,' in *Irénikon* XX (1947), 45. This term 'potential mystical Body' is based on the schema of Thomist ecclesiology. Since the relevant passage in St Thomas is so important we would cite it in full: 'This is the difference between the natural body of man and the Church's mystical body, that the members of the natural are all together, and the members of the mystical body are not all together: neither as regards their natural being, since the body of the Church is made up of the men who have been from the beginning of the world until its end—nor as regards its supernatural being, since, of those who are at any one time, some there are who are without grace, yet will afterwards obtain it, and some have it already. We must therefore consider the members of the mystical body, not only as they are in act, but as they are in potentiality. Nevertheless, some are in potentiality who will never be reduced to act, and some are reduced at some time to act; and this according to the triple class, of which the first is by faith, the second by the charity of this life, and the third by the fruition of the life to come. Hence we must say that if we take the whole time of the world in general, Christ is the Head of all men, but diversely. For, first and principally, He is the Head of such as are united to Him by glory; secondly, of those who are actually united to Him by charity; thirdly, of those who are actually united to Him by faith; fourthly, of those who are united to Him merely in potentiality, which is not yet reduced to act, yet will be reduced to act according to Divine predestination; fifthly, of those who are united to Him in potentiality, which will never be reduced to act; such are those men existing in the world, who are not predestined, who, yet, on their departure from this world, wholly cease to be members of Christ, as being no longer in potentiality to be united to Christ.' (*S.Th.* III, q. 8, a. 3. Literally translated by Fathers of the English Dominican Province, 1913.) The divergences between St Thomas's conception of the Church and that of the encyclical *Mystici Corporis* have already been mentioned and found to present no insuperable opposition. According to the encyclical's own words it is concerned to develop 'especially those aspects of it which concern the Church militant'. Nevertheless, different results will be obtained according to the starting-point of the speculation. For the point of departure of the encyclicals *Mystici Corporis* and *Humani Generis* cf. the work of T. Zapelena, S.J. *De Ecclesia Christi*, especially vol. II[2] (1954) which contains an extensive dogmatic treatise on the Church as the Mystical Body of Christ. This treatise develops the revealed theology of the teaching office of the Church and does not hesitate to abandon theses of scholastic speculation including some belonging to St Thomas, which represent the ideas of their time. The analysis begins with St Paul's conception of membership. This contains a moral and organic connexion with a social community, including co-operation in a common aim which is characterized by a definite action and attitude under a common and legitimate leadership. Further, there belongs to it a moral and organic union with Christ and a mutual and social connexion of the members with each other. According to St Paul, Church membership includes 1. Faith; 2. The one confession of faith made at baptism; 3. The confession of the one doctrine of the authentic teaching authority; 4. The one baptism; and 5. The mutual union of the members subordinated to the hierarchy. According to Zapelena the encyclical *Mystici Corporis* corresponds to this Pauline conception of membership (cf. *HK* IX (1955), 321–7).

[2] p. 93.

must still be perfected by other denominations. 'This must not be presented in such a way as to give the impression that their conversion would give the Church something essential she had so far been lacking.'

When discussing this passage we pointed out the peculiarity of the metaphysical style.[1] But apart from this, what matters is whether the Church is seen under the aspect of its fullness of being and its Christ-given essence, or from the point of view of the existential realization of this fullness. If we neglect this difference we shall miss the nature of the Church. If the dissident communities added something to the Church *quoad substantiam* we should have to say that through the separation the Church suffered a loss of substance. Thus she would have ceased to be the true Church of Christ, the gates of hell would have prevailed against her—but this would contradict the promises of Christ. The lack is not on the part of the Church but of the dissidents. Journet observes that the catholicity of the Church does not lack what the dissidents possess, but rather what they are still lacking and what they would possess if they were fully integrated in the Church.[2] But we have to reckon with the possibility that the catholicity of the Church is explicitly realized only in an imperfect manner. It may well be the case that values of catholicity are not fully actualized in the Church, which they would be if dissident communities were to return to it. Hence, as regards their return we may well speak of a 'vital expansion of the catholicity of the Church'[3] and of a 'greater fullness and richness of actualized Christian values which the Church contains in germ, but not always everywhere fully developed'.[4] Congar draws attention to the fact that the Church is lacking 'the Slav and Nordic expression of the one many-coloured grace of Christ' as long as Orthodox Russia and Lutheran Scandinavia are separated from Rome. These nations have their own characteristic way of being Christian, of belonging to Christ and of singing God's praises, which has no equivalent in the Latin or Anglo-Saxon nations; hence as long as they have not been completely integrated in the visible Church something of the

---

[1] p. 94.

[2] 'Ce qui manque alors à la catholicité de l'Église, ce n'est pas ce que détiennent les dissidents; c'est précisément ce qui leur manque encore, et qu'ils détrendraient s'ils étaient pleinement intégrés dans l'Église.' *L'Église du Verbe Incarné.* II (1951), 1222.

[3] 'La reconciliación de las cristiandades disidentes con la Iglesia representaría una expansión vital de su catolicidad en las nuevas expresiones raciales y culturales de su verdad y de su vida.' Llamera, o.p. in XII *Semana Española de Teología* 320.

[4] C. Colombo, 'E possibile la riunione dei Christiani?' in *La Scuola Cattolica* (1949), 302.

actual and effective realization of the Catholicity of the Church is evidently lacking. This does not imply a lack of substance, which is always truly Catholic, but a lack in the expression and incarnation of its living principles, or at least in the fullness of this expression and incarnation.[1]

In the case of a reunion the dissidents will bring to the Church their own expression of the *vestigia Ecclesiae*, their experience of the faith and their encounter with God, as well as the special way in which grace has formed their lives. As the Instruction *De motione oecumenica* says: 'On their return to the Church they will lose nothing of what God's grace has so far worked in their souls, but all this will be fulfilled and perfected through their return.' What is here said of individuals is also true by analogy of the Christian communities.

DIGRESSION

The Meaning of the Term Catholic

Just as today our Evangelical brethren are trying to clarify the meaning of 'evangelical', so we Catholics, too, must give an account of what we mean by 'Catholic'. This is all the more necessary as oecumenical Christians and evangelical theologians claim the concept of catholicity for themselves. The writings of the 'Michaelsbruderschaft' or the 'Sammlung' point in this direction. An evangelical clergyman said recently in a lecture: 'We are not the "Lutheran Church", we are the "Catholic Church of the Augsburg Confession".' Now the Catholic Church has no exact definition of catholicity, just as there is no strict definition of the Church. It is all the more important to clarify what 'Catholic' really means.

The traditional doctrine on the meaning of catholicity inclines to emphasize the geographical aspect. The Church is catholic, because it breaks through the narrow nationalism of the Old Testament People of God and sets up the universal kingdom of Christ; the partition between Jews and Gentiles is broken down (Eph. ii, 14f.), the frontiers between races and nations are abolished and one likes to use the 'numerical superiority of the Church over every other Christian community' (Algermissen) as an argument against the heretics. Some Catholic theologians such as, e.g., Algermissen (in the new edition of his *Konfessionskunde*) even go so far as to regard this geographical and arithmetical superiority of the Church as a sign by which to recognize the true Church. In view of the world-wide Protestant Oecumenical

[1] Cf. *Chrétiens désunis*, French edn., pp. 316–19.

Movement or even of the Lutheran World Alliance this is not really a satisfactory definition of catholicity. Within the Oecumene the view is gaining ground that the World Council represents true catholicity, because it contains all the experiences of the Christian faith.

The quantitative element, however, cannot be decisive for assessing the true catholicity of the Church. Michael Schmaus says rightly: 'The fact that the large number by itself cannot be regarded as proof of a divine institution militates against the purely quantitative conception of the spatial catholicity of the Church. This is easy to understand if we consider that communism, too, has conquered almost half the world and has a great number of adherents. Hence the spatial catholicity of the Church must involve something other than merely the large number of its members among all nations.'[1]

Hence modern Catholic theologians, especially the French, have laid more emphasis on the *qualitative concept of catholicity*, for example H de Lubac in his book *Catholicism*[2] or Congar in *Chrétiens désunis* (Paris, 1937).

It cannot be overlooked that, in the course of history, the concepts of unity, holiness, catholicity and apostolicity have undergone a development. This, however, was too much determined by an apologetical tendency. When comparing the Church with non-Catholic communions according to the accepted 'notes' Catholic apologists had to establish an argument which would allow them to distinguish the Church from all non-Roman denominations (including the Orthodox Church). For this purpose they had to revise the contents of the 'notes' and to remove such authentic Christian elements as could not serve their aim because they belonged to many Christian churches or confessions. Hence the apologists like to use 'negative notes' They are those visible qualities which are, indeed, essential to the true Church but are not found exclusively in her. Naturally, this apologetic argumentation emphasized the visibility and at the same time made it into an absolute. The World Council of Churches argues similarly when referring to the experiences of faith. The Church of Jesus Christ, including its catholicity, is far more than can be seen and experienced. The discussion of a series of theses will elucidate our subject.

1. Like the other notes of the Church, unity, holiness and apostolicity, her catholicity too, is both visible and invisible. It is realized first and primarily on the plane of faith, not of experience.

[1] *Katholische Dogmatik* III. 1 (1958), 604.

[2] *Catholicism* A Study of Dogma in relation to the Corporate Destiny of Mankind, London, 1950.

It is certainly true that the notes of the Church (unity, holiness, catholicity and apostolicity) are of a visible nature. Even in this, Catholic differs from Protestant doctrine. A passage from Ernst Wolf's book *Peregrinatio* is significant: 'The opposition between the doctrine of the Reformers and the Catholic doctrine of the *notae ecclesiae* is summed up in these words of Luther: *"Unica enim et perpetua et infallibilis ecclesiae nota semper fuit Verbum"*' ('The only perpetual and infallible note of the Church has always been the Word'.)

According to Wolf this 'unique note' is the 'most unequivocal expression of the Protestant view of the Church'; it is 'directly opposed to the essential Roman doctrine of the four notes of the Church'.[1]

As we have seen before, the Lutherans, too, do not identify the qualities of the Church and the *notae ecclesiae*. The qualities of the Church (hence also its catholicity) are referred to the sphere of faith; this means the 'catholic' quality belongs only to the 'Church properly so called', that is to the invisible Church. The visible Church can be recognized only by its 'notes', which are the proper preaching of the Word and the orderly administration of the sacraments. But here a possible misunderstanding must be avoided. According to the teaching of the confessional writings of the reformers '*ecclesia invisibilis*' does not mean 'invisible Church' but signifies rather that the Church of Jesus Christ cannot be understood. Luther uses the term '*unsichtiglich*', which means the Church does, indeed, exist in the world, but cannot be seen from our human point of view; it is an object of faith.

In the same way, however, we must also warn against another possible misunderstanding which might arise from the 'Catholic' emphasis on the visibility of the Church. For the Catholic, too, the Church is an object of faith. Thus we read for example in the Roman Catechism: 'Finally it must also here be taught about the Church, inhowfar it belongs to the articles of faith to believe in one Church. It is true, everyone perceives by his reason and his senses that there is a Church on earth, that is a community of men dedicated and consecrated to Christ the Lord, and it does not seem to need faith to apprehend it, because neither Jews nor Turks doubt it, nevertheless, only reason enlightened by faith and without being compelled by rational arguments can know these mysteries that are included in the Holy Church of God. Since, then, this article no less than the others transcends the power and forces of our reason, we confess with perfect right that we perceive the origin, the offices and the dignities of

[1] op. cit. pp. 150-57.

16

the Church not with human reason, but that we see them with the eyes of faith.'

As far as the catholicity of the Church is concerned this means that it cannot be proved by rational arguments. The Church is both visible and invisible also as regards its catholicity. If we were to argue only from the external or factual catholicity of the Church we would do the same as the World Council of Churches, we would regard the catholicity as a statement of experience. This is quite right if we are concerned with the living and existential realization of catholicity. But this aspect does not suffice to grasp what is Catholic.

2. The Catholicity of the Church is a christological concept: 'Where Christ is there is also the Catholic Church' (Ignatius of Antioch.).

But in how far is the catholicity of the Church a fact of faith, as is the teaching of the Catholic Church when speaking of catholicity? Perhaps our best point of departure will be the passage in Ignatius of Antioch's Letter to the Smyrnians, the first reference in history to the 'Catholic' Church. He writes: 'You must all follow the lead of the bishop, as Jesus Christ followed that of the Father; follow the presbytery as you would the Apostles; reverence the deacons as you would God's commandment. Let no one do anything touching the Church, apart from the bishop. Let that celebration of the Eucharist be considered valid which is held under the bishop or anyone to whom he has committed it. Where the bishop appears, there let the people be, just as where Jesus Christ is, there is the Catholic Church. It is not permitted without authorization from the bishop either to baptize or to hold an agape' (Ch. 8, trans. in *Ancient Christian Writers* vol. 1, p. 93). This shows that catholicity is a christological concept. Just as, generally speaking, the understanding of the Church develops from the correct notion of Christ, so also in this case. This christological aspect of the Church must be elaborated. Thus we shall arrive at a better interpretation of what can be regarded as typically 'Catholic'.

3. Because Jesus Christ has been the '*Verbum incarnandum*' (the Word to be incarnated) from the beginning of the world, the Christian Church can be understood only in the context of the economy of salvation, i.e. she is already present in the preparation of salvation in the Old Testament and reaches its peak in the fullness of time in Mary, the Mother of Christ.

Catholicity means universality, catholic means all-embracing. Because Jesus Christ reveals God He embraces all ages. Being the Word that is to become flesh He is the pre-existent Christ. When answering the question: 'Why did God become Man?' theologians divide into two schools of thought. The one school, represented by Thomas Aquinas, Bonaventure and the majority of later theologians, gave as the reason for the Incarnation the redemption of fallen humanity. They based their view on those texts of Scripture which speak of the actual order of salvation conditioned by sin, e.g. Col. i, 20. The others (Duns Scotus, following Rupert of Deutz and Albert the Great) taught that the Incarnation of Christ belonged to the original plan of creation. They refer e.g. to Hebr. ii, 10, according to which the world was created for the sake of Christ, or to Col. i, 15–17, where Christ is called the First-born of creation. Many contemporary Catholic theologians incline to this Scotist view. They can claim in support of their opinion the general Catholic teaching on the unity of the divine plan of salvation, according to which the Incarnation of Christ is contained in God's infinite counsel from all eternity. The mystery of creation, they say, is integrated into the comprehensive mystery of the Incarnation of God and, in the last resort, only intelligible from there. As regards the Church of Christ this means that she had been prepared in history (causality of the economy of salvation).[1] This view seems to us typically Catholic. Here are the roots of a spiritual-personalistic understanding of the Church as distinct from a juridically-hierarchic conception.

This relation of the Church to the economy of salvation has certain consequences in the sphere of doctrine. There is for example the question of the relation between Law and Gospel, which is the question of the relation between the Old and the New Covenants. Against the Lutheran antithesis of Law and Gospel the Council of Trent stressed in canon 21 that, though Jesus Christ was certainly given to men as the Saviour whom they were to trust, He was nevertheless also the Lawgiver, whom they had to obey.[2] The term Lawgiver suggests Moses, and whereas evangelical theologians have always refused to regard Christ as the second Moses, St. Thomas Aquinas speaks without restraint of the 'Law of the Gospel, which is also called the New Law'. There can be no question that Christ has taught commandments as well as counsels. The question is whether Christ's Law abrogates the Law of Moses or whether there exists a certain relation between the evangelical law-giving and the Old Covenant. Aquinas emphasizes the unity of the Old and the New Covenants without,

[1] Cf. M. Schmaus, *Katholische Dogmatik* III, 1 (1958) 6off.

[2] Denz. 831.

however, neglecting the difference between the two Laws. According to him they do not differ generically, because both are ordered to the same end. Considered in themselves, Old and New Testaments form a unity. For each law aims at making men just and virtuous, or as St Thomas says with reference to the Old and New Testaments, 'to subject men to God'. Faith in the New Testament is related to that in the Old as something fully developed and revealed to something as yet undeveloped and symbolic: one evolves from the other without changing its nature. This view is founded on the knowledge that the common factor of both promise and fulfilment is the 'message'. The Old Testament is a pre-message (cf. Hebr. i, 1), a message directed to something; the New Testament is the message itself. The promise of the Old Testament is directed towards Jesus Christ (cf. Gal. iii, 16). Thus this promise is, as it were, the pre-existence of Christ. For the Old Covenant is 'a shadow of things to come' (Col. ii, 17), just as, according to Rom. v, 14, Adam is the type of the Christ to come.

Even though contemporary Catholic theologians emphasize more strongly the difference between the Old and the New Testaments, they will never neglect the unity of Law and Gospel.

This economy of salvation also explains the prominent position of Mary in the doctrine of the Catholic Church, because the history of the Old Covenant is consummated in her. Hence Mary belongs to the apostolic Kerygma, as we see from Matth. i, 16: 'Mary, of whom was born Jesus, who is called Christ'.

As regards the catholicity of the Church this economy of salvation means that the Church is universal in her historical origin. If, therefore, we speak in a very exact sense of a 'Church from the beginning' (by which is meant the anterior form of the Church of Christ), we testify with this that the pre-existing *Verbum incarnandum* determines the history of mankind as a hidden entelechy. And if it be true that the mystery of Redemption includes the mystery of Creation, this would explain the fact that the Church protects the order of creation by proclaiming the validity of the laws of nature immanent in creation. So there exists indeed a christological foundation of the Natural Law.

4. The Word of God incarnate in time is the presence of the grace of God in the flesh. As the humanity of Christ is the instrument of God's redemption, so the Catholic Church is both the fruit and the means of salvation. Hence her catholicity means all-embracing Salvation.

The Son of God becomes man in the fullness of time. The Incarnation is an historical fact, but it differs from other historical facts in that not anyone, but the eternal God Himself was made Man. The Jesus of history cannot be separated or even torn away from the Christ of faith. The two are interchangeable: Christ is none other than Jesus. The Catholic Creed treats of this theme, history and faith, in many variations: historical statement: 'Born from Mary', statement of faith: 'conceived by the Holy Ghost'. Again, it is a fact of history that He was 'crucified under Pontius Pilate', while it is a profession of faith that He was 'crucified for us'. The doctrine of the nature of the Church, too, has a share in this interchangeability: according to Matthew xvi the historical person of Simon corresponds to the historical Jesus, whereas the name of 'Peter' corresponds to the statement of faith: 'Christ'. Christ and Peter are terms of office requiring the assent of faith.

Now the Incarnation of Jesus Christ means that 'God, sending His own Son in the likeness of sinful flesh . . . hath condemned sin in the flesh' (Rom. viii, 3). Thus the flesh of Jesus Christ condemns sin: 'The grace of God and the gift, by the grace of one man, Jesus Christ, hath abounded unto many.' (Rom. v, 15). Hence the grace of God is a gift which *is* (not only effects) the one Man Jesus. According to 2 Tim. i, 10 grace 'is now made manifest by the illumination' of our Saviour. God's grace is present in the Man Jesus as such; He is the 'present' of divine grace. Thus, according to St Paul (to say nothing of St John) the gift of grace is a historical person, a historical Man. This means that the grace of God is not only there as an event, but that, as revealed grace, it exists also, and antecedently, as Being. Grace appears in the flesh, it does not only happen now and again; this shows forth the measure of its self-emptying. For only with the Incarnation has grace entered the dimension of the flesh in which we live, that is to say the finite, vulnerable, palpable world. God has emptied Himself and has become present in the flesh of the man Jesus in a human life. True, this human life is not a simple being-there or absolute disposability. This misunderstanding has often threatened the true conception of grace, turning it into something that is simply there, instead of being someone meeting us in the flesh. There is a Monophysite misunderstanding of grace, though this is not abolished by a Nestorian attitude which, by rejecting grace as a material reality, would turn it into a mere dynamic event. A wrong view of the Incarnation implies also a wrong view of the Church, of the means of salvation, the Sacraments and the Word. But we speak of Christ and His grace, hence also of His Church, in ontic categories. With regard to the understanding of the term 'catholic' these mean that the Church is an institution and order of visible means of grace. The typically Catholic is signalized by the statement that grace has an incarnational structure.

5. The Church is the *pleroma* of Christ, 'the fullness of him who is filled all in all' (Eph. i, 23).

Grace is in the flesh, the fullness of Christ is in the Church, therefore the Letter to the Ephesians calls the Church the *pleroma* of Christ. *Pleroma* seems to be the corresponding Biblical term for catholicity. This expression '*pleroma* equals fulness' should be understood in an ambivalent sense, that is both in the active and the passive sense. Christ is the Head who Himself fills all in all (middle) and at the same time is fulfilled or complemented by the Church (passive). This latter meaning is made clear by the marriage metaphor (Eph. v, 22ff). Thus in this passage the Church is endowed with a *cosmic* function. If she is the renewed cosmos, then angels and spiritual powers also belong to her. Hence it does not seem to be true to say, as does the evangelical bishop W. Stählin in his essay on 'Catholicity, Protestantism and Catholicism' (*Die Katholizität der Kirche*): 'This fullness rests wholly in Christ; it is the work of the Holy Spirit and cannot be produced and secured by our own efforts; it is not, therefore, simply and completely given to the Church and at her disposal.' Certainly, the fullness cannot be established by our own efforts, but we may not attribute it to Christ alone either. The statement that the Church is the fullness of Christ is an ontic statement, and this seems to me typically Catholic. In the last resort this question of being is the fundamental difference which divides the Catholic Church from the separated communions. Leslie Newbigin, the Bishop of the Union of South India, writes in his book *The Household of God*: 'Being in Christ means being incorporated in a visible community which is—in principle—undivided and continuous, binding all men and all generations in the one Body of Christ . . .

' . . . I am myself wholly persuaded that there have been, and may be again, occasions when a break in the continuing structure is—. under the conditions created by human sin—inevitable if the truth of the Gospel is to be maintained. When the Church becomes corrupt and its message distorted, God does raise up prophets to speak His word afresh, and groups in whom His Spirit brings forth afresh His authentic fruits. When these new gifts can be assimilated within the old structure they serve to renew it all. But when a break occurs and a new structure is formed upon the basis of the particular doctrine of the reformer, or the particular spiritual experience of the group, something essential to the true being of the Church has been lost. The body which results is inevitably shaped by the limitations which mark even the greatest individual minds. It necessarily lacks the richness and completeness which belongs to the whole catholic Church. . . . It will inevitably begin . . . to develop its own structure. But this structure will be derivative and not primary. The primary thing will be a doctrine or an experience. But this means that structure will be related to faith and experience in a way fundamentally different from the way they are related in the New Testament.'

In view of these statements of Newbigin it is not surprising if Ernst Kinder, in his very important essay on Scripture and Tradition (in *Die Katholizität der Kirche*) speaks so much of 'experiences of faith' which are the answer to the revelation of salvation. The Church as the fullness of Christ is something transsubjective, it is an objective datum independent of any human limitation.

Catholicity means fullness, first and foremost fullness in an ontic sense. It is quite possible that this may not be fully and existentially realized, it is nevertheless there, because Christ is grace in the flesh and because the Church is founded on the Incarnation of Christ.

6. The glorified Christ is present in the Church sacramentally in word and sign and thus guarantees her catholicity both vertically and horizontally.

Hitherto we have spoken of the pre-existent and incarnate Christ; we must now consider the glorified Christ. It is the special concern of the Gospel according to St John to prove to the community the identity of the historical Jesus with the Lord and His presence in the Church. This presence of Christ requires a special category to prove it. It is un-Biblical to sever—as does e.g. O. Cullmann—*Endzeit* (end-time) from *Zeit in der Mitte* (mid-time). True, the pneumatically continuing Christ and the post-apostolic time which He rules must be distinguished from the historical figure of Jesus, but the two may not be separated. The sacramental presence of Christ in the Church irrupts into the earthly line of time. Christ promises the Church his Presence 'all days, even to the consummation of the world' (Matth. xxviii, 20). Because Christ is seated on the right hand of God the spiritual powers are vanquished and the Church is assured of its unfathomable union with her head; this, in its turn, ensures to the extra-human creation the desired share in the freedom of the children of God in the final consummation of all things. Ever since Pentecost the Church on earth has been a historical factor; our attitude to her decides which Master we follow. The formula of the Creed, 'sitting at the right hand of the Father' is in the present tense. Hence it visualizes all time until the end. This time is the time of God's Church on earth; hence this formula is a christological expression of the time of the Church. Here again, I think, we are in the presence of something typically Catholic. The Church of Jesus Christ can be understood only through the vertical line which links her to the glorified Lord. Christ is active in her. But it must not be overlooked that the Church is at the same time determined also by a horizontal line. On the one hand the Church is instituted from above. In concrete history she is born from the Word and the Sacrament. But whence are Word and Sacrament? In which space are they actualized? Has the Lord given power to his Church through the apostles which assures the preaching of the Word and the administration of the Sacraments?

A rightly understood Protestant ecclesiology will not deny this horizontal line, else it would be mere enthusiasm. But the Protestants understand the apostolic succession in a different way from the Catholic Church, and this is the point. In his essay 'Schrift und Tradition' Ernst Kinder has some fine remarks about the necessity and mode of the Christian tradition, to which we can agree. But his statements become questionable when he discusses the subject of the 'transmitting'. 'God Himself' he writes, 'wills to remain the Lord of tradition. True, faith and the Christian communities are the divinely willed and ordered "bed" and medium, including all they have known, experienced and lived of the whole complex of salvation. They are also the means of further tradition, of the future representation and effects of the *"Heilsgeschehen"* in Christ. But they are not the true *"spirtus rector"* and the actual subject of tradition. This is rather the glorified Lord Himself or the Holy Spirit' (pp. 36f.). But is not the Church also the subject, if she fulfils Christ according to Eph. i, 23 in the active sense? We quite understand the concern to preserve the distinction between Christ as the head and the Church. Catholic doctrine, too, makes this distinction. But it does not disregard human authority, because it remembers the Christ made flesh, the *whole* Christ who is both head and body. According to Catholic teaching the Church, guided by the Holy Spirit, that is to say the mystical body of Christ, is herself the subject of tradition, hence she guarantees the horizontal line.

7. The whole of the Church's history contains the fullness of her being. The unity of the Church, which embraces all countries and all

ages, is guaranteed by the apostolic succession of the ministry of the Church.

Here we must now discuss the essential and necessary connexion between the catholicity and the unity of the Church. Christ has assured the unity of the Church by introducing the ministry. According to Cardinal Newman the spiritual offices are the links which constitute the whole body of Christendom a unity. They are its organs; more, they are its moving principle. Without an uninterrupted continuance of the ministry there could be no uninterrupted existence of the Church throughout the centuries, no unity embracing all countries and ages. According to Newman the valid succession guarantees the catholicity of the Church. There is, indeed, in this respect a profound rift between Catholics and Protestants. The glorified Christ has bestowed 'gifts' on his Body which, according to Eph. iv, 11, are 'apostles, prophets, evangelists, pastors and doctors'. They are given 'to order the lives of the faithful, minister to their needs, build up the frame of Christ's body' (Eph. iv, 12).

Now we have to ask in what consists the continuity of these persons; what it means when the Pastoral Letters show a definite order, speaking of the power of the apostles to teach, govern and consecrate, of disciples of the apostles and presbyter-bishops, of the principle of succession and the tendency to a monarchical head? The Catholic Church will never admit that the constitution of the Church is something indifferent. Faith and order are not two different things. Hence the Church has no freedom to change her outer form in the essential question of her constitution. Protestantism, especially Lutheranism, also emphasizes the ministry; but Lutherans dare not attribute to it a dignity of its own. It seems to us that evangelical Christians with their tendency to concentrate on the Gospel in practice do pass over the centuries of the Church's history. In No. 41 of the study document on the third plenary session of the Lutheran World Alliance 'Christ liberates and unites', we read that in the Reformation there emerged again the authentic apostolic Church in which the Gospel alone is the supreme rule and guiding principle. But what is meant by 'the authentic apostolic Church' and by the 'Gospel'? What would the Apostolic Fathers say to the passage in No. 47 of this document according to which the Gospel cannot be pressed into a definite ecclesiastical form and be guaranteed by it? Is not—according to the Pastoral Letters—the teaching authority of the apostles and their successors a guarantee against errors and false doctrines (cf. 1 Tim. i, 8ff.; iv, 1ff.; 2 Tim. ii, 18; Tit. i, 13)? Indeed, St

Paul commends this guardianship to his disciples and successors. 'The Gospel and Christian doctrine do not work in the abstract, but in the concrete, in the words or decisions of the authorities. From the beginning the Gospel has been a living doctrine presupposing an authoritative teaching office'.[1] The Church has always exercised a doctrinal discipline through dogmatic decisions of a negative kind, i.e., through applying the anathema. Is it permissible to regard this teaching office as 'arbitrary human tradition besides the Gospel'?[2]

The continuity of the Church is not solely determined by an apostolic continuity of the Christian life or the experience of faith. As Newbigin says, the Word of God does not come to men naked. The office of preaching needs the preacher, and the sacraments one who is authorized to dispense them.

8. The catholicity of the Church is represented particularly through the successor of Peter, that is to say the Pope.

The Church of Jesus Christ is a cult community and a legal society. Hence the episcopal office is concerned above all with worship and the Eucharist, as Ignatius of Antioch (*d*.c. 107) writes in his Letter to the Philadelphians: 'Take care, then, to partake of one Eucharist; for one is the Flesh of Our Lord Jesus Christ, and one the cup to unite us with His Blood, and one altar, just as there is one bishop assisted by the presbytery and the deacons' (4; ACW translation p. 86). There is one bishop, because there is one Eucharist. Through the celebration of the Eucharist in one place the Church is linked to a locality. Now according to Ignatius the bishop reflects the love of his community; in him it appears as visible love. (The same idea is to be found in Cyprian and, in modern times, in J. A. Möhler.) On the other hand the bishop stands over against the community, because he represents the life-giving Father-God. Wherever, therefore, there is a local church, we meet the bishop.

The Catholic Church has repeatedly solemnly declared that the episcopate is of divine law, i.e. it is an essential constituent of the Church which cannot be abolished by anyone, not even by the Pope. New Testament evidence of the episcopate is to be found in 1 Peter ii, 25; v, 1–4; Acts xx, 28; Phil. i, 1 and the Pastoral Letters. We would, however, observe that these Scriptural passages furnish little material for a conclusive argument, since the earliest Church was a missionary Church; it was apostolic in the exact sense of the word. The position of the *presbyteroi* is to be understood in this context. This first age

[1] H. Schlier, *Die Zeit der Kirche* (d.*c*.107) (1956) 132.
[2] Studiendokument No. 19.

after the apostles was the time of itinerant missionaries. The monarchial episcopate developed only when the local churches were firmly established; but this does not mean that the episcopal office was founded only then. It is *jure divino*, of divine right, established by Christ when He sent the apostles as He Himself had been sent by the Father. This means that the office of the bishop stems directly from God and thus, according to Canon Law, the bishop has by divine law an independent pastoral authority over a local church. This probably agrees with the statements of article 28 of the Augsburg Confession.

The question now arises of how the episcopate is related to the Pope. The Pope as an individual has the full, direct, ordinary and universal pastoral authority (equalling the primacy of jurisdiction) over the whole Church and over each of her parts and members. This means that his direct and ordinary legal authority extends also to the individual bishops. The Pope decides who is to be consecreated bishop; he does not give the bishops their actual episcopal office, but he gives them their powers, which he can define, enlarge or limit. Despite its direct relation to God the episcopate is nevertheless dependent on the authority of the Papacy. Does this mean that, according to the declarations of the First Vatican Council on the primacy of the Pope, the bishops have now become officers or executive organs of the Pope? At present Catholic theologians are trying to elucidate this (as Karl Rahner says) 'peculiar doubleness and entanglement of papal and episcopal authority'. Rahner rightly emphasizes that there is a diffuse and almost instinctive general opinion that the papal Church is an absolute monarchy.[1] One reason for this unconscious feeling may be the talk of the 'monarchical constitution of the Church', suggesting parallels between an absolute monarchy in the political sense and the hierarchical constitution of the Church. But the relationship between Pope and bishop must be explained on a deeper level.

Canon Law says that the bishops are the successors of the apostles, in the plural. This means that a bishop exists only in the framework of the episcopate as a whole. At the consecration of a bishop this is expressed by the fact that at least three bishops must lay their hands on the one newly to be consecrated. As has been said before, the bishop is the chief pastor of his local church. The New Testament speaks of a local church and a universal Church; but the latter is not simply the sum of the local churches. The one Church appears in the individual localities, the whole is present in the part. Karl Rahner has

[1] 'Primat und Episkopat', *Stimmen der Zeit* 161 (1957/8) fasc. 8, 321-336.

pointed out that this relation between the universal and the local Church has its roots in pre-Christian Jewish theology. The people of Israel is still there and the divine promises given to it remain even if it exists only in a 'holy remnant'. Rahner, too, bases the local church on the celebration of the Eucharist. Because the celebration is localized, the Church is intended to become concrete in a locality. 'The local church does not exist through the atomizing division of the space of the universal Church, but through the concentration of the Church into its own local being.' Now because the office of the Papacy is coordinated to the universal Church, and because the individual bishops are such only in the whole context of the episcopate, therefore the Pope represents for the universal Church and the episcopate what the bishop represents for his diocese, that is to say the unity and the guarantee of the catholicity. In this way the Vatican Council also explained the position of the Papacy in its relation to the individual bishops.[1] Hence the Infallibility of the Pope, which was defined in 1870, must also be understood in the context of the universal Church, i.e. of its catholicity. The theologians of the Council had to prepare a draft on the 'Constitution of the Church of Christ' which has since been largely accepted as the foundation for the dogmatic treatment of the subject. In its ninth chapter we read: 'The Church of Christ would lose its immutability and dignity and would cease to be the community of life and the necessary means of salvation if she were to stray from the saving truth of faith and morals and to deceive herself or others in preaching and explaining them. She is the pillar and foundation of truth, hence completely free from all danger of error and deceit.—With the approval of the holy oecumenical Council of the Church we teach and declare: the gift of infallibility, revealed as the everlasting privilege of the Church of Christ—not to be confused with the gift of inspiration; nor is its meaning that it bestows new revelation on the Church—this infallibility is given to the Church so that the written and orally transmitted Word of God should remain authentic in her, untainted and preserved from novelty and change, as St Paul has commanded (1 Tim. vi, 20). We teach, therefore: Infallibility extends as far as the deposit of faith and the duty to protect it require. This privilege of infallibility which the Church of Christ possesses extends not only to the whole revealed Word of God but also to all that, though not itself revelation, is nevertheless indispensable for preserving what has been revealed, clearly defining it as a

[1] Cf. Denz. 1821, 1828f. Cf. also the declaration of the German episcopate of 1875, quoted in *Una Sancta* 12 (1957), 219–228.

dogma, explaining it or effectively asserting and defending it against human errors and the controversies of a false science. The meaning of this infallibility is the immaculate truth professed by the community of the faithful in the doctrine of faith and morals. It is based on the teaching office which Christ has instituted in his Church for all time when He said to his apostles: 'Going therefore, teach ye all nations: baptizing them in the name of the Father and of the Son and of the Holy Ghost. Teaching them to observe all things whatsoever I have commanded you. And behold I am with you all days, even to the consummation of the world' (Matth. xxviii, 19f).[1]

Thus the Pope represents the unity and catholicity of the universal Church, just as the bishop is the image of the love of his congregation. Hence communion with the Pope is necessary for true catholicity. True, the early Church did not express this in so many words, but only because the subject had not come up for discussion.

9. The Catholicity of the Church is expressed principally in her eucharistic worship.

The Church is essentially a community of worship, hence her offices and hierarchical structure must be understood from there. This means that the catholicity of the Church does not, in the first place, rest on her organization, but that its centre is the sacramental representation of the Cross, Resurrection and Ascension, i.e. the celebration of the Eucharist. Hence the universality of the Redemption is nowhere expressed so clearly as in the texts of the Mass. The Church's Eucharist is never celebrated in isolation. The universality in the past is expressed in the Canon of the Mass, which points to God's gracious acceptance of the gifts of Abel, the sacrifice of Abraham and the stainless gift of the High Priest Melchisedech. The historical continuity is further emphasized in the names of the apostles and martyrs. The Church's present action is at one with the past which she continues.

The heavenly dimension is opened up by the prayer after the consecration that God's holy angel may carry this sacrifice to the heavenly altar before the divine Majesty. The Church prays that her sacred action may penetrate through the heavenly sphere, even to the throne of God.

The future dimension is suggested by the Eucharist seen as celebrated until the Lord comes again. The catholicity of the Church shows itself in that her eucharistic action embraces all ages and places. But since she does nothing without Christ, because He is priest and

---

[1] Neuner-Roos, *Der Glaube der Kirche in den Urkunden der Lehrverkündigung* 1948², 367f.

victim in one, the christological importance of the catholicity of the Church is nowhere so apparent as just here, in the Eucharist.

At the beginning of the Canon we hear that this sacrifice is offered for God's holy Catholic Church. The priest prays that God may give peace to her throughout the world (here the geographical principle is evident), that He may preserve, unify and graciously guide her, one with the Pope (the universal Church appears) and the bishop (the local church appears). Beside the Pope and the bishops, mention is made of all those who confess the true Catholic and apostolic faith. And this brings us to the next section, which will discuss catholicity under the aspect of the unifying universal faith.

10. The catholicity of the Church is manifested in the Catholic consensus of doctrine and faith.

To make this clear we would point to the opposite view, which is represented by Karl Barth in his *Kirchliche Dogmatik* (I, 2; pp. 699–713). According to him the confession of faith has only a relative and particular validity. In Barth's view a creed of the Church is an insight into the Biblical revelation, formulated and proclaimed by the Church in a certain sphere after reaching a common decision. This 'certain sphere' is conditioned by space, time and object. The spatial limitation consists in this that creeds are always valid only in certain regions. (Barth is here influenced by his own reformed denomination, because the reformed church has no common formula of faith.) He wants to limit the authority of a creed: it is only relative and particular. In this *'Umkreistheorie'* of Barth it remains doubtful in how far one can still speak of authority, if this is not recognized by others. Barth considers the Apostles' Creed and the so-called Nicene Creed as typical formulations of West and East. According to him the Second council of Orange (529) represents a characteristically Western confession. The reformed creeds, on the other hand, express the faith of the North of Europe and 'thus the Council of Trent (and even the Vatican Council with its still essentially Italian majority) must be regarded as the reply of the South of Europe'.

Such a regional theory contradicts the catholicity of the Church. Certainly, the doctrines of the early Church show a geographical influence in their formulation, and there is a great variety in the ancient symbols and rules of faith. But right in the earliest part of the Apostolic Constitutions which was probably written in Syria in the third century we find the expression: *Katholike didaskalia*. In the New Testament *ekklesia* signifies the local community as well as the district and the universal Church; hence each of the three cases involves the whole Church on earth. If a local church formulates a creed this claims to be valid for the universal Church. Even a local creed is meant to be a catholic creed. The early Church has never regarded the various formulations of her Creed as contrary and contradictory statements. This disposes of the idea that a creed is decisively determined by a district.

We cannot imagine that the Lutherans share Barth's view. For their notion of the creed is always bound up with the spatial and temporal consensus with the Fathers and the Brethren. The consensus visualizes the content, a definite recognition and objective agreement. But though they see quite clearly that a creed claims to belong to the whole of Christendom and to be recognized by the other churches, we must yet ask who expresses this recognition. Lutherans will answer that this recognition is agreed by the other Churches and that Holy Scripture is the sole norm, pointing to the solution in the early Church. According to them the teaching office can also be exercised by a community of bishops and presbyters, assisted even by members of the congregation who have not been ordained. They point to the Lutheran World Alliance, which shows a certain affinity with the early Church in this respect. Nevertheless the question remains: who exactly authorizes this? Again this points to a binding teaching office.

11. In the sphere of experience the catholicity of the Church means in no way uniformity of the doctrinal formulae, of forms of worship or of devotion, nor is it to be equated with 'Roman' or 'Latin'.

The unity of doctrinal formulae has already been discussed; we need not repeat this here.

As regards the problem 'Roman and Catholic' this has been treated in *Una Sancta* 13, pp. 56ff. Just because of her catholicity the Catholic Church cannot visualize a unity that would not be a unity in truth, that is in doctrine. But we Catholics can agree that this unity is not necessarily uniformity; it does not mean a thoroughly centralized organization, a unity of administration or an identical liturgy, nor does it imply one standard theology, a uniform order of life or practice of piety. Anyone who knows the Catholic Church knows also that there is no uniformity in her. The ecclesiastical hierarchy is regarded as a collegiate order; the Primate, that is Peter or his successor, does not abolish the responsibilities and powers of the other apostles or bishops, but if he exercises his functions in the apostolic spirit he will confirm and protect the episcopal responsibilities and powers, as the Vatican Council itself expressed it. The other apostles were not delegates of Peter, the bishops are not delegates of the Pope, as if only one man were the shepherd of the flock[1]. Neither is there liturgical uniformity, as is shown by the many different rites; and the different theological schools bear witness to the fact that there is no standard theology either, while the orders afford convincing proof of the varieties of ways of life and pious practices.

Here, with regard to the factual catholicity of the Church, we certainly admit that it may be only imperfectly realized, as has been said before. We must let ourselves be questioned by our separated brethren, as was done by Bishop Stählin: 'In the Counter Reformation the old Church which wanted to be and remain "Catholic", has herself taken over characteristics of her adversary and thus exaggerated "Catholicism" to a kind of anti-attitude. As soon as separation from the "heterodox" and the preservation of one's own characteristics is raised into the only principle and thus turned into an -ism the unbiassed acceptance and all-embracing plenitude of true catholicity is lost and there comes into being that Catholicism which is itself a kind of Protest-Ism and thus an image of the ever-protesting Protestantism'.[2] In this way we can also speak in the Catholic Church of an 'ought' which the reality fails to accomplish. But it is a truly Catholic and hence also an oecumenical task to approach ever more closely towards it.

---

[1] O. Karrer, 'Das Petrusamt in ökumenischer Sicht', in Asmussen-Karrer, *Trennung und Einung im Glauben*, Stuttgart 1956, 64.

[2] 'Katholizität, Protestantismus und Katholizismus' in *Die Katholizität der Kirche*, 200f. Cf. also E. v. Kuehnelt-Leddihn 'Der katholische Ex-Zentriker oder der Katholizist' in *Una Sancta* 12, 192–201.

5. DIFFERENCES OF BEING

We must now discuss the formal difference between the Catholic Church and the other Christian communions. This can scarcely be reduced to a formula, since it involves too many different elements. There are for example anthropological premisses, historical circumstances, cultural implications, psychological factors, philosophical presuppositions and the great variety of theological doctrines. W. H. van de Pol regards 'the distinction between word-revelation and reality-revelation' as the deepest difference between Protestantism and the Catholic Church.[1] This distinction is undoubtedly insufficient, for a Protestant who does not subscribe to the forensic doctrine of justification would object to being told that the Word was no reality for him. Hence T. Strothmann rightly observes that the method used by van de Pol takes too little account of certain antinomies in the sphere of Catholic theology itself.[2] Nevertheless, van de Pol is not altogether wrong in considering Catholic 'reality' as a 'mystic-ontic' reality of a higher order of being, not perceptible to the senses, but so mysteriously connected with a visible reality as to be present and operative in it.[3] If we say that Protestantism narrows down the Christian revelation to the revelation of the Word, the opposite is not a Catholic 'revelation of nature'—the Vatican Council defends the *duplex ordo* and thus the unity—but what it means is, as van de Pol says, the reality of a higher order of being.

Now what is the meaning of this 'ontic reality' defended by Catholics? Can it be understood as opposed to personal reality, as Thielicke has attempted to show in his formula 'Catholic=ontic, Protestant=personal'?[4] The category corresponding to the ontic concept is that of objectivity or static being; that corresponding to the personal is the category of relation and dynamic event. Now this is not a real opposition, at least as far as theology is concerned. For in Catholic theology itself, as Urs von Balthasar observed, there has 'from early times been a tension between a more positive theology, which thinks strictly on the lines of the historical facts of revelation and hence is more inclined to use the categories of the event, and a

---

[1] *The Christian Dilemma*, 289.
[2] 'Conflit jusqu'au dilemme?' in *Irénikon* XXII (1949), 277.
[3] *The Christian Dilemma*, 289.
[4] *Theologische Ethik* I, 320.

more speculative theology, which is rather contemplatively detached from the actual event and prefers to take as its object the rationality of the event and the relations between the particular truths, hence uses rather the categories of essence and object.'[1] Nevertheless, Thielicke's intuition is not without truth as the question is posed from the point of view of man's relation to God. But this involves also the mystery of the Church.

The controversial question of the nature of the Church leads always to the fundamental problem of Christology and the doctrine of grace. Can the Church be understood only through the personal relation of the individual to God, or is she something prior to man and his attitude of faith? Or, formulated with our problem of unity in mind: Is the unity of the Church a synthesis of personal experiences of faith, a collective of individual believers, or is it a visible, objective entity continuing in time and appearing in history?

The answer to this question depends on what we understand by grace. The doctrine of the Reformers rejects all metaphysical considerations. Justification establishes a new relation with God, but does not effect an essential change. Protestant theology is concerned with the personal structure of sin and grace. Sin is always unbelief, by which a man clings to himself and refuses to give up his egocentric preoccupation. Hence it is quite foreign to the Reformers when St Thomas, for example, speaks of an essential relation even between God and the sinner through fear of punishment.[2] The *Apologie* says on the contrary: 'Servile fear is fear without faith, there is nothing but wrath and despair.'[3] For the Protestant, grace is 'Christ Himself in His presence, for He is the personified Yes of God passing judgement on man'.[4] Hence grace consists in God's speaking, in the event of the Word: 'We must firmly insist that God gives no one His spirit or grace except by or with the preceding external word.'[5] 'The word alone is the carriage in which God's grace rides.'[6]

P. Althaus reproaches Catholic theology for regarding grace not as the love of God but as its supernatural gift. He admits, though, that Catholic theologians also realize that in Scripture the term grace means first of all the gracious attitude and love of God. But, referring

---

[1] *Karl Barth*, 270.
[2] *S.Th.* II, 2, 19, 4.
[3] Apologie der Konfession XII. *Die Bekenntnisschriften*, 259.
[4] W. Jost, *Quellen zur Konfessionskunde*, Series A, 2, p. 72.
[5] Schmalkaldische Artikel VIII, 3. *Die Bekenntnisschriften*, 453.
[6] Luther, *Kommentar zum Galaterbrief*, on iii, 2 f. Calwer edn. of Luther V, 250.

to Diekamp, *Katholische Dogmatik* II, 398, he asserts that they quickly leave this meaning behind and affirm that when the New Testament speaks of the grace of Christ it means 'predominantly the gift that flows from benevolence'. According to Althaus this is wrong, for in the New Testament grace means, on the contrary, the free favour and benevolence of Christ as it appears and takes effect in His action. Only in the second place does it also mean the gift of grace, the state of grace and the share in salvation which grace bestows. In Catholic dogmatics the 'impersonal Roman conception of grace as a sacramental effect of divine power' predominates. In evangelical terminology, on the other hand, salvation is precisely 'the very favour of God grasped by faith, the beginning of a personal communion with God'.[1]

Grace is favour of God *and* gift of God. The Council of Trent opposed the exaggerations of the Reformers concerning the *sola imputatione* and 'favour (*Huld*) alone'. Following St Thomas and St Bonaventure, who teach an objective distinction between love and grace, the Council emphasizes the 'inherence' of grace. Grace takes hold of man in his inmost being, beyond understanding, will and emotion, it really reaches his essence, hence Catholic doctrine understands grace as a 'being' and speaks of *habitus entitativus*. Here appears a deep-seated opposition to Protestant doctrine. Only if grace is understood in this 'ontic' way will it be possible to speak of a real transformation of man into a 'new creature' (2 Cor. v, 17), even though 'the first element in man's life of grace seems to be the new relation to the Triune God, not the transformation. From the presence of the Triune God follows the transformation of human nature.'[2] Luther did not deny the inherence of grace,[3] even though, especially since 1535, he emphasized the teaching of imputed justice for pastoral and polemical reasons. The Augsburg Confession as well as the *Apologie* and the Formula of Concord speak of sanctification, renewal and rebirth, though less from the ontic than from the personal perspective. All the statements refer to the categories of salvation (*heilsgeschichtliche Kategorien*). According to Catholic doctrine grace is a state of being, hence concerned with a new, supernatural mode of human existence.[4] Protestant theologians start from man's situation in the history of salvation; hence they emphasize the

---

[1] *Die christliche Wahrheit*, 1952³, 280 f.
[2] Schmaus, *Kath. Dogmatik* III, 2, 91.
[3] Cf. *WA* 40, I, 283, 25; ibid., 30; 5, 311, 14.
[4] The Christian is truly made just: Rom. v, 9.16–19; Acts xiii, 38 f.; his sins are truly forgiven: Rom. vi, 6 f., 18.22; ᵛ ii, 1; he is truly renewed: 2 Cor. v, 17; Tit. iii, 5 f.

inchoate and imperfect character of rebirth, the growth of sanctification and the perfect renewal that will take place only with the
resurrection.

The character of grace as a *habitus* of being suggests an explanation of the union of the Christian with Christ by means of philosophical categories. Is this possible and useful? Schmaus answers:
'The categories worked out by Aristotle correspond to the being of
nature, though not to personal being. Despite this difficulty,
philosophy helps us to gain a clearer knowledge of the union of
Christ with the Christian.'[1] The *Dogmatik* of Schmaus shows clearly
that the Catholic theologian combines ontic and personal categories
and that for him, too, the first principal meaning of grace is the
favour of God; for the Council of Trent only corrected the exaggerations of the Reformers: 'If anyone says that the grace by which
we are justified is *only* favour (*gratiam, qua justificamur, esse tantum
favorem*), let him be anathema'.[2] The Council, too, describes
justification in personal categories when it speaks of being children
of God,[3] of the indwelling of the Holy Spirit[4] and the friendship of
God.[5]

Ontic and personal may be opposite terms, but they are not
contradictory. If the Biblical doctrine of grace implies a state of
being, an ontic philosophy will help to grasp Christian existence.
The Lutheran *Bekenntnisschriften* contain passages such as the following: 'The influence of philosophy on scholasticism has spoiled
Christian doctrine.'[6] Such statements might profitably be examined
afresh in the light of a centuries-old and partly very bad experience
of Protestant theologians with the influence of other philosophical
systems on Christian doctrine. 'Theology depends no less on
philosophy than vice versa; it must be thoroughly philosophic in its
formal structure, else it will become just edifying talk, very imagina-
tive perhaps, but narrowly sectarian.'[7] Here, however, it must be
asked which philosophy is best suited to serve theology.

The report of the Theological Commission on the Church preceding the Lund Conference mentioned existential philosophy as a
means of grasping the nature of the Church. It emphasized that such

---

[1] *Kath. Dogmatik* III, 2, 48.
[2] Denz., 821.
[3] cap. 4; Denz., 794.
[4] cap. 7; Denz., 799.
[5] cap. 10; Denz., 803.
[6] Cf. the subject index of *Die Bekenntnisschriften*, 1199, s.v. Philosophie.
[7] H. Echternach, 'Theologie und Ontologie,' *ELKZ* 6 (1952), 353.

a way of thought was anti-authoritarian and anti-institutional. But is not precisely this the great Protestant weakness, that it has no proper relation to ecclesiastical authority? Echternach comes to very different conclusions. According to him, theology gains by making use of ontology because, if being and knowledge are united, 'knowledge gives up its absolute claims and sees itself as a link and moment in a more comprehensive ontological process, which is that of grace'. Thus, he continues, 'subjection to authority—a *horrendum* for "pure" thought—becomes possible on principle, since the knowledge of truth, taken as a real event of grace, is a completely super-individual process in which the individual has but a limited part which it can carry out only as a member of the super-individual whole, i.e. the Church. Hence, whatever deviates from the whole is, by this very fact, proved to be untrue.'[1]

The religious intention of the Reformers was akin to 'existential' thought. For Protestants, the principle of human personality is an *esse coram Deo*, a being over against God, a 'personal correspondence' (E. Brunner). Consequently, the Church is 'a pneumatic community of persons', an existential community, which, 'being pneumatic, is always to be experienced only existentially but cannot be shown objectively'.[2] Thus Künneth concludes: 'The certainty of faith need by no means be reflected in moods or clear insights, for it is an awareness of the present Lord, but not at once a knowledge of the concrete content of His will.'[3] Here we sense the background of 'fiducial' faith, the Lutheran thesis of law and gospel, against which the Council of Trent formulated can. 21 of the *Canones de justificatione*: 'If anyone says Christ Jesus was given by God to men as the Redeemer whom they trust, but not also as the Law Giver whom they must obey, let him be anathema.'[4] The Protestant is afraid of any kind of objectivation, because in that case man might gain power over God. Thus Künneth sees in the Pope 'the objectivation of the dominion of the *Kyrios*', because in his opinion the Pope 'represents as a substitute the visibility of Christ the King who had been rehabilitated by the resurrection'.[5] To this, Protestants oppose the principle of hidden invisibility. We see how these questions are fundamentally concerned with the conception of grace and of the humanity of Christ.

[1] loc. cit., 353 f.
[2] W. Künneth, *Theologie der Auferstehung*, 173.
[3] ibid., 181.
[4] Denz., 831.
[5] loc. cit., 223 f.

The problem is in the words: How is Christ made present to us men today, nineteen hundred years after His death?

The Bishop of the Church of South India sharply criticized the Lutheran answer, according to which Christ becomes present in the event of Word and Sacrament. For this view leaves no room for the continued life of the Church as a community linking the generations to Christ. If we subscribe to an exclusively existential view of the Church, expressed, for example, by Karl Barth's definition at Amsterdam, 'The Church is an event', the Church becomes a series of completely disconnected events.[1] Word and Sacrament do not come to us 'naked', as it were, but through those who represent Christ and act with His authority. 'He is present in His people, His apostolic fellowship.'[2] They are the beginning of a real continuation of His redemptive work, 'an extension of the divine humanity through history, until its consummation at His coming again. This divine-human fellowship is a real visible community having its place in world history, even though the secret of its life is invisible and lies beyond world history'.[3] Word and Sacrament are administered in and by the Church. Indeed, the *nisi rite vocatus* of article 14 of the Augsburg Confession points to the authority of the Church. Newbigin's chapter on the Body of Christ makes it quite clear that he wants Christ's calling of the apostles to be taken seriously; and this implies that its rightful place must be given to the social structure of the Christian faith, the visible, continuous and historic structure of the Church. According to him, the Church is not constituted by a series of unconnected human answers to supernatural acts of divine grace in the Word and the Sacrament. Thus Newbigin defends the apostolic succession. If it is true that indivisibility and continuity belong to the nature of the Church, then a body that has lost the succession has also lost the right to call itself the Church.[4] An exclusively existential view of the Church founders on this. The personal relation of man to God must not be isolated and played off against the institution.[5]

---

[1] Cf. *The Household of God*, 50.

[2] ibid., 52.

[3] ibid., 57.

[4] ibid., 78.

[5] 'In attacks upon the Catholic position it is common to lay stress upon the fact that the relationship which God established with us in Christ is a purely personal relationship, constituted wholly by grace on His side and faith on ours, and that consequently impersonal and institutional conceptions must not be allowed to play a decisive part in our thinking about the Church. From this point of view both the sacraments and the institutional life of the Church are regarded as something less than central in the

However, Newbigin criticizes also the 'Catholic' position.[1] It is true that the Church is free from sin if considered as the Body of Christ, the extension of the Incarnation, the instrument of God's redemption, to which is given the promise that the gates of hell shall not prevail against her. But on the other hand, it cannot be said that the Church is free from sin, since her members are sinful. This dark paradox becomes bearable only if it is lit up by eschatological hope. The fundamental error into which, according to Newbigin, Catholic doctrines tend to fall is that 'of subordinating the eschatological to the historical'.[2] Here the Church seemed to become a purely historical institution. Nor is it true, according to Newbigin, that the Church contains the fullness of grace within itself. These criticisms have already been answered in this book. The Catholic, too, realizes the sinfulness of the Church, not only of its members,[3] its *status viatoris* and its eschatological aspect. He may even give a Catholic sense to Luther's somewhat unfortunate formula *simul justus et peccator* by considering it from a non-ontological point of view.[4] Thus Newbigin's criticism is directed more against a perhaps inadequate presentation, a shifting of emphasis and one-sided preaching. The main interest of his book is pastoral, and so we can

---

life of the Christian. In some statements of this view, the Church becomes merely a sort of framework within which such a true personal relationship between God and the souls of men, and between men and men, may develop, but which is purely instrumental to this purpose and to be altered, discarded, or replaced as the fulfilment of this purpose requires. To those who hold this view insistence upon the use of sacraments as essential to the being of the Church seems intolerable, and the doctrine that my relationship to Christ should be affected by the historic continuity or discontinuity of the Church to which I belong quite incredible. The exploration of the meaning of personal relationship is one of the great achievements of thought in our time, and one that has been immensely helpful in the understanding of the Christian faith. But is it not necessary also to insist that all personal relationships are given to us in an impersonal context and conditioned by impersonal factors? Is it not significant that the deepest, most fruitful, and most satisfying personal relationships are those in which the impersonal factors are at their maximum, in which the personal is most indissolubly connected with physical, biological and economic factors—namely in marriage and the family? And must we not assert that the attempt to isolate the personal, and to set it over against the legal and institutional, does violence to its nature? Must one not say that the attempt, in the conditions of human nature, to have a personal relation divorced from its proper impersonal context is futile? It is surely congruous with the whole nature of man that Christ, in giving us Himself, has given us a Church which is His body on earth and therefore marked by visible limits and a continuing structure, so that fellowship with Him should be by incorporation in it.' loc. cit., 76 f.

[1] ibid., 80 f.
[2] ibid., 82.
[3] Cf. K. Rahner, 'Die Kirche der Sünder,' in *Stimmen der Zeit* 140 (1947), 163–77.
[4] Cf. R. Grosche, *Pilgernde Kirche*, Freiburg, 1938, 147–58.

still understand such statements as that we must give up the attempt to define the being of the Church by concepts of something she has or is,[1] if we take into account his ascetic way of speaking; for otherwise he would contradict his own thesis.

Newbigin makes the decisive statement that communities severed from the Church suffer a loss of being. With regard to Luther and the Reformers he says that there may be circumstances produced by sin in which a breach in the continuity of the structure might be inevitable if the truth of the Gospel is to be preserved. Nevertheless, once the breach has been made and a new structure has been erected on the foundation of the particular doctrine of the Reformers or the particular spiritual experience of a group, something essential for the true being of the Church has been lost. The body that has come into being is inevitably formed according to the limitations to which even the greatest human personalities are necessarily subject. Hence the communions separated from the Church are marked by a loss of being. The deepest difference between them and the Church is a difference of being.

Here, however, we are faced with the question how we can explain this notion of being to our separated brethren. This seems to be particularly difficult in our own days, since certain schools of evangelical theology are increasingly drawn towards a theological personalism with subjectivity, relation and actuality as their leading concepts. Many evangelical theologians reject anything transsubjective, transrelational and transactual. For these views, however, they can certainly not claim Luther himself, as anyone who knows his writings will have to admit. For his concrete personalism 'presupposes the ontology of the doctrine of the Trinity and of the Christology of the ancient Church'.[2] Gloege has subjected the theological personalism in modern Protestant theology to vigorous criticism. He writes that 'there can and there must be no "pure", "consistent" and this means fundamentally "abstract" personalism '.[3] What Gloege says with regard to the Church is truly revolutionary in the Protestant conception of it; for he writes in the same article: 'We live in a Church that is not only "event" but "has" also "institution", which is both a visible and an invisible reality'.[4] Gloege shows also that this concept

---

[1] ibid., 74.
[2] Gerhard Gloege, 'Der theologische Personalismus als dogmatisches Problem. In *Kerygma und Dogma*, Zeitschrift für theologische Forschung und kirchliche Lehre I (1955) 39.
[3] ibid. 41.
[4] ibid.

of being is Biblical with regard to both the Old and the New Testament He asks for example:[1] 'What does it mean ontologically that John speaks not only in the categories of "becoming" but also of "being"? For he says that the Logos "became" flesh (i, 14), that grace and truth "appeared" (i, 14)—but that the "exegete", who acts personally, "is in the bosom of the Father" and describes Himself as "Ego eimi . . . " What does all this mean ontologically? What is the meaning of the paradoxical "Before Abraham was made (or became) I am?" (viii, 58) with its brusque juxtaposition of "being" and "becoming"?'

And, we would continue to ask with regard to the relation between Christ and the Church, what does it mean that Christ says of Himself: 'I am the true vine . . . Every branch in me that beareth not fruit the Father will take away . . . Abide in me and I in you. As the branch cannot bear fruit of itself, unless it abide in the vine, so neither can you, unless you abide in me' (John xv, 1–4). Even these few passages show that the ontic category can be found also by starting from Scripture.

Here, however, a new and important problem is introduced into theological controversy. What are the presuppositions with which we read the Bible? This question involves theology itself and its method. Two books would seem to be of special importance for this subject. They are *Teologiens metodfraga* by Gustaf Wingren, professor of theology at Lund,[2] and *Ceci est mon Corps. Explication de ces mots de Jesus-Christ* by F.-J. Leenhardt.[3]

Wingren attempts to criticize the methodical presuppositions of some contemporary theologians (Nygren, Bultmann and Barth). Confronting their theology with the New Testament he finds that they fail to do justice to the fullness of the Word of Scripture. Their methods prevent them from understanding the Biblical text in the way it understands itself. For Wingren theology is the science of faith in the sense that it must take the statements of faith just as seriously as the authentic believer; hence he opposes Nygren, Barth and Bultmann in the very name of faith. He says against Bultmann that the latter has read the New Testament with an eclecticism conditioned by pre-Biblical studies and that, moreover, he misinterprets it as a whole because of his wrong conception of the 'Law'. Similarly, he opposes Karl Barth because he lets himself be misled by his theological

[1] ibid. 36.
[2] Gleerup, Lund 1954.
[3] Delachaux et Niestlé, Neuchâtel/Paris 1955.

method. Finally he blames Nygren for accepting the epistemology of Kant and Schleiermacher without any reservations; he cuts out truth from religion.[1]

To these erroneous interpretations of Bultmann, Barth and Nygren Wingren opposes his own view of the New Testament. The result is that, what is meant to be a confrontation of, say, Barth's view of Scripture with the Bible itself, is actually a confrontation of Barth's interpretation with that of his critic. For Wingren, too, cannot help having a certain 'conception' of the New Testament. Here the Protestant dilemma becomes quite evident. For here it is not a question of conception against test, but of one conception against another. A Catholic critic of Wingren's book has rightly said: 'What is the basis of Wingren's interpretation of the Bible? Why should it be the only right one? By what criterion are we to judge that Barth's view is alien to the Bible, while that of Wingren is correct? Is it even possible that one particular interpretation of the New Testament could be proved to be the only one to correspond to the 'naked' word of the Bible? Does not every interpretation of a text add precision to its content? If this be so, the word as understood and interpreted by a living mind must needs contain more than the 'naked' word, and the word taken by itself cannot decide whether this 'more' is justified or not.'

This controversy which is taking place within one single school of thought (Nygren and Wingren are both professors at Lund) shows clearly that every theological system requires an epistemological foundation. This can only mean that every theologian, whether he wants to or not, approaches the statements of revelation on the basis of a certain philosophy. But most Protestant theologians detest philosophy within the framework of theology. In my opinion, however, a philosophy that *serves* theology is indispensable. Besides, Protestantism has always been influenced by certain philosophies; we may only remember nominalism, Kant, Schleiermacher, Hegel, Kierkegaard and Heidegger.[2] The above-mentioned book of Leenhardt is evidence of this.[3] There we find what seems at first sight 'Catholic' statements. The author uses e.g. terms such as 'transubstantiation' (p. 34), 'The Last Supper as a sacrifice' (p. 47f), 'efficacy of the rite' (p. 53), '*opus operatum*' (p. 55), 'objective character of the

---

[1] Wingren, loc. cit. 32.

[2] One of the most necessary 'oecumenical' books would be a comprehensive and critical study of the influence of the various philosophical systems on Protestant theology.

[3] S. G. Gloege, loc. cit. 36.

Church' (p. 59) and so forth. In my view the criticism of the French Dominicans[1] has gone straight to the weakest point of the book by questioning the meaning of these terms. Leenhardt, too, is concerned to determine what is reality. According to him it lies in the divine intention; only faith is capable of knowing what the things are in the will of God: 'The essence of things is . . . in the will of God, which keeps them in being'.[2] Thus the being of things has its foundation in the divine intention which is realized in them. For example, the *raison d'être* of the bread used in the Eucharist is no longer the nourishment of the body but the will of Jesus, that His Presence should be remaining in this bread.

This is the starting point of the criticism: if reality is based solely on the divine intention and can be changed also merely through the will of God, as Leenhardt alleges in the case of the eucharistic bread, then there is, strictly speaking, no real change in the bread at all. 'Nothing is changed in the bread. What is changed in only the role assigned to the bread, its *raison d'être*, its function in the thought of God.' This is the leading idea of Leenhardt's work.[3] It is rightly observed that such an 'extrinsecistic' (*extrinsezistisch*) interpretation of transubstantiation reveals a definite nominalism.

Thus we are here faced with a philosophy which places the reality of the essences outside themselves, in the will of God; the only thing that counts is what God wills. This voluntarism shows how thoroughly Leenhardt voids the 'Catholic' terms of transubstantiation etc. of their reality; and consequently he gives hardly any thought to the sacramental 'sign'.

I would sum up the fundamental problem at stake in the whole oecumenical conversation in the words of this French criticism: 'In general the Protestants take pleasure in denouncing the water of philosophy with which Catholics are supposed to mix the wine of Scripture, whereas they themselves claim to have preserved this wine in its purity. But they deceive themselves. For all of us, they as much as we, have a philosophy. And even the best philosophy may become most dangerous and destructive if one does not know what it is, indeed, if people are unaware that they have one at all. The nominalistic or idealistic preconceptions . . . may often be discovered in Protestantism. For is not even Karl Barth, who pretends to be such a stranger to philosophy, a very characteristic descendant of nineteenth

---

[1] 'Un débat sur l'Eucharistie', *Istina* 2, (1956) 210–40.
[2] Leenhardt, loc. cit. 33.
[3] 'Un débat...', loc. cit. 219.

century Idealism? It would be well worth while to analyze the implicit philosophical structures in the theologies of our Reformed or Lutheran brethren more thoroughly than has been done so far. It is greatly to be desired for the sake of a more fruitful result of the oecumenical dialogue to be less interested in determining the various exegetes of both sides and more in the philosophies that are at the base of all our religious ideas and modes of behaviour.'[1]

Now it has been said that the separation was brought about for the sake of truth. Here the question arises what truth is and how it is to be recognized? There can be no doubt that the question of truth is linked to the question of being and must be answered in connexion with this.

Christian truth is a being (*ein Sein*), an objectively transmitted reality. 'Like the λόγος τοῦ Θεοῦ, the ἀλήθεια too, is something objective, coming from God, a divine reality.'[2] Hence the question of truth does not in the first place belong to the doctrine of criteriology. 'The message is not a message *about* the event of Christ (*das Christusgeschehen*). . . . The message of Christ is not a doctrinal concept (in the philosophical sense). . . . The message of Christ is the New Life itself, and in and with the gift of the New Life we have also the doctrine and the example of the New Life.'[3] Hence the question of truth, of the true Church, is not in the first place the question of an idea—'a construction of Christianity from an idea, such as especially, a construction of the Church from the idea of a community of faith, is precisely "construction" in the pejorative sense of the word'[4]—it is a question of being, more precisely of the fullness of being and participation in it. The Christian truth, seen from Christ who is the truth, is the fullness of Christ; where the *totus Christus* is, there is truth. If a man does not live within this sphere of the fullness of Christ he cannot recognize the fullness of truth. According to St Thomas, there is a *cognitio per connaturalitatem*, a knowledge through connaturality of being. A greater share in being produces also a greater knowledge of truth. Because the Church is concerned with this sphere of the *totus Christus* and the whole truth, she calls the separated Christians to return to her fold.

---

[1] 'Un débat sur l'Eucharistie', loc. cit. 220.
[2] R. Schnackenburg, 'Die Johannesbriefe,' in *Herders Theol. Kommentar zum Neuen Testament*, Freiburg, 1953, 73, 136.
[3] R. Söhngen, *Die Einheit in der Theologie*, 365.
[4] ibid., 346.

Our separated brethren address questions to us; the Oecumenical Movement, especially in the form of Faith and Order, is such a question. All the forms of unity which are discussed as possibilities in the Oecumene contain a grain of truth. It is a mistake to believe that a Church could be built from these grains, but it would nevertheless be a good thing if, in our oecumenical conversations, we would listen to the justified concerns of the separated Christians. The man in search of the Church seeks besides the unity in truth also the unity in love; he wants to see the practical realization of this truth in a life of purity and truthfulness. Not satisfied with the principle of catholicity, he seeks in the Church the place where all the legitimate spirituality and religious experience of those who confess Christ are sheltered and united. For the unity of the Church does not imply intellectual uniformity. The Church contains a variety of elements; hence it must often synthesize great differences. In our doctrine of the Church we must show the separated Christians that besides the incarnational structure of the Church its eschatological aspect is not forgotten, that it consists not only of Pope, bishops and clergy but also of the faithful people, that the hierarchical offices are not without the charismata and that the law of the Church rests on a pneumatic basis. At first sight this diversity of aspects might appear as an agglomeration of contrasts. But contrasts need not be contradictions; they must not be played off against each other but synthesized.

We do not know by what means our separated brethren will find their way to the one Church, nor how far advanced we all are in it. However much we may criticize the Oecumenical Movement, the words of the Holy Office in the *Instructio De motione oecumenica* remain valid: 'God's Spirit is at work.' And God knows why this unhappy division has come over Christendom. In the end our guilt, too, can show forth His greater glory, when above all human error the glory He has given us will shine forth so that we may once more be one. It is our duty to have faith, hope and love. We could find no better conclusion for this book, meant to be a spur to further work, than the words of Pope Pius XII written in the foundation charter of the Russian College, which might be a motto for all oecumenical work: 'Our faith teaches us to hope even against all hope.'

Sources and Literature
(Works not included here are cited in full in the notes)

I. SOURCES

AAS:Acta Apostolicae Sedis, Commentarium Officiale, Rome 1909.

BATE (H. N.) ed.: *Faith and Order:* Proceedings of the World Conference, Lausanne, August 3 to 21, 1927, London 1927.

Bekenntnisschriften der Evangelisch-Lutherischen Kirche, Göttingen 1930.

BELL (G. K. A.) ed.: *Documents on Christian Unity*, 4 vols. London 1924, 1930, 1948, 1958.

CIC: Codex Iuris Canonici, Rome 1917.

Confessio Augustana, Tübingen Nottexte, Tübingen 1948.

DENZINGER, BANNWARTH, UMBERG, RAHNER: *Enchiridion symbolorum, definitionum et declarationum de rebus fidei et morum*, Freiburg/Br. 1960.[31]

Generalsynode der Niederländischen Reformierten Kirche über die Verhältnisse zur Römisch-Katholischen Kirche: *Der Römische Katholizismus—ein anderes Evangelium?* Zürich 1950.

HODGSON (L.) ed.: *The Second World Conference on Faith and Order* held at Edinburgh, August 3 to 18, 1937, London 1938.

Joint Committees of the Convocations of Canterbury and York, *The Church of South India*, Westminster 1950.

Lambeth Conference, The, 1948, Encyclical Letter from the Bishops, London 1948.

ROUSE (R.) and Neill (S. C.) eds.: *A History of the Ecumenica Movement 1517–1948*, London 1954.

TOMKINS (O.) ed.: *The Third World Conference on Faith and Order* held at Lund, August 15 to 28, 1952, London 1953.

Toronto, July 1950: *The Church, the Churches and the World Council of Churches. The ecclesiological significance of the World Council of Churches.* Geneva 1950.

VISSER 'T HOOFT (W. A.) ed.: *The First Assembly of the World Council of Churches* held at Amsterdam, August 22 to September 4, 1948, London 1949.

The Evanston Report: The Second Assembly of the World Council of Churches, 1954, London 1955.

WA: Luthers Werke. Weimar Edition, edited by J. KNAAKE, G. KAWARAU *et al.*, 54 vols., 1883 —.

II. LITERATURE

ADAM (K.) *One and Holy*, London 1954.

ASMUSSEN (H.) *Warum noch Lutherische Kirche?*, Stuttgart 1949.

——*Der Brief des Paulus an die Epheser*, Breklum 1949

——'Ganzheit und Mitte des Glaubens', *WuW* 5 (1950), 165–74.

BAILLIE (D.) and Marsh (J.) eds.: *Intercommunion:* The Report of the Theological Commission appointed by the Continuation Committee of the World Conference on Faith and Order together with a selection from the Material presented to the Commission, London 1952.

BARTH (K.), DANIÉLOU (J.), NIEBUHR (R.) *Amsterdamer Fragen und Antworten*, Theologische Existenz heute 15, München 1949

BARTSCH (H. W.) ed.: *Theologische Forschung.* Wissenschaftliche Beiträge zur theologischen Forschung, vols. 1 and 2, Hamburg 1951/2.

BAUM (G.) OSA. *That They many be One: A Study of Papal Doctrine* (Leo XIII–Pius XII), London 1958.

BELL (G. K. A.) *Christian Unity, the Anglican Position*, London 1948.

—— *The Kingship of Christ. The Story of the World Council of Churches*, Harmondsworth 1954.

BORNKAMM (G.) and CLAAS (W.) *Mythos und Evangelium. Zum Problem Bultmanns*, Theologische Existenz heute 26, München 1951.

BRAUN (F. M.) O.P. *Neues Licht auf die Kirche. Protestantische Kirchendogmatik in ihrer Auffassung*, Einsiedeln 1946.

BRENNECKE (G.) Amsterdam 1948. 'Die Bedeutung der ersten Vollversammlung des Oekymenischen Rates der Kirchen', *Die Zeichen der Zeit* 2 (1948), 352ff.

BRIDSTON (K. R.) 'The Future of Faith and Order', *ER* XI (1958/9) No. 3, 249ff.

BRUNNER (E.) 'Kirche als Lebensgemeinschaft', *Die Zeichen der Zeit* 2 (1948), 381ff.

—— 'Der Neue Barth. Bemerkungen zu Karl Barths Lehre vom Menschen', *Zeitschrift für Theologie und Kirche* 48 (1951), 89ff.

—— *The Misunderstanding of the Church*, London 1952 (o.p.).

BRUNNER (P.) 'The Realism of the Holy Spirit. Observations on the Theological Significance of the Toronto Statement', *ER* III (1950/51) 3, 221ff.

CERFAUX (L.) *The Church in the Theology of St. Paul*, London 1959.

CONGAR (Y. M-J.) O.P. *Divided Christendom. A Catholic Study of the Problem of Reunion*, London 1939 (o.p.).

—— *Christ, Our Lady and the Church.*

—— *Vraie et fausse Réforme dans l'Eglise*, Paris 1950.

—— 'A propos des "Vestigia ecclesiae" ', *Vers l'unité chrétiene*, No. 39 (Jan. 1952).

Constitution of the Church of South India, The, Madras 1956.

CRAIG (C. T.) 'The Church of the New Testament', *Christendom*, vol. 13, No. 3, 348–57.

—— 'The Reality of the Church and our Doctrines about the Church', *ER* III (1950/51) 3, 213ff.

CULLMANN (O.) *Early Christian Worship*, Studies in Biblical Theology No. 10, London 1953.

—— *Peter, Disciple, Apostle, Martyr*, rev. edn. London 1962.

DAVANDAN (P. D.) 'The Ecumenical Movement and the Younger Churches', *Christendom*, vol. 13, No. 3, 328–34.

DEJAIFVE (G.) S.J. ' "Sobornost" or Papacy?', *ECQ* X (1953/54) 1, 28ff.: 2, 75ff.: 3, 111ff.: 4, 168ff.

DILSCHNEIDER (O.) *Gegenwart Christi. Grundriss einer Dogmatik der Offenbarung*, 2 vols., Gütersloh 1948.

DUMONT (C-J.) O.P. *Approaches to Christian Unity*, London 1959.

DUN (A.) 'First Thoughts on Amsterdam and Lambeth 1948', *Christendom*, vol. 13, No. 4, 439–48.

EDWALL (P.), HAYMANN (E.) and MAXWELL (W. D.) eds.: *Ways of Worship. The Report of a Theological Commission on Faith and Order*, London 1951.

EICHMANN, and MORSDORF (K.) *Kirchenrecht*, 3 vols., Paderborn 1953[7].

Faith and Order Publications: *Reports on Intercommunion, Ways of Worship and the Church*, London 1951.

—— *Social and Cultural Factors in Church Divisions*, London 1952.

—— *One Lord, One Baptism. Report on the Divine Trinity and the Unity of the Church*, London 1960.

FECHTER (A.) 'Die Reformation im ökumenischen Gewissen', *WuW* 7 (1952) 1.

FLEW (N.) *The Nature of the Church*, Papers presented to the Theological Commission appointed by the Continuation Committee of the World Conference on Faith and Order, London 1952.

GOMMENGINGER (A.) S.J. 'Bedeutet die Exkommunikation Verlust der Kirchengliedschaft? Eine dogmatisch—kanonistiche Untersuchung', *ZkT* 73, No. 1, 1ff.

GOODALL (N.) *The Ecumenical Movement, What it is and what it does*, London 1961.

GRILLMEIER (A.) S.J. and BACHT (H.) S.J. eds.:*Das Konzil von Chalkedon, Geschichte und Gegenwart*, Vol. III Würzburg 1954 (includes articles in English and French).

HAMER (J.) O.P. 'Le Baptême et l'Eglise. A propos des "Vestigia Ecclesiae" ' *Irenikon* XXV (1952) 2, 142ff. and 3, 263ff.

HECKEL (J.) 'Initia iuris eeclesiatici Protestantium', *Sitzungsbericht der Bayerischen Akademie der Wissenschaften* (1949), No. 5, München 1950.

HEILER (F.) *Evangelische Katholizität. Gesammelte Aufsätze und Vorträge*, Vol. 1, München 1926.

HERNTRICH (V.) 'Die Kirche Jesu Christi und das Wort Gottes', *Bekennende Kirche*, No. 35, München 1935.

HODGSON (L.) 'The Task of the Third World Conference on Faith and Order', *ER* V (1952/3) 1, 1–14.

HOFMANN (F.) *Der Kirchenbegriff des heiligen Augustinus in seinen Grundlagen und in seiner Entwicklungen*, München 1933.

HOLL (K.) *Gesammelte Aufsätze zur Kirchengeschichte; Die Enstehung von Luthers Kirchenbegriff*, Vol. I, 288ff., Tubingen 1932.

JOURNET (C.) *L'Eglise du Verbe Incarné. Essai de Théologie Spéculative*, Vol. 1, Paris 1948: and especially Vol. 2, *Sa Structure interne et son unité Catholique*, Paris 1951.

—— *Primauté de Pierre dans la Perspective Protestante et dans la Perspective Catholique*, Paris 1953.

KÄSEMANN (E.) *Leib und Leib Christi*, Tübingen 1933.

KARRER (O.) *Um die Einheit der Christen. Die Petrusfrage—Ein Gespräch mit Emil Brunner, Oskar Cullmann, Hans von Campenhausen*, Frankfurt/M 1953.

KELLER-HÜSCHEMENGER (M.) 'Umfang und Grenzen der Kirche als der Leib Christi', *ELKZ* 4 (1950), No. 5, 66ff.

KIRK (K. E.) *The Apostolic Ministry, Essays on the History and Doctrine of Episcopacy*, London 1947[2].

KÖBERLE (A.) *Wort, Sakrament und Kirche im Luthertum*, Gütersloh 1934.

KOHLMEYER (E.) 'Charisma oder Recht? Vom Wesen des ältesten Kirchenrechts', *Zeitschrift der Savigny-Stiftung für Rechtsgeschichte*, Kan. Abt. 38 (1952), 1–38.

KÜNNETH (W.) *Theologie der Auferstehung*, München 1951[4].

LEEMING (B.) S.J. *The Churches and the Church, A Study of Ecumenism*, London 1960.

LINDE (H. VAN DER) 'The Nature and Significance of the World Council of Churches,' *ER* III (1950/1) 3, 238ff.

Lumière et Vie, Special edition, *Chrétiens Séparés devant L'Oecuménsime:* January 1955.

LUTHARDT (CH-R. E.) *Kompendium der Dogmatik*, edited by ROBERT JELKE, Leipzig 1937[2].

MASCALL (E.) *The Recovery of Unity*, London 1948.

MENN (W.) *Oekumenischer Katechismus, Eine kurze Unterweisung über Werden und Wesen der Oekumene*, Stuttgart 1950.[2]

MICHAEL J. P.) 'Der dritte Versuch, Das ökumenische Problem von Lausanne 1927 bis Lund 1952', *Orientierung* 16 (1952), No. 14/15, 151ff.

MÖHLER (J. A.) 'Die Einheit in der Kirche', edited by E. J. VIERNEISEL *Deutsche Klassiker der katholischen Theologie der neueren Zeit*, Mainz 1925.

—— *Symbolik, oder Darstellung der dogmatischen Gegensätze der Katholiken und Protestanten nach ihren öffentlichen Bekenntnisschriften*, Regensburg 1832[2].

MÖRSDORF (K.) 'Die Kirchengliedschaft im Licht der kirchlichen Rechtsordnung', *Theologie und Seelsorge* (1944), 151ff.

NEILL (S.) *Anglicanism*, Harmondsworth 1958.

NELSON (J. R.) *The Realm of Redemption*, London 1951.

NEWBIGIN (L.) *The Reunion of the Church*, London 1948.

—— *The Household of God. Lecture on the Nature of the Church*, London 1953.

NOTHOMB (D. M.) P.B. 'L'Eglise et le Corps mystique du Christ', *Irénikon* XXV (1952) 3, 226ff.

OEPKE (A.) 'Das Recht im Neuen Testament', *ELKZ* 5 (1951) 362ff.

ORTENBURGER (H.) 'Das Verhältnis der Gnadenmittel zur Kirche', *ELKZ* 4 (1950) No. 3.

PETERSON (E.) *Die Kirche*, München 1929.

PIUS XI (POPE) *True Religious Unity (Mortalium Animos)* London (CTS).

PIUS XII (POPE) *The Mystical Body of Christ (Mystici Corporis Christi)* London (CTS)

POL (W. H. VAN DE) *The Christian Dilemma: Catholic Church—Reformation*, London 1952.

PRIBILLA (M.) *Um kirchliche Einheit. Stockholm–Lausanne–Rome*, Freiburg/ Br. 1929.

RADEMACHER (A.) *Die Wiedervereinigung der christlichen Kirchen*, Bonn 1937.

RAHNER (K.) 'Gespräche über den "Zaun". Offener Brief an H. Asmussen'. *WuW* 5 (1950), 174ff.

RAWLINSON 'Lambeth 1948', *ER* II (1949/50) 2, 169ff.

RICHARD (L.) 'Une Thèse fondamentale de l'Oecumênisme: Le Baptême, Incorporation visible à l'Eglise', *Nouvelle Revue Théologique* 84ᵉ année (1952), vol. 74, No. 5, 485ff.

SCHLIER (H.) 'Über das Hauptanliegen des ersten Briefes an die Korinther' *Evangelische Theologie* 8 (1948/9), 462 ff.

SCHLINK (E.) 'Die Kirche in Gottes Heilsplan', *ThLZ* 73 (1948) No. 11.

—— 'The Church and the Churches', *ER* II (1949/50) 2, 150ff.

—— 'The Pilgrim People of God', *ER* V (1952/3) 1, 27ff.

SCHMAUS (M.) *Katholische Dogmatik*, München 1948⁴ (Vol. III, 1, München 1940²).

SCHREY (H-H.) 'Das Ringen um die Kirche in der schwedischen Theologie der Gegenwart', *Verkündigung und Forschung, Theologischer Jahresbericht* 1949/50, 136ff., München 1951.

SÖHNGEN (G.) *Die Einheit in der Theologie*, München 1952.

STÄHLIN (W.) 'Insights and Open Questions concerning Ways of Worship', *ER* V (1952/3) 3, 243ff.

STAUFFER (E.) 'Jüdisches Erbe im urchristlichen Kirchenrecht', *ThLZ* 77 (1952) No. 4, 201ff.

—— *The Theology of the New Testament*, London 1955.

Sundkler (B.) *The Church of South India. The Movement towards Union 1900–1947*, London 1954.

THIELICKE (H.) *Theologische Ethik./Dogmatisch-philosophisch-kontrovers-theologische Grundlegung*, Tübingen 1951.

THILS (G.) *Histoire Doctrinale du Mouvement Oecuménique*, Louvain 1955.

ThWzNT: Theologisches Wörterbuch zum Neuen Testament, Gerhard Kittel, Stuttgart, 1932.

TOMKINS (O.) *The Wholeness of the Church*, London 1949.

TOMKINS (O.) 'The Church, the Churches and the Council', *ER* IV (1951/2) 3, 259ff.

Treysa Conference, The 1950, on the theme: 'The Biblical Doctrine of Law and Justice: Geneva 1950.

TÜCHLE (H.) *Die Eine Kirche. Zum Gedenken J. A. Möhlers.* Paderborn 1939.

URS VON BALTHASAR (H.) *Karl Barth, Darstellung und Deutung seiner Theologie,* Köln 1951.

VILLAIN (M.) *Introduction à l'Oecuménisme,* Tournai-Paris 1960.[2]

VISSER 'T HOOFT (W. A.) *The Meaning of Ecumenical,* London 1953.

—— 'Super-Church and the Ecumenical Movement', *ER* X (1957/58) 4, 365ff.

VOGEL (H.) *Gott in Christo,* Berlin 1951.

VOLK (H.) 'Das Wirken Heiligen Geistes in den Gläubigen' *Catholica, Jahrbuch für Kontroverstheologie* (ed. ROBERT GROSCHE) IX, 1, (1952).

WEHRHAHN (H.) 'Die Grundlagenproblematik des deutschen evangelischen Kirchenrechts 1933–45', *Theologische Rundschau* 19 (1951), No. 3, 231ff.

WOLF (E.) 'Das Kirchliche Amt im Gericht der theologischen Existenz', *ET* 11 (1952) 10/11, 517ff.

ZANDER (L. A.) *Vision and Action, The Problems of Ecumenism,* London 1955.

III. PERIODICALS

Catholica: Jahrbuch für Kontroverstheologie, Ed ROBERT GROSCHE, Münster.

ECQ: The Eastern Churches Quarterly, Newman Bookshop, Oxford.

ELKZ: Evangelisch-Lutherische Kirchenzeitung, published for the Vereinigte Evangelisch-Lutherische Kirche Deutschlands, Berlin.

ER: The Ecumenical Review, a quarterly, published by the WCC, Geneva.

ET: Evangelische Theologie, monthly, published by Ernst Wolf, München.

Faith and Unity: the quarterly of the Church Union Committee for Faith and Unity, London.

HK: Herder-Korrespondenz. Orbis Catholicus, Freiburg/Br.

Heythrop Journal, The, a quarterly review of Philosophy and Theology, published by Heythrop College, Oxon.

Information Catholiques Internationales; fortnightly, Bd. Malesherbes, Paris.

Irénikon: a review, published three times a year by Prieuré Bénédictin d'Amay, Chèvetogne, Belgium.

Lumière et Vie: published by the Dominicans of the Province of Lyons.

ThLZ: Theologische Literaturzeitung, monthly journal, covering the whole field of theology and religion, Leipzig.

USR: Una Sancta, Rundbriefe für interkonfessionelle Begegnung. Published by the Una-Sancta-Arbeitsgemeinschaft Meitingen/Niederaltaich. Kyriosverlag Meitingen b. Augsburg.

Unitas: International quarterly of the Unitas Association (English Language Edition) of Rome.

Verbum Caro: quarterly published by the Community of Taizé.

Per l'Unité Chrétienne monthly, Paris.

WuW: Wort und Wahrheit, monthly, Vienna.

ZkT: Zeitschrift fur Katholoische Theologie, Innsbruck.

Index of Periodicals

Index of Names

Albertus Magnus, 223
Algermissen, 219
Allman, J.-J. von, 190
Althaus, P., 131, 183, 204, 239
Anselm, Abp. of Canterbury, 190
Anthony, Abp. of Kharkov, 12
Arnold, F. X., xiii, 186
Asmussen, H., xv, 15, 70, 77, 80, 82, 97, 161, 172, 178, 182, 184, 188ff., 200f., 212, 236
Athanasius, 119
Athenagoras, Metropolitan, 57
Aubrey, E., 86
Augustine, xiv, 110f., 117f., 185, 193, 202, 209
Aulén, G. 15, 109, 124, 174, 213
Azariah, V. S., 8

Bacht, H., 162, 165, 173
Baius, xiii, xix
Balthasar, H. U. von, xivf., 176f., 237
Barth, K., xv, xviii, 26, 29ff., 77, 91f., 111, 130, 132, 134, 161, 166, 175ff., 186, 189, 212, 234, 238, 242, 245ff.
Bartsch, W., 130
Bate, H. N., 5, 8, 10ff., 14, 20
Baumann, R., 192
Behrens, J., 183
Bell, G. K. A., 6
Bellarmine, R., 113, 116, 150
Benedict, XIV, 145, 147
Berdyaev, N., 175
Berggrav, Bp., 65
Bergendorff, K., 77
Bernard of Clairvaux, 127
Boegner, M., 15, 99
Bonaventure, 136, 223
Boyer, 57
Bouyer, vii
Braun, F. M., 129f., 131f.
Brennecke, G., 28, 70
Brent, Ch. H., 5, 8, 15
Brilioth, Y. T., 56
Bring, R., 80, 82, 210

Brunner, E., 97, 108f., 123f., 131, 170, 202f., 210, 241
Brunner, P., 96f., 181f., 209
Bulgakoff, S., 19, 125
Bultmann, R., 39, 130f., 137, 161, 245f.

Cajetan, 151
Calvin, J., 118, 157f.
Campbell, J. Y., 125
Campenhausen, H. von, 189, 213
Cerfaux, L., 122
Chavasse, 153
Clement, I., 170, 183, 184, 187, 194
Cletus, I., 170
Colombo, C., 218
Colson, J., 170
Congar, Y., M-J., xiii, xviii, 6, 13ff., 96, 129ff., 114, 135f., 138, 153, 156f., 162f., 173ff., 186, 193, 196, 212f., 215, 218
Conzelmann, H., 205
Craig, C. T., 25, 56, 119, 121, 124
Cullmann, O., 129, 131, 135, 184, 188f., 213, 227
Cyprian of Carthage, 126, 193, 209, 230

Dahl, N. A., 206
Dalmais, J.-H., 197
Daniélou, J., 91
Davanandan, P. D., 83
Deissmann, A., 128, 129
Dejaifve, G., 125, 127
Denzinger, H., xix, 98, 123, 145, 155, 168, 209, 223, 232, 240f.
Diekamp, 239
Diem, H., 210
Dilschneider, O., 122, 159ff., 201, 211
Dix, G., 190, 194
Dodd, H. C., 134
Dombois, H., 188
Döpfner, J., Cardinal, 153, 159
Duff, E., vii
Dulles, J. F, 30

General Index

Churches—*contd.*

33; continental, 30, 77; differences, 17, 33n, 40, 44, 52, 57, 58, 64; in Oecumenical Movement, 3, 8ff, 15, 21, 22, 25, 26, 28, 33n, 36, 37, 40, 42, 45, 47, 53, 55, 65, 81f, 91, 106, 160, 180; isolation, 25; local, 230, 231, 232, 234, 235; national, 12, 20, 31, 85; relations, 4, 6, 7, 12, 16f, 21, 24, 26, 39, 40, 41, 42f, 50, 52f, 55, 78, 81f, 141, 235; true Churches, 16, 42, 45, 141; use of terms, 43, 96, 126, 127; within Catholic Church, 127, 157, 230; young, 8, 29, 61, 65, 107

Churchmanship, 214

Cincinnati, 5, 76

Claim to totality: 3; to catholicity, 86, 219f; to superiority, 91

Clergy: 53, 64, 185; Anglican, viii; Catholic, 90, 249; medieval, 194

Clerical state, 184n

Cleveland (Ohio), Union (1950), 75

Code of Canon Law (CIC), 90, 91, 126n, 144f, 180n, 207n

Cognitio per connaturalitatem, 248

Collectivity, oecumenical, 107

Colossians, Epistle of St Paul to, 223, 224

Commandments: of Christ, 223; of God, 222

Commission on Faith and Order: 34, 35, 36, 55f, 57, 63, 133, 155, 180; geographical and confessional distribution, 56 [*see also Faith and Order*]

Commissions of WCC, 21, 22, 34, 37, 45, 61, 211, 240

Committee of Fourteen, 22

Committee of Thirty-five, 21, 22

Communicatio idiomatum, 161, 163

Communicatio in sacris, 91

Communication: 213; of grace, 150f, 152, 168; of Holy Spirit, 207, 208

Communio electorum, 111

Communio in sacris, 13

Communio in serviendo ecumenica, 34

Communio praedestinatorum, 111

Communio sacramentorum, 110, 111

Communio sanctorum, 49, 110, 118n, 123; derivation, 112 [*see also Communion of Saints*]

Communion: 50, 150, 202; between churches, 12, 52f, 80, 85; oecumenical, 34; of Catholic Church, 115, 144, 146, 168, 169; of faith and love, 117; of faithful, 112, 147; of love, 119; sacramental, *see*

Holy Communion; with Christ, 14, 78, 111; with God, 110, 239; with Holy See, 90, 159, 233

Communion of Saints, 19f, 51f, 193; of saints (Church), 49, 57, 110, 111

Communion Service, 77, 78, 188; sacrificial elements, 14, 51

Communions, vii, xi, xii, xx, 20, 36, 73, 81, 83, 89, 128, 133, 159, 214; American, 75; and Catholic Church, 96, 142, 156, 159, 216f, 220, 226, 237; and Church, 72, 146, 244; evangelical, 196; in oecumene, 26, 50, 89; with Apostolic Succession, 14n

Communism, 28, 35, 220

Communities, Christian: 143, 156, 158, 187, 193, 194, 216, 219, 228, 244; dissident, 148, 179, 196, 209, 214, 215, 217, 218; in Oecumenical Movement, 20, 43; membership of Catholic Church, 214ff; 'potential Mystical Body', 217; primitive, 230; Protestant, 198, 203; Reformed, 182n; return to Catholic Church, 217ff

COMMUNITY

I. Catholic Church: 95n, 111, 116, 148, 221; cult community, 230; exclusion from, 168, 169; of faithful, 109, 185, 233; of life, 232; of salvation, 115; of worship, 233

II. Church: 5, 7, 108, 109, 111, 121n, 123, 186, 188, 189, 226, 242, 248; Biblical concept, 32, 122, 211n, 217n; Christian, 33n, 59, 109, 164; external (large sense), 141, 210; of faith and worship, 16; of forgiven sinners, 48, 59, 135; of salvation, 121, 125; of supernatural grace, 124; pneumatic, 124, 125, 170, 241

III. Ecclesiastical group, 211, 214, 234; NT (primitive), xvi, 181, 188, 194, 205, 227; of perfect way, 27; Roman, 189, 193

IV. Secular: 7, 33n, 109, 146, 147f; World Community, 66

V. Oecumenical, 32; of bishops and presbyters, 235; of sacramental life, 23; of saints, 193

Comprehensiveness, 6, 13f, 28, 71, 83f, 85, 151

Compromise, xvii, 12, 14, 17f, 23, 24, 27, 30, 57, 81

Condemnation: of heresy, xix, 123n; of sin, 225

Conditio humani generis, 136

Truth(s)—*Contd.*

expression of, 167, 178, 249; fidelity to, 62; fullness of (whole), xviii, 20, 42, 45, 54, 66, 78, 81, 95, 107, 154, 248; ideal, 187; immutable, 165; infinite range, xvi; no compromise with, xvii; of Gospel, 62, 79, 82, 187, 226, 244; partial, xviii, xix, 20, 95; revealed, 54, 72, 81, 90, 93; 'truth' in itself, 81; unity in, 23, 42, 45, 119, 235, 249; visible, 25

U

Umkreistheorie, 234

Una Sancta, 22, 23, 24, 33, 40, 60

Una Sancta Movement, xi, xvii, 91, 190

Unction in Christ, 207f

Uniformity, 50, 103, 105, 118, 127, 165, 235f, 249; of doctrinal formulations, 166, 235

UNION: 3, 21, 40, 57, 60, 77, 90, 146, 154; corporate, 16f; in ministry, 11; of being and knowledge, 241; of Christ with Church, 47f, 69, 71, 160, 163, 200; of dissidents with Catholic Church, 214; of opposites, 125; organic, 17, 52, 75, 76, 83, 118, 121; practical attempts, 71, 75–86; premature, 52; sacramental, 11; ultimate, 78; will to, 8; with Christ, 57, 61, 69, 121, 122n, 152, 176n, 200, 208, 217n, 227, 240; with divine power, 206

Union of Churches, 12, 75, 78, 79, 81, 83

Union of South India [*see South India*]

Unionism, abstract, 33

Unitarianism, 22

Unitas caritatis, 118n

United Church of Christ, USA, 34n

United Evangelicals, 56, 77

United Free Liberal Church, 75

United States, 15, 56, 64, 75, 81, 107

UNITY: abstract idea, 33, 86, 98; already existing, 12, 16, 28, 43, 50, 53, 60, 92, 96; and continuity, 49, 71, 107; and Holy Spirit, 72, 76, 90, 117, 143, 148; and law, 120; and missions, 8, 55; and uniformity, 50, 103, 105, 165, 235, 249; as alliance, 16; as God's will, xx, 35, 73; as intercommunion, 16; beginning of, 4; 'bodily', 122; call to, 10, 216; Catholic conception, xx, 95, 98, 144, 150, 156, 215, 235; Christ's prayer for, viii, xi, xx, 8, 48, 87, 90, 93, 138; corporate, 16f, 18, 23, 67; desire for, xi, 4, 18, 21, 37, 52, 89, 92, 155, 156; development of concept, 220; diversity

in, 11, 13, 17, 83, 105n, 118, 165, 249; doctrinal, 3, 41, 44, 52, 53, 79, 80, 105, 165, 166, 217n; dynamic, 163; essence, 50; experience of, 11, 43, 61; expression of, 11, 18, 23, 26; faith in, 60n, 82, 137; false, 34, 87, 92; gift, 24, 26, 43, 50, 69, 105; historical, 81, 98. 113; horizontal, 107, 108; in Christ, 14, 26, 47, 48, 50, 54, 62, 66, 98, 106, 165, 176n; in Church, 47, 52, 119, 209, 249; in faith, 7n, 8, 10, 11, 13, 16, 17, 18, 33, 34, 41, 45, 71, 72, 88, 105, 113, 117, 125, 139, 146, 148, 150; in hope, 139; in love, xvii, 10, 11, 72, 87, 117, 125, 139, 249; in ministry, 11, 17, 18, 37, 53, 76, 83; in multiplicity, 194; in order, 8, 10, 34, 41, 45, 105; in service, 16, 34; in truth, 23, 42, 45, 119, 235, 249; in worship, 15, 16; inner and outer, 18; institutional, 18; interest in, 3; manifestation, 23, 24, 25, 35, 40, 41, 44, 48, 55, 69, 70, 96, 108; minimum basis, xvi; necessity, 8n, 55; objective, 124, 238; obstacles, 11, 15, 18, 37f, 51, 55; of administration, 235; of all baptized, 208; of Christ, 47, 104, 173, 207; of Christ with the Father, 138, 163; of compromise, 23, 30; of divine and human, 134; of dogmatic statements, 165f, 235; of episcopate, 72, 118, 126; of experience, 61; of grace, 113, 138; of Holy Spirit, 62, 117, 136; of laity and ministry, 38; of Law and Gospel, 224; of mutual recognition, 75; of Mystical Body, 151, 179n; of Old and New Covenants, 223f; of organization, 56, 113; organic, 16f, 18, 46, 50, 53, 75, 76; Orthodox view, 12f, 52, 71ff; pastoral, 35-political, 87; principles, 11, 80, 83, 84, 88, 120, 139; problems, 21, 45, 76, 238; progress towards, 5, 16, 25, 26, 37, 38, 42, 47, 55, 67, 78, 79, 107; sacramental 11, 17, 41, 45, 50, 52, 84, 88, 113, 123, 124, 150, 230; spiritual, 11, 18, 105, 108, 117, 123, 138; under primacy, 143, 150; use of term, 4; vertical, 17, 107, 108; visible, 23, 34, 41, 45, 50, 60, 98, 113, 115, 138, 238; willed by Christ, 90, 92, 93, 95

UNITY OF CATHOLIC CHURCH xx, 7n, 36, 88, 92, 94, 96, 98, 103, 104, 113, 115, 126, 141, 142, 146, 148, 155, 156, 214, 221, 228f, 232, 249; according to Möhler, 116–20, 194; and Eucharist, 69, 230; and Holy Spirit, 148, 180; eschatological aspect, 138; Newman's view, 229; object of faith, 137, 220, 221; reintegration into,